# SEASONAL FEASTS AND FESTIVALS

*By the same Author*

# SEASONAL FEASTS
# AND
# FESTIVALS

*by*
## E. O. JAMES
*D. Litt., Ph.D., F.S.A., Hon.D.D.*

*Professor Emeritus of the History and Philosophy of Religion
in the University of London
Fellow of University College, London
Fellow of King's College, London
Chaplain of All Souls College, Oxford*

UNIVERSITY PAPERBACK

BARNES & NOBLE, INC.    •    New York

*Publishers*   •   *Booksellers*     *Since 1873*

# CONTENTS

10 *Contents*

# PREFACE

It is hardly an exaggeration to say that the rhythm of nature reflected in the seasonal sequence has arrested the attention of mankind throughout the ages more intensively than any other phenomenon in the natural order. It is not surprising that this should be so when it is remembered how long subsistence depended almost entirely upon the products of the chase, and on such edible roots and fruits as could be gathered, or under later conditions on the flocks and herds kept on the grasslands, and the crops cultivated in the oases and fertile alluvial river valleys. Then the food supply and the means of livelihood were so dependent upon the vagaries of the environment and its climatic conditions, that every human group lived in a perpetual state of anxiety and uncertainty lest the breeding and the hunting seasons, or seed-time and harvest, should fail. And when in due course an urban civilization arose in the Fertile Crescent in the Ancient Near East in and after the third millennium B.C., the basic needs remained fundamentally the same, since the rapidly increasing population in the towns still had to be fed from the surrounding soil, making more and more demands upon its resources.

From the beginning it would seem that man did not rely wholly upon his own initiative and ingenuity to ensure that all his needs were met. Therefore, when nature appeared to be in the balance at the crucial and critical seasons, he performed the rites prescribed for the control of the growth of the crops, or the increase of the flocks and herds, at regular intervals. In the Fertile Crescent these were timed by the rise and fall of the Nile, or by the more erratic behaviour of the Tigris and Euphrates, and after the introduction of the calendar, often

calculated in relation to the phases of the moon. Thus, festivals
and feasts—and 'to feast' is simply to keep a 'festival'—tended
to occur at full moon, frequently on the twelfth day of the lunar
month, as in Greece, when one or more days were set apart for
the religious observances. These might be festal or ferial, gay or
grave, licentious or Lenten.

As most of them were agrarian in origin in the first instance
they were seasonal and periodic, either fixed or movable,
celebrated on a certain day or days at specified times in a
calendrical sequence, primarily for the ritual control of the food
supply, or as acts of public worship or propitiation of the
divine powers in whose honour they were held. In course of
time, however, these specifically sacred purposes acquired a
more secular character as games (*ludi*) and revels were added,
and soon they lost much of their earlier religious significance.
Moreover, as festivals increased in number and became
associated with particular events or gods independent of the
seasons, especially under urban conditions and State control,
although many of the old rites persisted, and often were carefully
preserved, they ceased to be seasonal feasts as such. New
festivals were instituted commemorating national, local,
religious, political and other occasions, divinities, heroes and
saints, frequently having little or nothing to do with the aspect
of the subject with which this volume is concerned.

Therefore, attention has been concentrated upon only those
observances which fall within the purview of the seasons.
Indeed, to attempt to cover the whole field would involve
writing the entire history of religion and of civilization. Even
keeping within the seasonal domain, it has been necessary to
impose limitations on the inquiry for the purpose of a reasonably
intensive investigation of the institutions in a culturally inter-
related region, and one with which I happen to be familiar.
It was tempting to go beyond the Fertile Crescent in the
Middle East and the Graeco-Roman world as the cradleland of
the subsequent calendrical developments in Christendom and
the folk cultures, extending the field of inquiry to Vedic India,
Mexico and Peru, where the parallels have been very close.

This, nevertheless, would have introduced a number of con﹍jectural and highly controversial issues concerning the problem of diffusion, and would have obscured rather than illuminated the development of the observances in the particular region under review. Therefore, for the present investigation it has been essential to confine the study to the seasonal ritual, myth and sacred drama, centred mainly in the Annual Festival in the ancient focus of civilization, in order to determine the course of development and their influence on our liturgical worship, dramatic art, social customs, popular pastimes, folk plays and traditions, which have persisted to the present day.

There is, of course, no dearth of books on all these various aspects of the subject, but so far as I am aware no systematic attempt has been made in a single volume to correlate in a historical sequence the archaeological and documentary data bearing on the origin and development of the observances with the ecclesiastical and folk material. In trying to fill this gap I have endeavoured to render the subject readily intelligible to readers who are not equipped with a highly specialized know﹍ledge of its technical details and terminology, without, it is hoped, diminishing the usefulness of the book to other workers in this field. Thus, in the documentation references have been given to the most authoritative literature, and to first﹍hand sources, while at the end a selected bibliography has been arranged for students wishing to go more deeply into the subject.

*All Souls College,*                                   E. O. JAMES
*Oxford*

# CHAPTER I

# The Emergence of Seasonal Ritual

FROM time immemorial the seasonal sequence has arrested the attention of mankind and aroused an intense emotional reaction in all states and stages of culture and types of society extending from the Upper Palaeolithic in prehistoric times to the higher civilizations of the Ancient Near East and the Graeco-Roman world, with repercussions on the subsequent development of custom, belief and behaviour in the intervening ages, not least in Christendom and the folk cultures in Europe. The reason is not far to seek. Everywhere and at all times the means of subsistence have been the primary concern and from this fundamental requirement recurrent seasonal periodic festivals have sprung, and by constant repetition they have assumed a variety of forms and acquired divers meanings and interpretations. But since food has always been an essential need it is in this context that the observances have exercised their primary functions.

## PALAEOLITHIC HUNTING RITUAL

Under Palaeolithic conditions life was necessarily hazardous and the food supply precarious, often determined by factors and circumstances outside human control. It is not surprising, therefore, that every effort should have been made to cause both edible plants and animals to increase and multiply and replenish the earth. And if, as is not at all improbable, the physiological process of generation was very imperfectly understood,[1] recourse would have to be made to supernatural means to promote and conserve the species. Thus, in the cave paintings and parietal art of the Upper Palaeolithic in France and Spain

---

[1] Cf. E. S. Hartland, *Primitive Paternity*, 1909-10; Malinowski, *The Father in Primitive Psychology*, 1927, pp. 28 ff.; 43 ff.; *Sexual Life of Savages in North-Western Melanesia*, 1929, pp. 146 ff.

four-fifths of the objects depicted are representations of animals mostly edible. Presumably they constituted the principal source of the food supply, and there can be little doubt that in the dark scarcely accessible recesses of the cavern-sanctuaries in which so many of them occur a variety of rites were per-formed in conjunction with the sacred designs. The pictures on the walls of these deep and tortuous decorated caves are often in nooks and crannies and other very obscure positions, as, for example, in the case of the woolly rhinoceros high up on the wall of a narrow crevice in the great cave known as Font-de-Gaume at Les Eyzies in the Dordogne. This, it would seem, was executed by the artist standing on the shoulders of his companion in the light of a flickering lamp burning marrow or fat with a wick of moss.

Or, again, at Tuc d'Audoubert in the commune of Montesquieu-Avantès, Ariège, on the French side of the Pyrenees, clay figures of a male and female bison in an attitude indicative of mating has been discovered at the end of a long passage, the entrance of which had been blocked by stalactites when it was first re-entered in 1912. In front of the figures heel-marks have been discerned, made by dancers engaged appar-ently in a fertility dance, probably similar to that called *duk-duk* in Melanesia. Near by, on the estate of the Count Bégouën, his three sons later wormed their way through a passage about the size of a drain-pipe at the end of a small cave, called Enlène, to a second cave, now appropriately named Les Trois Frères. There on a wall beside a sort of window overlooking an alcove, the walls of which are covered with engravings of bison, rein-deer, mammoth, rhinoceros and other Pleistocene animals, they found a masked figure of a man with a human face, the head of a stag, the eyes of an owl, the ears of a wolf, the claws of a lion and the tail of a horse, engraved and outlined in black pigments. Here apparently a cult was practised in which human beings and animals were brought together in a ritual action perhaps to establish a mystic relationship with the god or spirit, or supernatural forces controlling the food supply by means of a sacred dance, or to gain power over the animals simulated and to increase their fecundity.[1]

## The Ritual Control of the Food Supply

The mysterious forces of nutrition and propagation being sacred and the centres of emotional interest and concern, a reverent attitude was adopted towards them which found expression in a ritual technique devised for the purpose of bringing them under human control. That this often took the form of a dance may be explained mimetically. The ritual expert arrayed himself in the skin and antlers of a stag or the feathers of a bird and imitated the behaviour of the species he personified, or with which he became *en rapport*, believing that for the time being, and for the prescribed purpose of the rite, he was in fact what he represented or felt himself to be. He did not engage in imitative magic but actually did what he set out to do. He caught and killed his prey; he made the copulation of male and female to be effective in the production of offspring; he established a mystic relationship between man and the supernatural powers responsible for the maintenance of the food supply. Through a series of rhythmical muscular movements expression was given to strong emotional urges and desires which under Palaeolithic conditions were centred in fecundity and fertility, birth and generation, especially at critical junctures in the life of nature or of members of the human group. It was no doubt at these set times marking intense situations, some of which were of regular recurrence at different periods of the year, that the dances and the related rites were held. Then human beings and animals may have been brought together in a joint effort to conserve and promote the food supply by a ritual representation of their inmost urges and needs.

The desire to act discharged itself on the symbol so that ritual was at once a visual language and a vent of pentup emotions and longings. The primitive man it has been said

[1] Breuil, *Quatre cents siècles d'art pariétal*, Montignac, 1952, pp. 166, 176f.; Bégouën, *Antiquity*, iii, 1929, p. 17; James, *Prehistoric Religion*, 1957, pp. 148f., 173 ff.

with much truth 'dances out his religion', expressing his fundamental requirements and deepest emotional impulses in sacred
actions rather than in words, except perhaps for exclamations
and conventional utterances. As the artist externalizes a
feeling and mood, an inner quality of life, an emotional impulse, an interpretation of reality as he conceives it, by means
of his visual technique in paint or stone, or whatever medium
he may employ, so the ritual expert gives visual and dramatic
expression to the will to live, to the vital urge and rhythmic
relations to life, in response to concrete situations. It is not surprising, therefore, that ritual, art, dance and drama should have
conjoined in their earliest manifestations, and that from this
conjunction the seasonal sacred observances should have
emerged.

When life depended largely on the hazards of the chase, the
vagaries of the seasons, and similar circumstances and events
by no means wholly, or in some cases even partly, under human
control, the emotional tension was endemic in a perpetual
struggle for existence in a precarious environment. Therefore,
once a ritual technique had been devised to deal with the
situation and sublimate the strain, it became established and
organized to meet the various demands and to maintain a state
of equilibrium in an expanding social and religious structure.

This religious consciousness was projected into any natural
object, force or process that it identified with the mysterious
awesome sacred power transcending yet immanent in the
phenomenal world, in particular species of animals and in
physical features such as rivers, mountains and the constellations, and in the rhythm of nature. Around these various
symbols of divinity and divine activity a cultus collected,
designed to bring under control and to make efficacious the
forces with which the symbols were associated.

In their several capacities these transcendental symbols belonged to the 'other world' of ultimate reality which mysteri-
ously imposed itself on the phenomenal order of time and
space, and on physical processes, entities and events. With
their aid, and that of the rites performed in connexion with

them, the tension of the ever-present strain of uncontrollable and unpredictable occurrences was relieved and sublimated, thereby directing human energies into new activities affording emotional relief. By seeking the aid and intervention of a supra-mundane sacredness external to himself and society, and, indeed, of the phenomenal world at large, man endeavoured to establish efficacious relations with the ultimate source of life and well-being, stability and equilibrium through the prescribed ritual cultus. The emphasis seems to have been on fecundity to secure abundance of the species on which the human groups depended for their means of subsistence. This is shown by the symbolism displayed at Tuc d'Audoubert and Les Trois Frères, and in the numerous representations of men wearing animal masks or heads, such as the three figures masquerading in the skin of a chamois at Abri Mège, Dordogne, and those with animal heads at Marsoulas, Hornos de la Pena, Altamira, and Lourdes, engaged apparently in a mimetic dance.

## The Mimetic Masked Dance and the Magic of the Chase

The figures of the masked dancers in animal disguises suggest that a cult was in vogue in which the hunter would appear to have impersonated the 'spirit' of the animals he embodied, and to have represented dramatically in a series of ritual actions a rehearsal of what it was earnestly hoped would be accomplished in the chase. The will to live as a primary emotion was discharged by anticipatory rites as a pre-presentation of a successful hunt. To these actions a magical efficacy was given, not because 'like produces like' but because a ritual that involved a more or less realistic reproduction of some practical activity established the *ex post facto* notion of 'sympathetic causation' as a secondary interpretation of the rites performed in the first instance to produce abundance of the food supply and successful hunting. The situation, however, was complicated by an inherent sense of kinship which man felt existed between himself and the sacrosanct animals on which he was so dependent, and yet which he was compelled to hunt, thereby condoning their killing. It may have been this aspect of the emotional tension that was given expression in the mimetic masked dances for the purpose of establishing a 'mystical union' with the source of bounty.

In Palaeolithic sanctuaries like Niaux, Lascaux or Les Trois Frères the ceremonies probably involved an organized effort on the part of the community in a collective attempt to control natural forces and processes by seasonal observances, directed to the common good in an attempt to maintain and secure the means of subsistence by an economic ritual.

At Lascaux, for instance, situated in the valley of the Vézère near Montignac, some eighteen miles from Les Eyzies, the most important centre of the decorated caves in the Dordogne, the remarkable series of paintings extend from the Aurignacian, the opening phase of the Upper Palaeolithic (sometimes now called Gravettian), to the final stage of Périgordian art at the end of the Magdalenian, placed by the radio-carbon 14 dating test as late as 15,000 years ago.[1] This Versailles of Palaeolithic art, as Lascaux has been described by the Abbé Breuil, with its galaxy of styles in mauve and purple as well as in the more familiar black and red pigments, must have been a cult-centre for some thousands of years in view of this succession of paint-ings, with their distinguishing features and techniques. There-fore, in it a great variety of rites must have been performed, ranging probably from hunting magic to some mysterious commemorative symbolism depicting the hazards of the chase. Thus, in the secluded 'crypt' of the cavern-sanctuary, reached by a perilous descent of some twenty-five feet, a scene is por-trayed showing a man delineated in a schematic manner, killed by a bison, and a rhinoceros painted in a different style, lumbering away after having ripped up the bison. Below the man is a bird on a pole, not unlike similar cult-objects repre-senting the external soul of the deceased in mortuary ritual among the Eskimo and the North American Indians. Indeed, the Abbé Breuil has conjectured that the scene is a votive painting of a hunter who may have been buried in the

[1] F. Windels, *The Lascaux Cave Paintings*, 1949, pp. 17 ff., 49 ff.

cave.[1] But whatever was the original purpose of this 'problem picture' it was executed in this very difficult position presumably because it was at that sacred spot that great potency was thought to reside for the control of the chase and its fortunes, alike for the hunters and their prey.

More accessible on the left-hand side of the main hall is a mythical animal with a large sagging body resembling a rhinoceros, and a head like that of an antelope, with oval rings on the flanks and two long horns projecting from the forehead and terminating in a tuft. To describe this strange composite creature as a 'unicorn' is a misnomer, but it certainly does not represent any known living beast. It could be a sorcerer, as at Les Trois Frères, clad in a spotted skin of some Bovidae, impersonating perhaps an ancestral being believed to be responsible for fertility and success in the chase; bearing some relation to Chinese paintings of horses with short legs and protruding barrel-like bodies. If the large oval spots represented marks of wounds, as in the reproduction of the dying bison at Niaux, and not natural dappling, then the purpose no doubt was destruction rather than veneration. But no other animal design at Lascaux is portrayed in this manner, though at the end of the axial passage a horse is shown falling over a precipice, or into a pit, and the tectiform and other magical signs which frequently appear on the paintings may indicate traps, unless, as Breuil suggests, they are local tribal marks.

In spite of the conjectural nature of much of the symbolism in these Palaeolithic cave paintings, there can be little doubt that the caverns were in fact sanctuaries to which resort was made before setting out on hunting expeditions to achieve success in the chase by magico-religious devices. Hunting was the essential pursuit in the Old Stone Age and upon it depended the principal means of subsistence, and, indeed, the entire life of mankind including his clothing, bone and horn for artefacts, needles and tendons for sewing, fat for lamps and hooks and harpoons for fishing, as well as meat for daily consumption. But it was a precarious undertaking requiring, in addition to

[1] Breuil, *op. cit.*, pp. 131, 134ff.

human ingenuity and skill, superhuman knowledge and power, for in so many respects the animals were superior in strength and cunning to man. Hence the many examples at Lascaux, and in most of the other decorated caves in France and Spain, of paintings, or occasionally, as at Montespan in Haute-Garonne, of clay models of wounded animals marked with spears, darts and stabs from javelins and other missiles. Before setting out on an expedition the images were pierced or mutilated to cast a spell on the prey, the effigies being completely identified with the creatures portrayed. Thus, the same model was used repeatedly for this purpose as is shown by that of a headless bear covered with spear-marks at Montespan.

This also applied to some of the feline representations. In the case of Marsoulas, also in Haute-Garonne near Salies-du-Salat, a series of polychrome paintings, outlines in black or brown with spear-markings, are massed on the highly polished rock surface of the left wall as if they had been constantly renewed time after time. The oldest were very thin black line-drawings beneath a large polychrome horse overlaid by some more black drawings shaded and figures of bison. Above these are the large polychromes in black or brown, and successive layers of conventionalized signs and symbols, first brown and then red.[1] In a recess at Les Trois Frères the head of a lion engraved on a stalactite had been redrawn three times in different positions, and the tail was shown at first as straight and then as curling. Judging from the number of spear-heads engraved upon it it must have been in constant use.

Sometimes it sufficed only to depict particular parts of the animal such as the head or the horns, as for the purposes of magical control they could be employed efficaciously as symbols to convey the spell to the prey with which they were identified. The occurrence of figures of mammoth and cattle without eyes and ears at Pech-Merle, near the village of Cabrerets in the valley of the Lot in Corrèze, has led the Abbé Lémozi to conclude that they were so portrayed that their living counterparts in the chase would be deprived of sight and hearing and so

[1] Cartailhac and Breuil, *L'Anthrop.*, xv, 1904, pp. 625; xvi, 1905, pp. 431 ff.

become an easy prey for the hunters.[1] But on the roof of the
galleries in this cave headless figures of women also occur, and
it would seem to be more likely that just as female figurines
used as fertility charms not infrequently lack heads or faces
because they were regarded as superfluous, for the same reason
it was not thought to be necessary to include eyes and ears in
the animal designs. In any case, it was to control the chase
that they were executed, sometimes with consummate artistic
skill as at Altamira and Font-de-Gaume, at other times in
outline or in part as at Pech-Merle, Enlène and Tuc d'Audoubert, or in conventionalized geometric patterns as at Marsoulas
and on the Azilian pebbles.

## Seasonal Rites of Increase

Securing the prey required for food, however, was only one
purpose of the ritual control of the chase. The supply had to be
maintained as well as procured. Therefore, it was to perform
rites of increase to ensure abundance in addition to bringing
success in hunting that the sanctuaries were visited by those
who had the necessary qualifications to perform the prescribed
ritual. Propagation rather than destruction was then the aim
of the ceremonies, as is realistically shown by the clay bisons
at Tuc d'Audoubert, and in the representation of a male reindeer
pursuing a female at Les Trois Frères. Thus, in primitive states
of culture today people like the Australian aborigines who live
by the chase, hold seasonal rites at prescribed times and places
for this purpose, and it is highly probable that their Palaeolithic
forebears resorted to their cavern-sanctuaries with the same
intent on similar occasions. The preponderance of examples
of hunting magic over those connected with propagation may
be explained by the fact that the chase was a continuous occupation to meet the everyday needs of the food supply, whereas
breeding was confined to particular seasons.

Some primitive peoples still live today in the cultural and
economic conditions of the Old Stone Age. The aboriginal
inhabitants of Australia appear to have reached their present

[1] Abbé Lémozi, *La Grotte-Temple du Pech-Merle*, Paris, 1929.

habitat towards the end of the Pleistocene period.[1] It is true some Neolithic traits (e.g. hafted polished stone hammers, the domestication of the dingo) occur in their cultural equipment and, therefore, they cannot be regarded as strictly Palaeolithic survivals, corresponding to the Aurignacians or the Magda⁄lenians. Nevertheless, their ancestors appear to have reached Australia from south⁄east Asia in the Late Pleistocene when the sea⁄levels were relatively low and while they were still in a food⁄gathering state of culture, akin to that of pre⁄Neolithic peoples all over the world. Since then they have remained ignorant of agriculture, herding, pottery⁄making and the use of the bow; their flint and stone industries resemble in their techniques those of the Solutreans and Magdalenians; their awls and pins are also reminiscent of the Upper Palaeolithic types; likewise their geometrical designs on stones and cere⁄monial objects (e.g. *churinga* and bull⁄roarers), their zoo⁄morphic and phytomorphic totemic delineations; tectiforms; scutiforms, and stencilled outlines of hands—occasionally with mutilated fingers as in the Pyrenaean and Cantabrian Palaeo⁄lithic caves at Gargas and Castillo, and at Peche⁄Merle, in Corrèze—which are often concealed in obscure positions.[2]

At such sacred spots as Emily Gap near Alice Springs in the Arunta country in Central Australia some of the rocks taboo to the uninitiated are still believed to be full of the spirit⁄parts of animals awaiting reincarnation, and are adorned with drawings of the totems. Some are painted and repainted as part of the fertility ritual to make the species increase and multiply, ceremonial superpositions as practised at Les Trois Frères, Marsoulas and Teyjat. In the rock shelters in north⁄west Australia realistic drawings of animals occur executed in white pipe⁄clay, charcoal and red or yellow ochre, together with representations of mythical heroes connected with rain and fertility, as, for example, that of Katuru, or the 'lightning

[1] MacCurdy, *Early Man*, 1937, pp. 269 ff.; S. A. Smith, *Phil. Trans. Royal Society*, 1923, p. 370.

[2] Spencer and Gillen, *Native Tribes of Central Australia*, 1938, pp. 171 ff.; *Northern Tribes of Central Australia*, 1904, pp. 436 f.

man', at Kalurungari on the Calder river; and of Wond'ina at Robudda shelter, Walcott Inlet, the ancestor responsible for rain, the increase in nature and spirit-children.[1]

Now it is true that among the native tribes of Australia these sacred drawings are quite definitely associated with the practice of totemism which involves a highly complicated socio-religious system and a kinship organization presupposing a very considerable period of cultural and social development.[2] Thus, the classificatory system that determines the social structure in relation to marriage and kinship, and the totemic magico-religious cultus with its elaborate ceremonial and mythology, is not at all likely to have obtained in the Upper Palaeolithic. Moreover, the representation of many different varieties of animals not only in the same cave but in the same painting is not indicative of a totemic system as each totem would perform its rites in relation to the figure of its own sacred ally, just as the members of the Witchetty Grub totem assembled at its own sacred sites at Alice Springs. It is also to be noted that among the Bushmen of South Africa, where cave paintings are a very prominent feature of the culture, totemism has not been practised.

Nevertheless, although it is not very probable that such a specialized institution was in vogue in the Old Stone Age in Europe, the rites held in the seclusion of the decorated caves would seem to have had certain resemblances to the food-producing ceremonies of which those known as Intichiuma, held by the Arunta in Central Australia in the spring, are a typical example. On those arid steppes during the long barren season of drought there are few signs of life, only the scrub and a few acacia trees are able to survive. Then come the torrential rains making the desert blossom as a rose, when luxuriant vegetation suddenly bursts forth and birds, insects, frogs and wild life in general appear in profusion as though by

[1] *Northern Tribes of Central Australia*, pp. 436ff.
[2] *Native Tribes of Central Australia*, pp. 55ff.; Elkin, *The Australian Aborigines*, 1938, pp. 125ff.; Mainage, *Les Religions de la Préhistoire*, Paris, 1921, pp. 241ff.

magic. Small wonder that this remarkable transformation should be hailed as a supernatural event, the recurrence of which year after year at the appointed season has to be ensured by due performance of the rites believed to be responsible for the annual renewal of fertility in plants and animals alike.

Thus, it is at this critical juncture in the sequence of the seasons when the rains are due to begin that a selected group of men of the Witchetty Grub totemic clan assemble at Emily Gap near Alice Springs where their divine ancestors in the Alcheringa, or 'dream time' of long ago, produced a shallow cave high up on the western wall of the ravine with a large block of quartzite surrounded with small stones, representing the fully grown grub (*maegwa*) and its eggs. On the western side of the Gap are the sacred drawings on the rock face, to which reference already has been made, supposed to have been placed there by a mythical ancestral being Numbakallu, during his wanderings over the country establishing the sacred places for all time. Thither the little company make their way secretly and in silence after having observed and still maintaining a rigid fast, each carrying a twig of the Udniringa bush, and following their leader in single file. On arrival at the cave songs are sung invoking the grub to lay eggs, and the stones are struck with the twigs carried by the men. Then the leader rubs the stomach of each of them with one of the small stones saying, 'You have eaten much food', a formula that is repeated on the way back at other sacred spots where stones occur representing the chrysalis stage of the grub. Since actually they have eaten nothing, being in a state of fasting, this ceremony symbolizes the purpose of the rites, namely to produce much food for general consumption.

About a mile from the camp on the return procession a halt is made to enable the party to decorate themselves with sacred designs of the grub, hair-strings, nose-bones, bunches of feathers and twigs of the Udniringa bush. Meanwhile the old men who had remained behind in the camp had constructed a long narrow hut, or *wurley*, to represent the chrysalis from which the witchetty grub emerges. Into this structure the party wriggle their way on their arrival and sing of the insect in its various stages, and of the sacred stones they have visited in the cave to produce its multiplication. Food and water are then brought to them which they consume in the hut after their prolonged fast. At dusk they shuffle out of the *wurley* and sit round a fire till daybreak singing of the grub. The ceremonies are brought to an abrupt end by the leader suddenly announcing, 'Our Intichiuma is finished, the *mulyanuka* [men of the other moiety of the tribe] must have these things or else our Intichiuma would not be successful, and some harm would happen to us.' They all reply, 'Yes, yes, certainly', and the ornaments are handed over to the *mulyanuka*, and the designs are removed from their faces and bodies by rubbing them with red ochre before the performers return to their respective camps.[1]

The purpose of the rites is to increase the supply of the insects, which are a favourite article of diet, for the benefit of the whole community, even though it may be eaten only very sparingly by those who have engaged in the rites. This is accomplished by a dramatic representation of the principal events in the sacred lore of the group, and the repetition of the processes upon which its production is thought to depend, including what the ancestors are supposed to have done in the Alcheringa when they lived and roamed about on the earth 'giving the blackfellow all that he has'. By the performance of rites of this nature each group makes its contribution towards the food supply of the community as a whole because upon their efforts the fertility of the particular species, in which they stand in a peculiar relationship, is promoted at the proper season of the year.

Thus, analogous ceremonies are held in the neighbouring clans with the same aims and taboos imposed upon those who engage in the rites for the common good. In the Undiara kangaroo totem in the Arunta tribe, for instance, the men proceed to the foot of a hill where there are two rocks believed

[1] Spencer and Gillen, *Native Tribes of Central Australia*, pp. 170 ff.; *The Arunta*, i, 1927, pp. 148 ff.

to be full of the spirits of kangaroos awaiting reincarnation. One of the rocks is thought to represent a male kangaroo, the other a female, and at the appropriate season they are decorated with vertical stripes of red and white pigment to indicate the red fur and white bones of the animal. The headman of the clan and his maternal uncle having rubbed them with a stone, young men sit on the ledge and open veins in their arms to allow the blood to fall over the edge of the rock in order to drive out the spirits of the kangaroos in all directions, and so to increase their number. They then go and hunt them and bring back their spoils to the camp. The leader and the old men eat a little of the flesh of the animal and anoint with its fat the bodies of those who have taken part in the Intichiuma. The rest of the meat is divided among them and the night is spent in dancing and singing songs relating to the exploits of the Alcheringa ancestors.[1] After this the sacred species may be eaten sparingly.

As in the Witchetty Grub ceremonies, the purpose of the rite is to maintain and increase the food supply at the breeding season, and to establish a mystic bond with the source of all beneficence sealed in the ritual shedding of blood. The life-giving essence is poured out on the sacred stones to promote and conserve life, and to consolidate the sacramental relation-ship on which the continuance and well-being of the com-munity depend. Natural means of hunting and collecting animals, plants and insects not sufficing to meet every emerg-ency and need, magico-religious methods have to be employed to ensure an adequate food supply, and to maintain a correct attitude towards the supramundane source of beneficence and bounty. This will to live finds a practical and emotional outlet and mode of expression in the ritual control of the means of subsistence and increase, and while in Australia it was centred in the institution of totemism, the same primary urge was apparently discharged in the Old Stone Age by anticipatory rites at the natural periodic seasonal cycles as a pre-presentation of this intense desire for food and fertility on which life and survival depended.

[1] Spencer and Gillen, *Native Tribes of Central Australia*, pp. 204 ff.

In the Upper Palaeolithic for the reasons which have been considered totemism in all probability can be eliminated as the socio‐religious setting of the rites of increase, but, nevertheless, there can be little doubt that seasonal ceremonies with much the same intent were held in the cavern‐sanctuaries, and under very similar conditions. In both cases the purpose was the promotion of fecundity concentrated on the food supply as a pre‐presentation of forthcoming events and their results. Therefore, they were brought into relation with the periodic sequence in nature as a constantly recurring phenomenon. At certain times in the year the animals and plants are prolific and at other times there may be a scarcity often bordering on famine. The dates and circumstances vary according to climatic conditions in different localities and periods in the history of the world. In the Upper Palaeolithic in western Europe, for instance, the weather and surroundings were very different from those that obtained in the valley of the Nile, or in Mesopotamia, when civilization arose there in and after the fifth millennium B.C., or in more recent times on the dry steppes of Central Australia. A nearer parallel with the Palaeolithic Magdalenian cultural phase would be perhaps the Arctic environment of the proto‐Eskimo and the Palaeo‐Asiatic cultures where the perpetual dread of ice and snow, and the long dismal winter rather than the hope of spring predominated. While the modern Eskimo cannot be regarded as descendants of the Magdalenians, as sometimes has been suggested,[1] nevertheless, besides resemblances in their imple‐ments and weapons of ivory and bone, the two cultures resemble each other in respect of their climatic conditions and depend‐ence on the reindeer.

In the Arctic regions the reindeer herds migrate to their northerly feeding grounds from the forest belt at the end of May in search of fresh vegetation, returning at the approach of winter to the woodlands in the south. It is then that the hunting expeditions are in full force to capture the well‐fed herds and their young, particularly at the river crossings, and to lay in

[1] W. J. Sollas, *Ancient Hunters*, 1915, pp. 485 ff.

stores of meat dried in the sun and fat and hides for the long
winter ahead. It would be at such times and occasions that the
ritual of the chase would be most likely to be performed under
these circumstances, though the increase rites might be held
more appropriately at the breeding season in the early summer.
Anyway, the climatic conditions and local peculiarities in
such matters as breeding, migration and other habits of the
animals have been largely responsible for determining the
timing of the seasonal ritual observances everywhere and at all
times, and there is no reason to suppose that the Upper Palaeolithic was an exception to this rule.

### THE VEGETATION CULTUS

It was not, however, until the ice retreated northwards at the
end of the Pleistocene period, some 14,000 years ago, that a
fundamental change came over the situation as a result of a
climatic crisis. With milder inter-glacial oscillations the steppes
and tundras in Europe became forested, and the prairies of
North Africa and Western Asia were transformed into deserts
with fertile oases. It was then, after the Magdalenians had
evacuated their former haunts following the reindeer and the
cold-loving animals towards the Arctic regions, that settlers
from an original Asiatic cradleland with Gravettian cultural
affinities began to infiltrate into Europe, perhaps by way of
North Africa. Eventually when they had adopted a sedentary
life, their descendants took up their abode in small groups in
the open glades of the forests and on the banks of rivers or
on lakesides, eking out a precarious existence by hunting or
fishing, snaring game and wild fowl with the aid of the jackal
in the Mesolithic phase between the Palaeolithic and Neolithic
periods.

### The Beginnings of Agriculture

In these settlements, and particularly those on the edge of the
deserts in the Near East, as more and more animals became
attached to the human habitations they acquired a domestic
status. Similarly, the storing of fruits, berries, and wild grasses

may have led to their seeds having been collected, and, like edible roots, germinating until at length an accidental event became a deliberate practice, once it was recognized that fresh supplies could be grown by sowing the seeds in the soil and cultivating the resultant crops. But the transition from hunting to herding and from food-gathering to agriculture was a gradual process, at first confined to favourable localities, and then only very slowly adopted. As the dog had become the companion of man in the chase in the Mesolithic, so it is not improbable that other animals may have been tamed and admitted to the family circle before systematic attempts were made at stock-rearing and dairy farming. A few cows and goats may have been milked when men and animals were brought together in a closer intimacy in the oases and river valleys as the deserts spread in North Africa, the southern flatlands and Western Asia. Similarly, the process of germination having been observed in these reserves, seeds of wheat and barley doubtless were sown in the fertile soil so that a regular cereal harvest might be obtained for future use.

At this stage of mixed farming, the prevailing economy may have been husbanding resources rather than organized husbandry, supplemented with a few tamed cows, goats, sheep or pigs, and pursued in conjunction with snaring, fowling, trapping or hunting any prey that happened to be available. Therefore, the transition from food-gathering to food-production did not constitute a 'Neolithic revolution' at all comparable to that which characterized the Industrial Revolution in Western Europe in the last century of our present era, as has often been erroneously affirmed in Marxist circles. Where the new methods of securing a permanent supply were adopted in particular localities they were at most supplementary to the hazards of hunting, fishing and collecting the means of subsistence from day to day, brought about very largely by dire necessity of conserving the very meagre resources available under the climatic and environmental conditions, and dependent upon local circumstances often hardly less precarious than those governing the chase.

Wheat and barley grew wild in South-West Asia chiefly on the Syrian hills and on the Persian highlands, and in the caves at Wadi el Natuf in Mount Carmel; and elsewhere in Palestine the remains of a culture have come to light in which hunting was combined with the use of sickles employed for cutting straw or the stems of grass, and of mortars and rubbers for grinding corn—perhaps the wheat and barley that still grew wild there. These Natufians had tamed the dog but there are no traces of any other domesticated animals in their settlements, or of a knowledge of the art of making pottery.[1] If they were not actually engaged in cultivating grain at least they harvested the grasses that grew wild, and since their date probably is somewhere between 8000 and 6000 B.C. they represent a very early stage in the beginnings of agriculture. Now Miss Kenyon has found an agricultural settlement at Jericho without pottery belonging apparently to this period (i.e. 8000–6000 B.C.),[2] though Dr Braidwood would reduce the estimate to about 5000 B.C. to bring it into line with his own excavation at Qalat Jarmo, dated by radio carbon 14 analysis at approximately 4750 B.C.[3]

Whether the lowest levels in the mound at Jericho containing mortars and grinding stones for milling corn but no pottery belong to the eighth millennium B.C., as Miss Kenyon and Sir Mortimer Wheeler believe,[4] or to the second half of the fifth millennium B.C. contemporary with the parallel pre-pottery village-farming community at Jarmo on the Kurdish foothills of north-eastern Iraq,[5] it is becoming apparent that it is to the fertile oases rather than to the great river valleys like the Nile and the Euphrates that we have to look for the earliest phases of agriculture, and 'urbanization'. At Jericho a settled community defended by a strong stone wall and a tower had become firmly established within a fortified enclosure contain-

[1] D. A. E. Garrod and D. M. A. Bates, *The Stone Age of Mount Carmel*, O.U.P., 1937; *B.S.A.*, xxxvii, 1936-7, pp. 123 ff.
[2] K. M. Kenyon, *Digging up Jericho*, 1957, pp. 51 ff.; *Antiquity*, xxx, 1956, pp. 184 ff.     [3] *Antiquity*, xxxi, 1957, pp. 78 ff.
[4] *Ibid.*, xxx, 1956, pp. 134 ff.     [5] *Ibid.*, xxiv, 1950, pp. 190 ff.

ing a spring, said to produce a thousand gallons of water a minute, which still supports the town and irrigates the luxurious oasis.[1] This perpetual supply of water would account for the location of the early settlement at the western edge of the desert with its fertile alluvium covered with trees and corn fields, in striking contrast to the surrounding wilderness. Such a supply of life-giving water in the midst of an arid plain stimulating the practice of agriculture could hardly have failed at this early period to have attracted the attention and veneration of the pre-ceramic Neolithic population in this singularly favoured spot. Among their permanent houses are the remains of structures which seem to have been shrines with cult-objects which include a menhir, or *mazzebah*, comparable to those found in Semitic sanctuaries, a ceremonial basin used perhaps in connexion with ablutions, and female figurines suggestive of the worship of the Mother-goddess, with emblems of the male generative organ prominent in Near Eastern religion everywhere. It seems, therefore, that in this very ancient settled community so dependent upon the productivity of the soil for its existence, a fertility vegetation cult was in vogue in which maternal and phallic symbols played their customary roles.

## The Emergence of the Vegetation Cultus

As food-gathering dropped more and more into the background until finally it was abandoned, or became only very sparsely contributory to agriculture and herding, the fertility of the soil and the succession of summer and winter, springtime and harvest, together with the associated pursuits—tilling and ploughing, sowing and reaping—became the centre of interest and of the ritual organization. Under these new conditions the regular growth of the crops was a matter of vital concern, as had been the hazards of the chase in Palaeolithic and Mesolithic times. Nature was no less precarious for the farmer than for the hunter, consequently at the critical seasons an emotional reaction to the prevailing tension called forth a

[1] Kenyon, *Antiquity*, xxx, 1956, p. 184.

ritual response to ensure success in the food-producing activities at their several stages, and overcome the unpredictable elements in the situation outside human control by natural means. Thus, a ritual technique was devised to prepare the ground for the sowing of the crops to prevent sterility and promote fertility, and subsequently to secure a safely gathered and abundant harvest and the renewal of the generative process in nature. Around this cultus a death and resurrection drama in due course developed.

When food-production along these lines began to supplant food-gathering in the Fertile Crescent in the fourth millennium B.C. attention was concentrated increasingly on the ritual control of husbandry in its various aspects and phases. This is apparent in Tells like Sialk near Kashan on the western edge of the arid Iranian plateau, at Jarmo on the Kurdish foothills to the east of the Tigris, at Hassuna in northern Iraq, Halaf on the Upper Khabur river in eastern Syria, at Merimde to the west of the Nile Delta north of Cairo, at Badari and Deir Tasa in Middle Egypt, and in other sites on the more habitable spurs of the desert near the eastern bank of the Nile. It was then when copper was coming into general use and finely painted pottery was being widely distributed through northern Mesopotamia, Iran and Kurdistan that female figurines became prevalent. At Hassuna they have been found in the earliest levels of the mound and at Arpachiyah in the Mosul district of northern Iraq near the ancient city of Nineveh clay statuettes were abundant before 4000 B.C.

## The Cult of the Mother-goddess

Some of these so-called 'idols' are roughly modelled in the round, others of the 'fiddle-shaped' variety are flat, but they all resemble their Palaeolithic prototypes generally known as 'Venuses' (e.g. the Willendorf, Lespugne, Brassempouy and Laussel female figurines) in having the maternal organs especially emphasized, often with pendulous breasts, a pro-tuberant navel, and sometimes highly developed buttocks. Most of them are in a squatting posture this being a normal attitude adopted in childbirth; others seem to indicate a state of pregnancy. Frequently no attempt has been made to fashion the face or head, and the body has been reduced to a peg or cone. They tend to be inferior in design and technique, in fact, to the earlier examples from the Upper Palaeolithic and the excessive conventionalization suggests that they were used as amulets rather than images emblematic of the maternal divine principle, if not portraying the actual Mother-goddess, symbolizing her functions and attributes.[1]

From their abundance at Arpachiyah it would seem that the cult was firmly established in northern Iraq, probably in the fifth millennium B.C., before it became very prominent in the rest of Western Asia. Thus, only a few have been recovered from the pre-Halaf stratum at Tell Hassuna, whereas in the late Halaf deposits they became prevalent everywhere from the Syrian coast to the Zagros mountains,[2] spreading eventually to Persia, Baluchistan and the Indus valley in the east, and to Anatolia, Crete and the Aegean in the west; often so badly modelled that they can have been employed only as charms to facilitate accouchement and the increase of fruitfulness. At Tell Beit Mirsim in the south of Palestine, for example, in an Israelite Iron Age occupation level, Dr Albright has discovered a group of five statuettes representing nude women in what he believes to be the act of childbirth to hasten parturition by a magical device.[3]

While figures of this nature are hardly likely to be representa-tions of the Goddess herself, once the maternal principle had been personified it was either a single goddess who eventually became the Great Mother with her various functions and symbols, such as genitalia, doves, the double axe and serpents, or a number of independent gods and goddesses exercising their

[1] James, *The Cult of the Mother Goddess*, 1959, pp. 23 ff.; E. Douglas van Buren, *Clay Figurines of Babylonia and Assyria*, New Haven, 1930, pp. xlixf.

[2] Mallowan and Cruikshank Rose, *Iraq*, ii, 1935, pp. 79ff.; cf. *Syria*, iii, 1936, pp. 19ff.

[3] Albright, *The Archaeology of Palestine and the Bible*, 1932, p. 109; *Annual of American Schools of Oriental Research*, xxi–xxii, 1943, pp. 23 ff.

several roles in the processes of generation, fertility and birth, in whom the cult was centred. At first it would seem to have been concentrated mainly on the mystery of birth and the major aspects of fecundity, propagation and nutrition since the principal concern of man throughout the ages always has been food and children. Therefore, the veneration of the maternal principle and the worship of the Mother-goddess constitute one of the oldest and most persistent elements in the history of religion around which the seasonal ritual has developed.

Behind the complex figure of the life-producing Mother lay all that is involved in the processes of birth and generation, alike in the human and animal orders, in the struggle for existence and survival. Under Palaeolithic conditions maternal symbolism was predominant because it gave expression to this life urge and woman was its essential instrument playing the indispensable role in propagation. When food-gathering gave place to food-production as agriculture and herding became established the two poles of creative energy, the one female and receptive, and the other male and begettive, could not fail to be recognized. Then the network of emotions and sentiments and their ritual representations that had gathered round the maternal centre acquired a dual significance. Phallic emblems became increasingly prominent in the Neolithic and subsequent cultures but the maternal principle, now personified in the Mother-goddess, continued to assume the leading role in Western Asia, Crete and the Aegean, where the male god was subordinate to the Goddess. With the rise of the practice of agriculture women apparently were mainly responsible for hoeing and the cultivation of the crops on a small scale around the homestead, and it is by no means improbable that the very deeply laid association of their maternal functions with the fertility of the soil made it singularly appropriate for them to engage in these operations.

It was not, in fact, until sowing and reaping expanded involving heavy manual labour that it was transferred to the male section of the community. Then the plough acquired a phallic significance being the instrument by which the earth was broken up and made ready to receive the seeds to be sown in it. But originally the soil being regarded as the womb of Mother-earth, it was exclusively her own domain, and to disturb it was a perilous undertaking often demanding appease-ment by a sacrificial offering or ritual expiation of some kind. Even when the ground had been cleared and farmed by men the breaking of the soil and the planting were done by women who as the child-bearers alone could enable the earth to bring forth abundantly.

## The Worship of the Sky-father and the Earth-mother

As the inexhaustible repository of all the vital forces responsible for the manifestations of life and maternity, the earth retained its procreative significance long after the self-fertilizing female principle had been abandoned and the male paternal functions had been recognized and given their part and place in the vegetation cultus. The Earth-mother then became associated with the Sky-father who was regarded as sending the rain to fertilize the soil through a sacred marriage with the Goddess. When the existence of an extra-mundane celestial Supreme Being was recognized and made the source of creative activity and centred in the god of the all-encompassing sky, who was the creator and sustainer of the universe, the various aspects and attributes of nature were related to him directly or indirectly as the head of the pantheon in the polytheistic systems in the Near East and their derivatives in the Ancient World.

Everywhere the same linguistic root connects the heavens, the clouds and the rain with their personifications in the Sky-god and his manifestations in the revivification of nature, the storm and the thunder. For example, the very ancient Indo-European Sky- and Weather-god Dyaus Pitar, who personi-fied the heavens, the prototype of the Greek Zeus and the Roman Jupiter, was the source of the fertilizing rain in his procreative capacity. So in India he was united with Prithivi the Earth-mother, and they were vaguely conceived as the universal parents of mankind, Dyavaprithivi, personifying respectively the physical heavens and earth, themselves having

been fashioned from the primeval cosmic waters.[1] Although
Dyaus faded into the background and in the Vedas became
little more than the designation of the 'bright sky', the sky was
always regarded as creative—the bull fertilizing the earth in a
sacred marriage of the primeval pair. But it was his consort
Prithivi who was the chief object of devotion in the cultus,
Dyaus not being even mentioned in the hymns celebrating
Heaven and Earth.[2] In the ritual before sowing, ploughing
and at milking the sacred cow, the Earth-mother was revered
as the dynamic source of all life. After each successive harvest
the soil having become exhausted it had to be renewed by the
performance of fertility dances, sometimes involving human
sacrifice, to obtain 'good crops, good weather and good
health' by the aid of the Goddess. So fundamental was the
sacrifice to her of the human Meriah, as the victim was called
among the Khonds of Bengal, that it persisted until it was
suppressed under British rule.

For the Greeks, again, it was Ge or Gaia, the Earth-goddess,
who gave birth to Ouranus, the heavens, and they became the
primeval pair long before Zeus was coupled with one or other
of her personifications—Aphrodite, Semele, Artemis, Demeter,
etc.—with whom he contracted so many alliances. In his
Cretan form he was a much more primitive figure than the
Indo-European Sky-god who was worshipped under a variety
of names derived from the root 'to shine', and who was finally
known as Zeus 'the Sky' when the migrants from the Eurasian
grasslands settled on the pastures of Thessaly. There on the
misty heights of Mount Olympus he was 'the cloud-gatherer'
sending rain and manifesting his presence in lightning and
thunder, though his proper home was in the celestial realms.
But instead of becoming an obscure figure like Dyaus Pitar
and many other High Gods or Supreme Beings, he assumed
the role of a composite deity incorporating the nature and
attributes and cultus of a great many gods connected with his
several functions. Legends grew up around him which had

[1] *Rig-veda*, x, 110, 9; iii, 3, 11; N. Brown, *J.A.O.S.*, lxii, 1942, pp. 86ff.
[2] *Rig-veda*, v, 84, 1ff.

little or nothing to do with his original aspects, such as the Cretan story of his birth by Rhea, the consort of Kronos and an early form of the Anatolian Mother-goddess Kybele, and his suckling by a goat. In this capacity he embodied the processes of fecundity as the year-god, the spirit of fertility, and the new life of spring.[1] Therefore, it is not surprising that a vegetation legend and cultus should have developed in connexion with this version of his birth and infancy, or that a Sky- and Weather-god should be identified with the flocks and herds as well as with the vitalizing rains fecundating the earth at the appropriate seasons.

Such a coalescence frequently had occurred from the Fertile Crescent and Anatolia to the Indo-Iranian region, and when the Olympian myth and ritual of the Indo-Europeans reached Greece and were fused with the Goddess worship of the Aegean basin Zeus continued to exercise his customary functions without any very substantial change in combination with those of the indigenous chthonian vegetation cultus in which the goddesses from below were fecundated by the gods from above. Behind this mythology and its ritual enactment may lie reminiscences of a historical situation when the Olympian Sky-religion defeated to some extent the chthonian goddess cult of the soil and incorporated it into its own system of faith and practice. Thus, Zeus combined his original celestial attributes and characteristic features with his vitalizing functions in connexion with the fertility of the earth and of vegetation when the Indo-European invaders had established themselves in Greece and lived on the product of the soil, and so had to adapt themselves and their cultus to the conditions of the land of their adoption.

The various unions of Zeus with Earth- and Corn-goddesses—Hera, Dione, Semele, Kore (Persephone)—suggest that in the background of these traditions lay the widespread conception of the marriage of Heaven and Earth in which he played the role of the Sky-father in alliance with his many

---

[1] Nilsson, *Minoan-Mycenaean Religion*, Lund, 1950, pp. 543 ff.; Hesiod, *Theogony*, 453 ff.; *Antoninus Liberalis*, chap. 19.

divine consorts. In due course one of them was exalted to the
status of his official wife while the rest were regarded as his
mistresses in accordance with the custom then in vogue in the
Greek states where monogamy was established with con-
cubinage as an accepted practice.[1] In this way Zeus and the
Olympian mythology were brought into very intimate relations
with the seasonal festivals, and especially with those observances connected with vegetation expressing the sacred marriage
of Heaven and Earth interpreted in terms of the fertilization of
the ground by the life-giving rain.[2] In this syncretism, however, Zeus was always predominant his consorts being
relatively minor figures. Even the cult of Hera, his official wife,
had little to do with him, and the union was effected merely
because it was fitting for the chief god to have for his partner
the chief goddess.

## The Goddess and the Young God

In Western Asia, on the other hand, the Goddess retained her
pre-eminence, assuming the status of the mother and bride of
the young and virile male god rather than that of the Earth-
mother. Thus, in Mesopotamia when the maternal cult was
brought into relation with the seasonal cycle and its vegetation
ritual, the Goddess remained the ultimate source of generative
power in nature as a whole and so she was responsible for the
periodic renewal of life in the spring after the blight of the
winter or after the summer drought. Therefore, she was both
mother and bride with many different names and epithets, such
as Ninhursaga, Ninmah, Inanna-Ishtar, Nintu, Aruru,
Mah. In Sumerian mythology for instance Ninhursaga, 'the
mother of the land', was Ninsikil-la, 'the pure lady', until she
was approached by the Water-god of Wisdom, Enki, and
gave birth to a number of deities. Then she became Nintu ama
Kalamma, 'the lady who gives birth, the mother of the land'.
When she had accepted him as her husband she was Dam-
gal-nunna, 'the great spouse of the prince' (i.e. of Enki), and

[1] Minucius Felix, *Octavius*, xxii, 1.
[2] Cf. Tacitus, *Hist.*, iv, 81; Plutarch, *Moralia*, 361-2e.

having conceived as the fertile soil and given birth to vegetation she was Ninhursaga, 'the lady of the mountain', where nature manifested its powers of fecundity in the spring on its lush slopes.[1]

Similarly, the nuptials of Inanna, the Sumerian counterpart of the Akkadian Ishtar, were celebrated annually at the Spring Festival in Isin to revive the vital forces in nature because the ritual situation required the union of the goddess who incarnated fertility in general with the god who embodied the creative powers of spring in order to arouse the dormant earth and the process of fecundity at this season. Therefore, it was her marriage with Dumuzi, 'the faithful son of the waters that came forth from the earth'—the Sumerian equivalent of the youthful suffering Shepherd-god Tammuz, the son-lover of Ishtar—that gave expression to the vegetation cycle. The widespread and basic figure of Dumuzi-Tammuz recurring in a number of forms and names in the various versions of his legend, embodied the seasonal sequence, personifying the recreative powers of spring and the autumnal decline in nature, celebrated at the appropriate times in the year, according to local conditions and circumstances. His nature and significance in calendrical ritual will be considered in their various aspects as the inquiry proceeds. Suffice it to say at this juncture that he represented essentially the Young God who in the rotation of the seasons passed into the nether regions, typifying death for ritual purposes, and was rescued by the Goddess. Therefore, it was she who was responsible for his recovery and resuscitation on which the renewal of nature depended. So that in the last analysis Inanna-Ishtar not Dumuzi-Tammuz was the ultimate source of life and regeneration though the Young God as her agent was instrumental in the process. In short, she was the supreme embodiment of the creative powers in nature; he was the personification of the seasonal decline and revival in the generative process.

In Egypt, on the other hand, the position was reversed, as in

[1] Kramer, *Sumerian Mythology*, Philad., 1944, pp. 56ff.; *A.N.E.T.*, pp. 37ff.; Jacobsen, *J.N.E.S.*, iv, 1946, p. 150.

the case of Zeus. When the official priesthood systematized
theological speculation and organized the local cults and the
calendar on the basis of the unified rule of the 'Two Lands'
under one Pharaoh from the Fifth Dynasty (*c.* 2580 B.C.) the
king became the incarnation and the physical son of the Sun-
god Re at Heliopolis, and later of Amon-Re at Thebes.
Moreover, when the Osiris myth was solarized he reigned as
the living Horus, the posthumous son and avenger of Osiris,
the god of vegetation and the judge of the dead. Therefore, in
both his solar and Osirian capacities he was the epitome of all
that was divine in the Nile valley and never was subordinate
or subservient to the Goddess like the Mesopotamian kings.

Although Isis eventually became the syncretistic 'Goddess
of many names' she was not in fact a Mother-goddess. Rather
was it with the Sky- and Cow-goddess Hathor, the mother of
Horus the Elder, and in the Heliopolitan tradition the wife of
Re, that all the reproductive goddesses were identified. It was
she who was essentially the Mother-goddess *par excellence.*
Eventually Isis incorporated her horns in her symbolism but
originally Isis was 'the throne woman' personifying the sacred
coronation stool which was charged with the mysterious power
of kinship.[1] To this extent she was the source of royal vitality,
but, nevertheless, the Pharaohs exercised their functions because
they were divine in their own right. Thus, to beget an heir to
the throne the reigning sovereign visited the queen in his divine
majesty rather than himself acquiring divinity by being
summoned by the Goddess to share her couch, as in Mesopotamia.

Isis provided the royal descent which gave the occupant of
the throne his right of succession through the instrumentality
of his human mother, the queen, but she was only the vehicle
of his incarnation, his divinity coming from his solar and
Osirian lineage derived from the royal god Horus and his
mother Hathor. Thus, in the Hellenistic period the marriage

[1] Sethe, *Urgeschichte und Aelteste Religion der Aegypter*, Leipzig, 1930, p.
85; M. A. Murray, *Journal of the Royal Anthropological Institute*, xlv, 1915,
pp. 308f.

of Hathor and Horus was celebrated at the festival at Edfu (Behdet) when the image of Hathor was taken there by ship from her temple at Denderah on the western bank of the Nile, forty miles north of Thebes, for a ritual visit to her husband Horus with whom she consorted for a fortnight, apparently on mutual terms, the Goddess enjoying 'the beauteous embrace with her Horus'.[1] As 'the Bull of Heaven' the Pharaoh in his divine capacity was the dominant male, the embodiment of virile fertility impregnating the queen, 'the cow who bore the bull'.[2]

From prehistoric times onwards Horus was worshipped all over Egypt, usually in association with his ancient symbol the falcon, to which was added that of the disk of the sun with outstretched wings when he and his followers conquered Upper Egypt. References to his festivals and their processions constantly occur in the records and inscriptions,[3] and while there were many Horus falcon gods worshipped at various places, it was mainly Horus the Elder and Horus the son of Osiris and Isis in whose honour the calendrical festivals were held with their ceremonial voyages of the images of the god in his boat, and litanies, often including the enactment of the resurrection of Osiris by his son.[4] It was this recurrent theme, and its ritual representation that was fundamental in the seasonal observances in the Nile valley, and in them the predominant role was played by the male year-god and his associates; the Goddess had her part but this was not as conspicuous as it was in Western Asia.

[1] Junker, *Die Onurislegende*, Vienna, 1917, p. 116. Erman, *Handbook of Egyptian Religion*, 1907, pp. 215ff.

[2] *P.T.*, 282c, 990d.

[3] Bayer, 'Die Religion der aeltesten aegyptischen Inschriften', *Anthropos*, xx–xxiii, 1925, pp. 417ff.

[4] L. Moret, *Rituel du culte divin journalier en Egypte*, Paris, 1902.

## CHAPTER II

# The Calendrical Festivals in Egypt

SINCE so much depended upon the rise and fall of the Nile in Egypt the agricultural calendrical observances were based on its inundations at regular intervals. As Herodotus recognized, the country was in fact 'the gift of the Nile', and upon it all phases of Egyptian life depended. Flowing out of the streams which rise in the vast African lakes and the mountains of Abyssinia, it becomes flooded in the spring with the heavy African rains and melting Abyssinian snows, and overflows its banks leaving behind a very fertile deposit of silt which renews the soil and creates a highly fertile oasis in the surrounding desert, extending from the First Cataract at Aswan to the Mediterranean, broadening into the flat marshes of the Delta near the ancient city of Memphis where Lower Egypt begins. In all, the 'Two Lands' of Upper and Lower Egypt cover less than ten thousand square miles.

## THE SEASONAL SEQUENCE IN THE NILE VALLEY

In May the level of the river is at its lowest and the parched soil would be in danger of becoming arid were it not for the annual inundation which begins in June. Then it is covered first with a vegetable detritus followed a month later by a rich humus containing minerals and potash. The rising waters continue their beneficent functions until they begin to recede in October, though the irrigation canals and their dykes, with the aid of water wheels, keep the water in reserve for the rest of the year. In such a land of perpetual summer, where rain is virtually unknown and the sun shines by day continually, its heat tempered with cool and drying winds, a stable agricultural civilization hardly could fail to develop, with every natural resource in its favour maintaining the regular rhythm of the seasons, in striking contrast to the wilderness all around.

Therefore, that the sun and the river, upon the conjunction of which everything depended, were deified and the rise and fall of the Nile was carefully observed and measured and brought into relation with the Osirian ritual is not surprising, notwith-standing the fact that the civil calendar bore little or no connexion with the seasons.

## The Invention of the Calendar

In theory the year began on the nineteenth of July thereby co-inciding with the rise of the Nile at 'The Season of Inundation' (Thoth) in the peasants' calendar. Through observation of the heavens and the recurrence of the inundation in 4241 B.C. it appears that the earliest astronomers in the Delta noticed that Sothis, the Dog Star (i.e. Sirius) rose just before the sun on the same day as that on which the inundation began. Thus, on the basis of that star a calendar year of three hundred and sixty-five days was established, and arbitrarily divided into twelve months of thirty days, each with five feast days at the end. Actually, however, the year was nearly six hours too short, but despite the growing discrepancy between the rising of the star and the inundations and the seasons the date was retained as the beginning of the official year. This is the earliest fixed date in the history of the world, and the first attempt to devise a calendar artificially divorced from nature except in the accept-ance of the day and the year, and in spite of the lunar month and the solar year being incommensurable quantities.[1]

Side by side with this official calendar there was doubtless a civil year that followed the seasons. Thus, four months after 'The Season of Inundation' in the peasants' calendar 'The Season of Coming Forth' (Tybi) was celebrated when the waters were at their height, and in February and March 'The Season of Deficiency' (Pakhen) marked their decline after the grain sown in November had disappeared and the summer was approaching, from March until June. Although in its de-veloped form the calendar involved highly complex computa-tion based on the solar year reckoned from the heliacal rising

[1] Breasted, *A History of Egypt*, New York, 1905, pp. 32f.

of the Dog Star Sothis related to the annual inundation of the
Nile, dependent upon observations carried on for a prolonged
period, it is not improbable that it was based on much simpler
calculations respecting the Nilotic year.[1]

References to the five epagomenal days correcting the mis-
calculations of the length of the solar year in the Pyramid
Texts at Sakkara at the beginning of the Old Kingdom in
connexion with the birthdays of the Osirian gods suggest that
the civil calendar went back to an earlier period, calculated at
4241 B.C.[2] But if in fact the Sothic version was a later elaboration, the Nilotic original must have been in vogue far back in the
Predynastic era. Be this as it may, it was the rise and fall of the
Nile that was of supreme importance for Egypt, and sooner or
later the beginning of the season of inundation was made the
commencement of the year. Having observed its coincidence
with the heliacal rising of the Dog Star which occurred on
July 19th (in the Julian calendar), the chronologists started
their calculations for a year of three hundred and sixty-five days
divided into twelve months from this date, with five days
intercalated at the end.

If as it would seem this calendar was instituted in Early
Dynastic times, it was based on a long period of observation
and notational recording going back no doubt in origin to the
Predynastic period. But for the practical purposes of agriculture
and the inseparable calendrical observances, it was the rise and
fall of the Nile and the lunar sequence that were of vital
importance and remained the determining factor in daily life.
Thus, the oldest calendar divided the year into three periods of
four months related to the agricultural course of events determined by the inundations, and the behaviour of the river was
sufficiently erratic to cause the rising of its waters to be watched
with anxiety during the early months of the inundation until
the maximum, on which the prosperity of the country depended, was reached. If it was low all the land could not be

[1] Neugebauer, *Acta Orientalia*, vii, 1939, pp. 169 ff.

[2] E. J. Drioton and J. Vandier, *L'Egypte*, p. 50; Sethe, *Urgeschichte und Aelteste
Religion der Aegypter*, p. 110.

cultivated, everywhere the crops would be light, and there was always the danger of famine, as in the Joseph story in the book of Genesis. Similarly, if it was too high flooding resulted, and the seeds were washed out of the ground before germinating. Therefore, a 'good Nile', when the correct level would be maintained and everyone be content was anxiously sought.

Under these uncertain circumstances June opened every year with apprehension, the river then being reduced to a mere trickle and the desert threatening to engulf the valley. True, by comparison with the Tigris and Euphrates the Nile was remarkably uniform and very seldom brought disaster upon the country, but since there was always the possibility of drought or flooding, offerings in the form of seals, pendants and statuettes were made to the god of the river, Hapi, and his consort Repit, by the Pharaoh and in the temples, both at the beginning of June and two months later when the inundation was at its height, before the waters receded, and ploughing began. The Dog Star Sirius was identified with Isis, and as the Nile was thought to be the fluids that exuded from Osiris[1] so the inundation was supposed to have been caused by the tears of Isis.[2] In the calendar on one of the walls at the temple of Ramesses III at Medinet Habu it is definitely stated that the Festival of Sirius celebrated on this day coincided with that of the New Year,[3] which was observed throughout Egypt as a holiday and the occasion for the offering of gifts to the gods, and to the Pharaoh.[4]

## The Festival of Opet

The sequence of festivals extended throughout the year cele-brating in addition to the agricultural observances the birth-days of gods and men, legendary episodes in their lives, the coronation and royal jubilees and mortuary rituals. They were

[1] Blackman, *Zeitschrift für aegyptische Sprache und Altertumskunde*, l, 1912, pp. 69f.    [2] A. H. Gardiner, *J.E.A.*, xxiv, 1938, pp. 170ff.
[3] Wilson, *Medinet Habu III*, Chicago, 1940, pl. 152.
[4] N. de Davies, *Tomb of Ken-Amun at Thebes*, i, Metropolitan Museum of Art, New York, 1930, pl. 38-9.

most numerous, however, in the first month (Thoth or Akhit) when work in the fields was at a standstill owing to the inundation. It was then when the floods were at their height that the Feast of Opet in honour of Amon was held at Karnak and Thebes, lasting usually for twenty-four days. This was a New Year event in which almost the entire population appear to have taken part, having plenty of leisure to greet the bark of the god on the swollen waters of the Nile in the flotilla that was pressed into service to accompany it and the gods on their triumphant voyage from Karnak to 'Southern Opet' (i.e. Luxor). There Amon was going to remain for nearly a month in the 'Southern Harim', the headquarters in all probability of the secondary wives or concubines of his high priest.

From the series of reliefs on the walls on either side of the court of Amenhotep III at Luxor, executed in the reign of Tutankhamen (*c.* 1366–57 B.C.), the ceremonies began with food and drink offerings to Amon, his consort Mut, and their son Khonsu, in the temple at Karnak. The shrines of each of the gods were in the form of a boat with the image of the god in the cabin in the centre. On that of Amon at the bow and stern were ornaments of ram's head, that of Mut was adorned with two women's heads and a vulture skin, and there were two falcon heads on that of Khonsu. Poles were attached to the shrines to enable the priests to carry them in solemn procession to the quayside with a *flabellifer*, or ceremonial fan, in front and behind each boat, and a pair of attendants clad in panther-skins. The Pharaoh followed the boat of Amon and a trumpeter and drummer led the way. On reaching the water's edge the boat-shrines were placed on large and elaborately decorated vessels, some sixty to seventy feet in length, in the form of a temple, with a central shrine, obelisks, sphinxes, statues and bas-reliefs depicting the king performing rites in honour of Amon. On the bow and stern were two huge rams, while the boats of Mut and Khonsu were similarly decorated, their animal symbols replacing the ram and crowns of that of Amon.

When all was ready for the voyage to begin the soldiers who had been marshalled to tow the vessels to the main stream of the Nile began their arduous task headed by a priest chanting a hymn to Amon, and accompanied by a Negro drummer and Negro dancers, some carrying trumpets, others performing antics among the crowd, together with priests rattling castanets and priestesses jingling sistra, while the citizens on the east bank of the river clapped their hands and beat tambourines in time with the music. On reaching the main stream the vessels containing the images were taken over by the flotilla of small boats, and both the banks were thronged with spectators from far and near as they proceeded in triumph to Luxor, 'the southern Opet'. There the images were taken off the ships and carried in procession to the temple on the shoulders of the priests behind the drummer and trumpeter, the concubines of Amon dancing and rattling their sistra.

Within, the gods were the recipients of lavish food and drink offerings presented to them by the Pharaoh. But precisely what took place during their stay of twenty-four days at Luxor has not been recorded. That it included excessive eating and drinking—the characteristic feature of all great festivals in Ancient Egypt—is suggested by the quantities of food and liquor amassed for the occasion. But in addition to these not very edifying jollifications it is probable that the rites included the enactment of episodes in the legend of Amon, borrowed in the first instance, perhaps, from that of Min, the very ancient fertility god of Koptos in Upper Egypt, of whom Amon may have become a localized form before he was identified with the Heliopolitan Sun-god Re in the Middle Kingdom.[1] Be this as it may, whatever had taken place during this month of festivities at Luxor, when they came to an end the sacred fleet made its way back to Karnak where the images were reinstated in their shrines in the temple, following the same procedure and with similar accompaniments, though probably with less enthusiasm now that the objects of the visit had been achieved and

[1] Newberry, *Annals of Anthropology and Archaeology*, iii, Liverpool, 1916, p. 50.

prosperity for the forthcoming year had been secured, with the king safely renewed on the throne of Horus.[1]

How firmly established was this festival is shown by its survival in a degraded condition in the annual procession in honour of an obscure Muslim patron saint of Luxor, Sheykh Yusef Abu'l-Haggag, on the fourteenth of the month of Sha'ban. On the western side of the first court of the temple of Ramesses II a mosque has been erected containing the tomb of the saint, and to it two beflagged boats mounted on four-wheeled lorries drawn by men and boys hauling ropes attached to the shafts, are taken with flags inscribed with sacred texts carried in front and behind. Starting from the market place the procession, in which the decorated boats are supported by soldiers, musicians, dancers, readers of the Qur'an, gaily adorned camels, men, women and children singing hymns in honour of the saint, proceeds through the streets. Stations are made at the tombs of the other local saints and prayers recited. Finally the boats are deposited in the mosque of Sheykh Yusel Abu'l Haggag where they remain for the rest of the year.[2] Various legends appear from time to time by way of explanation of the observance, but it is clearly a rather outworn and therefore meaningless relic of the ancient Festival of Opet depicted on the western wall outside the temple of Ramesses III.

## The Harvest Festival of Min

When the season of enforced leisure came to an end the preparations for the harvest began with 'The Coming Forth of Min', the god of fertility and the lord of Koptos and the desert regions, who since Predynastic times had personified the generative force in nature as the bestower of procreative power. Therefore, although several commemorations were observed in connexion with Min during the course of the year, the

[1] Wolf, *Das schöne Fest von Opet*, Leipzig, 1931; Blackman, *Luxor and its Temples*, 1923, pp. 70 ff.

[2] Blackman, *Luxor and its Temples*, p. 78; G. Legrain, *Louqsor dans les Pharaons*, Paris, 1919, pp. 81 ff.; J. Hornell, *Man*, xxxviii, 1938, pp. 145 f.

harvest month of Shemou (April) was the principal and most appropriate occasion for the Harvest Festival to be held over which in the official calendar he presided. As the god of fertility, and especially of sexual reproduction, he was repre-sented as an ithyphallic bearded man, but as he was also a storm and weather-god his emblem was the thunderbolt. Traditionally he was regarded as the son of Osiris and Isis and of Re, and also of Shu, the god of the atmosphere who held up the heavens with his arms and dwelt between heaven and earth. His connexions with Horus began in prehistoric times when in the Gerzean period he was a sky and fertility god associated with both the falcon as a symbol of heaven and with meteorites, two drawings of the thunderbolt appearing on colossal mono-liths of Min at Koptos.[1] His special care was the corn and the hoeing of the soil, and so his principal festival was celebrated at the beginning of the harvest.[2]

As the local god at a strategic point where the Nile and the Red Sea most closely approach each other, and the caravan route to the east begins, Min early acquired a wider cultus in the form of Min-Horus and eventually Min-Amon, identified with both fertility worship and the sky religion. Thus, by the time of the Middle Kingdom the lord of Koptos and the desert region had become a composite deity whose principal festival acquired a wider significance as a universal observance in which the king played the leading role. As depicted on the sculptures of the temple of Medinet Habu at Thebes on the west bank of the Nile, the ithyphallic statue of Min was carried on poles on the shoulders of the priests who were concealed under the hangings decorated with the names of the reigning Pharaoh (i.e. Ramesses III) and preceded by a white bull sacred to the god, with the solar disk surmounted by two feathers be-tween its horns. Behind it a bundle of lettuces, the plant of Min, was carried, and the Pharaoh walked in front of the statue.[3]

[1] Petrie, *The Making of Egypt*, 1939, p. 46, pl. xxxiv.; Wainwright, *J.E.A.*, xvii, 1931, pp. 185 f.

[2] Gauthier, *Les fêtes du dieu Min*, Cairo, 1931, pp. 194, 235.

[3] Wilson, *Medinet Habu III*, Chicago, 1940.

As the anniversary of the coronation of Ramesses III coincided with the festival the Pharaoh and the god were the two
principal figures in the procession. Thus, the king as the living
Horus went forth in triumph from his 'palace of life, health and
strength', shining like the rising sun in his splendour, to meet
and contemplate the beauty of his father Min who personified
the fertility of the newly sown fields, and to perform his royal
functions at the beginning of harvest. Like the statue of the
god, he is depicted seated on a litter in a chair decorated with
a sphinx and a lion, and the symbol of two winged goddesses,
borne by his sons and high dignitaries, and headed by priests
and important officials carrying the royal insignia, sunshades
and fans. Immediately in front of the litter the eldest son as the
heir-apparent walked, and behind it were the royal servants
and troops and a stool-bearer.

On reaching the dwelling of Min the king descended and
stood facing the shrine containing the image of the god. After
censings and libations he made the prescribed offerings, in
return for which he received the divine gift of renewed life. The
doors of the shrine were then opened and the statue in all its
beauty and magnificence was placed on its litter, after due
veneration, to be carried by the twenty-two priests, and escorted
by very many more waving bunches of flowers and fans, with
the Pharaoh wearing the crown of Lower Egypt, and accompanied by the queen and the white bull, and the bearers of the
various emblems of the ancestors and gods who had been
associated with Min and his cultus in their long and chequered
history. These included Menes, the traditional founder of the
Dynasty, Nebkheroure who reunited the country, and many
of the rulers of the Eighteenth and Nineteenth Dynasties,
excluding Ikhnaton and Queen Hatshepsut who were by no
means in favour at court in the time of Ramesses III. Among
the name signs were jackals, falcons and an ibis.

Halts were made from time to time *en route*, apparently for
the purpose of performing dances and similar rites, and for the
recitation of liturgical hymns, until at length the shrine of Min
was reached where the god was duly installed on a throne

under a canopy and offerings were made to him by the king. Exactly what then took place is conjectural. It is not improbable that a sacred marriage was enacted by the Pharaoh and the queen at this point in the rite, Min being so very intimately connected with the maintenance of the royal lineage. Thus, at the end of the festival a priest proclaimed, 'Hail to thee Min, who impregnates his mother! How mysterious is that which thou hast done to her in the darkness.'[1] That at this Festival an heir to the throne should have been begotten is strictly in line with the royal accession ritual in Ancient Egypt, and Min who was called 'the Bull of his Mother'—the marital substitute of Osiris, *ka-mutef*—was thought to have been responsible for the conception of Horus by Isis.

It was to commemorate this event that at the Harvest Festival with its coronation affinities the sovereign assumed the double crown of Upper and Lower Egypt, and after his enthronement shot arrows north and south, east and west to destroy his enemies, and then released four birds, called after the children of Horus, Amseti, Hapi, Duamutef, and Qebehsenouf, to carry to the four cardinal points of the earth the proclamation: 'Horus son of Min and Osiris has assumed the Great Crown of Upper and Lower Egypt', just as the announcement of the accession of a new king was heralded by a similar release of birds.[2] At the Min Festival it was the union of the god with the king that was acclaimed rather than the actual accession, probably because at this annual observance the reaping of the crops was celebrated in conjunction with the worship of the god who symbolized the harmonious interlocking of nature and society in a divine source of fertility independent of the chances and changes of the seasonal sequence, and infinitely more dynamic than Osiris.

Thus, when Min had been installed, the statues were placed on the ground, the king and queen standing in the centre of a circle of officiants. A copper sickle was then handed to the Pharaoh who proceeded to cut a sheaf of spelt (*boti*) rooted in

---

[1] Gauthier, *op. cit.*, pp. 230f., 239f.

[2] Moret, *Du caractère religieux de la royauté pharaonique*, Paris, 1902, pp. 104ff.

the soil, which he may have offered to the bull to strengthen his virility and avert sterility.[1] But since Min was a form of Horus,[2] it would seem more likely that when it was said that the sheaf of barley was reaped by the king 'for his father' he was in fact acting in the capacity of the son of Osiris, and, therefore, he was impersonating Horus.[3] The reigning sovereign (Ramesses III) as the living Horus being equated with Min who personified the fertility of the newly sown fields, he exercised his royal functions at this seasonal ritual to secure a plentiful supply of the crops in the ensuing years. To this end for the king and queen to engage in a sacred marriage would be in accord with long-established and widely diffused custom in the Ancient East in what was primarily and essentially a royal seasonal ritual.

## Rites of Irrigation

A more popular method of dealing with the situation occurred when at the commencement of the agricultural year in the first half of August the irrigation canals were opened to enable the rising waters of the Nile to pass into the interior, allegorically interpreted in terms of the union of Osiris and Isis. So vital for the prosperity of the country was this cutting of the dams that every care had to be taken to ensure that it was done each year at the most auspicious moment and under the most propitious conditions. This appears to have involved throwing into the river a virgin attractively dressed as a sacrifice to obtain a plentiful inundation, a relic of which practice has survived in the casting of offerings of gold into it near Philae for this purpose, and to secure the growth of the crops by the union of the fructifying waters with the fertilized earth.[4] This custom has persisted throughout the ages as a popular observance, and the fact that a truncated cone of earth in front of the dam on the

---

[1] Frankfort, *Kingship and the Gods*, p. 188.

[2] Erman and Blackman, *The Literature of the Ancient Egyptians*, 1927, p. 137.

[3] Gardiner, *J.E.A.*, ii, 1915, p. 175.

[4] E. W. Lane, *Manners and Customs of Modern Egyptians*, 1895, pp. 499f.; J. G. Wilkinson, *Manners and Customs of the Ancient Egyptians*, ii, 1878, p. 366; Seneca, *Naturales Quaestiones*, iv, pp. 2, 7.

side of the river near Cairo is called 'the bride' (*aroosch*) and is erected to be washed down the Nile by the rising tide, suggests that originally a nuptial ritual was in vogue to effect the union of the river with his bride.

## The Osirian Festivals in the month of Khoiak

It was, however, on the first day of the first month of winter (Khoiak) that the great autumnal festival was held in commemoration of the death of Osiris described in some detail in a long inscription belonging to the Ptolemaic period inscribed on the walls of the temple at Denderah on the western bank of the river north of Thebes.[1] Although the order of the rites is by no means clear the enactment of the drama of Osiris is amplified in an inscription on a mortuary stele at Abydos where he was thought to have been buried, recording the performance of a combat between the followers and enemies of Osiris during a procession of the god in his barge. His foes were smitten but in the next act Osiris was killed by Seth, and after several days of mourning his body represented by an effigy adorned with funerary ornaments was transported to his tomb at Peker on the southeast of the temple, to the singing of dirges. In a third play the slaying of Seth and his followers was enacted, together with the return of Osiris restored to life and taken in triumph amid general rejoicing to his palace at Abydos.[2]

At Busiris in Lower Egypt, the original home of Osiris in the Delta, where the relic of his backbone was alleged to have been preserved, on the twentieth day of Khoiak barley and sand were placed in a flowerpot, and water from the inundation was poured over it, and over the headless image of a cow, perhaps representing Isis, to make the grain sprout. This symbolized the resurrection of Osiris after his burial, the growth of the 'garden' being the growth of his divine substance.[3]

[1] V. Loret, *Recueil de Travaux relatifs à la Philologie et à l'archéologie égyptiennes*, iii, 1882, pp. 43 ff.; 1883, iv, pp. 21 ff.; 1884, v, pp. 85 ff.

[2] A. Moret, *Mystères égyptiens*, Paris, 1912, p. 11; H. Schaefer, *Die Mysterien des Osiris in Abydos*, Leipzig, 1904.

[3] M. A. Murray, *The Osireion at Abydos*, 1904, p. 28.

At Philae the god is represented on a bier with water being poured over him by a priest, while at Abydos the barley and sand were put into a hollow gold statuette of Osiris in the form of a mummy on the twelfth day of Khoiak and laid in the 'garden' with rushes over and under it in the presence of the corn-goddess Shanty. It was wrapped in rushes and nine days later the sand and barley were removed. Incense was then inserted and the effigy was bandaged with strips of linen adorned with a necklace and a blue flower. Until the twenty-fifth day of the month it was exposed to the sun when its predecessor was brought out of its place of burial and laid on a bier. It was then buried in the tomb of Osiris (*Arq-heh*).[1]

At Denderah the representations of the resurrection were distinct from the Osiris-beds of barley which were watered from the eighteenth to the twenty-fifth of Khoiak, or a few days later. Unlike the 'beds' the grain in the hollow effigies instead of being allowed to sprout was exposed to the sun daily, and on the twenty-second it was sent on a mysterious voyage with other images of gods in thirty-four small boats illuminated by three hundred and sixty-five candles, representing presumably the days of the year. This coincided with a ceremony known as the 'hacking up of the earth',[2] and was preceded by a ploughing and sowing rite on the twelfth day of Khoiak when barley was sown at one end of a field, spelt at the other, and flax in the middle. Seed was scattered by a boy, and a ritual text, 'The Sowing of the Fields', was recited by the celebrant.[3] On the twenty-fourth day when the boats returned the effigy of Osiris was removed, placed in a coffin of mulberry wood, and laid in a grave two hours after sunset. At the ninth hour of the night the image of the previous year was put in the branches of a sycamore tree. On the thirteenth day of the month, when the inundation was due to subside and the sowing of the grain to begin, the effigy in its box was taken to a

[1] Murray, *op. cit.*; Davies and Gardiner, *The Tomb of Amenembet*, 1915, p. 115.
[2] Brugsch, *Thesaurus*, ii, 1891, p. 364.
[3] Brugsch, *Zeitschrift für aegyptische Sprache und Altertumskunde*, xix, 1881, pp. 90, 96ff.

subterranean chamber and placed on a bed of sand, there to rest until the ceremony was re-enacted the following year with its successor.[1]

The sequel to these burial rites is depicted on the bas-reliefs which accompany the inscription at Denderah. There a series of scenes exhibit the ithyphallic dead god swathed as a mummy on a bier gradually raising himself up with the assistance of Nephthys, Isis, and Horus, while before him a male attendant holds the *crux ansata*, the sign of life. In another representation Horus presents to him a lotus flower, and he is also shown with his soul in the form of a hawk with outstretched wings above him and the faithful Isis standing behind him.[2] In her temple at Philae Osiris is portrayed with stalks of corn sprouting from his dead body and a priest watering from a pitcher the germinating grain. In the inscription it is explained that 'this is the form of him whom one may not name, Osiris of the Mysteries, who springs from the waters'.[3] In this guise he was the personification of the corn that sprang from the inundated soil, but, nevertheless, he remained the dead god resuscitated in conjunction with the seasonal sequence rather than the young virile god of vegetation—a role played by Horus his son.

Now it was on the thirtieth day of Khoiak that his resurrection was enacted in the raising of the *Djed*-column at Busiris, Thebes, Memphis and elsewhere. This very ancient pillar resembling a telegraph-pole with four or five cross-bars at the top unquestionably was a symbol of Osiris before it was identified with Ptah at Memphis, representing perhaps a tree with the branches lopped off.[4] On the tomb of Kheryaf at Thebes it is shown in process of being raised with ropes by the Pharaoh with the help of the high priest of Memphis in the presence of the queen and her sixteen daughters

[1] Brugsch, *Zeitschrift*, xix, 1881, pp. 94, 99.

[2] Budge, *The Gods of the Egyptians*, ii, 1904, pp. 131 ff.

[3] Brugsch, *Religion und Mythologie der alten Aegypter*, Leipzig, 1885–8, pp. 621 ff.; V. Lanzone, *Dizionario di Mitologia Egizia*, Turin, 1881–4, pl. cclxi.

[4] Moret, *The Nile and Egyptian Civilization*, 1927, p. 81.

and a number of courtiers. A sham fight is depicted as in progress between the inhabitants of Buto, the Predynastic capital of Lower Egypt, while the king and his subjects, together with herds of cattle and asses process round the walls of the city.[1] At Abydos in the Hall of the Osirian Mysteries, the reputed home of the body of Osiris, a similar combat occurred and Seti I and Isis are represented setting up the *Djed*-column (swathed in a cloth) between them.[2]

In the Denderah inscriptions it is definitely stated to have been raised at Busiris on 'the day of the interment of Osiris'[3] when the coffin containing the effigy was placed in the sub-terranean tomb. If, as it seems, it was originally a lopped tree, perhaps a cedar representing the symbol of a Syrian vegetation god with whom Osiris was equated at a very early period, its ceremonial elevation may have been a seasonal rite in the Delta in prehistoric times, and so became the final act in the Dynastic Osirian festival in the month of Khoiak com-memorating the restoration to life of the dead king in his sepulchre. As Gardiner has pointed out 'the resurrection of Osiris on this thirtieth and last day of the month was not that of a young and vigorous god of vegetation, but that of a dead king recalled in the tomb to a semblance of his former life'.[4]

Osiris, in fact, was not strictly a vegetation deity but he was immanent in the annual germination of the crops in the soil. Thus, in the Memphite Mystery play performed at the accession of Senusert I in the Twelfth Dynasty (*c.* 1900 B.C.), the text of which contained material from much earlier than the Middle Kingdom,[5] he was identified with the barley and the emmer that nourished the gods in heaven and mankind on earth, and in the Ptolemaic temple at Denderah he was said to have

[1] Sethe, *Untersuchungen zur Geschichte und Altertumskunde Aegyptens*, iii, 1905, p. 134; Brugsch, *Thesaurus*, ii, 1891, pp. 1190ff.

[2] Murray, *op. cit.*, p. 28.

[3] Brugsch, *Recueil de Travaux relatifs*. iv, 1882, pp. 32f.

[4] *J.E.A.*, ii, 1915, p. 125.

[5] Frankfort, *op. cit.*, pp. 123ff.

made the corn from the liquid that was in him.[1] Therefore, from the Dynastic period to Roman times belief in the resus-citation and life-giving power of Osiris persisted in the Nile valley. All the gods connected with vegetation and fertilization were identified with him and he with them, as were all those associated with the dead, while his *Djed*-column remained his ancient symbol until eventually it was deified at Memphis and transferred to Ptah, the head of the Memphite pantheon. Inherent in the Osirian cultus was the death, burial and resurrection of the culture hero; and his association with the sprouting grain, taken in conjunction with the rites at his festival in the month of Khoiak, show how very intimately the annual renewal in nature was related to his restoration inter-preted in terms of the rise and fall of the Nile with which his ritual observances and their symbolism coincided. This was most apparent in those depicted on the walls of the temple at Denderah and dramatically enacted in the sixteen provinces of Egypt during the last eighteen days of the month of Khoiak. But so numerous were the Osirian festivals that they were celebrated throughout the seasons of the agricultural year at a great many places, notable at Abydos and Busiris, his two principal centres.

THE ROYAL OBSERVANCES

*The Sed Festival*

It is also significant that it was at 'The Season of Coming Forth', after the raising of the *Djed*-column at the Khoiak festival when the inundation was subsiding, that the very ancient Feast of Sed was held periodically to rejuvenate the occupant of the throne. Precisely at what intervals it was celebrated is difficult to determine. It has usually been assumed to have been thirty years,[2] but in the reigns of Ikhnaton, Thutmose II, and Ramesses II references are made to the repetition of the rite much more frequently.[3] It is probably the

---

[1] Blackman, *Analecta Orientalia*, xvii, 1938, p. 2.
[2] Moret, *Du caractère religieux de la royauté pharaonique*, pp. 256 ff.
[3] Griffith, *J.E.A.*, v, 1918, pp. 61 ff.; xxi, 1935, p. 248.

oldest festival of which any traces have survived,[1] going back
before the time of Menes. If Osiris himself did not play any
part in the observance, it was very intimately associated with
his Mysteries, and the vestures and insignia of the king were
unquestionably Osirian in appearance, even though as Dr
Kees has contended, the robe, crook and flail were the characteristic adornments of the king in his festive garb, and Osiris
was so arrayed because he was the king *par excellence*.[2]

The Sed Festival, in fact, was essentially a royal rite held for
the purpose of rejuvenating the reigning Pharaoh by a reinvestiture to confirm his beneficent rule over Upper and Lower
Egypt as first accomplished by Menes. What may have lain
behind it in the prehistoric past cannot be ascertained, but in
the Dynastic period it was held in a Festival Hall containing a
large throne equipped with obelisks and a robing chamber,
called 'the palace' of the 'House of the Morning' (*per duat*). On
the day after the raising of the *Djed*-column—usually coinciding
with the date of the coronation held on the first day of 'The
Season of Coming Forth'[3]—the gods from their respective
shrines, personified in their statues, arrived in the courtyard
where they were met by the king and his court. After purifications had been performed offerings of the royal bounty were
made to them in return for which they gave 'life and prosperity' to the king.[4] For the next few days the Pharaoh and the
priesthoods with the statues of the gods and their attendants
and fan-bearers engaged in processions in which the standard
of the Royal Placenta was carried. The king, seated on his
throne, then received pledges of loyalty, and his feet were washed
by two courtiers before he entered 'the palace' (i.e. the robing
chamber) for his reinvestiture.

Proceeding to a double throne he sat alternately upon each

---

[1] Breasted, *Development of Religion and Thought in Ancient Egypt*, 1914, p. 39;
Murray, *Ancient Egypt*, iii, 1932, pp. 70 ff.; Moret, *Du caractère religieux*, pp. 211,
235 f.; Griffiths, *J.E.A.*, v, 1918, pp. 61 ff.

[2] Kees, *Der Opfertanz des ägyptischen Königs*, Leipzig, 1912, pp. 163 ff.

[3] Van der Waller, *La Nouvelle Clio*, vi, 1954, pp. 283 ff.

[4] Gardiner, *J.E.A.*, xxx, 1944, pp. 28 f.

of them to symbolize his rule over Upper and Lower Egypt. To assert his double authority over the entire land he ceremonially crossed the area of the temple court called 'the field' (i.e. the whole of Egypt), and then he was carried on a litter preceded by the ensign of the jackal-god Upuaut of Siut to the chapel of Horus of Libya to receive the sceptre, the flail and the crook. There wrapped in a cloak and holding these symbols of his royal office and its powers, he sat on a throne and was given the blessing of the gods and proclaimed four times. Homage was made to him by his subjects and in return he made appropriate offerings to the gods. Taking off his cloak and clad only in a kilt having the tail of an animal, but still wearing the crown of Upper Egypt and carrying a short sceptre and whisk, he ran four ritual courses in 'the field'. Finally, he offered his insignia to Upuaut and the ceremonies were concluded with a visit to the chapels of Horus of Edfu and of Seth of Ombos, where he was given a bow and arrow by the priests to shoot four arrows of victory to the four cardinal points. This was in accord with his having been enthroned four times facing the four points of the compass.[1]

As the purpose of the Sed Festival appears to have been the renewal of the occupant of the throne in the kingship, and all that this involved for the country and the seasonal sequence in the agricultural year, rather than the establishment of the succession as in the coronation rite,[2] it was dominion over the forces of nature which he controlled and the maintenance of the beneficial relations between heaven and earth, that had to be secured by the periodic regeneration ritual. The Osiris myth does not seem to have been re-enacted in the Mysteries, and it is more likely that the Pharaoh functioned in the capacity of Horus rather than in that of Osiris, notwithstanding his investiture with the costume and insignia of Osiris. Nevertheless, the Osirian theme was inherent in the observance as it was performed to renew and strengthen the life of the king and to

---

[1] Moret, *Du caractère religieux*, p. 105, fig. 21; Seligman, *Egypt and Negro Africa*, 1934, pp. 15 ff.

[2] Griffith, *J.E.A.*, xxviii, 1942, p. 71; Frankfort, *op. cit.*, p. 79.

re-establish him in his divine office. Indeed, not a few Egypto-
logists and anthropologists have maintained that the essence of
the rite was the identification of the Pharaoh with Osiris.[1] What,
however, is clear is that it was essentially a royal regenerative
jubilee rite to bestow renewed vigour upon the occupant of the
throne as the divine dynamic centre of the nation. Hence the
declaration: 'Thou beginnest thy renewal, beginnest to flourish
again like the infant god of the Moon, thou art young again
year by year, like Nun at the beginning of the ages, thou art
reborn by renewing thy Festival of Sed.'[2]

In the Nile valley the monarchy was the consolidating and
stabilizing element in a static civilization, the cosmic centre of
the divine order established at the creation, so that the Pharaohs
were regarded as the gods they embodied in their several
manifestations and syncretisms. They were, in fact, virtually the
incarnation of all the deities of Upper and Lower Egypt, and
when the royal solar theology was Osirianized in the Sixth
Dynasty (c. 2440 B.C.) and they reigned as the living Horus,
they succeeded to all the divine prerogatives conferred upon
the son of Osiris by decree of the heavenly tribunal, as well as
those of the solar creator Amon-Re in his cosmic aspects. It
was this fulness of divinity that gave the throne its amazing
strength, vitality and cohesive influence, and made the
Pharaoh a unique personality isolated from the rest of the
community and yet the dynamic centre and the mediator
between heaven and earth.

## The Royal Accession Rites

When the Dynastic rulers succeeded the ancient god-kings of
the Predynastic nomes in the Nile valley about 3200 B.C.,
and were still regarded as the heirs of their divine predecessors,
from birth onwards the sacred qualities they had inherited had
to be carefully nurtured; accession to the throne being a per-
fectly normal procedure, the son inheriting the office and status

[1] Breasted, *Development of Religion and Thought in Ancient Egypt*, p. 39; Mercer,
*Religion in Ancient Egypt*, 1954, pp. 122, 361; Seligman, *op. cit.*, p. 2; G.B.,
pt. iv, pp. 153 ff.                          [2] Moret, *Du caractère religieux*, p. 256.

from his royal father at his decease. When he came of age he underwent a ceremonial purification before he was crowned at the Dual Shrines of Upper and Lower Egypt respectively. Our knowledge of precisely what took place at the coronation ceremony is incomplete and uncertain because so long as the royal lineage was maintained without question the transition from one reign to another was made in an orderly sequence without apparently much comment or detailed information about the course of events. The rites seem to have been held at the beginning of the three seasons, especially the fifth month (i.e. the first month of winter, Piret) because of the intimate connexion between the kingship and the agricultural year. Thus, in the temple of Medinet Habu the festival of Khoiak is mentioned as the theoretical date of the accession of Ramesses III though this does not coincide with the actual date of accession given elsewhere.[1] Evidently, however, the festival of Khoiak was considered to be the proper occasion for the reign to begin, and for this reason the Sed Festival, as we have seen, was held at its conclusion.

The first requisite for a valid succession was divine father-hood, the Pharaohs being born as a result of a union between a god and the queen.[2] This was taken as axiomatic, at any rate from the Fifth Dynasty onwards, when the Heliopolitan fiction of royal solar paternity was established. It was only when some unusual circumstances arose, as in the case of the accession to the throne of a woman in the person of Hatshepsut, the daughter of Thutmose I in the Eighteenth Dynasty, that the validity of divine descent had to be established beyond doubt to regularize the claims. It was this situation which gave rise to the representation of the divine birth through the paternity of Amon-Re in the bas-reliefs engraved on the walls of the middle terrace of her temple at Deir el-Bahri at Thebes. Here is displayed the visitation of the Sun-god Amon-Re to the queen-mother 'placing in her body' his daughter that she might 'exercise the beneficent kingship in this entire land'.[3] The god Khnum

---

[1] Brugsch, *Thesaurus*, ii, p. 364.      [2] Moret, *Du caractère religieux*, pp. 49, 72.
[3] Sethe, *Urkunden des aegyptischen Altertums*, iv, 1903, pp. 219 ff.

was commanded to fashion in surpassing beauty her body and her *Ka*, and Hekel his wife to give her life.[1] Next are depicted the preparations for the delivery of the infant, her birth and presentation to the protecting goddesses and to her heavenly father Amon-Re who welcomed her as the daughter of his loins whom he loved, and who would 'make real his risings on the throne of the Horus of the living for ever'.[2]

Thus, 'beautiful to look upon' and 'like unto a god' Hatshepsut in due course was crowned by her father Thutmose I at Heliopolis and seated on his throne before Amon-Re in the presence of the nobles and state officials, who did homage to her. The main episodes in the coronation rite are represented in the reliefs which show the white crown of Lower Egypt, and the red crown of Upper Egypt being placed on her head by the priests impersonating Horus and Seth, or Horus and Thoth, after preliminary purifications. So arrayed she sat on a throne in the sanctuary between the two gods of the south and the north (i.e. Horus and Seth) with the lotus flower and bunches of papyrus as emblems of Lower and Upper Egypt tied together under her feet to symbolize the union of the 'Two Lands' over which she was to rule. Holding the scourge and flail of Osiris she is shown in the next scene led in procession round the walls of the sanctuary to indicate her taking possession of the domains of Horus and Seth, before being led to the shrine of Amon to be embraced by her celestial father.[3]

On these bas-reliefs the normal procedure in the coronation ceremony has been indicated as there is no reason to doubt that the accession of Hatshepsut followed the established order. It was only in relation to her divine descent and selection that particular emphasis was given to her conception in order that her ascendancy of the throne should be made quite secure in spite of her sex. Her position having been regularized as the divine heir to the throne the rest proceeded in the usual manner.

---

[1] Naville, *Deir el-Bahari*, pt. ii, 1894, pp. 12 ff.

[2] Naville, *op. cit.*, pt. ii, pl. li–liii; Moret, *Du caractère religieux*, pp. 53 ff.; Sethe, *Urkunden des aegyptischen Altertums*, iv, pp. 244 f.

[3] Naville, *op. cit.*, pt. iii, pl. lxi, pp. 3–11; Moret, *Du caractère religieux*, pp. 79 ff.

This is confirmed and amplified by the evidence from the Mystery Play of the Accession of Senusert, the second king of the Twelfth Dynasty (*c.* 2000 B.C.),[1] from which it appears that before the coronation the Pharaoh visited a number of cities in his royal barge. In the enactment of the installation rite he played the role of Horus at each town supported by the princes, officials and courtiers, to establish the bond between the throne and the land over which he was to reign on which its prosperity depended. The scenes performed included the victory over Seth by Horus in the Osiris myth, and the treading of barley by oxen on the threshing floor, symbolizing the dismemberment of Osiris by Seth and his conspirators in a vegetation setting. Then followed the avenging of Horus, involving the loss of his eye, the symbol of royal power, which had been bestowed upon his father (Osiris) to revivify him. After these mythological preludes, the actual accession rites were enacted in a series of scenes which included the investiture of the Pharaoh with the insignia, censings and the distribution of half-loaves of bread as the symbol of life to those who made homage to him.

'The affixing of the crown' with the Predynastic two feathers, without specific description of the purpose for which this was done, suggests it was the survival of a very ancient custom deriving from the Delta, its origin and meaning having been forgotten. Dirges were then sung by two women in the guise of Isis and Nephthys as a prologue to the burial rites when the body of Osiris had been found by the priests impersonating Thoth. Articles were offered to them which suggest 'The Opening of the Mouth Ceremony' to restore the faculties to the mummified corpse, before the final scene portraying the ascent of Osiris to the sky and a celestial banquet. By the performance of this fundamental cult-drama integral to the kingship the new occupant was installed in the throne of Horus with all that this involved for the well-being of the nation, mankind and the natural order.

[1] Sethe, *Dramatische Texte zu altaegyptischen Mysterienspielen*, Leipzig, 1928, pp. i–ii.

In the Pyramid Texts, the inscriptions of the first two Dynasties, those on the Palermo stone and on the back of the statue of King Haremhab in the Turin Museum, in which as the successor of Tutankhamen his doubtful claims are indicated, it is shown that the coronation ceremonial included a number of episodes depicted in the scenes of the Mystery play.[1] The proceedings opened with the purification of the sovereign by two priests impersonating Horus and Thoth (or Seth), and by those representing the gods of the four cardinal points wearing their masks. He was then taken to the Dual Shrines, presented with the two crowns of Upper and Lower Egypt, and embraced by the chief officiant in the capacity of Amon-Re. In the Mystery play the embrace was effected by the king putting around his chest and back a sacred object containing the vital power of Horus, as this was transferred to Osiris by the eye of Horus, and now made operative in his royal counterpart, the reigning Horus. After a sacrifice had been offered and eaten, the endowment of the new Pharaoh with all the divine qualities of his sacred office was completed by a priest in the guise of Yahes (*I'bo*) pouring a libation from vessels with the words, 'I purify thee with the water of life and good fortune, all stability, all wealth and happiness.' Invested with the crook and flail and standing in all his regalia as the ruler of the 'Two Lands' he was presented first to the gods, and then to the people, his official names were proclaimed and he circumambulated the walls of the city.[2]

## The Toilet Ceremonies and the Daily Temple Liturgy

So fundamental were these accession rites for all that the kingship signified in the Nile valley that they had to be repeated by the Pharaoh every morning and in the daily temple liturgy. Thus, each day the sovereign had to be asperged in 'the

---

[1] *P.T.*, *Ut.*, 222; Moret, *Du caractère religieux*, pp. 75ff., 86ff., 213; Sethe, *Urgeschichte*, pp. 180ff.; *Untersuchungen*, iii, pp. 133ff.

[2] Moret, *Du caractère religieux*, pp. 77f.; Breasted, *Ancient Records of Egypt*, ii, p. 99; Blackman, *Proceedings of the Society of Biblical Archaeology*, xl, 1918, p. 90; Sethe, *Urkunden*, iv, p. 262, n.b.

palace' of the 'House of the Morning', censed to unite him with Horus, and to chew balls of natron to complete his rebirth. After these preliminary rites had been duly performed, he ascended the stairs to behold and greet his celestial father, the Sun-god, at the great window constructed for the purpose, thereby symbolizing the rising of the morning sun from the waters. As Re in his several forms and aspects was purified and reborn every morning in 'House beneath the Horizon', so his incarnation on earth had to undergo the same daily ritual renewal in the 'House of the Morning' to identify himself with the lord and giver of life before he was ceremoniously vested and exercised his royal functions in his divine capacity.[1]

In the daily temple liturgy these episodes had their counter-parts in relation to the cult-image of the Sun-god which took the place of the Pharaoh in the solar temple at Heliopolis. There every morning it was solemnly asperged, censed and anointed at dawn before it was vested and crowned with the diadem of Upper and Lower Egypt and presented with the flail, the crook and the sceptre. The priest proceeded to the sanctuary in which the image was enshrined at dawn, and having kindled a fire and holding in his hand a censer contain-ing charcoal and incense, he unbolted the doors of the shrine containing the image in its sacred bark. After censing and venerating it, he sang a hymn in its honour and in that of the goddess Hathor, offered to it scented honey, and took it out of the bark, sprinkled it with water from the sacred pool, cleansed its mouth with natron, again censed it, and then arrayed it in white, green, red and darker red cloths in succession. After adorning it with ornaments he anointed it with unguents and painted the eyelids with green and black cosmetics, investing it with the royal insignia.[2]

What had been done to the Sun-god and his son on the

[1] Blackman, *Journal of the Manchester Egyptian and Oriental Society*, 1918–19, pp. 51 ff.

[2] *Ibid.*, p. 30; *E.R.E.*, xii, 1921, pp. 777 ff.; v, 1918, pp. 162 ff.; *Recueil de Travaux*, xxxix, 1920, pp. 44 ff.; Moret, *Le rituel du culte divin journalier en Égypte*, Paris, 1902, pp. 9, 66.

throne had to be done to his image in the shrine as their embodiment. All three were virtually one and the same divine
entity, and so they had to receive identical treatment. When,
however, the solar theology was Osirianized under the influence of the Osiris myth and ritual it was to some extent
transformed. The god in the shrine became the dead Osiris
who was revivified every morning in much the same way
as was the Pharaoh himself in the 'House of the Morning'
with censings, lustrations, cleansing with natron, investiture,
anointing with unguents and adornment with cosmetics, and
the presentation of food and drink offerings as in the mortuary
ritual.

## The Royal Priesthood

In fact, the same mode of worship was adopted in relation to
the chief god of any temple by the local priest representing the
Pharaoh, who was the priest *par excellence* everywhere and at all
times. But when the two great cults of Re and Osiris were
democratized and the royal worship was extended to com-
moners, the Toilet ritual set the patterns for the daily temple
liturgy, and especially for that celebrated on the feasts and
festivals of most of the gods, notwithstanding the recurrence of
the cults of Horus, Amon and the short-lived triumph of the
Aton. But the royal origin and significance are shown by the
king being represented in most of the reliefs as the sole celebrant
in spite of the fact that it was only on rare occasions that he
officiated in person at the rites as in the case of the bishop today who exercises his 'cure of souls' and pastoral ministrations
through his deputy the parish priest and his assistants. Doubtless when he did himself officiate the ceremonial was appropriately elaborate, as at a pontifical High Mass sung by or in
the presence of the bishop of the diocese, calling for a number
of priests to perform their respective functions. Thus, in a relief
at Luxor four officiants are depicted in front of the Pharaoh,
one holding what may be a libation vessel while the others
present the king's offering to Amon, and a *sem*-priest and the
high priestess of Amon summon the gods to the repast prepared

for them by Amenhotep.[1] But when a priest impersonated the king in his Horus capacity he had to undergo the same purification as the Pharaoh since for the time being and for the purposes of the rite he was virtually himself the Pharaoh, performing his functions to secure the favour of the gods for the reigning son of Osiris and of Re, bestowing upon him health, victory, stability and an 'eternity of jubilees' and life everlasting.[2]

As the Pharaoh was the official intermediary between the people and the gods, the representative of the country in the heavenly realms, endowed with divinity and so becoming any god the occasion required, the seasonal rites were essentially his concern, and that of the local priest who deputized for him and shared to some extent his divine personality. The power of the throne over natural forces made its occupant the dispenser of bounty 'filling the "Two Lands" with strength and life', and making them 'more green than a high Nile', giving food and sustenance by causing the earth to bring forth in abundance. Hence the stress laid on his influence over the inundation and his part in its festivals. At his coronation he had been identified with Horus the living king, and Osiris the dead king, and having become the recipient of divine vitality and procreative power he ensured the fertility of the land over which he reigned, and that of his subjects, their fields, flocks and herds. At death the office and all that it signified was transferred to his son and successor who thereby continued to exercise the royal functions and perform its rites in the prescribed manner at the specified times and seasons, on which the stability and prosperity of the nation depended.

[1] A. Gayet, *Le Temple de Louxor*, Paris, 1894, pl. xxxv, fig. 138.
[2] Gauthier, *La grande Inscription dédicatoire d'Abydos*, Cairo, 1912, pp. 1 (line 4), 6.

CHAPTER III

# The New Year Festival in Mesopotamia

So distinctive were the geographical and climatic conditions in Mesopotamia, 'the land between the rivers', and so uncertain was the behaviour of the Tigris and Euphrates, that they could not be made a reliable index for the determination of the calendar and its ritual observances like the Nile in Ancient Egypt. At the close of the Ice Age the melting snows and glaciers covered with water the plain at the head of the Persian Gulf, which later became Babylonia and parts of Assyria. Its northern shores were the highlands with glaciers extending along the southern slope of the Highland Zone between Samarra and Hit towards the southern diluvial flatlands, with no sea like the Mediterranean to separate them, as in the case of Egypt, from the retreating ice. As these snows and glaciers melted at the end of the Pleistocene devastating torrents raged over what is now Mesopotamia bringing with them quantities of silt which gradually produced the flat alluvial plain of Shinar (i.e. Sumer), eventually called Babylonia.

## THE INFLUENCE OF ENVIRONMENT IN MESOPOTAMIA

Taking their rise in the Armenian mountains in the Highland Zone the two great rivers of the region, the Tigris and Euphrates, were the main channels along which the waters from these lofty slopes were conveyed in a south-westerly direction for the first part of their course, and then south-eastwards, converging as they approached the ancient coastline at Samarra and Hit respectively, to empty their waters in the Persian Gulf. As the plain emerged with the filling up of the Gulf for 125 miles north of Basra, and became habitable, on its fertile

70

alluvial soil the great Mesopotamian civilization arose. The older part of the country had been farmed while Southern Mesopotamia was still under the Persian Gulf. It was not until the third millennium B.C. that the northern agriculturists moved south, and having irrigated the newly formed plain, established the Sumerian civilization, a thousand years before the Babylonian culture developed.

When this Sumerian colonization began only a very small part of the reclaimed area was cultivable, and the pluvial conditions had given place to an arid climate with a scanty rainfall in winter and devastatingly hot and dry summers. Tidal lagoons extended inland nearly to the limestone ridge on which the ancient city of Eridu was erected by the Sumerians, but irrigation was required to ripen the grain grown on the prodigiously fertile soil. This was accomplished by the non-Semitic highlanders who had reclaimed the southern alluvial marshes before 3000 B.C., and in addition to cultivating barley and wheat, and engaging in mixed farming with cattle, sheep and goats combined with agriculture, invented the art of writing on clay tablets with the wedge-shaped characters of their cuneiform script.

Thus, in this not very promising land of Sumer, which at first was a region of swamps, written history began, and, unlike Egyptian, cuneiform became the medium for many different languages, mostly non-Semitic, in Western Asia. For at least a thousand years (*c*. 3500–2500 B.C.) Sumerian was the only written tongue in Mesopotamia, and it remained the learned language of the entire region for the next two and a half millennia. 'Sumerian', however, is a linguistic term having no relation to a particular physical type of mankind, and in Mesopotamia it was replaced by Semitic Akkadian speech in the second half of the third millennium B.C. when political power was transferred from the south to Babylonia in the centre and later to Assyria in the north. But the script in which it was written originally survived those changes in the fortunes of Western Asian history, being employed to write Hittite and Hurrian in Anatolia, Elamite in Susiana, Ugaritic in

Syria, and occasionally Hebrew, Aramaic, Egyptian and Old
Persian texts, as well as those of Mesopotamia. Consequently,
the decipherment of cuneiform since the middle of the last
century (1846–55) by Grotefend, Rawlinson, Hincks and
Oppert, has made available a vast literature preserved on the
thousands of clay tablets which have been discovered throughout the area, throwing much light on the rise and development
of civilization in Hither Asia, the climatic and geographical
conditions, customs, beliefs and seasonal observances.

From these contemporary sources of information the environment of the dwellers in Mesopotamia and those in the surrounding region has clearly been a determining factor in
their cultural development and general outlook. Those who
settled on the banks of the Tigris and Euphrates with their
vagaries of climate, scorching winds, torrential rainfall and
devastating floods, were confronted continually with forces
over which they had little if any control. Yet they proved
themselves to be capable of establishing an urban literate
civilization in and after the third millennium B.C. on the
foundations of a peasant agricultural society, an achievement
all the more remarkable since it was accomplished in the face
of so many adverse natural conditions. Heavy falls of snow in
the Armenian mountains or of rain in the south, spring tides in
the Persian Gulf, or landslides in the narrow channels of
the Tigris and Euphrates, clamming up and then suddenly
releasing their waters, were always liable to have very serious
results not only for the crops but also for the permanent human
settlements in the plain, especially when these became towns
and cities.

## The Climate and the Cultus

It is not surprising, therefore, that each city as it developed
under these precarious conditions was placed under the
patronage and protection of its own god, who was regarded as
owning it and its inhabitants. Around its temple an elaborate
political, civil and ecclesiastical organization grew up, which
on its socio-religious side was centred upon the *ziqqurat*, or

temple tower. The latter was formed of a large artificial mound composed of sun-dried bricks, such as that at Ur, or at Babylon where the remains of the staged tower described by Herodotus in the fifth century B.C. is generally regarded as the Biblical Tower of Babel. On the top stood the shrine of the god, and the name *ziqquratu* meaning 'pinnacle' or the 'summit of a mountain', identifies the structure with the 'high place' or elevated sanctuary where the mysterious sacred potency of the universe was located, as at the 'primeval hill' from which creation took its beginning in Egyptian cosmology. Therefore, it was here that creative energy was concentrated, and made accessible at certain times and seasons by the due performance of the prescribed cultus in accordance with the peculiar climatic conditions.

Thus, in Mesopotamia the fertility god personifying the cosmic forces in the universe in their vegetation aspects, most familiar under the title of Tammuz, was represented emerging from the mountain-shrine to a newness of life and vitality at the New Year after the devastating heat and drought of summer had come to an end and nature had begun to revive. Indeed, it was from the mountain that the life-giving rain was thought to be brought forth by the weather-god, very much as it was from this sacred rendezvous in the East that the Sun-god began his daily course across the horizon. To make it the 'Holy of Holies' in the temple, therefore, was a very natural procedure, and as each sunrise and each New Year's Day was regarded as the repetition of the initial creation when the current sequence of events began by divine initiative, they were the appropriate occasions for the celebration of the renewal rites. In Egypt, as we have seen, this was observed in the daily Toilet ceremonies of the Pharaoh to ensure the course of the sun across the horizon. In Mesopotamia the accession rites were held in the month of Nisan in the spring at the New Year Festival, when the rains had renewed vegetation, or in Tishri in the autumn when the harvest had been gathered. Either of these constituted the beginning of the year, and at Ur and Erech New Year Festivals were observed on both these occasions.

## The Babylonian Calendar

As the Egyptians divided the year into three seasons of four months duration so in all probability the Babylonian seasonal sequence originally was dependent upon the priestly computations in their attempts to adjust the lunar year of 354 days and the solar year of $365\frac{1}{4}$ days. By about 3000 B.C. the Sumerians had devised lunar calendars based on the first appearance of the moon after sunset until its disappearance on the morning of the twenty-eighth day to keep the harvest season in its proper place in the agricultural year. This necessitated intercalating a month before the twelfth month (*segurkud*, the barley harvest) every fifth or sixth year, as required, or, as at Ur where the lunar year of 354 days prevailed, every second or third year, in place of the Egyptian system of inserting five epagomenal days at the end of every year.

Each month was associated with the festival of a particular god or goddess, and with the development of the zodiacal system with the constellations that rose heliacally at the time of the monthly festivals. Thus, the first month was connected with the rising heliacally of Taurus and the Pleiades soon after the spring equinox, while in the Sargon calendar the year began in the autumn, the intercalary month being placed after Tammuz at the summer solstice and the New Year Festival observed on the first of Tishri at the autumnal equinox in September. The Sumerians celebrated the death of Tammuz in the fourth month, Dumuzi (July), when the decline in vegetation in the heat of summer was interpreted in terms of the dying year-god (Tammuz), and weeping and lamentation for him prevailed everywhere.[1]

From the time of Hammurabi (*c.* 1728 B.C.), the founder of the Dynasty of Babylon, the Sumerian names of the months were sometimes given Semitic renderings, but the earlier calendrical sequence, its myths, festivals and terminology, survived little changed in form or significance, and was adopted

[1] S. Langdon, *Babylonian Menologies and the Semitic Calendar*, Schweich Lectures, 1933, O.U.P., 1958, pp. 120f.

by the Hebrews, especially after their exile in Mesopotamia, and so became a permanent feature in Jewish tradition, as will be considered later,[1] recurring in the Talmud and in the rest of the Rabbinical literature. As a result it may be that a double New Year Festival, the one in the autumn and the other in the spring, was observed in those cultures that came under Meso-potamian influence because in the Ancient Near East the event marked the end of winter and the end of the devastating summer, followed in each case by a new season. In Babylon the starting-point was in the month of Nisan at the time of the spring rains, but in Ur, Erech, and east of the Tigris the Chaldaean practice of beginning the year in the autumn was adopted also. Therefore, the festival was held in Tishri as well as in Nisan when two new epochs in the year were opening, the one in the autumn, the other in the spring. On both of these important occasions the New Year ritual attached to the sacral kingship was enacted.

## The Kingship

Although in Mesopotamia the Kingship never had the importance and predominance it exercised in the Nile valley, the ruler of the city-state was generally the principal officiant at the cult-festivals, assuming the role of Dumuzi or Tammuz, the Young Shepherd-god incarnating the creative powers of spring. No Sumerian *lugal* or *patesi* was a consolidating force in the country as a whole it is true because neither Sumer nor Akkad was organized on a national basis. Before the Flood in the third millennium B.C. royalty, it was said, was conferred only on very few Sumerian kings who as 'shepherds of the people' reigned by divine prerogative and lived to fabulous ages like Methuselah in Hebrew tradition. After the deluge Dumuzi alone continued the antediluvian régime in Erech, where, according to the Gilgamesh Epic, from time im-memorial, a permanent dynasty had reigned which survived in the legendary figures of Lugal-banda and Gilgamesh.[2]

[1] Cf. Chap. iv, pp. 110ff.
[2] Jacobsen, *The Sumerian King Lists*, Chicago, 1939, pp. 88ff., 142ff.

It was not, however, until the ruler of Uruk and Umma, Lugal-zaggisi, at the end of the Early Dynastic period had sub-dued Lagash, that the new title 'King of the Land' was introduced on the authority of Enlil, the Storm-god. As the 'son born of Nisa-ba, fed by the holy milk of Ninhursaga', he assumed dominion over the entire country, and prayed that he might fulfil his destiny and always be 'the shepherd at the head of the flock'.[1] This he accomplished, gaining ascendancy over all the countries from the Persian Gulf ('the Lower Sea') to the Mediterranean ('the Upper Sea'). At length he was conquered by Sargon of Akkad who had founded a new city, Agade, and called himself 'the ruler of the Four Quarters', his son, Naram-Sin, assuming the title of 'King of the Four Quarters' with the sanction of the great Babylonian triad of deities, Anu, Enlil and Shamash.[2] Though these rulers were not actually equated with these gods, the new title implied universal rule on earth comparable with that exercised by the supreme deities in the heavens. It was not an uncommon practice, in fact, for Sumerian rulers to claim divine parentage, while the kings of the Isin and Kassite Dynasties sometimes re-garded themselves as the spouses of the Goddess, and performed nuptial rites with her earthly embodiment at the New Year Festival.[3]

The city-states, however, were ruled over by the *patesi*, the 'tenant farmers' of the chief local god, the office being renewed annually at the New Year Festival. The real sovereign was the city-god and the human ruler acted as his steward in the capacity of the chief priest of the temple and civic admini-strator with a staff of officials which included the *sangu mah*, who was concerned with the temple revenues and its organization, and the *ensi* as high priest, who as the governor managed the

[1] Thureau-Dangin, *Sumerische und Akkadische Königinschriften*, Leipzig, 1907, pp. 156 ff.

[2] *Ibid.*, p. 219; Barton, *The Royal Inscriptions of Sumer and Akkad*, New Haven, 1929, pp. 137 ff.

[3] Gadd, *Ideas of Divine Rule in the Ancient East*, 1948, pp. 45 f.; Labat, *Caractère religieux de la royauté assyro-babylonienne*, Paris, 1939, pp. 248 ff.

estate of the god. It was he who maintained law and order and dealt with defence, trade and foreign affairs generally. These offices were often held by the same person but in times of crisis the king exercised the powers of a *lugal*, i.e. 'great ruler', though only a few of the Early Dynastic rulers adopted the title. The first to do so was Ur-Nina of Lagash (*c.* 2900 B.C.), who was engaged mainly in building temples, digging irrigation canals and fortifications. But his grandson Eannatum claimed to have become Lord of Sumer and Akkad by the grace of Enlil, the strength of Ningirsu, the city-god of Lagash, and to have been suckled by Ninhursaga, the Mother-goddess.[1] The permanent control of the city-state was, in theory, in the hands of the *patesi* and *ensi*, the *lugal* representing the kingship holding office only for a limited period and in times of crisis. As these, however, were almost perennial in their occurrence, in practice the institution acquired a more or less permanent status in some cities, especially when it included priestly functions, as in the case of Lugal-zaggisi who ruled in the name of Anu and Enlil. In southern Babylonia Gilgamesh, although the despotic human king of Erech, was two-thirds a divine being, and Gudea, the *ensi* of Lagash (*c.* 2400 B.C.), was the steward of Ningirsu whose temple he was commissioned to build.

It was not, however, until Anu and Enlil, the two leaders of the pantheon, exalted Marduk above all the gods of the earth and authorized him to exercise the administrative func-tions of Enlil, that in Mesopotamia a ruler acquired a status at all comparable to that of the Pharaoh in Egypt. This was accomplished when at the beginning of the second millennium B.C. Hammurabi conquered Naram-Sin of Larsa and having subdued Mari in the north, on the route to the Mediterranean, established his unified rule at Babylon as the steward of Marduk. Raised up, as he declared, by the great gods to be 'a shepherd who brings peace, whose sceptre is just that the strong may not oppress the weak', he had been given pre-eminence among the kings that 'justice might appear in the lands'.[2] If neither he

[1] Thureau-Dangin, *Les inscriptions de Sumer et d'Akkad*, pp. 47, 49.
[2] Driver and Miles, *The Babylonian Laws*, ii, O.U.P., 1955, p. 97.

nor the Lord of Babylon, Marduk, occupied the position in
Mesopotamia that the Pharaoh and Osiris held in the Nile
valley, the centralization of authority in Hammurabi as the
steward of Marduk made him 'the father to his people' whose
name would be for ever favourably mentioned in Esagila, the
temple in Babylon where his statue had been set up by command of Marduk.[1]

It is not surprising, therefore, that it was he who functioned
at the New Year Festival and the other great seasonal rituals,
and that he and his queen became identified with Tammuz
and Ishtar (Dumuzi-Innana) in the annual renewal rites to
maintain the creative powers of spring, 'He was "the life of all
lands"' being the embodiment of deity in perpetuity, the
epitome of all the divine qualities incarnate in him, and so
in the calendrical sequence he played the role of Marduk,
Ashur or Enlil, who at the threshold of creation vanquished the malign powers of chaos and ever after controlled
the cosmic forces, and the cycle of decline and renewal in
nature.

## The Tammuz Celebrations

This involved a complicated ritual representation of the
original events in which a number of gods and goddesses were
involved, exercising similar and yet distinct functions, brought
into relation with the king and his consort in their several
capacities, their divine embodiments for specific purposes yet
still their servants. As the generative force in nature the predominant figure was Tammuz-Dumuzi, the son and lover of
Ishtar-Innana, who was the source of all life. When Babylon
became the capital under the powerful rule of Hammurabi,
Marduk replaced Tammuz as the central male figure, and the
king performed the essential role in the New Year Festival. As
the Tigris and Euphrates, unlike the Nile, were too unreliable
in their rise and fall to be the determining factor in the calendrical observances, the beginning of the year in Mesopotamia
was fixed in relation to the rains in the spring. Thus, the

[1] *Code of Hammurabi*, col. xxiv, 11 ff., pp. 84 ff.

Akkadian Akitu Festival was held in the capital (Babylon) during the first eleven days of the month of Nisan when the crops were appearing, while in Ur and Erech the New Year rites were repeated in Tishri at the time of the autumnal rains which produced a new harvest.

In the interval between these two periods of germination and ingathering the stifling heat of summer brought all growth to an end on the parched and sun-baked soil. The prevailing mood of desolation coupled with the anxious desire for the breaking of the drought found expression in the lamentations and wailings echoing the cries of Ishtar-Innana for Tammuz-Dumuzi when she as the Mater dolorosa sought her lover-son imprisoned in the mountain of the nether regions.[1] Then the absent god of vegetation, personifying the generative forces in nature, was mourned in tune with the prevailing state of aridity, exhaustion and stagnation. While the Tammuz liturgies were being recited and the dirges sung it is very probable that the fate of the suffering and incarcerated Young God was enacted by committing to the waters of the Tigris or the Euphrates a wooden effigy of Tammuz in commemoration of his 'lying in the submerged grain' when he had perished in his boat beneath the waves of the flood by the shore of the Euphrates,[2] to induce him to send the much-needed refreshing and reinvigorating rains to replenish the parched earth. When this was accomplished and the shepherd returned to his flock, sorrow was turned into joy and life emerged from death, decay and desolation.

Although in the later seasonal festivals Tammuz was not at all prominent, his cultus and its theme lay in the background of the Babylonian and Assyrian calendrical rituals. The antiphonal laments over the woe and desolation of the land, and the universal mourning for the 'Shepherd of his people' at the instigation of the sorrowing mother Ishtar, reflected in the blight upon nature and the cessation of fertility everywhere, interpreted in relation to her descent into the underworld

[1] Langdon, *Tammuz and Ishtar*, O.U.P., 1914, pp. 9ff.
[2] Langdon, *Babylonian Liturgies*, Paris, 1913, p. 95.

and his delivery,[1] constitute the characteristic recurrent features of the Tammuz liturgies, and the associated myths everywhere and at all times, because they give expression to the climatic conditions and the urgent needs of the nation. Thus, the calendrical sequence of fast and festival, of mourning and rejoicing, represented the collective effort of the community personified in the king to effect a safe passage from one phase to another, beset at all the critical junctures in the year by so many and great dangers and hazards.

## THE NEW YEAR FESTIVAL

Although the king never occupied the dynamic position of the Pharaoh in Egypt, he began his reign on New Year's Day, and by virtue of his supernatural endowment at his birth and his sacred status with its ritual obligations, he was the most conspicuous figure in the Annual Festival. This was most apparent in the seasonal drama that was held at the beginning of the month of Nisan, and which in due course became the pattern of this event throughout Mesopotamia and the rest of Western Asia. The Akkadian texts from which we get our information about the Akitu in Babylon are relatively late, belonging to the Seleucid ritual texts of the third and second centuries B.C.[2] But these are copies of earlier documents which at any rate in some of their sections may go back to Sumerian times.

Thus, the Creation story is an ancient version of the emergence of the world from a state of chaos in which the 'sweet waters' personified as Apsu, the primeval male, mingled with the salt waters of the ocean, i.e. Tiamat his consort. From this union their son Mummu was born, representing the mist and clouds arising from the waters. So as the Euphrates and Tigris merged with the sea to produce luxuriant growth in the

[1] M. Witzel, 'Tammuzliturgien und Verwandtes,' *Analecta Orientalia*, Rome, 1935; Ebling, *Tod und Leben nach den Vorstellungen der Babylonier*, Leipzig, 1931.

[2] ThureauDangin, *Rituels Accadiens*, Paris, 1921, pp. 127ff.; A. Sachs, *A.N.E.T.*, pp. 513ff.

southern Mesopotamian marshes, all life was regarded as having sprung spontaneously from the primeval watery abyss, together with the gods Lahmu and Lahamu, followed by a second pair, Amshar and Kishar, who in due course produced the Sky-god Anu. From him sprang Ea, the god of water and of wisdom, the patron deity of the ancient city of Eridu at the head of the Persian Gulf. His original surname in Sumerian was Enki, 'lord of the earth', having reference to his abode in the Apsu from which the fresh water of the rivers was supposed to flow. In another Sumerian text it was the goddess Nammu, written in cuneiform with the ideogram for 'sea', who is said to have been 'the mother who gave birth to heaven and earth',[1] the process of creation having been carried on by a succession of generations of divine pairs derived ultimately from the primeval Goddess who was the source of all life.

In the New Year Festival in Babylon the celebration of the annual renewal in nature and society was enacted in very intimate association with the Creation Epic as this was recorded in the text known as *Enuma elish*. The story, in fact, was recited twice during the performance of the rites which concluded with the commemoration of the building of the temple of Marduk (i.e. Esagila) in heaven after he had conquered Tiamat and the powers of chaos. At first, however, it seems to have centred round the Storm-god Enlil of Nippur, the second member of the Great Triad of Babylonian deities. In this earlier version it was he who was elected the leader of the gods and subdued Tiamat by the storms he commanded, and it was not until Babylon became the capital that Marduk succeeded Enlil as the hero of the Epic, until in due course, when Assyria became the dominant power, he was replaced by Ashur. But while the names of the principal figures in the drama changed with the fortunes of the cities or lands with which they were connected, the ritual was enacted with the same intention and followed the same general pattern, though often it had very little if anything to do with the original nature and functions of the gods before they were incorporated in the

[1] Kramer, *Sumerian Mythology*, Philadelphia, 1944, p. 39.

cultus. Thus, Marduk was a very different deity from Enlil before he assumed a Tammuz role and usurped the position previously occupied by his opposite number at Nippur. But once he was established at Babylon it was with him that the kings from Hammurabi onwards sought to be iden- tified, and his victory over Tiamat and Kingu which they shared, with all that this entailed in the supernatural control of nature, the revival of vegetation in the spring, the main- tenance of the cosmic processes and the right ordering of society.

## The Akitu Festival in Babylon

The Akitu opened on the first days of the month of Nisan with the preliminary preparations. Arising two hours before dawn on the second day the *Urigallu*-priest of E-Kua, to whom alone were known the secrets of the temple called Esagila, performed his ablutions with water from the river before vesting in a linen garment. He then called upon Marduk as 'the Lord of Kings, light of mankind, and the fixer of destinies', to bless the city and 'to turn his face to the temple of Esagila', before opening the doors of the sanctuary for the priests and singers to enter.[1] At this point a break in the text occurs, but when the account is resumed reference is made to the summoning of a metal worker and a wood worker on the third day three hours after sunrise. They were given precious stones and gold from the treasury of Marduk to make two images for the ceremonies on the sixth day; the one to be constructed of cedar and the other of tamarisk, ornamented with the stones set in gold. A snake fashioned in cedar was held in the left hand of one image, and the other holds a scorpion with his right hand raised to the son of Marduk. Clad in red garments the images were placed in the temple of Daian, the Judge, and given food from the table of the god. The next day the *urigallu* continued his prayers for the blessing of Marduk on Babylon, adding a petition to Sar- penit, the consort of Marduk, in her exalted dwelling in the heavens, 'the brightest of the stars', to 'fix the destinies of the

[1] Thureau-Dangin, *Rituels Accadiens*, pp. 129f.

king, to give life to the children of Babel [Babylon]', to plead for them before Marduk, 'the king of the gods'. He then went out into the courtyard and blessed three times Esagila, 'image of heaven and earth'.

Late in the afternoon he recited the Creation Epic (the *Enuma elish*) in its entirety, very much as in the Holy Saturday ceremonies in Catholic Christendom the creation story in the Book of Genesis, together with the prophecies concerning the Incarnation and the redemption of mankind, are read at the transition from the mourning on Good Friday to the triumphant joy of the Easter Festival.[1] So in the Babylonian Akitu the death and revival of Marduk were celebrated amid the outward signs and symbols of intense sorrow and chaos and those of joy and victory, to re-enact the primeval battle with Chaos and make atonement for the king as an act of renewal. As in the Christian rite the statues in the church remain veiled in the purple of Passiontide until the new fire has been kindled and the 'light of Christ', symbolized by the tripartite candle, shines forth in the darkness, so in the Akitu the crown of Anu and the throne of Enlil were covered during the recitation of the Creation Epic.

## The Rites of Atonement

The fifth day being the Babylonian counterpart of Good Friday, it was characterized by lamentations and 'search for Marduk' who was incarcerated in the mountain (i.e. the nether regions) while the city was in an increasing state of commotion and the temple was cleansed and sprinkled with holy water from the Tigris and Euphrates. The sacred drum was beaten by the exorcist (*mashmashu*) and the court was censed. This completed, the chapel of Nabu, the son of Marduk, was purified in the same manner, and the doors were smeared with cedar-oil, and the sanctuary was censed. An executioner was then summoned to cut off the head of a sheep, and the exorcist wiped the temple with the carcass, reciting spells, before taking the body of the sheep to the river and

[1] Cf. Chap. vii, p. 215.

throwing it into the water facing the west. The same was done with the head by the executioner. Both being in a taboo condition, they had to retire to the country until Nabu had left the city on the twelfth day. The *urigallu* also was forbidden to see the purifying of the temple lest he too should become defiled.

Three and a third hours after sunrise he had to summon the craftsmen to bring the baldachin from the treasury of Marduk with which to cover the chapel of Nabu, reciting a cathartic invocation calling upon Marduk to purify his temple and expel all evil that was within it. He then prepared the table of offerings and placed upon it roast meats, twelve loaves, salt and honey, and a golden censer before it, pouring out wine before 'the most exalted among the gods'. The craftsmen carried the table to the banks of the canal to await the arrival of Nabu in his boat and to offer to him the loaves. They then escorted the king to Esagila where he entered the shrine of Marduk to undergo a ritual abdication. The *urigallu* emerged from 'the Holy of Holies' which contained the statue of Marduk, and removed the crown, ring, sceptre and *harpé* from the king and put them upon a 'seat' before the statue of the god. The *urigallu* returned, struck the king a blow on his face and forced him to his knees to make an act of penitence and expiation in the presence of Marduk. This included a negative confession, or declaration of innocence.

> *I have not sinned, O Lord of the lands,*
> *I have not been negligent regarding thy divinity,*
> *I have not destroyed Babylon; I have not caused its overthrow;*
> *I have not neglected the temple Esagila; I have not forgotten*
>     *its ritual.*
> *I have not rained blows on the cheek of a subordinate;*
> *I have not humiliated them;*
> *I have cared for Babylon; I have not broken its walls.*

After a short break of about five lines in the text, the reply of the *urigallu* is recorded in the name of Marduk as a sort of absolution and renewal blessing:

*Have no fear—for Marduk has spoken—*
*He will listen to your prayer. He will increase thy dominion—*
*He will exalt thy kingship—*
*On the day of the feast of the new moon thou shalt—*
*Day and night—*
*Thou whose city is Babylon, whose temple is Esagila;*
*Whose suppliants are the children of Babylon.*
*Thy god Bel will bless you—for ever.*
*He will destroy thy enemies; he will beat down thy adversaries.*

The *urigallu* then restored the insignia, struck the king on the cheek with the intention of making tears flow as a sign of the favour and good-will of Marduk towards him. Forty minutes after sunset he (the *urigallu*) bound together with a palm branch forty reeds of three cubits each in length, dug a hole in the courtyard and planted them in it with honey, cream and oil of the best quality. A white bull was placed before the hole, and the king kindled a fire in it with a reed. A prayer was recited the contents of which are lost apart from the opening lines addressed to the bull of Anu as 'the shining light who doth illuminate the darkness'.[1]

It is clear that the abdication and reinvestiture constituted a renewal rite at a critical juncture in the seasonal sequence. Thus, while all this was taking place in the Esagila the city was in a state of increasing confusion because the god had disappeared and was held captive in the nether world like Tammuz or Kore or Aleyan-Baal, with reciprocal effects on the decline of life in nature and the uncertainties always felt concerning the seasons. Ritual combats were in progress in the streets symbolizing the ascendancy of Chaos, very much as in the earlier New Year Festival at Erech, held in honour of Ishtar in the autumn, a Saturnalian carnival like the Persian Sacaea, may have been enacted, in which a mock king reigned for five days while everything was in uproar.[2]

[1] Zimmern, *Der alte Orient*, xxv, Leipzig, 1926, pp. 12 ff.
[2] Langdon, *J.R.A.S.*, 1924, pp. 68 ff.

*The Procession and Drama in the Festival House*

However this may have been, in Babylonia once the king was restored to his royal office by the high priest and the god had been released by his son Nabu on the seventh day of Nisan, the revival of vegetation was assured and the first rains were due to begin. Then the statues of the gods were assembled in the Chamber of Destinies in order of precedence to confer upon Marduk their strength and power in the conquest of the forces of evil, as at the creation when he was elected leader of the pantheon. The king acting as the master of ceremonies and holding in his hand his sceptre summoned each of the gods and led him to his place in the Great Hall. He then himself 'took the hand' of Marduk, upon whom the panoply of divine might had been bestowed, and led the way in the procession from the Esagila to the Bit Akitu, or Festival House, on the outskirts of the city. On the copper doors the conflict between Marduk and Tiamat was portrayed by the Assyrian kings for their annual visit, when they went forth in triumph along the sacred way like the victorious armies of the gods. Thus, Sargon recorded his joy at making the pilgrimage to the Bit Akitu, and Sennacherib caused his own figure to be inserted in the chariot of Ashur on the copper doors he erected at the House of the New Year Festival as the Assyrian form of Marduk under the name of Ashur, regarding himself perhaps as the 'victorious prince' who had conquered the forces of evil and drought.[1]

Having arrived at the Bit Akitu on the tenth day of Nisan the king and those who had taken part in the procession remained in the Festival House until they returned to the Esagila two days later. Exactly what took place there can only be conjectured from the few extracts in the texts available. Since each new year threatened to bring back the watery chaos that prevailed when the primeval battle between Marduk and Tiamat depicted on the doors was fought, it is by no means improbable that this crucial event was celebrated in a sacred

[1] Zimmern, *Zum babylonischen Neujahrsfest*, Leipzig, 1906–18; D. D. Luckenbill, *Ancient Records of Assyria*, ii, Chicago, 1927, p. 70.

drama in which the king played the role of Marduk. The triumphal procession following the release of the god and the reinstatement of the king accords with such an inter, pretation of the observance, as does the ceremonial 'fixing of the destinies', though the precise form in which it was carried out is not known. Moreover, the rites in the Bit Akitu con, cluded with a banquet, partaken of by the king, the gods, the priests and attendants, upon which considerable stress is laid in the texts.[1] It was apparently held on the tenth day of Nisan before the return to the Esagila, and Early Dynastic reliefs show that banquets of this nature were a very prominent feature of the New Year Festival in Mesopotamia, usually connected with the consummation of the marriage of the god and goddess to promote the fertility of the crops and herds in the ensuing year.[2]

## The Sacred Nuptials of the King and Queen

That such sacred nuptials were held at the end of the Baby, lonian Akitu Festival is suggested by the king and queen repairing to a chamber called *gigunu*, decorated with greenery, situated it would seem on one of the stages of the *ziqqurat*. The nature, position and purpose of this building has been a matter of much discussion since Herodotus called attention to the erection he saw on the top of the tower of Babel.[3] These speculations have ranged from identifying it with a lofty shrine containing a couch on a temple tower, to an underground tomb of a god.[4] But so far as the Akitu is concerned, it would seem to have been at the Esagila after the return from the Bit Akitu on the tenth evening of the Festival that the newly reinstated king cohabited with his spouse to engage in a ritual marital intercourse symbolizing the union of the Goddess with the Young God to reinforce the creative powers of spring in nature,

[1] Pallis, *The Babylonian Akitu Festival*, 1926, pp. 173 ff.

[2] Frankfort, *Sculpture of the Third Millennium B.C. from Tell Asmar and Khafajah*, xliv, Chicago, Oriental Institute Publications, 1939, pp. 45 f.

[3] Herodotus, i, pp. 182f.

[4] cf. S. Smith, *J.R.A.S.*, 1928, pp. 849 ff.; E. Douglas van Buren, *Orientalia*, xiii, N.S. 1944, pp. 17 f.

the flocks and mankind. It was in such a *gigunu* as 'the seat of joy' that the nuptials of Enlil took place for this purpose,[1] and the adornment with greenery enhanced the efficacy of the rite and warded off evil influences. Therefore, the sacral king enacted the role of the divine bridegroom in the seclusion of the *gigunu* with all its safeguards to renew vegetation as the culmination of the Akitu Festival.

## The Determination of Destinies

This accomplished, on the twelfth day of Nisan the gods again assembled in the Chamber of Destinies to resolve their fears concerning the fate of society during the forthcoming year, and to establish all that had been achieved by the due performance of the prescribed rites. The divine decree was ratified as in the Epic of Creation, when the gods foregathered after the victory of Marduk over Tiamat and the demoniac powers to elect him the leader of the pantheon, and to determine his functions and the destiny of the cosmic order for all eternity. When the universe had been formed, and the calendar organized in relation to the constellations of the stars that had been set in the sky to determine the years, months and days, it was decided to create mankind to serve the gods and to keep them supplied with nourishment by sacrificial offerings.[2] It remained henceforth the lot of man to carry out these decrees with the aid of the calendrical ritual, evermindful of the precarious conditions under which they lived, always liable to fluctuation and disasters. It was upon the fulfilment of these obligations as the servants of the gods that the fates were determined at the Annual Festival when the rejuvenation of nature was in the balance for the ensuing year.

Generative force having been once more made to flow freely to sustain nature, the gods returned to their respective cities, the king went to his palace to continue his vital functions, and the men to the cultivation of the revitalized soil in sure and certain hope that now all would be well in the new year, the prosperity

[1] F. Nötscher, *Ellil in Sumer und Akkad*, Hanover, 1927, pp. 19 ff.
[2] *Enuma elish*, tablets v, vi.

of which had been assured. So important, in fact, was the observance for the country as a whole that, although we are most adequately informed about the Akitu in Babylon, the Festival was celebrated in all or most of the principal Meso-potamian cities—e.g. Ur, Nippur, Ashur, Harran, Dilbat, Erech, Nineveh and Arbela—from the third millennium B.C. onwards.[1]

The relative importance of the local celebrations depended upon the status of its principal god and the ruler, but notwith-standing the constantly changing fortunes of the cult-centres, the New Year Festival gave stability to a fluid situation, being performed with the same rites and for the same purpose every-where, whatever might be the designation of the vegetation deity and his entourage. They were all Tammuz figures personi-fying the dying and reviving of plant life in its annual ebb and flow, represented as the disappearance of the year-god, the search for him by his bereaved mother or spouse amid universal mourning and lamentation, so very prominent in the Sumerian liturgies, culminating in this restoration and the marriage of the god and goddess to assure a prosperous 'destiny' in the new year. Then sorrow was turned into rejoicing and defeat into victory.

## THE CALENDRICAL RITUALS

Although in some of the older cities the earlier Chaldaean New Year Festival was still held in the autumn when, under Hammurabi and his successors, the Babylonian Akitu was firmly established in the spring, the monthly and lesser feasts for every occasion of daily life were for the most part associated with Marduk and his companions in the Babylonian pantheon. These festivals covered a great variety of occasions and incidents, ranging from lucky and unlucky days and their taboos and rites, to pregnancy observances and protective incantations at specified times believed to be under the guidance and control of particular gods or demons, adjusted to the lunar months and days of the year with their prescribed festivals. While some of

[1] Thureau-Dangin, *Rituels Accadiens*, pp. 86ff.; Pallis, *op. cit.*, pp. 19ff.

them had a personal application, divination was essentially an integral part of the civic administration in a carefully devised calendrical scheme spread over the whole year.

While the earliest Mesopotamian city-states had their own calendars and different order, dates and names of the month, they conformed to the same pattern, beginning invariably with either Nisan or Tishri. When the Nippur calendar was imposed on all the cities under the rule of the kings of Sumer and Akkad a different set of names for the months and their observances was adopted based on Sumerian designations, and became recognized throughout Babylonia from the time of Hammurabi. The Assyrians, on the other hand, being an agricultural people who had not come out of Sumer and Akkad, had their own calendar which was Semitic in origin and content, and was not equated with the Akkadian Nisan sequence and its intercalation, or, in fact, with that of any other Sumerian calendar. The year began in the spring about the time of the equinox, and the festivals were related to the agricultural seasonal events before astrological terminology was introduced. Therefore, although the Assyrian festivals and rituals resembled their Babylonian counterparts, they were distinct from them in their nomenclature, chronology and cultural background and significance. When the Assyrians settled in southern Mesopotamia they adopted the Sumerian customs and the existing organization of the theocratic city-state, but they preserved their own established usages in the designation and intent of the calendrical sequence, as, indeed, in most of their other social customs, religious institutions, their legal practices and art.

Thus, in Mesopotamia the names of the months and their ritual significance and observances varied according to the period and locality, though the Nippur calendar held the field from the Third Dynasty of Ur (*c.* 2079–1960 B.C.), and superseded all the others, notwithstanding the Chaldaean variations, those in the hemerologies (i.e. the texts prescribing sacrifices and taboos for the days of the month), and in the methods of intercalation of the months. Apart from the seasonal festivals already considered, certain days in each month were set apart as sacred to Marduk and his consort Sarpenit, to Shamash, Enlil and Ninlil, Nannar and Nergal, the moon-god of Ur and his spouse. These were, in fact, for the most part connected with the moon and the constellations, and were probably astral in their origin, Marduk as head of the pantheon occupying a unique position in the calendrical ritual. In addition to being a year-god in the agricultural cycle, he too was also associated with the heavenly bodies, eclipses and similar phenomena through the months of the year, as he was a constellation in the third month, Simanu, and in the tenth month, Tebitum, he was the star Lugal, and repeatedly he was Jupiter.

Astrology no doubt played some part in these identifications especially as it seems that the practice goes back to the Sumerian period in the middle of the third millennium B.C., and the moon probably was the first of the heavenly bodies to come under observation. Its periodic movements and those of the other constellations, together with the concurrence of the sun and the moon in the sky between the twelfth and the twentieth days of the month, were calculated and tabulated very early, and the occult character of each month was determined by the Chaldaean astrologers. But before a zodiacal calendar was drawn up and organized, the course of the moon, the stars and the planets were brought into relation with the Babylonian pantheon of which Marduk was the leader, and with the calendrical cycle so closely connected with the seasonal sequence and human destinies. The seasonal vegetation rituals, however, were prior to the formation of calendars, and were only gradually brought into conjunction with them when attempts were made to divide the year into months and days with the aid of the moon and the sun, and the movements of the other heavenly bodies.

## CHAPTER IV

# Palestinian Festivals

PASSING from Mesopotamia to Palestine and Syria, originally known as Canaan before it was called 'the land of the Philistines' ('Peleste' from which the Greek form 'Palestine' is derived) after their settlements along the southern coast in the twelfth century B.C., we encounter again a fertile oasis surrounded by desert on the east and south, the Mediterranean on the west, and the Taurus mountains on the north. It may be that the term 'Canaan' was applied in the first instance only to the northern coastal region which the Greeks described as Phoenicia, but it was soon extended to cover the whole country west of the Jordan.[1] With the discovery of the murex shellfish on the eastern Mediterranean coast and the manufacture from it of a valuable and much sought after purple dye, 'the land of the purple' (Canaan) was given this wider connotation, the dividing line being the Jordan separating Canaan (i.e. the whole SyrioPalestinian region from Dan to Beersheba) from Transjordania on the east of the river.

## THE CLIMATIC CONDITIONS IN PALESTINE

Although the lower valley of the Jordan is subtropical the rest of the country, which is up to two thousand feet above sealevel, has a temperate climate. From the end of October to the middle of April is the rainy season with snow on Mount Hermon in the north of the central mountain range. From the latter runs the Lebanon to the hills of Judaea in the south, where the Jordan sinks to nearly 2,600 feet below sealevel. In the spring (April) the hillsides in Galilee are decked with a profusion of wild flowers, such as the scarlet pimpernel, crimson anemones and cyclamen, with the green corn waving in the

[1] Herodotus, vii, p. 89.

cool breezes on the fields below. For it is and always has been the north that is essentially 'a good land, a land of brooks of water, of fountains and depths that spring out of valleys and hills; . . . a land of oil olive, and honey'.[1]

It is true as Gordon contended that in Palestine in no part of the year is the land as sterile as in Mesopotamia.[2] Figs and grapes ripen in the long rainless summer, and it is only at times of abnormally prolonged drought that famine prevails. Nevertheless, the recurrence of these conditions has been an ever-present fear in Palestine, since they have been always in the offing, as the Elijah and other similar stories in the Old Testament indicate.[3] Thus there was likely to be tension when the seasonal rains were pending however much a normal summer with only partial drought might be expected. What had happened in the past at fairly frequent intervals could occur again, and so a seasonal ritual of the Tammuz type had been devised and was duly performed if not annually at least periodically when the rains failed to materialize at the approach of the cool season.

Moreover, although summer fruits like figs and grapes might ripen as a matter of course, it was the grain that was the chief concern. Wheat and barley required the maintenance of the climatic rhythm in nature without interruption, be it in the dry or in the wet seasons. The fact that bad years were relatively exceptional and serious drought when it did occur was devastating and prolonged, often apparently of seven years duration or thereabouts, made the emotional reaction all the more intense, so that every precaution was likely to be taken to avoid so serious a catastrophe. It was this situation that found expression in the seasonal drama, of which traces recur in the texts on the clay tablets discovered since 1929 at Ras Shamra, the ancient city of Ugarit, on the coast of northern Syria near the modern seaport of Latakia, dating from the middle of the second millennium B.C.

[1] Deut. viii, 7 ff.
[2] *Ugaritic Literature*, Rome, 1949, p. 4.
[3] 1 Kings, xvii; Gen. xii, 10; Ruth 1.

## The Canaanite Cult-Drama

At present the texts, written in a hitherto unknown alphabetic cuneiform script recording a Canaanite dialect akin to Phoenician and an early form of Hebrew, are too fragmentary, and their decipherment is too incomplete to enable us to arrive at very definite conclusions about the precise nature of their contents. Nevertheless, about fifty per cent of the documents have been read and interpreted, and it is now becoming apparent that in this region a Canaanite and Phoenician myth and ritual were in vogue which despite local variations conformed in their general content and purpose to those of Mesopotamia and the rest of the Near East. As in Babylonia, the texts belonged to the archives of a temple prior to the fourteenth century B.C., and the Semitic alphabetic script in which they were written is similar to that which has been discovered at Beth Shemesh and Mount Tabor. It represents a Canaanite-Hurrian dialectal adaptation of cuneiform suitable for use only on clay tablets, unusual in Palestine and of short duration, but while it existed it was an active and prolific literary enterprise dealing largely with the gods and heroes and their exploits.[1]

For our present inquiry the Baal-Anat cycle, the epic of the dying god of fertility, Aleyan-Baal, is the most illuminating in spite of the fragmentary state of the tablets and the considerable number of lacunae at important points in the narratives. The central theme, however, seems to have been the story of the struggle between two opposed forces, in which the antagonists, Baal and Mot, represent personifications of the figures playing the leading roles in the seasonal drama elsewhere in Western Asia. In the Ugaritic version prominence is given to Baal's intention to build himself a palace of silver and gold, and the way in which the consent of his father El, the Supreme

[1] C. H. Gordon, *Ugaritic Handbook*, Rome, 1947; *Ugaritic Literature*, Rome, 1949; C. F. A. Schaeffer, *Ugaritica*, Paris, 1939, pp. 154 ff.; R. de Langhe, *Les Textes de Ras Shamra-Ugarit*, Paris, 1944–5; T. H. Gaster, *Thespis*, New York, 1950; G. R. Driver, *Canaanite Myths and Legends*, Edinburgh, 1956.

God, was obtained with the help of his ferocious wife and
sister, the goddess Anat, and the gentler Asherah, the consort
of El. The scheme was kept secret from Mot, the god of death
and sterility, another son of El, until it was *fait accompli*, and
this exploit may have been the principal cause of the subsequent
conflict between Baal and Mot.[1]

Mot, however, was not the only adversary with whom Baal
had to contend. He was the young weather-god, the son of El,
and, like Marduk in Babylonia, he had to wrest the pre-
eminence from the older father of the gods (i.e. El or Anu).
In the prolonged struggle between the two generations El was
always conspiring against Baal to undermine his growing
power and authority and regain for himself the supremacy.
To this end he lent his aid to Mot and to Prince Sea, the
monster with whom Baal had to fight as a rival claimant
to the lordship of the gods. Thus, El declared that the Sea
was Baal's slave and ordered a house for his rival to be
built in Baal's domain by Hayin, an Egyptian master-
builder.[2] Lotan, the writhing serpent, was another of Baal's
adversaries, crushed by Anat who cursed one of his
seven heads. Mot thereupon vowed that he would be avenged
upon Baal, Lotan being equated with the forces of death and
desolation.[3]

Beset with supernatural foes on all sides, Baal was compelled to take up the challenge as the divine warrior in the
guise of the dying and reviving god of vegetation in the
seasonal drama. Exactly what transpired cannot be determined
in the present condition of the tablets, but it would seem that
unlike Marduk he was at first petrified with fear and returned
to his house weeping at the approach of the enemy, ready
to become his slave without resistance.[4] Somehow or another
he was killed, Mot having contrived to cause him to descend
to the nether regions with disastrous effects on vegetation, all

[1] 2 *A.B.*, viii, 40-2; 51:1:13 ff.; 51:iv:52 ff.
[2] 49, vi, 27 ff.; 129:8, 22, i; 'nt: pl. x: iv, 14 ff; 137; 17, 33, 36; Obermann, *J.A.O.S.*, lxvii, 1947, p. 196.     [3] 'nt., iii, 38 f.; 67, 1, 1 ff.
[4] 67:11, 10 ff; 51, vii, 42.

life on the earth languishing. With the help of the Sun-goddess Shapsh, Anat went in search of her brother-spouse, searching every mountain in the land, and crying 'Baal is dead', lamenting as bitterly as Demeter or Adonis grieved for Kore or Attis, 'desiring him as a cow her calf or a ewe her lamb'.[1] Eventually his body was found prostrate in the pastures of Shlmmt and taken by Anat to the heights of Sapan, his former abode; and there she buried him.[2]

Although Baal's demise removed the rival of El, the latter came down from his celestial home under the name of Ltpn and sat on the ground with his head covered with the 'dust of mourning', girt in sackcloth and lacerating himself as he too cried 'Baal is dead, perished is the Prince, the Lord of Earth!' Anat then poured out her complaint to El, forestalling Asherah who rejoiced at his death and tried to get her son Attar appointed in his stead. Attar, however, eventually was made to recognize his incapacity to rule in the heights of Sapan.[3] Knowing that Mot had been responsible for slaying Baal, Anat continued her search for him, and when he was found he admitted that he had killed his brother, making him like a lamb in his mouth and crushing him in his jaws like a kid. Thereupon she seized Mot, clave him with a ritual sickle (*harpé*), winnowed him in a sieve, scorched him, ground him in a mill, scattered his flesh over the fields like the dismembered body of Osiris, and gave it to the birds to eat.[4] In short, she treated him as the reaped grain.

By avenging the death of her lover in this way she treated his murderer in the same manner as the corn at harvest, reaping, threshing and winnowing him, baking him as bread, and grinding him to meal, and finally sowing him in the field like the seed. This was an anomaly as Mot was the god of death, drought and sterility whose abode was in the underworld, turning every hill into desolation by robbing all living things of the breath of life.[5] By making him a corn spirit who was

[1] *A.B.* 49:11:5ff., iv, *A.B.*, ii, 26.     [2] *A.B.*, 67; vi, 8ff.; 1: 62: 12ff., 154.

[3] *A.B.*, 62:1:12, 15; 67:vi, 8ff.     [4] 49:ii:10ff.

[5] 1. *A.B.*, ii, 15–20.

slain at the ingathering of harvest,[1] an inconsistency was intro-duced into the theme. Nevertheless, apart from the fact that consistency is never a characteristic feature of mythological tradition, in equating Mot with the reaped grain the ritual slaying of the corn spirit was in accord with the seasonal situation, the purpose being to revive not Mot but Baal by a sympathetic magical action, thereby bringing him into line with Adonis and other vegetation gods. It was after his (Baal's) release from the nether regions whither he had taken the rain-producing clouds, that 'the heavens rained oil and the wadis ran with honey'.[2]

How this was accomplished is not recorded, but both Baal and Mot were brought back to life, and continued their peren-nial struggle. But whereas in their earlier encounters Baal had been paralysed with fear and eager to surrender, typifying his declining vigour in the dry season, after the return of the rains he is represented as full of strength and vitality fighting furiously with his adversary, biting like a serpent and kicking like a steed. El, in fact, recognized that the time had come for Baal to bring life on the earth and so he 'overturned Mot's throne and broke the sceptre of his dominion', forcing him to surrender and acknowledge the sovereignty of Baal.[3] So ended the drought because Baal was the god of rain and fertility who ruled upon earth from September to May. Mot as the god of death and aridity supplanted Baal in the summer, but only to be driven out once more with the coming of autumn and the re-establish-ment of fertility in the seasonal sequence.

## The Chronology of the Calendrical Ritual

It may be true as Gordon maintains that in Syria severe drought and famine were sporadic, septennial rather than annual occurrences, but the end of summer and the opening of the rainy season were in all probability celebrated in Ugarit as elsewhere by the calendrical cult-drama so widespread in Western Asia. If this were so, the combat between Aleyan-Baal

---

[1] *G.B.*, pt. vii, pp. 216ff.; V. Jacob, *Harvard Theological Review.*

[2] 49; iii, 6f., 12.          [3] 49, v, 1 ff.

and Mot was doubtless enacted to establish the dominion of the beneficent Storm and Weather god (Baal) upon which fertility and prosperity depended not only at times of serious drought but in the normal course of events. Every year the return of the refreshing and life giving rains was eagerly awaited since they were the primary source of fertility, and to this recurrent phenomenon the cultic rituals were related in the temple of Baal, with Mot as the antithesis to the Weather god in a vegetation setting, personifying the dreaded sterility and aridity, and yet treated as the reaped grain in the guise of the corn spirit dying at the ingathering of harvest.

The struggle being perennial neither of the contending forces could be ultimately destroyed. When the reign of Baal returned fecundity was restored by his opening the lattice in his mountain palace to enable the rain to fall on the parched ground. Indeed, as King of Sapan, his main task seems to have been the rejuvenation of vegetation and the maintenance of the succession of the seasons. In this capacity he was identified in all probability with the Hurrian Weather god Hadad and the Akkadian Adad, the ancient Semitic Storm god, before he was introduced into northern Syria, the early home of the god of thunder and rain.[1] This may account for his having no palace temple unlike the rest of the Ugaritic divinities. Hence his urgent efforts to secure a house and to establish himself as the most virile figure in the pantheon, dwarfing in strength and status all other gods and goddesses. Therefore, it was around him that the cult drama developed, conforming in its essential features to the customary seasonal pattern.

### The Drama of 'the Gracious Gods'

In text 52, first published by Virolleaud in 1933, the birth of the gods Shr (Dawn) and Slm (Sunset) is described in a manner that has led Dr Gaster to regard it as the libretto of a sacred drama addressed to 'Gracious Gods' called 'princes' and 'high ones', written for performance at the Canaanite festival of first fruits in the spring; the prototype of the Hebrew Feast

[1] Schaeffer, *The Cuneiform Texts of Ras-Shamra-Ugarit*, p. 8.

of Weeks, or Pentecost, at the beginning of the wheat harvest.[1] The obverse side of the tablet contains the ritual consisting of an introductory invocation (1–7), a viticulture song of the Vinedressers (8–11) sung in a near-by chantry in Dionysiac terms representing the emasculation of the vine by pruning. Then follows a threefold rite performed seven times celebrating the astronomical, pastoral and agricultural aspects of the festival (12–15), leading on to the induction and enthronement of the gods, identified with Anat, the Virgin goddess, and Asherah, the consort of El, under the names Rhmy and Atrt. Their identity is open to question, but whoever they may have been, their statues appear to have been carried in procession gorgeously attired and solemnly enthroned (16–19).

The sacred drama then begins on the reverse side of the tablet with a prologue invoking the 'Gracious Gods' and the sun, and the greeting of the worshippers assembled with their offerings (23–27). The action of the play, it is explained, opens with a scene on the seashore before the house of El where the aged supreme deity demonstrates his virility to two girls, identified with Anat and Asherah, who watched him carrying water into his house, and with accurate marksmanship shoot an arrow into the air and bring down a bird, which he then plucks and boils for his meal. As these events are recorded in the text, so impressed were they with his youthful strength and adroitness that they offered him their devoted service as either his brides or his daughters (30–36). It was as wives that he accepted them, and an erotic scene follows in which after passionate intercourse they conceive and bring forth the two gods, Dawn (Shr) and Sunset (Slm) (49–52a). This episode is repeated with the offspring called the 'Gracious Gods' (55–61a), the children and their mothers feeding voraciously for seven years on the fruitful earth (61b–76).

It seems very likely that this is a cultic text with a ritual background giving instructions for the performance of the

[1] Virolleaud, *Syria*, xiv, 1933, fasc. 2, pp. 128 ff.; Gaster, *J.A.O.S.*, lxvi, 1946, pp. 49 ff.

seasonal pantomime, depicting a sacred marriage resulting in the birth of certain gods for the purpose of promoting fertility at the ingathering of the first-fruits in the spring. The literary structure, as Dr Gaster maintains, supports this contention,[1] and the theme is in accord with what is known about the myth and ritual of the sacred marriage throughout the Ancient Near East and the adjacent regions. Furthermore, the most appropriate occasion for the celebration would have been at the Canaanite festival of the first-fruits, as is suggested by the rubrics and dominant features of the text, especially if the two women do in fact represent Anat and Asherah under the designations of Rhmy and Atrt, with El playing the leading part.

### The Ugaritic Baal Cult and its Theme

In the background of these Ugaritic texts lies the Tammuz theme, even though owing to the climatic conditions in Palestine the rites may have been celebrated with less frequency and regularity than in Mesopotamia. Of this, however, we cannot be certain, and it is by no means improbable that the conflict between Baal and Prince Sea may have been enacted at the autumnal festival when the rains were due to begin, Baal playing a role not unlike that of Marduk in his victory over Tiamat in the Babylonian *Enuma elish*. It was he who appointed the seasons, and fixed the time for the refreshing rains and showers to fall upon the earth,[2] and in the absence of a river like the Tigris or Euphrates, it was upon the rain and dew that Syria depended for its fertility.

Baal, 'the Rider on the Clouds', personifying the storm and the rain, controlled the weather, and ordered a rift to be opened in the clouds and a lattice within his palace in the heavens to enable the rain to descend. The installation of windows in his house represent the mythological background of a rain-making ceremony at the autumnal festival, when the windows in the temple at Ras Shamra were opened to simulate the opening of the windows of heaven and the clefts in the clouds.

---

[1] Gaster, *J.A.O.S.*, lxvi, 1946, pp. 75 ff.          [2] 51; v, 68 ff.

Schaeffer, in fact, has suggested that the rain was intended to descend through the skylight in the roof on the face of the god depicted on a stele which stood in the sanctuary, a representation of Baal armed with lightning.[1]

In any case, Baal was 'the lord of the furrows of the field',[2] and although he was not the only fertility god in the Ugaritic pantheon, he was responsible for the rain and for everything growing in the soil. Consequently, when he was slain all vegetation languished and fecundity was suspended on the earth because he had taken the clouds with him to the under⁄world. It was these events which were celebrated in the calen⁄drical ritual at the critical junctures in the agricultural year in which he and his adversary were the predominant figures. The battle between life and death in nature being the central theme, the sacred drama can hardly have been other than the Canaan⁄ite version of the Tammuz⁄Adonis cult which unquestionably was firmly established in Syria, whatever variations in chro⁄nology and content may have occurred in the Ugaritc observances. At all costs the rhythm of the seasons had to be maintained and Baal was the god who controlled the processes of vegetation.

He was a composite deity and his name was derived from *ba'lu*, a generic term for 'lord', and so applicable to a variety of gods exercising generative functions closely connected with rain and fertility. Even so, he was not without his rivals, and his rule did not go unchallenged. However, he was the emotional centre of the Ugaritic drama of nature, being its most prominent figure, and the calendrical ritual connected with nature and the seasonal cycle of ploughing, sowing, reaping and ingathering were brought into relation with, and inter⁄preted in terms of, his legend, enacted at the appropriate festivals and dramatic occasions in the normal course of events and at times of great emotional tension such as during a severe drought, or at the erection of a new temple. The climax in the yearly cycle doubtless was reached at the New Year Festival,

[1] Schaeffer, *The Cuneiform Texts of Ras⁄Shamra⁄Ugarit*, p. 68.
[2] 49; iv; 27, 29.

when the destinies of the coming year were fixed, and the conflict between life and death was resolved by the return of the life-giving rains at the end of the hot dry summer. Once again Baal had revived and been restored, and all would be well during the forthcoming year.

## THE HEBREW OCCUPATION OF PALESTINE

It is against this Canaanite background that the Hebrew festivals and their cultus have to be set, since the Ugaritic tradition and its myth and ritual were firmly established when the Israelites settled in the land in the middle of the second millennium B.C. Their origin and ethnology are still obscure, and it has yet to be determined whether or not they are to be equated with a widely dispersed nomadic people in Mesopotamia and Syria, known as the Habiru in cuneiform inscriptions from 1720 to 1570 B.C., from whom Hammurabi wrested the mastery of Sumer.[1] In any case, it was not until the beginning of the Iron Age (*c.* 1200–900 B.C.) that the Hebrew invasion of Palestine began. Prior to the final settlement in the country the ancestors of these roving people, following their flocks and herds between Mesopotamia and Syria, may have infiltrated in small groups from the north-west, as is suggested in the Patriarchal narratives in the book of Genesis.

The traditional account of these events, however, is largely mythological in its setting, but, nevertheless, behind the legends lies a hard core of fact interpreted and embellished in terms of later beliefs, observances and ethnological situations concerning place-names and sacred sites and sanctuaries. In their present form the narratives for the most part have been drawn up to explain current events, customs and festivals in relation to occurrences alleged to have taken place in the distant past, many of them some five hundred years or more before the documents were compiled, between about 850 B.C. and the re-settlement of the exiled Jews in and around Jerusalem after their return from Mesopotamia at the end of the sixth century

[1] Kraeling, *B.A.S.O.R.*, no. 77, 1940, pp. 47f.; Rowley, *From Joseph to Joshua* (Schweich Lectures, 1950).

B.C.[1] As regards the conquest and occupation of Palestine, some of the complications have arisen from there having been more than one entry of the Hebrew tribes, and because their penetration and establishment was a very gradual process, involving a fusion with the indigenous population which produced a composite culture and cultus.

This occurred at a time when Western Asia and Egypt were in a state of unrest and the eastern Mediterranean littoral was subject to constant attack by the raiding 'people of the sea' known as the Philistines. These events are reflected in the vicissitudes in the history of Israel and Judah, and their institutions were constantly subjected to extraneous influences, first from one direction then from another. When they entered Palestine the Hebrew tribes were already in possession of a religious tradition which they attributed to Moses and their sojourn in the desert, with roots going back into the nebulous Patriarchal age of their remote ancestors, Abraham, Isaac, Jacob and Joseph. In the absence of archaeological or reliable documentary evidence it is exceedingly difficult, and often impossible, to assess the historicity of the characters and events which have been handed down from time immemorial prior to the written records. In recent years, however, the former practice among Old Testament scholars of dismissing the Patriarchal and Mosaic traditions as fabrications of later compilers of the narratives has given place to a much more conservative view, their historicity being now maintained to a much greater extent by Orientalists like Professor Albright, Sidney Smith, C. H. Gordon, S. H. Hooke, and E. A. Speiser.[2]

It is all too easy for the veracity of the narratives to be assumed or over-emphasized by those who attach a particular religious significance to the Scriptures as divinely disclosed revelations, and to draw from this change of attitude on the part of scholars unjustifiable conclusions. Thus, while in view of our present

---

[1] Rowley, *op. cit.* Meek, *Hebrew Origins*, 1950; Albright, *Archaeology and the Religion of Israel*, Baltimore, 1953; *From the Stone Age to Christianity*, new ed., Doubleday Anchor Books, N.Y., 1957.

[2] Cf. C. H. Gordon, *The Biblical Archaeologist*, iii, 1940, no. 1.

knowledge of what was happening in the Fertile Crescent in
the early part of the second millennium B.C. it is very likely that
deeply laid traditions concerning the sojourn of the Hebrew
tribes in Egypt and their subsequent exodus under Moses
may be substantially correct in broad outline, nevertheless, as
Professor Rowley has pointed out, 'there is no feature in the
reconstruction of the date of the Exodus, the route followed
to the Holy Mountain, its location, and the duration of the
sojourn in the desert, or which among the Hebrew tribes were
involved in the conquest of Palestine, that has not been
challenged in recent years'.[1]

The tradition fits into the general framework of events in the
Near East at the time, but every attempt to adjust it to contemporary chronology and to find corroborative evidence has
failed. Thus, the assignment of the date and circumstances of
the Exodus and the conquest of Palestine by Garstang and
J. W. Jack to 1475–1400 B.C., hailed with such delight by Sir
Charles Marston and his co-religionists in the early thirties, has
now been superseded by a dating two hundred years later, in
favour of the Pharaoh of the oppression being Ramesses II
(c. 1299–32 B.C.) and the accession of his successor Merenptah
(c. 1299–21 B.C.) the occasion of the escape into the desert.
The fact is that the problem is of such complexity that in
the present state of the data it is insoluble. Every attempt to
arrive at a solution encounters insuperable difficulties in trying
to reconcile the archaeological and Biblical evidence. But a
tradition so firmly established in the annals of the nation requires
an explanation in fact, and few competent authorities would
deny that some of the Hebrew tribes were enslaved in Egypt
and did escape, however obscure may be the time and occasion
of the event, and embellished with supernatural adornments
the way in which it was accomplished.

### The Cult of Yahweh in Israel

Moreover, it would seem that the tribes which were in the
desert were welded together into a theocratic confederacy under

[1] *op. cit.*, p. 2.

the leadership of Moses, who may have brought them into a covenant relationship with the Western Semitic deity whose name occurs on a number of Aramaean, Babylonian, Hebrew and Canaanite inscriptions and documents as *Ya, Yami,* or *Yaum-ilum,*[1] although there is no conclusive evidence of the name of Yahweh in cuneiform literature before the eighth century B.C.[2] He was, however, primarily a desert deity, probably worshipped among the Kenites, before the encounter with Moses recorded in the Elohist document in the book of Exodus (E) belonging to the northern kingdom of Israel, and repeated in the post-exilic Priestly Code (P).[3] On the other hand, in the Yahwist (J) narrative current in Judah in the middle of the eighth century B.C., before it was combined in the JE recension probably in about 700 B.C., he is said to have been known to the Hebrew ancestors from the time of the mythical Enoch, and even to the first parents of the human race in Eden.[4] Why the northern tribes, who apparently did not embrace Yahwism until after the time of Moses, should have attributed the covenant and the Sinaitic cultus to him is not explained. Professor Rowley suggests that the tribes which were not with Moses at the time of the Exodus did not ascribe the beginnings of their Yahwism to him, while those which were with him did make him the source of the revelation.[5] But notwithstanding these obscurities, however and wherever the cult may have arisen it stood primarily in the desert tradition, and in it the conception of the Exodus and the Sinaitic covenant was fundamental.

After the settlement in Palestine Yahweh eventually assumed the role and functions of the indigenous vegetation gods, and often was hardly distinguishable from Aleyan-Baal and Hadad as the 'Rider on the Clouds' sending the rain to nourish

[1] Albright, *Archaeology and the Religion of Israel,* p. 64; *Journal of Biblical Literature,* lxvii, 1948, p. 380.

[2] Luckenbill, *American Journal of Theology,* xxii, 1918, pp. 24ff.; Driver, *Zeitschrift für die alttestamentliche Wissenschaft,* xlvi, 1928, pp. 7ff.

[3] Ex. iii, 13–15; vi, 2f.; cf. Meek, *op. cit.,* pp. 93ff.; Rowley *op. cit.,* pp. 149f.

[4] Gen. ii, 4–25; iv, 26.          [5] *op. cit.,* p. 144.

the earth, speaking in the thunder and manifest in the lightning, and engaging in battle with primeval monsters like Leviathan and Rahab.[1] This made it easy for the agricultural festivals of Canaan to be taken over by the Hebrews, and to be given an historical interpretation in terms of the earlier Mosaic desert tradition when Palestine became officially 'the land of Yahweh'. But attractive and indispensable as were the vegetation observances at the local shrines, and firmly established among that section of the Hebrew community which had lived in the country continually since long before the invasions in the second millennium B.C., the Sinaitic covenant (*berith*) remained the distinguishing feature in the faith and worship of Israel, with its monolatrous implications, until at length after the Exile the nation was weaned away altogether from the Canaanite gods and their vegetation cultus.

In their present form the accounts of the festivals and calendrical rites have been worked over and reinterpreted in the Deuteronomic literature of the seventh century B.C. and onwards, to bring them into line with the monotheistic position strenuously maintained by the prophetic movement. Nevertheless, there is no reason to suppose that Yahweh was originally a vegetation deity like Baal, or that his worship conformed to the Canaanite pattern until he was firmly installed in Palestine, conforming then only with important differences. In Canaan he may have been a minor divinity before the Israelite occupation under the name of *Yau* or *Yo*. Thus, on a cuneiform tablet from Taanach, dated between 3000 and 2000 B.C., the name *Ahi-yahu* occurs, and the abbreviation *Yo* has been found on a Palestinian jug handle of a rather later period, while, if Virolleaud is correct, it recurs in the form *yw* at Ugarit.[2] But as the Phoenicians like the Israelites probably came from the deserts south of Palestine, it is not surprising that they should both be acquainted with the same deity, though he had a different status in the two groups. When eventually he became pre

---

[1] Ps. xlviii, 14; xvii, 4ff.; Jud. ii, 6–iii, 6; v, 4f., 23.

[2] Virolleaud, *La Déesse d'Anat*, Paris, 1938, p. 98; cf. Albright, *B.A.S.O.R.*, 1936, no. 63, p. 29, n. 36; no. 71, 1938, p. 39, n. 38.

dominant in Palestine his cultus and its calendrical observances readily became adapted to the needs of an agricultural
society without discarding its earlier desert inheritance.

## THE HEBREW SPRING FESTIVAL

### (a) *The Pesach*

Thus, the Spring Festival which became known as the
Passover (*Pesach*) and the Feast of Unleavened Bread (*Maṣṣôth*)
was a composite rite which began at the full moon nearest to
the vernal equinox when the firstlings of the lambing season
were offered. The sacrifice of the lamb represented the shepherd's natural offering to his fertility divinity of the first-fruits
of his flocks in the spring in a lunar setting, and it was this
pastoral sacrifice that was interpreted in terms of the Exodus
from Egypt arising out of a command to go a three days'
journey into the desert to sacrifice to Yahweh.[1] But, as Frazer
says, in the very involved narratives 'the one thing that looms
clear through the haze of his weird tradition is the memory of a
great massacre of firstborn'.[2] This was the outstanding feature
of the annual commemoration of the historic night on which
the angel of Yahweh was alleged to have set forth on his bloody
campaign against the Egyptians,[3] and it may well have been
originally a sacrifice of the firstlings on the 14th of Nisan at the
opening of the rainy season in the spring, whether or not, as
Frazer contends, the offering of the firstborn of man was
required, which later was softened into a vicarious sacrifice of
a lamb of the flocks, and the payment of a ransom for each
child. With this *Pesach* was combined the *Maṣṣôth*, or Feast of
Unleavened Bread, which was an agricultural rite celebrated
at barley harvest but so interwoven with the *Pesach* that the
Paschal lamb had to be kept apart from the leaven and eaten
in haste with bitter herbs and unleavened bread, none being
left until the morning.[4] Moreover, it was strictly forbidden to
eat the flesh of the victim raw, a taboo that Robertson Smith
considered to be indicative of the 'living flesh' with the warm

[1] Ex. v, 3.                     [2] *G.B.*, pt. iv, p. 176.
[3] Ex. xii, 12 f.; xvi, 1–8.     [4] Ex. xiii, 15 ff.; xxiii, 18; xxxiv, 25.

blood still in it originally having been consumed sacra‚
mentally.[1]

According to the narratives in the books of Exodus and
Deuteronomy the lamb had to be slain at 'the going down of
the sun' in the evening of the 14th of Nisan when the moon
was full, and the barley was ripening.[2] This injunction indicates
a combination of a solar and a lunar chronology brought into
relation with the agricultural year. To make certain that the
rites were held at the right moment in the spring, it was neces‚
sary to intercalate before the month of Nisan. The sprinkling
of the blood of the lamb on the lintel and the two doorposts
of the house[3] was, however, unquestionably a later addition to
the Paschal ritual, borrowed from the widespread ancient
practice of smearing houses with blood as a protective apotro‚
paic rite to repel demons.[4] It had nothing to do with the Spring
Paschal Festival as such, and the explanations given for it are
inconsistent, the 'destroyer' and Yahweh being confused.[5] It is
not clear, moreover, whether it was to be a sign to the Israelites
or to the destroying 'angel'.[6] As Buchanan Gray says, 'either
the story is intended to correct a popular conception of Yah‚
weh, or to counteract a popular recognition of other divine
powers than Yahweh'.[7] But in any case, it was a very primitive
and ancient practice for the purpose of repelling from houses
evil spirits and influences quite independent of the Paschal
Feast with which it was in every respect inconsistent in its
occurrence and application.

## (b) *The Maṣṣôth*

The *Maṣṣôth*, or Feast of Unleavened Bread, on the other
hand, became an integral part of the Passover, though its
association with the Exodus probably was an afterthought.
Its setting and timing, however, presupposed agricultural

---

[1] *The Religion of the Semites*, 1927, p. 345.
[2] Ex. xii, 6; Deut. xvi, 6; Ex. xiii, 4; xxiii, 15.      [3] Ex. xii, 21 f.
[4] Ex. xii, 22 ff.; Curtiss, *Primitive Semitic Religion Today* 1902, pp., 226 ff.
[5] Ex. xii, 13, 23, 27; xi, 4.          [6] Ex. xii, 21 ff., cf. xi, 4.
[7] *Sacrifice in the Old Testament*, O.U.P., 1925, p. 364.

rather than pastoral conditions connected with the barley harvest when in Babylonia the Annual Festival in honour of Shamash, the Sun-god, was held in Sippar on the 7th of Nisan. In Israel it was observed in the month of Abib (Nisan) approximately in April at the vernal equinox, as an offering of the first-fruits.[1] As it was in this month that the deliverance from bondage in Egypt was alleged to have occurred it was readily associated with the Exodus. Although special import-ance was attached to the first day of the feast before the harvest period, for a week unleavened bread only might be eaten; an injunction that was in no way connected with the nomadic Paschal observance, the association being merely a coincidence in the time of the celebration of the two rites. This eventually led to their amalgamation in a composite Spring Festival called either *Pesach* or *Maṣṣôth*, and interpreted in the books of Exodus and Deuteronomy as the annual commemoration of the great release from the Egyptian yoke.[2]

That the two ordinances were originally distinct is indicated in the story of the supplementary Passover service in the second month, recorded in the book of Numbers (chap. i, 1–14), held for the benefit of those prevented by ceremonial uncleanness or absence from home from taking part in the festival on the 14th of Nisan. Here no mention is made of the Feast of Unleavened Bread, the *Pesach* offering of the firstborn being regarded as the earlier and really significant institution before the two had coalesced, in spite of the fact that in both the J document in Exodus and in Deuteronomy the *Maṣṣôth* is given precedence.[3] If, as is not improbable, the agricultural observance was taken over from the Canaanites and tacked on to the pastoral *Pesach*, having made its way into Syria under Mesopotamian influence, originally it may have been a solar festival. The *Pesach*, on the other hand, would appear to have had lunar affinities, to ensure the increase of the flocks and herds by the aid and intervention of the Moon-god who was so widely associated with fertility.[4]

[1] Ex. xxxiv, 18, 26.  [2] Ex. xii; Deut. xvi, 1–8, 16f.
[3] Ex. xxxiv, 18; Deut. xvi, 3 ff.
[4] Cf. Nielsen, *Handbuch der altarabischen Altertumskunde*, i, 1927, pp. 213 ff.

Thus, it was celebrated in the evening at the full moon on the 14th of Nisan,[1] and the sacrifice had to be consumed in its entirety before the presence of the moon in all its glory had been withdrawn. Everything was to be done in haste—aetiologically reinterpreted in terms of the speedy escape from Egypt with girded loins ready for flight—whereas the Feast of Unleavened Bread was a leisurely affair, extended over a week devoted solely to the performance of the prescribed rites.[2] These included in the post-exilic Priestly Code the offering of special sacrifices for seven days,[3] and apparently it was on the second day of this week that a sheaf of the new crop of barley (*'omer*) was waved before Yahweh as an act of sanctification and to promote fertility,[4] concluding with a holy convocation on the seventh day.[5] Thus, it is evident that the Spring Festival was a combination of two originally independent observances, the one pastoral, the other agricultural, brought together at the time of barley harvest and amalgamated under the influence of an annual commemoration of the Exodus after the settlement of the tribes in Palestine.

## (c) *The Post-Exilic Passover*

While the sources of these various strands in the complex pattern of the Hebrew Spring Festival are still obscure, unquestionably the resultant product was a seasonal sacrificial and sacramental observance in which pastoral and agricultural elements were combined for the purpose of consecrating and renewing the flocks, herds and crops at the turn of the year. This was reinterpreted as a commemoration of the deliverance from Egypt when under Deuteronomic influence the Yahwistic and Elohistic documents of the southern and northern kingdoms respectively were revised and brought together in a composite narrative. To this the Priestly sections were added after the Exile, and the Paschal festival then became a temple feast beginning on the 14th of Nisan and lasting seven days with a prescribed routine of sacrifices as a part of its expiation

[1] Deut. xvi, 1, 4, 6; Ex. xii, 6; Lev. xxiii, 5.     [2] Lev. xxiii, 5–8.
[3] Num. xxviii, 16ff.     [4] Lev. xxiii, 10ff.     [5] Deut. xvi, 8.

system.[1] In this later literature the temple observance is referred back to the reforms undertaken by Hezekiah and Josiah before the Exile[2] when the cultus was centralized at Jerusalem, and this procedure was carried on in the re-established Jewish community with the emphasis on the Exodus. In the books of the Chronicles the Priestly writer rested the festival on the authority of Moses but its celebration was made to begin with the building of the temple in Jerusalem as the only place where Yahweh might be legitimately worshipped.[3]

Although the feast then ceased to be a domestic observance held in private houses, the oblation and eating of the Paschal lamb, sheep or goat remained the chief feature, the blood being offered on the altar in the temple where the victims were slain by the priests. Nevertheless, the earlier practice survived in the custom of small groups of the pilgrims to Jerusalem assembling together in a house that had been carefully swept to remove any traces of leaven to eat the communal Paschal meal. During the eating of an unleavened cake (*mazuoth*) with bitter herbs the story of the deliverance from Egypt recorded in Exodus was recited, and Psalms cxiii–cxviii were sung as the Hallel. In this rite the *Maṣṣôth* Feast of Canaanite origin was commemorated in remembrance of the Exodus,[4] brought into conjunction with the rites of barley harvest and followed by those of wheat harvest a month later at the Feast of Weeks. Thus, those who partook of it had to eat it with haste with sandals on their feet, a staff in their hands, and their loins girded, like their forefathers on the night of their escape from Egypt.[5] Other incidents in the cult-legend may have been re-enacted in the imagery employed in the course of the observance, such as the blood-smearing rite, the nocturnal flight after the slaughter of the firstborn, the pursuit and the victorious passage across the river. But of this we have no knowledge. All we know is that the various traditions connected with the Spring Festival were amalgamated and reinterpreted in terms of the Exodus legend and its ritual,

---

[1] Lev. xxiii, 4–8.  [2] Num. xxviii, 16–25.
[3] Cf. W. Rudolph, *Chronikbücher*, Tübingen, 1955, pp. viii–xxiv.
[4] Ex. xxiii, 15; xxxiv, 18.  [5] Ex. xii, 11.

involving many discrepancies and contradictions, in which the original calendrical observances were obscured though not obliterated; the feast of the firstlings and the first-fruits remained in the background.

In the post-exilic community the temple ritual predominated until the destruction of the central sanctuary on Mount Sion in A.D. 70 when of necessity the sacrificial and sacerdotal aspects of the Passover ceased. Then it reassumed its earlier domestic character. The head of each family in the presence of his children and guests gave the prescribed answer to the question, 'Why is this night different from other nights?'[1] emphasizing the spiritual significance of the annual commemoration of the deliverance of their forefathers from oppression in Egypt.[2] But the elimination of the sacrificial element removed the grimmer side of the Festival, with the offering of the firstborn in its background, and brought into greater prominence the agricultural aspect of the *Maṣṣôth* and its sequel in the vegetation cultus. Thus, the Passover became eventually the Feast of Unleavened Bread rather than the *Pesach*.

## (d) *The Feast of Weeks* (*Shabuoth*)

Seven weeks after the Paschal observances, at the end of wheat harvest, the Feast of Weeks, or Pentecost, was kept when a sheaf of wheat analogous to the sheaf of barley, and two 'wave loaves' made of fine flour of the new corn and baked with leaven were offered to Yahweh as first-fruits.[3] No doubt originally the midsummer rite was celebrated independently everywhere all over the country as soon as the harvest was ready to be gathered. When, however, the worship of the nation was centralized in the temple at Jerusalem after the Deuteronomic reforms in the seventh century B.C., and all males were required 'to appear before the face of Yahweh' at his central sanctuary three times a year,[4] it became a fixed calendrical

---

[1] Ex. xii, 26ff.                    [2] *Pesahim.*, x.
[3] Ex. xxxiv, 22; Lev. xxiii, 17; Deut. xvi, 9, 12.
[4] Ex. xxiii, 14, 15, 17.

observance seven weeks after the *Maṣṣôth*[1] as a modification of the harvest-sheaf ritual, introduced perhaps through a Canaanite medium from Babylonian sources. Oesterley, on the other hand, has suggested with less probability, possible Egyptian contacts, connecting the two 'wave loaves' with a similar rite in a Mystery drama in the Ramesseum Papyrus in which two cakes of spelt were presented to the Pharaoh in the coronation ceremony accompanied by a dance. These represented the eye of Horus with which Osiris was revivified, and so became life-giving agents in the renewal of vegetation in the spring, and at mid-summer, offered to Yahweh as the giver of the fruits of the earth.[2]

## THE AUTUMNAL FEAST OF INGATHERING ('ASITH)

### (a) *Sukkôth*

At the end of harvest time in the autumn a third feast was kept. This was a feast of ingathering known as *Sukkôth*, commonly called The Feast of Tabernacles or Booths.[3] It was observed at full moon in the month of Ethanim, described after the Exile as 'the seventh month' (Tishri), corresponding to our October to November, when the vintage had been completed. Both the time and setting of the event suggest a Canaanite origin connected with the grape harvest and celebrated at the autumnal equinox when the agricultural work of the season had come to an end, and the urgently needed 'former rains' in October were due to begin.[4]

When the Babylonian calendar was adopted after the Exile the earlier hilarious rites at 'the going out of the year' continued to be observed for seven days as a pilgrimage feast closely associated with viticulture, beginning on the fifteenth day of

[1] In the Priestly calendar the Feast of Weeks was reckoned at fifty days from the beginning of barley harvest: hence the name Feast of Pentecost.

[2] *Myth and Ritual*, O.U.P., 1933, p. 121.

[3] Ex. xxiii, 16; xxxiv, 22.

[4] Zech., xiv, 16ff.; 1 Kings viii, 2; xii, 32; 2 Chron. vi, 26; Mowinckel, *Psalmenstudien II*, Kristiania, 1922, pp. 102ff., 230; P. Volz, *Das Neujahrs-fest Jahwas*, Tübingen, 1912, p. 15; Snaith, *The Jewish New Year Festival*, 1947, pp. 62ff.

Tishri with a holy convocation and the cessation of all servile work, as also on the last day of the festival. Boughs of fruit‑trees, branches of palm‑trees, of leaf‑trees and of Arabah‑trees from the river beds were taken, and from them and their foliage, booths were constructed in which the congregation of Israel dwelt during the Feast of Tabernacles.[1] The later texts alleged that this was done to commemorate the deliverance from Egypt, but this was clearly a reinterpretation of an earlier agricultural practice, the purpose of which was to promote fertility at the end of harvest, and to secure the much‑needed rain at a critical moment marked by the Rosh hashShanah (New Year's Day) on the first of Tishri, when the autumnal rites began.

No doubt in their Canaanite form they included feasting and erotic dancing such as obtained outside the vineyards at these seasons, referred to in the book of Judges,[2] when ecstatic revels not very different from those engaged in by the Maenads of Dionysus in Thrace and Phrygia, were held in joyous abandon for the bounty received, and to secure a fresh outpour‑ing of vital energy in the crops and in mankind in the forth‑coming season. Since not infrequently nuptial rites were performed in booths of greenery at the Annual Festival in agricultural communities it would not be surprising if behind the post‑exilic 'booths' lay the very ancient and widespread custom of resorting to bridal‑chambers at the time of in‑gathering to engage in a *connubium* as an integral element in the riotous erotic viticulture festival. But if it was in this context that the practice arose, it had lost its connexion with its original significance when it was revived after the Exile, and became the distinguishing feature and designation of one of the three major festivals in the Jewish calendar.

It was, in fact, referred to as 'the Feast'[3] being at once a feast of ingathering at the end of the season, and an inauguration of the year that was about to open with its routine of observances, very largely connected with vegetation and the climatic con‑

[1] Lev. xxiii, 39 ff.; Neh. viii, 15.  [2] Judges ix, 27; xxi, 20 f.
[3] 1 Kings viii, 2; Neh. viii, 14; Num. xxix, 12 (lxx).

ditions. Thus, the anxiety for the recurrent rains found expression in the rites in pre-exilic and post-exilic times[1] in which libations played a part. The nocturnal torch dances and the illumination of the women's court of the temple are reminiscent of a light festival at the autumnal equinox, and may have had a similar fertility significance. It is very difficult, however, to determine precisely what took place at the pre-exilic Feast of 'Asith before it was reconstructed after the Exile and brought into relation with the Rosh hashShanah on the first of Tishri and the Day of Atonement on the tenth. It is generally agreed, nevertheless, that it was the principal festival in the Hebrew calendar held at the turn of the year in the autumn when rain was the urgent requirement. Thus, at the Feast of Booths the altar was dedicated when the temple was rebuilt in the days of Joshua, the Zadokite high priest, and the prophet Haggai,[2] in a rain-making context.

## (b) *The Rosh hashShanah* (*New Year Festival*)

In the post-exilic Priestly literature the Festival of Rosh hash-Shanah, the Feast of Trumpets, assigned to the first day of the seventh month, was associated with the Jewish New Year Festival, which has led Mowinckel to regard it as the beginning of the year, and to connect it with the annual commemoration of the coronation of Yahweh when his victory over the forces of primeval chaos, and his dominion over the kings and nations on earth were celebrated. This triumph was re-enacted in a solemn procession to the temple in Jerusalem where he was acclaimed as the universal sovereign Lord of the universe.[3] To secure his blessing on the forthcoming year the covenant (*berith*, i.e. cultus) with the House of David was renewed, a right relationship between the nation and its god being the indispensable condition for prosperity.

[1] Ezra x, 9; Zech. xiv, 16f.; Jer. viii, 20; *Sukkah*, iv, 9; v, 4; *Bereshith Rabba*, lxx, 8.     [2] Ezra iii, 3, 4; Haggai ii, 2, cf. i, 10f.

[3] *op. cit.*, pp. 102ff.; Volz, *Das Neujahr Jahves*, 1927, p. 13; Hans Schmidt, *Die Thronfahrt Jahves am Fest der Jahreswende*, Tübingen, 1927; Engnell, *Studies in Divine Kingship in the Ancient Near East*, 1943, pp. 176f.; Johnson, *Sacral Kingship in Ancient Israel*, 1955, pp. 53ff.

It is true that in the Hebrew monarchy the king was never the dynamic centre of the social structure like the Pharaoh in Egypt, and most of the available evidence based on the 'enthronement Psalms' (Ps. xciii, xcv–xcix) and the book of Zechariah come from post-exilic sources. Moreover, these Psalms do not occur in the Rosh hashShanah liturgy or in the synagogue commemoration, where they were used in late post-exilic worship as Sabbath Psalms. Nevertheless, some of the Psalms listed by Mowinckel may go back to the time of the monarchy (e.g. xlvii, xciii, xcv–c) emphasızing as they do the enthronement of Yahweh over the physical universe, and the manifestation of his sovereign rule in the bestowal of the seasonal rains and of the prosperity of the nation. But if, in fact, originally they did belong to the New Year liturgy, which is by no means improbable, they had lost their earlier significance before the destruction of the temple in A.D. 70, when the New Year Festival had become associated with the kingdom of God.

There is good reason to think, however, that Psalm lxxxi (which is parallel to Psalm xcv) was composed for the Feast of Ingathering at the full moon in the month of Tishri,[1] whatever may be said about the rest of the collection. The poem in the form of a folk song opens on a festal note eminently suited to a harvest feast in praise of the god of the field and the vine, in whose honour it was sung in recognition of the bountiful crops and abundant yield produced by his divine power. So on the Day of Trumpet-blowing initiating the Feast of Tabernacles when the new moon was appearing, the chief musician uttered a call to sing aloud to Yahweh, and to make a joyful noise with timbrel and harp and psaltery, and to blow upon the trumpet on the solemn feast day. The merry-making was in response to a divine decree, and so became a liturgical ordinance in which the debauchery so prominent in these seasonal revelries was restrained, and the pilgrims called to remember the bitter experiences of their forefathers in the land of Egypt at the time of their bondage, lest they should be led astray by all the debasing associations of the vintage festival.

[1] Snaith, *op. cit.*, pp. 99 ff.; Johnson, *op. cit.*, p. 61, n. 2.

There can be little doubt that this Psalm is composed of a number of fragments of folk songs put together for use at the autumnal festival, and under Yahwist influence it was brought into relation with the story of the Exodus and the sovereign power of the god of Israel. As in Psalm xcv the worship of Yahweh as the great King and Creator, Lord over all the gods, was stressed, and the strength of his power magnified, bringing forth wheat and honey in abundance. It is not surprising, therefore, that it was connected with the Feast of Tabernacles and the Rosh hashShanah[1] in which it may have been used as an 'Enthronement Psalm', as Mowinckel suggests.[2]

While there is no reason to suppose that in Israel the king ever assumed the role of a divine being in the calendrical observances, the equation of the Davidic monarchy with the Canaanite royal priesthood of Melchizedek suggests that the ancient kingship theme was deeply laid in pre-exilic Israel, and in its conception of the nature and function of the Davidic dynasty.[3] When Jerusalem, as a Jebusite fortress, was captured, its priesthood and at least some of the elements of its cultus could hardly fail to have been transmitted to Yahwistic worship, however much they may have been modified and re-interpreted. Indeed, eventually the Davidic covenant (i.e. the cultus) was transformed into the Messianic reign of the adopted son of Yahweh as 'a priest for ever after the order of Mel-chizedek' enthroned on Mount Zion as Yahweh's viceregent 'having neither beginning nor end of life'.[4] Furthermore, as Mr Snaith says, 'it is clear that the well-being of the nation was regarded as being intimately bound up with the well-being of the king',[5] and this found cultic expression in the seasonal festivals.[6] Hence the survival of some of the earlier harvest

---

[1] *Tamid*, vii, 4; Talmud, *Rosh ha-Shanah*, 30b.

[2] *op. cit.*, pp. 152ff.     [3] Johnson, *op. cit.*, pp. 32, 46.

[4] Ps. cx, 4; Gen. xiv, 18ff.; Heb. vii, 13; Ezek. xvi, 3.

[5] Snaith, *op. cit.*, p. 218.

[6] Widengren, *Sakrales Koenigtum im Alten Testament und im Judentum*, Stuttgart, 1955, pp. 44ff.

observances at the end of the time of ingathering originally set against a lunar, solar, and fertility background.[1]

## (c) *The Day of Atonement*

Although the dominant note was that of joy and triumph there was an underlying minor key of sorrow and weeping, as in the Tammuz liturgies,[2] of which the 'lamentation psalms' may be regarded as the Hebrew equivalent.[3] Thus, the annual expiation known as the Day of Atonement in the post-exilic community, with its primitive expulsion ritual, was very closely associated with the Feast of Tabernacles, being held from the evening of the 9th of Tishri to that of the 10th, between the Rosh hashShanah on the first day of the seventh month and the Feast of Booths on the 15th to 22nd.[4] Late as was its introduction in the post-exilic calendrical sequence, its ceremonial and underlying purpose must go back to a very remote period when evil was regarded as a substantive pollution or miasma, removable by cathartic agents (e.g. blood, censing, and lustration) and transferable to an animal as a sin-carrier. Indeed, in the book of Leviticus it is represented as having originated in the desert as a part of the Mosaic tradition when the rites were divinely ordained. In fact, it seems most likely that they were an integral part of the agricultural autumnal festival, 'Asith, connected with the full moon,[5] which combined both rejoicing and lamentation at the turn of the year. It was appropriate therefore, that at the harvest moon in addition to hilarious merriment and festivities which annually accompanied the vintage rites, a period should be set apart for 'afflicting the soul' and expelling evil influences, so dangerously rampant at this season with dire effects on the well-being of the

[1] Ezek. viii, 16; Ps. xxiv, 7 ff.; lxxxvi, 1; Thackeray, *The Septuagint and Jewish Worship*, 1921, pp. 547 ff.

[2] Ezek. viii, 14–16; Hvidberg, *Graad og latter i det Gamle Testamente*, Copenhagen, 1938, pp. 85 f., 115 f.; *The Expositor*, ix, 3, 1925, p. 422.

[3] Neh. viii–ix. Cf. Widengren, *op. cit.*, pp. 63 ff.

[4] Morgenstern, *Hebrew Union College Annual*, i, Cincinnati, 1924, pp. 13 ff.

[5] Cf. Lev. xvi, 20; xxiii, 27, 34–6, 39–44; Num. xxix, 7, 12, 38; *Rosh ha-Shanah*, i.

community and its crops, flocks and herds. Then too, was the time for the celebration of the triumph of Yahweh over the forces of death and destruction, and for the cleansing of the sanctuary, the priesthood and the whole congregation of Israel from the defilements contracted during the year that was coming to an end.

In the book of Ezekiel the sanctuary is said to have been cleansed twice a year—on the first day of the first month and on the first day of the seventh month[1]—but no mention is made of the Day of Atonement as described in the Levitical narrative.[2] Therefore, the post-exilic observance would seem to have been an addition to the autumnal festival after the return from Babylon when the Jewish calendrical sequence was established, the symbolism of which was borrowed from earlier sources. At first it appears to have been a relatively simple expiation instituted in the fourth century B.C., consisting of the sacrificing of a bullock as a sin-offering for the priesthood and a ram for a burnt-offering. Two he-goats were 'set before Yahweh' and lots cast over them for the purpose of assigning one to Yahweh as a sin-offering, and the other to the demon Azazel as the sin-receiver. Yahweh's victim was then slain and Azazel's goat was dispatched alive to 'a solitary land' laden with the uncleanness of Israel and its sanctuary (Lev. xvi, 3, 5–10).

This rite was elaborated when detailed regulations were drawn up concerning the manipulation of the sacrificial blood, censings and the transference of the iniquities of the people to the 'scapegoat' by the laying on of the hands of the priest upon it, and confessing all their sins over it. The carcasses of the bullock and the goat slain as a sin-offering were to be destroyed by fire 'outside the camp' (i.e. the city), and the man responsible for this was required to undergo a thorough ablution of himself and his clothes to remove the contagion he had contracted before he returned to the community (verses 11–28). Finally, a note was added ordering the Day of Atonement to be observed as a 'high sabbath' on which the people

[1] Ezek. xlv, 13, 20.   [2] Lev. xvi; xvii, 10.

were to 'afflict their souls' and 'do no manner of work' (verses 29–34a).

This very primitive ceremonial was interpreted in terms of ethical and spiritual concepts in the Rabbinical literature, the piacular being represented as demonstrating repentance. Because the violation of the law and commandments of Yahweh was an affront to his holiness, genuine penitence and amendment in addition to ritual expiation were required. Furthermore, when the temple was destroyed in A.D. 70 and sacrificial worship inevitably came to an end, the provisions made, before this catastrophe occurred, for special confessions of sin and prayers for forgiveness in the synagogue liturgy for those prevented from attending the Atonement rites in the temple, alone remained to perpetuate the observance. This placed the emphasis on the deeper significance of the cathartic expulsion ritual and its later interpretations. And it is in this form that 'the sabbath of great sanctity' has been observed ever since in Judaism on the tenth day of the seventh month.

## THE WINTER FESTIVALS

### (a) *The Hanukka Dedication Festival*

Among the minor festivals of later origin in the Jewish calendar was that kept for eight days from the 25th day of the ninth month, Kislev, to commemorate the re-dedication of the temple and of the altar of burnt-offering after their defilement by Antiochus Epiphanes in 168 B.C.[1] Though the designation Hanukka of the Dedication Festival is very obscure, the practice of lighting candles in the Temple and in houses during the weeks of the feast is suggestive of the Feast of Lights at the winter solstice, which had behind it a long history with its roots deeply laid in solar myth and ritual,[2] and, as will be considered in a later chapter,[3] recurrent in the Christian observance of Candlemas at the end of the Christmas Festival. It also contained traces of elements in the Dionysian and

---

[1] 1 Macc. iv, 36ff., 52ff.          [2] Josephus, *Ant.*, xii, vii.
[3] Chap. vii.

Apolline cults,[1] and in the Saturnalia,[2] of which it was a Judaized version arising out of the victorious Maccabaean revolt in 161 B.C., brought into the canonical sequence of festivals by its connexion with the Feast of Tabernacles, with Judas Maccabaeus as the principal figure.[3] The book of Judith may have ended with this festival.[4]

## (b) *The Feast of Purim*

Similarly, on the 13th of Adar, the twelfth and last month of the year, known as Nicanor's Day, the victory of Judas Maccabaeus over the Syrian general Nicanor of Adasa was celebrated in very close association with the Feast of Purim on the 14th and 15th of this month (Adar). This latter observance ostensibly commemorated, as it was alleged, the vengeance taken by the Jews on their Persian enemies in the days of King Ahasuerus (i.e. Artaxerxes I) in 473 B.C. after Haman had been hanged on the gallows he had erected for Mordecai, as recorded in the book of Esther.[5] The Esther story, however, represents the cult-legend of the Festival (i.e. Purim) devoid of any historical significance. Thus, there are no grounds for supposing that an incident of this kind ever occurred in the reign of Xerxes, when the Jews in Persia were an exceedingly small community of little or no importance. Moreover, no reference is made to Esther or Mordecai by Ben Sira in his hymn in praise of the Jewish fathers in Ecclesiasticus (xliv–xlix) compiled about 180 B.C. Indeed, the first mention of Mordecai is in 2 Maccabees xv, 36, written about 50 B.C., when the Feast of Purim is described as Mordecai's Day and said to commemorate the victory of Nicanor.

If the book of Esther assumed its present form during the Maccabaean revolt, as is suggested by the internal evidence, the festival with which it was associated (i.e. Purim) probably was adopted as a secular feast by the Jews at that time and interpreted

---

[1] Rankin, *The Origins of the Festival of Hanukkah*, Edinburgh, 1930, pp. 109ff., 140, 142.    [2] Chap. vi, pp. 175ff.    [3] 2 Macc. x, 6–8.

[4] Judith xvi, 20. Cf. Van Goudoever, *Biblical Calendars*, Leiden, 1959, p. 91.    [5] Esther ix, 15–32.

in terms of the Mordecai story.[1] Since the episode is given a Persian setting doubtless it was from this source that Purim was derived. Clearly the designation is a Hebraized form of the word *Pur*, said to mean 'lot'.[2] Attempts have been made to connect the term with the Babylonian *Puhru* meaning 'feast' or 'assembly', and only very conjecturally can it be made to refer to 'lot', as Zimmern has suggested.[3] A better case can be made for the equation of Mordecai and Esther with Marduk and Ishtar, and Haman with the Elamite god Humba, his wife Zeresh with the goddess Kirisha, and the queen Vashti with the Elamite goddess of that name (Mashti),[4] though not without some reservations.

While to equate the legend with the Babylonian Marduk and Ishtar myth in terms of the conflict between light and darkness at the mid-winter solstice, or even of the liberation of Babylonia from Elamite domination in 2300 B.C., is highly conjectural, and awaits confirmation by more convincing evidence than has so far been produced, it is by no means improbable that behind the Esther story lies a Mesopotamian Saturnalian cultus and its legend in which Marduk and Ishtar were the principal figures. This at least is in accord with the general character of Purim as a winter festival of merry-making closely connected with the Hanukka and the Day of Nicanor. Against this is the fact that in Babylonia rites of this nature were held in conjunction with the Spring Festival whereas Purim was a winter observance. To overcome this discrepancy Jastrow has suggested that the Babylonian myth was transformed in the book of Esther in such a manner as to make it the basis of a festal legend to justify the adoption of a foreign festival into the Jewish calendar.[5] The association with the Maccabaean victory assisted the assimulation, and by holding it in the middle of the month of Adar it

[1] L. B. Paton, *A Critical and Exegetical Commentary on the Book of Esther*, 1908, pp. 64ff.  [2] Esther iii, 7; ix, 24, 26.

[3] *Zeitschrift für die alttestamentliche Wissenschaft*, xi, 1891, pp. 158f.; cf. Gunkel, *Schöpfung und Chaos in Urzeit und Endzeit*, 1895, p. 310; Paton, *op. cit.*, pp. 84ff.

[4] Gunkel, *op. cit.*, p. 313; P. Jensen, *Wiener Zeitschrift für Kunde des Morgenlandes*, vi, 1892, pp. 47ff., 209ff.  [5] *E.R.E.*, x, pp. 505b, 506a.

became a precursor of the triumph of the Young God over the hostile destructive forces of winter, and of the rainy season, accompanied by Saturnalian customs reminiscent of the Babylonian festival of Sacaea.

This was apparent in the feasting and revelry which were the conspicuous feature of the Jewish winter festivals. Thus, the two days of Purim were designated as days of feasting and gladness, and of sending portions one to another and making gifts to the poor.[1] It was, in fact, the only festival that did not have a more sombre aspect corresponding to the Paschal massacre or the Day of Atonement expulsion ritual. On the 14th and 15th of Adar the popular rejoicing took the form of excessive drinking, men masquerading as women contrary to the Deuteronomic Law, and boisterous behaviour in the synagogue at the mention of the name of Haman and through-out the night, which was spent in unrestrained ribaldry in Saturnalian fashion.[2] All this was reminiscent of the practices employed on such occasions to drive away evil influences by noises, and to seek protection from them by adopting disguises and reversing the normal procedure, as in the changing fortunes of Haman and Mordecai, and Vashti and Esther in the Biblical legend, representing perhaps the deep-seated rivalries between their Mesopotamian counterparts, if these comparisons can be sustained.

[1] Esther ix, 22.
[2] I. Abrahams, *Jewish Life in the Middle Ages*, 1896, pp. 261 ff.; Talmud, Bab. M'gillah, 76, 18a.

# CHAPTER V

# The Festivals in Asia Minor and Greece

## ANATOLIA

In Anatolia a number of tablets in the royal archives of Hattusas, the ancient Hittite capital near the Turkish village of Boghazköy, contain very fragmentary accounts of ceremonies called festivals, having a variety of names but very similar rituals. Those that can be deciphered are mostly connected with the seasonal sequence, and its agricultural processes (i.e. sowing and harvest); the king, often accompanied by the queen, played the leading role; together or separately, they poured out libations to the temple and its contents, and drank to the god. When he celebrated in person particular care had to be taken to fulfil in every detail the prescribed ceremonial, and for this purpose minute instructions were issued for all concerned, as is recorded on the tablets that have survived.

### Hittite Festival Ritual

First the king himself had to perform a series of Toilet ceremonies, not unlike those of the Pharaoh in Egypt, before setting forth in a solemn procession to the temple where the seasonal rites were held. Leaving the palace with the queen, the king was preceded by a member of his bodyguard, and two palace servants; the rest of the servants, the bodyguards and the lords, walked behind. In front and behind musical instruments were played by the 'statue-worshippers', and a ritual dance was performed by them. On reaching the temple the king and queen knelt before the sacred golden spear and sat down on their thrones. They then ceremonially washed their hands and the king commanded the 'Ishtar instruments' to be brought forth. When they had been placed in position the cooks entered with dishes of meat and water. These were uncovered by the king and presumably a sacred meal followed though no mention of it is made in the texts. All that is said is that at a given sign from the king the ground was swept by a sweeper, the presumption being that at this point in the ritual there had been a sacramental meal accompanied in all probability with a sacrificial offering at which the king acted as the chief priest.[1]

## The Purulli Festival

The principal Anatolian festival was that known as *Purulliyas*, probably a Hattian term meaning 'of the earth', celebrated in the spring when the cult-legend, the myth of the dragon Illuyankas was enacted. According to this story, so far as it can be ascertained from the fragments that have survived on the badly broken tablets, an encounter ensued between the Weather-god of Hatti and a dragon Illuyankas in which the hero (i.e. the Weather-god) was defeated by his formidable adversary. He then appealed to the gods for help. In response the goddess Inaras prepared a great banquet with wine in abundance to which she invited the Dragon and his children together with a man called Hupasiyas who was to be her ally. When they had eaten and emptied every barrel of wine Illu-yankas and his brood were incapable of returning through the hole in the ground to the underworld. Thereupon Hupasiyas trussed them with a rope and the Weather-god slew them. As a reward Inaras built her ally (Hupasiyas) a house on a cliff in the land of Tarukka, but gave him strict injunctions not to look out of the window lest he should see his wife and children. But after twenty days he disobeyed these instructions, pushed open the window and saw them. What happened on the return of Inaras is not explained as the tablet becomes frag-mentary at this crucial point. A quarrel seems to have ensued and apparently the man was killed, and the Weather-god sowed a weed (*sabla*) over the ruins of the house.[2]

[1] Sturtevant, *A Hittite Text on the Duties of Priests and Temple Servants*, Phila-delphia, 1934.

[2] Goetze, *A.N.E.T.*, pp. 125f.

In a second version of the story the Weather-god was completely incapacitated by the Dragon who took away his heart
and eyes when he vanquished him in the fight in which they
engaged. To recover them the Weather-god married a mortal
woman and had a son by her, who eventually married the
daughter of Illuyankas. His father instructed him to demand
the stolen heart and eyes as a bride price when he entered his
bride's house. This he did and restored them to his father who
recovered his former strength and this time defeated the Dragon
in battle. The son thereupon asked his father to kill him with
Illuyankas because he thought he had betrayed the Dragon's
hospitality.[1]

These two cult-legends bear a striking resemblance to the
Babylonian Creation Epic, to the Egyptian Osiris, Isis, Horus
myth, and to the Greek story of Zeus losing his sinews in his
struggle with Typhon and recovering them through the agency
of Hermes and Hegipan with the help of Typhon's daughter,
and then killing the Dragon.[2] That they were recited at the
*Purulli* Festival is definitely affirmed, though it is said that the
first version was no longer recited on this occasion when the
winter rains had ceased and the summer drought was immanent.[3] Dr Gaster, in fact, regards the myth of the festival as
the libretto of an ancient Hittite ritual drama in five parts, of
about 1350 B.C., written by a priest named Killas at Nerik, an
important centre of the cult of the Weather-god in the eastern
part of the Hittite country.[4] As in the *Enuma elish*, or the
Mumming play of the folk traditions, the leading theme was
a sacred combat between the forces of good and evil personified,
resulting in the victory of the Weather-god responsible for the
control of the rainfall over the Dragon of drought or flood.
The basic structure, as he says, connects the festival and its
legend with the folk customs that have long been associated
with Rogationtide, the Ascension and St Georges's Day in
Europe, originally devised to protect the crops from damage by

[1] Goetze, *op. cit.*, p. 126; *K.U.B.*, xvii, 5, 6.
[2] W. Porzig, in *Kleinasiatische Forschungen*, i, 1930, pp. 379ff.
[3] Goetze, *Kleinasien*, p. 131f.          [4] Gaster, *Thespis*, pp. 317ff.

storm and drought.[1] Typical of folklore also are the motifs of the stupidity and gluttony of the Dragon, who invariably has been represented as falling a victim to the sort of trickery indicated in the case of Illuyankas. The concludin gfragment may be a ritual epilogue describing the procession of the gods and goddesses and the installation of the Weather-god in the temple at Nerik, as in the Babylonian Akitu rites.

Whether or not the myth was the libretto of a cult-drama, as has been very plausibly suggested, unquestionably it was the legend of the festival, as the text affirms. The king was the celebrant, and the royal ritual recorded on the tablets follows the usual procedure. So important, in fact, was this annual event that Mursilis II (*c.* 1339–1306), having already per-formed his royal ritual functions in honour of the Weather-god of Hatti and the Weather-god of Zippalanda earlier in the year, felt compelled to interrupt a military campaign in order to return to Hattusas to officiate at 'the Great Festival of *Purulli*'.[2] Indeed, it is not improbable that its purpose may have been to renew the life of the king and queen and all that this involved for the prosperity and well-being of the community of which they were such a vital and integral part. We know from other sources that rites were celebrated by and for the king for these ends at the vernal equinox, when in all probability the year began in the Hittite as in the Babylonian calendar.[3]

## The Telipinu Myth and the Spring Festival

Moreover, in the closely related Telipinu myth the episode turns on the renewal of the life of the king. Thus, 'the god of agriculture' (Telipinu) as the patron deity of Mursilis II,[4] is represented as having left the land in a rage and taken with him 'all good things' including the grain and fecundity. As a result

[1] Cf. Chap. vii, pp. 220 ff.    [2] *Keilschrifttexte aus-Boghazköi*, ii, 5, iii, 38 ff.
[3] Goetze, *Language*, xxvii, 1951, p. 467; Otten, *Orientalistische Literatur-zeitung*, li, 1956, cols. 102–5; *K.U.B.*, xxxvi, 95; H. Ehelolf, in *Kleinasiatische Forschungen*, i, p. 149.
[4] Gurney, *Annals of Archaeology and Anthropology*, xxvii, Liverpool, 1940, p. 45.

vegetation withered, cattle, sheep and mankind no longer conceived, and those with young could not bring forth. Famine prevailed everywhere so that both man and the gods were in danger of perishing from hunger. The Sun-god then arranged a banquet and invited to it 'the thousand gods' great and small. They ate but they did not satisfy their hunger; they drank but they did not quench their thirst. The Weather-god, remembering that his son Telipinu was not in the land, attributed their plight to his withdrawal. Thereupon he ordered his messenger the eagle to make a search for him in 'the high mountains, the shallow valleys and the dark-blue waters'. When this proved unsuccessful he consulted the Grandmother Hannahanna (i.e. the Mother-goddess) who urged the Weather-god to go himself in quest of his son. He too, however, failed, and the Goddess then sent forth the bee who found him in his own town (either at Lihzina or Hattusas), and stung him on his feet and hands. This only increased his fury, and it was not until Kamrusepas, the goddess of healing, exorcized his malice that he returned on the wings of the eagle. Then, after further exorcizing, his anger was allayed and 'the sheep went to the fold, the cattle to the pen, the mother tended her child, the ewe her lamb, the cow her calf', Telipinu re-entered his temple, restored fertility and 'tended the king and queen and provided them with enduring life and vigour'. An evergreen was set up before him, and a fleece, and on it the skin of a sheep was hung to secure abundance, long life and progeny.[1]

This myth in its several recensions, corresponds to that of Tammuz and his counterparts (e.g. of Adonis, Attis, Baal and Osiris), both as regards the disastrous effect caused by his absence, the diligent search for him, and the reinvigoration of the earth upon his return. It represents, therefore, the typical cult-legend of the Spring Festival, though no specific reference is made to a seasonal rite in the texts, and here, unlike the Tammuz story, the god neither died nor descended to the underworld. Nevertheless, the points of contact with the cult-

[1] *K.U.B.*, xvii, 10; Otten, *K.U.B.*, xxxiii, 1-12; Goetze, *A.N.E.T.*, pp. 126ff.; Gaster, *op. cit.*, pp. 316ff.

drama are so apparent in respect of the theme, the magical ceremonies and exorcisms, their form and purpose, the gods and goddesses in the episode, and the setting of the myth and ritual directed to the renewal of the king and queen on the throne, that it has every appearance of having been originally a seasonal performance, probably at the Spring Festival. The story and its dramatic action centre in the blight caused by the vanished god, and the various attempts made to bring him back in order that fertility might be restored. The devices employed to this end included the use of cathartic agents, exorcisms, and regenerative ceremonies, including the erection of an evergreen pole adorned with a fleece, and perhaps sacrificial offerings, though the text is defective at this point, leading up to the climax of the rite in the bestowal of abun/dance, prosperity and new life and strength for the occupants of the throne. Thus the king and queen, the Weather/god and the Mother/goddess, and their retinues, assume their customary roles in the cult/drama, and in the background there would seem to be the perennial cosmic struggle among the gods.

*The Hurrian Kumarbi Theogony and the Song of Ullikummi*

This is apparent in the Hurrian cycle of myths recording the way in which Kumarbi, 'the father of the gods', acquired the leadership in heaven. In the beginning the king of heaven, Alalu, reigned for nine years, and then Anu conspired against him causing him to flee to the underworld. For the next nine years Anu held sway in heaven until in his turn he was attacked by Kumarbi who bit off his generative organ and consumed it, so becoming pregnant with three great gods—the Storm/god (?), the River/god Aranzakh (the Tigris), and Tasmisu, a servant of the Weather/god. Kumarbi spat out of his mouth the seed of these gods and impregnated the Earth/goddess who gave birth to them in due course, as Gaia in the Hesiodic theogony produced Heaven, and Kronos emasculated his father at her injunction. The rest of the Kumarbi tablet is unintelligible, but it seems from the fragments that, like the Greek counterpart, the goddess gave birth to the Storm/ and

Weather-god, Teshub, who fought enemies and finally be-came king in the place of Kumarbi.[1]

The account of the conspiracy of Kumarbi and his son Teshub is equally mutilated, but from the few short passages available of what is known as 'The Song of Ullikummi' it appears that Kumarbi begot a monster of diorite stone, Ulli-kummi, to fight Teshub and the other gods. He was taken down to earth and placed on the shoulders of Upelluri, an Atlas-like figure, where he grew with such tremendous rapidity that in a fortnight the water came only up to his knees when he stood on the bottom of the sea. This phenomenal growth was viewed by the Sun-god with alarm, and he sought the advice and aid of the Storm-god, Teshub, who with his sister Ishtar went to the top of Mount Hazzi, probably Mount Casius on the Syrian coast, the Sapan in the Ugaritic texts, to inspect the situation. Having decided to attack the monster, battle was joined but the gods proved to be powerless against Ullikummi. Teshub was compelled to abdicate, and, following the advice of his minister Tasmisa, he appealed to Ea for help. The gods were then summoned to Apsu to consider what could be done to meet the crisis, but without success. Ea then consulted Enlil, and went to Upelluri on whose shoulder Ullikummi had grown unperceived by the old man (i.e. Upelluri). Thereupon Ea sent for a copper knife and severed the diorite stone at its feet. Having thereby rendered Ullikummi powerless, the gods may be regarded as completing their victory over him and establishing the rule of Teshub, though the final section of the text is unintelligible.[2]

These ritual myths give indications of having been the cultic enactment of a sacred combat in the seasonal drama at the Spring Festival. The story of Illuyankas we know was recited as the cult-legend at the *Purulli* Festival, probably at the New

---

[1] Goetze, *A.N.E.T.*, pp. 120f.; *American Journal of Archaeology*, lii, 1948, pp. 123 ff.; *K.U.B.*, xxxiii, p. 120; Güterbock, *Kumarbi Efsanesi*, Ankara, 1945, pp. 11–16; Otten, *Mythen vom Gotte Kumarbi*, Berlin, 1950, pp. 5 ff.

[2] Goetze, *A.N.E.T.*, pp. 121f.; *J.A.O.S.* 69, 1949, pp. 178 ff.; Güterbock, *The Song of Ullikummi*, New Haven, 1952.

Year, and in the closely related combat stories connected with the names of Telipinu and Kumarbi, and their Babylonian and Hellenic counterparts, the same seasonal theme recurs as a ritual representation of the perennial struggle between the two opposed forces in nature and the cosmic processes. As Güterbock has shown, the Hurrian god Kumarbi corresponds to the Greek Kronos, Anu to Ouranus, and Teshub to Zeus. In spite of certain distinguishing features in the two traditions, such as the two generations of gods in the Anatolian version centred in Alalu who stands behind Anu, the similarities are too apparent to be merely accidental. In the cult-legends in both theogonies 'the father of the gods' having begotten a son became afraid that he would dethrone him and so a struggle ensued between them, the older god being defeated by his emasculation by his younger successor.

## The Anatolian and Hesiodic Theogonies

Similarly, in the Song of Ullikummi another battle between gods occurs resembling in some measure that between Zeus and the Titans; both Teshub and Zeus were led to seek the help of the god of the nether regions against their adversaries. In fact, primeval gods and monsters descended from Ouranus engaged in a spate of concealing and swallowing their offspring lest they should dethrone their respective fathers. Zeus alone remained through a ruse of his mother Rhea, and on growing to maturity set free those who had been imprisoned in the subterranean Tartarus. Equipped with thunderbolts forged for him by the Cyclopes, and armed with lightning, he set forth on his campaign against the older brothers of Kronos, the Titans, like Anu against Alalu. The conflict was pursued for years, and not until he had secured the aid of Hekatoncheiros in Tartarus, who hurled stones at the Titans, was he able to subdue them.[1]

It may be that behind this Greek version of the story lies the struggle between the pantheons of the invading Indo-Europeans headed by Zeus and the Olympian gods, and those of the

[1] Hesiod, *Theogony*, 501 ff.

indigenous population with its Goddess tradition, and their subsequent merging in a composite culture. Nevertheless, the theme assumed the form of the Anatolian and Mesopotamian theogonies and was enacted in the cult-drama in the dualistic sacred combat. It was this which provided the basis for Hesiod's *Theogony*, both Zeus and Teshub being powerless to overcome their adversaries until they gained assistance from the subterranean regions.

In its Greek form, however, the Ullikummi episode is more clearly reproduced in Apollodorus' version of the struggle of Zeus with Typhoeus (Typhon), the son of Gaia and Tartarus, with a hundred snakes' heads.[1] This half-human half-animal untameable dragon bellowed like a bull but spoke the language of the gods, and although he was not made of stone, as in the case of Ullikummi, he was so tall that he reached to the sky. After conquering the Titans and becoming king of the universe Zeus made a violent assault upon Typhoeus with his thunderbolts and lightning, and cast him into Tartarus. In another version, however, Typhoeus is said to have wrested from Zeus his sacred *harpé* on Mount Kasion on the Syrian coast, and cut the sinews of his hands and feet. Having rendered Zeus helpless he carried him across the sea to Cilicia and deposited him in the Corycian cave under the surveillance of a monster, Delphyna. Hermes and Hegipan (or Cadmus) then restored the sinews to Zeus and conveyed him to the sky in a winged chariot. Pelting his adversary with thunderbolts, Zeus pursued him to Mount Nysa, and beguiled him into eating human food to reduce his strength. The struggle continued until finally Typhoeus was chased to Sicily and buried under Mount Etna.[2]

The contacts with the Hittite Illuyankas myth and the Ullikummi story are unmistakable, and the end of the Anatolian dragon in the western Mediterranean suggests the course of the diffusion of the myth from Asia Minor to Sicily.

[1] Hesiod, *Theogony*, 820 ff.; Roscher, 'Typhoeus' in *Lexikon der griech. und röm. Mythologie*, i.

[2] Apollodorus, *Bibliotheca*, i, 6, 3.

In its passage through the Aegean, perhaps by Hurrian, Mycenaean and Phoenician traders,[1] it was adapted to local traditions and circumstances, enacted in all probability in a recurrent cult-drama in which the sacred combat was such a prominent feature throughout the region of its distribution. The fundamental theme remained the same in spite of the many variations in the characters and their exploits, because the perennial conflict was a constant occurrence, finding ritual expression in the seasonal rites everywhere.

## GREECE

### The Rural Rites and Festivals

Thus, in Greece the principal events in the agricultural year—those of sowing, ploughing and reaping—were the occasions of special rites to control the processes of vegetation at these important and often critical junctures in the seasonal sequence. Nearly all the early Greek festivals, in fact, were agrarian, Greece being essentially a country of peasants and herdsmen overlaid by a higher culture and subject to external influences, notably from Western Asia, Crete and Egypt. An urban civilization became established in certain centres at an early period as towns were industrialized. Nevertheless, the greater part of Greece was and remained agricultural, subsisting on the none too fertile soil, depending on the grain it produced, together with figs, olives and a not very abundant vintage.

Under these conditions rain was an urgent need, and it is no small wonder that when the Indo-Europeans brought with them their Sky- and Weather-god Zeus, and installed him on the misty heights of Mount Olympus in Thessaly, it was to the lofty 'cloud-gatherer' and rain-giver that they looked for sustenance. In the late autumn and winter rain was as regular an occurrence as were sunshine and drought in the summer. But although this course of events was a constant feature, the precise moment in the year when the drought would break or the rains would cease was not to be determined with such accuracy

[1] Güterbock, *A.J.A.*, lii, 52, 1948, p. 133; R. D. Barnett, *J.H.S.*, lxv, 1945, p. 101.

that specific days could be set apart in spring and autumn for the performance of the appropriate seasonal rites. Zeus had singularly few festivals in his capacity as the Weather-god, though not infrequently he was approached when drought, storm or flood caused alarm.[1]

So far as everyday life in rural Greece was concerned it was the lesser gods and spirits, and the activities of the farm and the fields in the spring and autumn with which they were especially connected, that constituted the festal occasions of the year. Rustic rites and communal feasts known as *panegyreis* were held at village sanctuaries dedicated to a particular god appropriate to the occasion. These included simple offerings of food, drink and incense, though they might involve costly sacrifices of cattle on a grand scale, when all the members of the community assembled for a communal feast on the victims, in which the gods and their worshippers shared. This was one of the relatively few occasions on which meat was eaten by the peasants. Thus, a festival was in very truth a feast, as indeed it often still is in the more rustic and remote parts of Greece, feasting being combined with music, dancing, games and merry-making, especially after the ingathering of harvest when, as Aristotle says, there was more leisure to engage in these festivities.[2]

## The Calendar

It was from this seasonal routine of agricultural rites that the Greek calendar emerged and eventually, when the urban civilization gained control over the social and religious organization a calendar of festivals was promulgated under the protection of Apollo at Delphi so that the rites of the gods might be celebrated at the correct time. But as originally the sequence was based on the principal events in the agricultural routine and the rites that were connected with them, the official lunar calendar was drawn up with the year divided into twelve months of twenty-nine or thirty days, making a total of 354 days. On this calculation it was eleven and a quarter days

---

[1] Cf. Herodotus, vii, 197; Theophrastus in Porphyrius, *De abstenentia*, ii, 27.
[2] *Ethica Nicomachea*, viii, p. 1160a.

short, thereby requiring adjustment by the introduction of an intercalating system in which the years were arranged in groups of eight containing three leap years of thirty days. Then three intercalary days were added in two groups of eight years (*oktaeteris*) to bring the calendar into relation with the seasons and the solar year, making up the total number of days more or less accurately.

In the meantime, however, there might be a considerable discrepancy between the sowing or ingathering in the fields and the calendrical celebration in the towns; the one being determined by rural observations, the other by lunar inter-calationary devices. As the Athenian months bore the names of the festivals with which they were supposed to be associated, this anomaly caused confusion in practice between town and country, the months being reckoned by the moon, and the year by the sun, with the seasonal sequence cutting across both periods of time and their calendrical celebrations.[1]

The Athenian year was supposed to begin with the summer solstice in June, but it never did because its first month had to start with a new moon, perhaps several weeks later. This led to a double system of dating, one in accordance with the civic year, the other with the position of the heavenly bodies. But despite several efforts to reform the system the old calendar was retained officially while the festivals continued to be celebrated in relation to the seasons, being essentially agricultural observances instituted in the ancient peasant culture and never losing their character and functions. Thus in Athens two very archaic rites, the Thesmophoria and the Skirophoria, were held in conjunction with the urban festivals.

*The Thesmophoria*

The Thesmophoria occurred at the autumn sowing of the new crops between the 11th and the 13th of the month Pyanopsion (October) in honour of Demeter and was performed solely by women. In the background would seem to have been the great Corn-goddess and Earth-mother Demeter, and her daughter

[1] Aristophanes, *Clouds*, 610ff.

Kore, the Corn-maiden, embodying the new harvest and controlling the processes of vegetation, causing the grain to germinate and the fruits of the earth to spring forth in due season.
Demeter, in fact, is sometimes referred to in the literature as
Thesmophorus, and her own Mysteries at Eleusis were held
originally at the time of the autumn sowing in the last half of
the month of Boedromion.

In Athens and in other places where it was celebrated, the
Thesmophoria opened with women erecting bowers with
couches made of plants, like the Babylonian *gigunu*, and sitting
on the ground to promote the fertility of the corn that had just
been sown and to secure their own fecundity. The next day
was observed as a fast, and on the third day, that known as the
Day of Fair Increase, pigs sacred to Demeter were thrown into
subterranean chasms (μέγαρα), probably to represent the
descent of Kore into the nether regions. Thus, in the scholiast on
the dialogue of Lucian,[1] where the festival is discussed in some
detail, it is connected with the abduction of the Corn-maiden
while she was gathering flowers in the meadows on the Rarian
plain near Eleusis, and was carried away by Pluto to his subterranean domain. To commemorate this event, in which the
swineherd Eubouleus was said to have been swallowed up,
according to the scholiast pigs were let down into the clefts,
together with dough-cakes and branches of pine trees, by
women who had undergone purification for the purpose. They
then descended into the underground chambers and brought
up the putrified remains of those that had been cast into the
*megata* the previous year, and left there to rot and to be
devoured by snakes which guarded the caverns. The rotten
flesh was placed on altars and mixed with seed-corn which was
sown in the fields as a magical manure to produce a good crop.[2]

Since it was at this season that ploughing began in Attica

---

[1] *Dial. Meretr.*, ii, 1.

[2] J. E. Harrison, *Prolegomena to the Study of Greek Religion*, 3rd ed., C.U.P.,
1903, pp. 120ff.; Nilsson, *Griechische Feste von religiöser Bedeutung*, 1906, pp.
106ff.; Deübner, *Attische Feste*, Berlin, 1932, pp. 179ff.; *G.B.*, pt. viii,
pp. 17ff.; *C.G.S.*, iii, pp. 75ff.

it was an appropriate time to fertilize the ground in this manner, a practice which survived long after its original purpose had been abandoned and forgotten. Behind it, as Nilsson has suggested, lay in all probability a still more ancient festival which celebrated the bringing up of the corn from the sub-terranean silos in which it had been stored after it had been threshed in June, until the fields were ready to be sown in October.[1] During the four months when the grain was con-cealed in the silos the fields in Attica were barren, parched by the scorching sun, and it was not until the winter rains began in October that they could be ploughed and sown. Then in the mild climate they sprouted immediately for a few weeks in January. When the fields were becoming green again after the summer drought, it was the time for the celebration of the release of the Corn-maiden Kore from the realms of Plouton, originally the god of the wealth of the fertile earth who later became confused with Pluto, the ruler of the underworld.

Now it would seem to have been around these events in the agricultural year that the Thesmophorian and the Eleusinian agrarian rituals and their myths arose to promote the fertility of the corn sown in the earth. The opening of the silos was equated with the swallowing up of the swine of the herdsman Eubouleus in the Thesmophoria, and the abduction of Kore by Pluto, who in the so-called *Homeric Hymn* is said to have suddenly appeared in his chariot from his subterranean abode through a cleft in the ground while the Corn-maiden was picking flowers in the meadows. Therefore, originally the two autumnal sowing rites were in all probability very closely related to each other, both being connected with the same annual seasonal event. Hence the reason why Demeter was called Thesmophoros, and she and her daughter were the two Thesmophori.

## The Skirophoria

In the last month of the year a closely allied festival, the Skiro-phoria, from which the month Skirophorion took its name, was held at the time of threshing. In this summer observance

[1] *Greek Popular Religion*, Columbia Press, 1940, pp. 51 ff.

very young girls of noble birth called Arrephoroi, whose chastity by reason of their tender years was indubitable and who had lived a year on the Acropolis at Athens, were clad in white robes and given at night sacred objects called *skira*, consisting of sucking-pigs and cakes made in the shape of serpents, probably having a phallic significance. These they carried by a natural descent in 'the Gardens of the sanctuary of Aphrodite' leading presumably to her temple. Having deposited the fertility charms there they returned through the same passage with others, wrapped up to be concealed from public gaze. In addition to performing this rite the Arrephoroi are said to have baked cakes called *anastiato*, probably in the form of *phalloi*, and to have begun the weaving of the sacred garment, the *peplos*, which was periodically presented to Athena, in whose honour the Arrephoria (taking its name from them) was performed at the Skirophoria.[1]

Although the accounts of the event are obscure, the festival seems to have been a form of the Thesmophoria held just before the harvest to renew the soil. This is suggested by the solemn carrying of fertility charms by specially selected girls whose virginity was not in question to a subterranean destination connected with the goddesses Aphrodite and Athena. In origin undoubtedly it goes back to the agricultural ritual when rites of this nature were held, generally by women, who always were mainly responsible for the performance of fertility rites, to prepare the ground for the autumnal sowing, not infrequently by the introduction of phallic images and symbols to impregnate mother-earth and so to make the soil bring forth its new crops in abundance.

## The Thalysia and the Thargelia

Of the same character and equally primitive was the Thalysia, the festival of the harvest, when according to Homer and Theocritus sacrifices were offered on the threshing-floor at the altar of Demeter in recognition of her bounty.[2] It appears

[1] Frazer, *Pausanias's Description of Greece*, i, 1913, pp. 344 ff.
[2] *Iliad*, ix, 534; *Idyll*, vii, 31.

to have been a domestic observance—a kind of 'harvest home'—rather than a state festival like the autumn sowing rites. Therefore, its original rustic nature survived little changed. It remained a domestic affair held at no fixed date when the threshing was concluded, and the first loaf was baked from the new corn—the *thalysion arton* with which Demeter was associated as 'the Goddess of the great loaves'. In Attica, where a loaf of this nature was called *thargelos*, a similar rite known as the Thargelia was celebrated in the last month but one of the year (May), which was therefore called Thargelion.

The Thargelia, however, was associated with Apollo rather than Demeter and assumed a different character. The central figure was the *pharmakos* who was a criminal, or selected for his ugliness, and treated as a scapegoat. He was led through the streets and alternatively fed and flogged with green branches, and finally either expelled or killed. In Athens, where two *pharmakoi* were selected, the supreme penalty was not required.[1] Originally it appears to have been an expiation rite to expel the evil that had accumulated during the year, and to allay the supernatural dangers consequent upon the slaying of the corn-spirit at the forthcoming harvest. Thus, the *pharmakos* exercised the functions of a sin-carrier and a sacrificial victim in a vegetation rite. The cleansing of the city was followed by the cooking and presentation to Apollo of the *thargelia*—the first-fruits of the new crops—in the hope that thereby a good harvest would be secured. The purpose of the festival, therefore, was to protect and to promote the successful ingathering of the crops.

## The Anthesteria

Rather earlier in the month Anthesterion when the crops were ripening, the vines were being pruned and the spring flowers were appearing, the Anthesteria, or Festival of Flowers, was held in honour of Dionysus as the god of spring, in which,

[1] *Tzetzes Historum variarum Chiliades*, xxiii, pp. 726 ff.; Deübner, *op. cit.*, pp. 179 ff.; Harrison, *op. cit.*, pp. 77 ff.

again, rejoicing and gloom were combined. The ceremonies opened on the 11th of the month which bears its name, corresponding approximately to our February, when the second fermentation of the wine came to an end and it was ready for drinking. Then the jars in which it had been kept were opened amid general rejoicing and rustic merrymaking. Heavy drinking followed, lads jumping on the wineskins and girls being swung in swings to promote fertility.

On the next day, the Day of the Cups (Choes), the wine from the jars was taken from Athens to the sanctuary of Dionysus in the marshes, where in silence it was distributed in small jugs among all the citizens over the age of four. The Archon, or magistrate who bore the title of king, presided over a drinking contest, and his wife was married to Dionysus. For this purpose she was taken to the official residence of her husband, called the Bukoleion or Oxstall, attended by women who had taken vows of chastity in the service of Dionysus. There she made certain unspecified sacrificial offerings. Thither the image of Dionysus, possibly in bovine form, or an actor wearing horns and a hide, was brought on a boatlike structure on wheels to complete the nuptial rites in the consummation of the marriage of the wife of the Archon and the god. How this was accomplished is not revealed. The king himself may have visited the Oxstall in person, and played the part of Dionysus. But whatever was done and by whom, the ritual no doubt had the same purpose and function as elsewhere in the vegetation drama, though in this case it was very closely associated with another and different aspect of the Anthesteria.

Thus, on the evening of the second day and during the third and last day, that known as the Pots (Chytrori), a sort of cereal porridge was prepared and placed in pots as an offering to Hermes, who among his many offices was the guide of the souls of the dead escorting them to the underworld. It was, in fact, to the dead that the libations were poured out on this day, and while the Dionysian nuptial rites were being performed in the Bukoleion ghosts were thought to be hovering about in the streets of the city. To keep them at bay whitethorn was chewed, pitch was smeared on the doorposts of the houses, and many public and private activities were suspended. At the end of the proceedings at midnight on the third day, as in the Lemuria in Ancient Rome, the ghosts were summarily dismissed with the formula, 'Be gone ghosts [*keres*], the Anthesteria is over.'[1]

Originally it may have been a placation and renewal of ancestral spirits summoned from the grave on the first day of the Festival, the jars being burial urns, or *pithoi*, which were frequently sunk in the ground and regarded as graves from which the dead could be released when the lids were removed. Then they fluttered forth and returned in due course when their visits to earth were over.[2] At the Anthesteria Pithoigia the jars were opened to enable the ghosts to leave their tombs and to be feasted by their relatives. While they were about every precaution had to be taken to prevent their causing harm to the living, and when they had been duly fêted and appeased at the end of the third day, after they had partaken of the *pan-spermia*, or 'pot-of-all-seeds', specially prepared for them, they were summarily dispatched from the houses and sent back whence they came. The streets and houses in Athens were then cleansed from the taint of death, and all its attendant perils, and life in the city resumed its normal course.

It may be that this annual 'Feast of All Souls' in the spring was held to renew as well as to placate the ancestors, since it was incorporated in the Dionysian rites in which the sacred marriage of the wife of the Archon with Dionysus in the Ox-stall occupied such a prominent and significant place and function. This was combined with viticulture revels and contests, and with fear of pollution and attack from the ghosts. Thus, as in so many spring festivals, there was a joyous and sinister side to proceedings represented by the Dionysian and the funerary aspects; the one Bacchic and hilarious, the other chthonian,

[1] Harrison, *op. cit.*, pp. 32 ff.; *C.G.S.*, v, pp. 214 ff.
[2] Harrison, *op. cit.*, pp. 43 ff.; *Themis*, C.U.P., 1912, p. 276; Gilbert Murray, *Five Stages in Greek Religion*, O.U.P., 1912, p. 31.

sombre and protective. But the *keres* also were venerated and given a sacred meal, the *panspermia*, cooked exclusively for them, not even the priest being allowed to partake of the con⁄tents of the holy pots,[1] this being in the nature of an offering to them of the first⁄fruits, like the first loaf baked after the thresh⁄ing at the Thargelia. It may have been thought to have been carried by them to Hermes in the underworld, and Miss Harrison suggests that they brought it back in the autumn as a *pankarpia*—a pot of all kinds of fruits for the nourishment of the living on earth.[2] If this were so, the Anthesteria had within it an element of renewal as in most primitive agrarian festivals in the seasonal cycle.

## The Lenaia and the Greater Dionysia

Two other important Athenian feasts were connected with Dionysus, the Lenaia in the month of Gamelion (January), and the Greater Dionysia in Elaphebolion (March). The Lenaia was preceded by a Rural Dionysia in Poseidon (December) in which *phalloi* were carried in procession amid general merry⁄making and joking to promote the fertility of the autumn⁄sown seed, and of the soil in general during the winter recess. A sacred basket containing sacrificial implements was borne on the head of a *kanephoros* to the place where the offering was to be made, later reduced to pouring a libation over a flat loaf before the image of Dionysus. But the rite must have been performed in Attica long before it came under Dionysian influences, or had any connexions with the viti⁄culture, the vintage being well over and the new wine not ready when it was celebrated in December.

When in historical times it was held in honour of Dionysus as the god of wine and of the fertility of the fields, it consisted of the phallic procession, described by Aristophanes in the *Acharnians* (ii, 241–79), in which it was headed by the daughter of Dikaiopolis as *kanephoros* carrying a flat loaf as an offering on which she poured porridge with a ladle. Behind her were two slaves holding a pole surmounted by the emblem of a phallus,  .

[1] Aristophanes, scholiast on *Frogs*, p. 218.        [2] *Themis*, p. 292.

while Dikaiopolis representing the chorus and revellers singing a song to Phales, the personified symbol of fertility, the com-panion of Dionysus in his nocturnal revels. From this account of the scene in the *Acharnians* it seems that the Rural Dionysia consisted of a procession bearing a phallus, a sacrificial offering and a Phallic Song to Phales. While it was hardly from these *komoi*, or phallic songs, in particular that comedy was derived,[1] it would seem that in these mimetic vegetation rites, rural revels, phallic and goat songs connected with Dionysus, the origins of comedy and tragedy should be sought. In them, in addition to the procession, the sacrifice and the *komos*, were contests between groups of revellers, dances and a sacred marriage; in short all the essential elements of the ritual drama and its subsequent developments from the dithyramb to the last degeneration in the Mumming plays of relatively recent times.

It was from this Rural Dionysia that the Lenaia emerged on the 12th, 13th and 14th of the following month, Gamelion (January) as the winter festival to arouse the slumbering vegetation. The ceremonies described in the *Acharnians* were, in fact, the rustic versions of the Lenaia, very much as rural revels, Mumming plays and Rogationtide processions survive today chiefly in the country rather than in the towns. But as the English centre of folk dancing is at Cecil Sharp House in Regent's Park in London, so Attic comedy and tragedy, the ritual of the Lenaia and the Greater Dionysia became urban observances in spite of their rustic origins in agrarian folk dramas. The Lenaia was the winter domestic festival confined to the Athenians themselves, and may have included an ecstatic nocturnal element in which female Maenads exercised their Dionysian functions, as is depicted on the vases. Plays of some kind were performed during the course of the rites, but as Sir Arthur Pickard-Cambridge has shown,[2] they included an

---

[1] Deübner, *op. cit.*, p. 136; A. Pickard-Cambridge, *The Dramatic Festivals of Athens*, O.U.P., 1953 , pp. 42 f.; Cornford, *The Origins of Attic Comedy*, 1914, pp. 20, 38 ff.

[2] Pickard-Cambridge, *Dithyramb, Tragedy and Comedy*, O.U.P., 1927, pp. 268 ff.

elaborate passion play representing the rebirth of Dionysus, and regarded as the origin of tragedy, along the lines of A. B. Cook's theory.[1] On this hypothesis it was supposed that the dithyramb performed at the Greater Dionysia in March represented the begetting of the god, and the Lenaia his birth ten lunar months later. But while the festival included a procession conducted by the Archon Basileus (i.e. the annual magistrate) there are no indications of phallic symbolism in connexion with it, or revels like the *komos* as in the Rural Dionysia. Comedy appears to have been preferred to tragedy originally, though a possible reference to contests of tragedies at a Lenaian festival occurs in a late inscription outside Athens.[2] In the city the Lenaia may normally have been held in the sanctuary to the west of the Acropolis called the Lenaion, though the scholiast on Aristophanes places it outside Athens. But little is known with any degree of certainty about either its location or in what the rites consisted that were performed at the festival. Contests among poets in comedy and tragedy occurred from about the middle of the fifth century B.C., but what lies behind this rise to fame of the Lenaia in dramatic art is very obscure. Among the gods Demeter, Kore and Pluto were brought into conjunction with Bacchus, but the festival remained essentially Dionysian.

The Greater Dionysia in full spring, which lasted from the ninth to the thirteenth of Elaphebolion (March), was the last of the festivals of Dionysus to be instituted in Athens, and became the principal occasion for staging new tragedies, probably under the influence of Peisistratus in the sixth century B.C. About 534 B.C. a prize for tragedy was won by Thespis of Ikaria in Attica, who centred his theme on the episodes in the adventures of the god, played by one actor, and a chorus of mortals or divine beings in human form. Contests of dithyramb danced by fifty singers gradually came to be performed at the festival, and to tragedies and comedies satyric plays were added early in the next century. By the end of the fourth century

[1] *Zeus*, i, Cambridge, 1914, pp. 665 ff.
[2] *C.I.G.*, 2483.

contests for dithyramb at the Greater Dionysia appear from the inscriptions to have been in process of decline, though choruses of this nature continued to be held elsewhere in Greece, surviving in some cases until the beginning of the Christian era.

But although Greek drama began largely as an act of worship of Dionysus, the actual plays that developed out of the Dionysian contests soon had little or nothing to do with or say about the god. This is apparent in the tragedies of Aeschylus, Sophocles and Euripides performed at Athens at this festival. Yet in the background was a spring dithyrambic ritual with its flower-crowned and ivy-clad dancers and choruses, having a long history behind it of the rustic revels, of the *komos*, and of the more sombre and serious tragic cultus out of which tragedy appears to have sprung, eventually forming an integral part of the festivals of Dionysus. But tragedy was not an act of worship of a particular god like the seasonal drama, or the dithyramb. Its concern was with religious and other problems of universal appeal and significance, as Aristotle recognized, but neither its theme nor its chorus was specifically Dionysian. Nevertheless, the performances were confined to the Dionysian festivals and the actors continued to call themselves the craftsmen of Dionysus, the plays being secularized in content but retaining their ritual setting.

In Greece the Thraco-Phrygian orgiastic and ecstatic Dionysian rites, so prominent in the vintage festivals, were sobered in spite of the wild revels on Mount Parnassus, and became occasions of the presentation of the finest literary achievements of the poets and dramatists of the fifth century B.C. and onwards. This was to some extent due to their gaining a place in the Olympian tradition, and in the Orphic movement under the restraining influence of Delphi. Thus, when the festivals of Dionysus were included in the calendar of Athens they had undergone a very considerable change, the esoteric nocturnal orgies having become dramatic performances played in public in the city in broad daylight; though a good deal of the earlier frenzy, or its symbolism, survived in the Anthesterion rites in the marshes, in the Lenaia and in the

Attic rural feasts in a modified and more restrained form. On the heights of Mount Parnassus an officially recognized band of Delphic Maenads and of Athenian Thyiades celebrated ecstatic dances at night by torchlight (i.e. the *oreibasia*), at midwinter in alternate years,[1] involving no small risk and great discomfort at a height of 8,000 feet at that time of year. Only a very strong impulse to become *en rapport* with Dionysus could have induced them to set forth on such a journey to the barren mountain-tops under the worse possible climatic conditions. Mere commemoration of ancient orgies, as the later writers suggest,[2] is not sufficient to explain the phenomenon. A deeper primeval urge, so widespread in Shamanistic cultus and mass hysteria, is required. It was this that found expression in the Thraco-Phrygian Dionysian winter dance culminating in the *omophagia*, when a bull or calf was torn to pieces and the flesh consumed by the demented dancers,[3] in order to become *Bacchoi*, or god-possessed. So profound had been the experience, at once fascinating and repulsive, holy and horrible, that it lived on and found a vent in the biennial festival in which the traditional elements survived, if in due course they became more restrained. The rites, however, were only sporadic, and were condoned as foreign to Hellas, permitted but not encouraged.

Greek tragedy or comedy began, therefore, as a religious service held at the festivals of Dionysus, in the country in December, in the city in March, and at the Lenaia in January. At first when the city Dionysia was a State observance the plays with their dithyrambs performed during it continued to be rendered to one of the gods, beginning with a sacrifice to Dionysus. But as it lost its seasonal character, by the third century B.C., the drama became secularized, very much as the medieval Mystery and Miracle plays were dissociated from the Church and lost their sacred significance and character when in the secularized versions they were enacted in the market-

[1] Pausanias, x, 4, 2; 32, 5.

[2] Firmicus Maternus, *De errore prof. rel.*, vi, 5; Diodorus Siculus, iv, 3.

[3] Cf. Dodds, *Euripides Bacchae*, O.U.P., 1944, p. xv; *Harvard Theological Review*, xxxiii, 1940, pp. 155 ff.

place by strolling players. Though many elements were combined in Greek drama, the Thraco-Phrygian Dionysus was
the principal figure in the complex pattern, the Eleutherae
being held on his birthday, and at Delphi he was as much
at home as was Apollo. There in the religious capital of Hellas,
his resurrection and the birth of the new-born child Iakchos
after his winter sleep were celebrated. Beside the statue of
Apollo stood his coffin, for before Greek tragedy went its own
way, Dionysus was the god of sorrow and death as well as of
joy and life, of tragedy and of comedy, and only in the satyr-
drama did he continue to figure in his original role. And in
origin the satyr-drama and tragedy were separated from Attic
comedy with its phallic Bacchic dancers and revellers.

## The Eleusinian Festivals

The most important and influential agricultural or quasi-agri-
cultural festivals however, were those held annually in Attica in
honour of Demeter and Kore; the Lesser and Greater Eleusinian Mysteries. Thus, in the spring in the month of Anthesterion
(January–February) the first of these two observances, about
which unfortunately very little is known, was held at a
suburb of Athens, Agrae on the Ilissus. In the absence of any
traces of a sanctuary or temple, and from the general character
of the rites at Eleusis, it is not improbable that the Lesser
Mysteries were held in the open air for the benefit of the newly
sown seed-corn, before they became the first stage in the initiation of the *mystae*. At the approach of the summer drought,
personified in the descent of Kore to the subterranean realms of
Pluto, and while the grain was still stored away in the silos
beneath the ground it would be appropriate to perform rites to
facilitate both the renewal of the sprouting new crops and the
return of Kore and her reunion with Demeter, with the subsequent inferences respecting a blissful immortality for those
who partook therein.[1]

It was, however, in the autumn from the thirteenth to the

[1] *C.G.S.*, iii, p. 169; Nilsson, *Geschichte der griechischen Religion*, Munich, 1941, pp. 427 ff.

twenty-second of the month of Boedromion, at the time of the sowing in September and October, that the Great Eleusinian festival occurred, beginning with a procession to fetch certain sacred objects from the sanctuary of Demeter at Eleusis, including in all probability the statues of the two goddesses (Demeter and Kore), to bring them to the capital where the *mystae* were assembled. Having undergone preliminary purifications, and instructions from a mystagogue, on the sixteenth they were addressed and scrutinized by the Archon-king, the hierophant and the torch-bearers to make sure that they had duly fulfilled their ritual preparations, could speak Greek, and had not been deprived of civil rights for murder or similar crimes, these being the conditions required for initiation into the Mysteries.[1] This accomplished they were led to the sea at Phaleron to bathe and wash their pigs, and on the seventeenth a sucking-pig was sacrificed to the goddesses. How the rest of the time was spent until the formation of the procession to Eleusis on the night of the nineteenth is by no means clear. It seems that there were small processions in honour of gods like Asklepios, as in Crete where processions of sacral kings on portable thrones followed by their worshippers made their way along the *via sacra* to the enclosed paved 'theatrical area' in the Minoan palace sanctuaries, as depicted on the frescoes.[2] It would seem, in fact, that it is to Crete that we have to look for the beginnings of the Eleusinian ritual, and there at Knossos, Phaestos, and Gournia, the sanctuaries were designed for small gatherings of carefully selected persons who stood or sat on stone steps in a rectangular hall resembling the *telesterion*, or hall of initiation at Eleusis, to behold a sacred drama or dances enacted on the 'orchestra' in which probably the Minoan Mother-goddess played the principal role.

Of what happened in the Eleusinian *telesterion*, however, little is known for certain. On the nineteenth, late in the evening, the *mystae* were led in procession along the Sacred Way from Athens to Eleusis calling at certain shrines, and at the bridge

---

[1] Aristophanes, *Frogs*, 354 ff.
[2] Evans, *Palace of Minos*, ii, 1928, pp. 578 ff.

over the river Kephissos, where ceremonial obscene cursing and jesting occurred. The chief object of veneration was the statue of Iakchos-Dionysus which, with repeated shouts of 'Iache!', was carried amid the other sacred objects that had been previously taken to Athens on the thirteenth, and were now returned to their home in Eleusis. On arrival the *mystae* bathed in the sea, then roamed about the shore with lighted torches, enacting the search of Demeter for her abducted daughter. In the evening they assembled in the *telesterion* and in darkness and complete silence, sitting on stools covered with sheepskins, they beheld sacred sights which might never be revealed. Apart from a few scattered allusions to the cult by later, mainly Christian, writers such as Hippolytus and Clement of Alexandria, of very doubtful veracity, what was displayed or enacted during this final spectacle, which constituted the climax of the initiation, can be only conjectured.

The iconography throws little light on what was done, but it seems likely that the cult-legend recorded in the so-called *Homeric Hymn* assigned to the seventh century B.C., in which the Mystery was centred, was enacted in a sacred drama portraying the rape of Kore in the rich Rarian meadows, and the wanderings of the sorrowful mother in search of her, carrying a lighted torch. Eventually, disguising herself as an old woman who, she said, had escaped from pirates who had brought her from Crete to Greece, Demeter reached Eleusis. There sitting on a seat covered with a ram's skin by a wayside well she encountered the daughters of the ruler, Keleos, to whom she told her fictitious story and she was taken by them to their home. There she became nurse to their infant brother Domophoon, and endeavoured secretly to make him immortal by anointing him day by day with ambrosia, the food of the gods, and at night putting him in the fire to consume his mortal nature. Disturbed in these fiery operations by his mother, who screamed in terror at the agonizing sight, Demeter revealed her identity, and abandoned her intention of making Domophoon into an immortal. Before leaving the royal household, however, she commanded the people of Eleusis to build her a sanctuary on the hill above 'the fountain of maidenhood', where she first met the daughters of Keleos. There the rites she would teach her votaries were to be performed for the purpose of bestowing upon them a blissful immortality.[1] The drought and famine caused by her grief at the abduction of Kore nevertheless continued for another year, until in despair Zeus intervened and secured the return of Kore, but not before Pluto had con-trived to make her eat some pomegranate seeds which bound her to him for a third of the year. Then as long as Kore was above ground with her, Demeter allowed the fructifying rain to fall on the parched ground and life to spring forth again. But on the return of Kore to the nether regions sterility once more prevailed in the arid months of summer, pending her ascent in October when the crops began to germinate in Attica.

In this complex legend a number of myths and traditions have been incorporated, but behind it was the agrarian festival centred in the goddess of vegetation and fertility, who at Eleusis was primarily concerned with the growth of the corn, and who became the giver of immortality to her initiates, individually and collectively. In all probability she was at once the goddess of vegetation in general and the Corn-mother in particular, in spite of the emphasis given to her latter function by Nilsson.[2] In the Eleusinian *telesterion* no doubt the several outstanding episodes in the cult-story were enacted, prominence being given probably to the abduction of Kore, the grief of Demeter, the birth of a holy child called Brimos (i.e. Iakchos), the reaping of an ear of corn in profound silence and in a blaze of light, culminating perhaps in a sacred marriage of the hierophant and the chief priestess in the roles of Zeus and Demeter, or of Plouton and Persephone.[3]

Although Hippolytus seems to have confused the Phrygian Attis rites with those of Demeter in his account of the initiation

[1] T. W. Allen, E. E. Sykes, T. W. Halliday, *The Homeric Hymn*, 3rd ed., O.U.P., 1936, pp. 10ff.

[2] *Popular Greek Religion*, pp. 52ff.

[3] Hippolytus, *Refutatio omnium haeresium*, v, 8.

ceremonies,[1] a corn-token symbolism and a sacred marriage were in keeping with the idea of rebirth alike in nature and in man.[2] These two motifs were fundamental in the Eleusinian Mysteries throughout their long and chequered history, from their beginnings in the agrarian rites which almost certainly go back to the Minoan-Mycenaean substratum of the cult and its manifestations in Crete, whence Demeter said she had come in her story about the pirates. The *telesterion*, in fact, was erected over a Mycenaean *megaron*,[3] and Hesiod attributed the birth of Plouton, the god of wealth, to Demeter and Iasion in Crete.[4]

So deeply laid was this purpose and significance in the rites that a Neoplatonic writer, Proclus, in the fifth century A.D., in a passage emended by Lobeck, records that the hierophant was said to have uttered a sacred formula as he gazed up to the sky, 'Rain (O Sky) conceive (O Earth), be fruitful.'[5] This, as Farnell says, 'savours of a very primitive liturgy that closely resembles the famous Dodenaean invocation to Zeus and Mother-earth; and it belongs to that part of the Eleusinian ritual "*quod ad frumentum attinet*"'. Late though it be, it has every indication of being 'the genuine ore of an old religious stratum sparkling all the more for being found in a waste deposit of Neoplatonic metaphysic'.[6]

Therefore, it is highly probable that the seasonal cult-drama was enacted at Eleusis from very ancient times, vested probably as a hereditary possession in the ancient priestly family of the Eumolpidae with its mythical ancestry, who like the *kerykes* (heralds) as the successors of the Archon-king, had their definite functions in the rites long before it was transformed into a death and resurrection esoteric mystery to bestow eternal life on its initiates. As a family cult it involved an element of secrecy, being a carefully and jealously preserved agrarian ritual for specific purposes and particular occasions, which included

---

[1] Cf. *C.G.S.*, iii, pp. 177, 183.

[2] Cicero, *De legibus*, ii, 63; Plutarch, *De facie in orbe lunae*, 943b.

[3] Nilsson, *Geschichte der Griechischen Religion*, pp. 316ff.

[4] *Theogony*, 970.

[5] Proclus, *Ad Plato, Timaeus*, Lobeck, p. 293.     [6] *C.G.S.*, iii, p. 185.

a preliminary fast and the drinking of a sacred gruel known as *kykeon* before the regenerative renewal rites proper began at the appropriate seasons in the agricultural year; in the case of the Lesser Mysteries at Agrae in the spring, and of the Greater Mysteries at Eleusis at the time of the autumn sowing. As the rites acquired a more personal and individual application as a means of securing a blessed eternity, they lost their earlier rustic and agrarian character, and became more essentially an esoteric cult-drama hedged round with taboos and inviolable secrets concerning the things seen and perhaps done at the supreme moment of initiation. But they continued to be held at their traditional dates in the calendar, preserving thereby their original place in the spring and autumn seasonal ritual observances.

## The Panathenaia

Among other important events in the Attic year was the Panathenaia held in the height of summer, from the twenty-first to the twenty-eighth of Hekatombaion (July–August), the traditional birthday of Athena. In the sixth century B.C., when Athens rose to pre-eminence after driving back the Persian invaders, Peisistratus remodelled the old Athenaia under the name of the Panathenaia as an annual celebration of the union of Athens in the worship of its patroness Athena, especially splendid every fourth year. At this Great Panathenaia the Homeric poems were recited to set forth the pageantry of the Olympian gods, and contests were engaged in on several days with prizes of jars of oil for the winners. On the first three days there were musical competitions, then came athletic and gymnastic exercises which included boxing and wrestling matches, horse and chariot races, concluding with a torchlight procession, sacrifices and games on the seventh day (i.e. the 28th of Hekatombaion).

On the Panathenaia vases of the sixth to the fourth centuries B.C. these contests are depicted, and on the frieze on the Parthenon in Athens (originally in coloured relief with bronze reins and bridles on the horses), probably designed by Pheidias about 440 B.C., the procession to the Acropolis at the Great Panathenaia is portrayed. This may now be seen in the skilfully rearranged representation of the scene in the Elgin Galleries in the British Museum. On the West Frieze the preparations are shown for the procession, which starts from the south-west corner of the Parthenon in two groups, going in either direction to end in the east. The horsemen and their attendants are shown preparing themselves and their horses, fastening their boots and the harness, and mounting their steeds. Their speed increases as they move northwards along the side of the temple in tumult, and the group gets denser when they are joined by other horsemen, almost riding abreast. On the next slab chariots appear with their charioteers and armed men leaping with great agility on and off them while they are in rapid motion. The troops are directed by marshals, and though at this point the frieze was badly damaged by an explosion in 1687 during the Turkish war, it seems that in front of them came the elders, or *thallophori*, bearing olive branches preceded by musicians playing lyres and flutes, and boys carrying water-pots for libations, while three bear trays of offerings. Before them are the animals for sacrifice with their attendants, led by a heifer.

On the East Freize, where the convergence of the two streams is reconstructed, girls carrying jugs, incense-burners and libation bowls lead the way, two in the centre holding stools or cushions on their heads which are taken down by the priestess of Athena, perhaps to be used as seats for the gods on either side. At the head of each section of the procession are maidens empty-handed, who may represent those of good birth who had been carefully selected to embroider the robe, or *peplos*, woven every four years to drape the statue of Athena, and conveyed by them to the temple in the procession on the mast of a ship set on wheels. This vessel is not shown on the frieze, but the handing up of the *peplos* to the priest by a small boy is depicted in the centre directly above the main eastern doorway of the Parthenon. The priestess of Athena prepares one of the two stools, apparently for the attendant gods who are seated in two groups and include Artemis, Apollo, Poseidon with his trident, Hephaestus, and Eros holding a parasol over his mother Aphrodite. Athena near the *peplos* is in pacific guise without her helmet and holding her breastplate bearing the Gorgon's head, and opposite her is her father Zeus with his consort Hera in front of him. To her left is a young girl with wings, probably Nike or Iris, as the messenger of the gods. The heavily draped goddess in front of Ares holding her torch is Demeter, and opposite her is Dionysus leaning on the shoulder of Hermes, the herald of the gods, often associated with him.[1] The clothing of the Goddess on her birthday in the presence of the twelve Olympian gods was the climax of the festival held in her honour at the opening of the Attic year, and with great magnificence, amid general rejoicing, athletic contests and games every fourth year; similarly at the biennial Eleusinia (not to be confused with the Eleusinian Mysteries) when in the next month, Metageitnion, games were held on a grand scale on the fourth year, with a procession and prizes of grain from the Rarian cornland. Again, at Olympia in Elis, the principal sanctuary of Zeus, the sacred games were celebrated in his honour quadrennially from the eighth century B.C. in connexion with the Olympic Festival founded according to tradition either by Heracles or Pelops. At first they were confined to a single day and consisted of wrestling and racing, chariot-racing having been a feature in the funeral games in the north-west Peloponnese from early times. Whether the games began as funeral rites of this nature, or a ritual contest for the throne,[2] either to gratify a deceased hero or to enable a divine king to defend his title to the throne by engaging in a conflict with his rival claimant, by the fifth century B.C. they had become an established Hellenic institution.

[1] A. S. Murray, *The Sculptures of the Parthenon*, 1903; B. Ashmole, *Short Guide to the Sculptures of the Parthenon*, new ed., 1950; A. Mommsen, *Feste der Stadt Athen*, 1898; Deübner, *op. cit.*, pp. 22 ff.; E. N. Gardiner, *Greek Athletic Sports and Festivals*, 1910, pp. 229 ff.; *J.H.S.*, xxxii, 1912, pp. 179 ff.

[2] Gardiner, *B.S.A.*, xxii, 1916–17, pp. 85 ff.; *Olympia*, O.U.P., 1925, pp. 63 ff.; Cornford, *Origin of Greek Tragedy*, pp. 36, 38; Harrison, *Themis*, pp. 212 ff.; Ridgeway, *J.H.S.*, xxxi, 1911, pp. xlvi f.; *G.B.*, pt. iv, pp. 92 ff.

## The Olympic Festival and the Panegyreis

Everywhere athletic sports and exercises accompanied by sacrifices tended to find a place in the greater festivals known as *panegyreis* in honour of Zeus, Apollo or Poseidon, respectively at Nemea, Delphi, Corinth and Olympia, the greatest of them all being the Olympian games attracting streams of visitors and participants. Some came to compete in or watch the games, others either to sell or to purchase at the booths of the traders, while the great temples bear witness to the many cults that found a spiritual centre there. It was, in short, a sort of combination of Wembley, Widecombe and Walsingham, frequented by all men who spoke Greek. So important was this great assembly, in fact, as a unifying force in the very diverse and loosely federated citystates that a truce was proclaimed at the time of the festival to enable all who wished to to visit Olympia and take part in the sacred games, ceremonies and circuses. And the response was widespread as it included delegates and contestants from all the Greek colonies scattered over the Aegean and the eastern Mediterranean, as well as from Hellas proper.

Nevertheless, the *panegyreis* were primarily religious gatherings in their foundation and purpose, centred in the cult of the Olympian gods, even though their chief attraction often may have been the fact that they were also fairs and athletic contests. It is only, however, under modern postReformation conditions, in which the sacred and the secular are kept in watertight compartments, that a rigid distinction has been made between religious and profane institutions and observances. In medieval Europe and in the less sophisticated regions of Catholic Christendom today, the two were and still are blended in a happy and natural combination of holy days and holidays, of ecclesiastical festivals and social feasts and revels. So deeply laid and natural was this union that in Britain at the Restoration in 1660, when south of the border the dead hand of Puritanism was removed, there was a speedy and spontaneous return to the tradition of Merrie England.

Indeed, in Greece many of the *panegyreis* are still celebrated,

as are their counterparts elsewhere in southern Europe, little
changed in character and content, apart from the substitution
of a local saint for the Olympian god. The same medley of
religion, athletics, trading and revels persists, centred in the
parish church or a miraculous shrine, with contests, competitions and dancing intermingled with pious exercises, rhap-
sodies, topical recitations by skilled raconteurs, and the cries
of the pedlars boasting their wares. Thus, the ancient gatherings at Olympia, Delphi, Nemea and Corinth have lived on
throughout the ages. If in the passage of years they have lost their
more serious intent, they have retained their original place, and
to some extent their function in the sacred seasonal sequence of
calendrical events.

When, however, the festival belonged to the chthonian
rather than to the Olympian tradition its purpose was usually
to drive away, rather than to establish, intimate beneficial relations with the gods whose abode was under the earth or in the
nether regions. In the sacrificial offerings the victims were
differently selected and treated, generally being black instead of
white, and given wholly to the god as a piacular to appease his
anger and restrain his machinations. But here again a hard and
fast line cannot be drawn as the chthonian and Olympian
traditions frequently were in some measure fused or inter-
related, so that the two existed side by side on the same occasion.
Even so, their respective rites tended to retain their more characteristic features. But when the cultus of a powerful Olympian
god was superimposed on that of a lesser chthonian divinity
or hero, often the name of the higher deity was adopted, as in
the case of the heroic Zeus-Agamemnon, but the chthonian
ritual still survived in the cultus.

*The Hyakinthia*

Thus, the Hyakinthia at Amyklai in Lakonia was a joint
celebration in honour of Apollo and Hyakinthos, an ancient
vegetation god who according to the later saga was killed
accidentally by Apollo with a discus while he was playing at
quoits with him. He was then alleged to have been buried in a

tomb under what later became the throne of Apollo at Amyklai, south of Sparta, at a site which has been found to contain Mycenaean remains.[1] On it stood the ancient bronze image of Apollo, and beside the altar-tomb was a low bronze door through which portions of the animals sacrificed during the festival were sent down to Hyakinthos.

The setting suggests that the Hyakinthia was a pre-Hellenic cult in which the ancient god eventually was overshadowed by Apollo and reduced to the status of a youthful hero beloved of the Greek deity (Apollo). His name is pre-Hellenic, having the suffix *nth* which belongs to the language of the indigenous inhabitants of the country, and the cult-statue depicts him as a mature bearded man. The relief on the base of the throne shows his being led to the heavenly realms by a number of fertility divinities (e.g. Demeter, Kore, Pluto, Aphrodite, Artemis and Athena) in which Apollo is con-spicuous by his absence. It was not until Apollo, though a late addition to the pantheon of Hellas and probably Anatolian in origin, became the dominant figure that he usurped the name and festival of Hyakinthos, and had his throne placed above the tomb of the original occupant of the sacred site. Neverthe-less, the memory of the ancient vegetation god was retained since the newcomer was called Apollo Hyakinthos, and the festival continued to be known as the Hyakinthia, celebrated in honour of a vegetation deity.[2]

So important was the annual event that it became one of the chief festivals of Sparta, and was observed throughout the Dorian region. Beginning probably on the seventh day of the month Kekatombaion, corresponding to the latter part of May, it lasted for three days which were devoted to demonstrations of grief for the dead hero-god (Hyakinthos). On the first day there was general mourning; no wreaths were worn or paeans sung at the solemn banquet, nor were bread or cakes eaten. It was no doubt then that offerings were made at the tomb of

[1] Nilsson, *Minoan-Mycenaean Religion*, 1950, pp. 470, 556.
[2] Pausanias, iii, 1, 3; 19, 1-5; Greve, 'Hyakinthos' in Roscher's *Lexikon der griech. und röm. Mythologie*, i, 2762f.; Nonnos, *Dionysos*, xi, 330; xix, 104.

Hyakinthos. The next day there was a sudden change in the procedure. Boys with their tunics tucked up played on the lyre, and sang to the flute with dancers mingling with them, while others in gay apparel paraded on horseback through the theatre, the citizens feasting in Saturnalian fashion with their slaves as well as with their friends. Sorrow, in short, had given place to joy because the god had been restored to life and all was once more well with the course of nature.[1] From the blood of Hyakinthos sprang a purple iris resembling a fritillary, inscribed with the letters of lamentation AI (alas!) on its petals, which blooms in the spring after the violets and before the roses. But this should not be confused with the flower that now bears his name, the hyacinth.

There is a marked similarity to the cultus of Adonis, Attis and Osiris in the mourning for the dead god with abstinence from cereals and taboos against wearing crowns and garlands, until his fortunes were reversed and he was restored to life and conducted to a blissful immortality, with corresponding outbursts of gaiety and hilarity. These festivities included the principal actors in the drama wreathing themselves with ivy at a banquet, like Dionysus and the slain and revived 'Jack-in-the-Green', the garlanded personification of vegetation in the folk festivals of later days.[2] The joyous music and gorgeous pageantry are also suggestive of a spring vegetation festival, as is the name Hyakinthos denoting a flower. All this was in keeping with the celebration of the passing away of winter and the appearance of the first verdure brought into relation with the later Apolline ritual and its story. For Apollo too was connected with agriculture to some extent, in addition to his oracular, pastoral, Orphic, Dionysian, and many other aspects. But before it came under his influence and was absorbed in his cultus the Hyakinthia was the annual seasonal festival of the ancient god of vegetation heralding the advent of spring.

[1] Athenaeus, iv, 17ff., 139ff.; *C.G.S.*, iv, pp. 125, 264ff.; Nilsson, *Griechische Feste von religiöser Bedeutung*, Leipzig, 1906, pp. 139ff.
[2] Cf. Chap. ix.

## CHAPTER VI

# The Roman Festivals

THE position of Rome on the most important river in Central Italy, and in close proximity to the excellent harbourage on the west coast, laid the city open to invasion at a very early period, and made immigration and cultural contact recurrent features throughout its history. It must not be forgotten, however, that behind these incursions lay a developing indigenous civilization, extending back to prehistoric times, of which the classical writers like Livy appear to have been unaware; or at any rate, of which they took no account. Yet it was in this pre-Roman era that so many of the subsequent institutions, beliefs and practices took their origin, and these can be rightly understood only in relation to their foundations in the remote and often obscure past. This is particularly apparent in the case of the Roman, the Graeco-Roman and Graeco-Oriental festivals, and of the calendar in which they occur as seasonal observances.

## THE ROMAN CALENDAR

### The Earliest Festival Calendar

In the public cults almost all the gods were worshipped sporadically, in connexion with particular occasions and events in the annual round of feast and fast with which they had some special association. Indeed, our knowledge of the original character of Roman religion is derived very largely from the *Fasti*, or sacred calendars and priestly lists, written mainly on stone between the middle of the first centuries B.C. and A.D., but containing much earlier material, going back in one case to the outline of the original Republican calendar traditionally assigned to 304 B.C.[1] In this pre-Julian fragment the names of

[1] *C.I.L.*, i, and Commentary on *Fasti divini* by Mommsen, 1893; W. Warde Fowler, *The Roman Festivals*, 1899, pp. 11 ff.; F. Altheim, *A History of Roman Religion*, 1938, pp. 104 ff.

the fixed festivals were recorded and annotated copies were displayed from time to time in public places. From these, numbering some thirty fragments and one all but complete, a general idea can be obtained of the nature of Ancient Roman religion and its cultus before it was subjected to foreign influences on a large scale. To this evidence has to be added the relevant references in the Roman and Greek literature, which throw light upon the fragmentary information supplied by the earliest calendars, and in the inscriptions of the Arval Brethren, a very old priesthood revived by Augustus, whose records were carved on stone in the grove of their goddess, the Dea Dia.

Though their precise date is a matter of dispute, the numerous fragments of a Republican stucco calendar with coloured lettering (*Fasti Antiates*) found in a heap of building debris in Antium, show that pre-Julian calendars early in the first century B.C. were essentially a list of festivals. Since they contain a thirteenth intercalary month (Mercedonius) they belong to the earlier mode of calculation, and yet they conform in their general structure and contents to the later types, so that it is clear that there was a continuity in calendrical tradition in the Roman Republic and in the Empire. Nevertheless, all the calendars that still survive belong to the early Empire and represent the form assumed after the revision by Julius Caesar when the unsuccessful compromise between a solar year of 365 days and a lunar year of twelve months of twenty-nine days was brought to an end. As long as the earlier method prevailed the organization of the year was in the hands of the *pontifices* who were responsible for the administration of the state cults and the ordering of the calendar and its observances. It was they who kept the knowledge of the feast days throughout the year, and on the Kalends, or first day of the month, they had to announce publicly whether the Nones of each month were to fall on the fifth or the seventh day,[1] and the days on which the festivals were to be kept.

[1] Macrobius, *Saturn*, i, 15, 9. In March, May, July and October the Nones fell on the 7th, and in the rest of the months on the 5th. The Ides were on either the 13th or 15th and the Nones were the ninth day before the Ides.

*The Julian Calendar*

The Roman calendar on which our present calendar is ultimately based originally consisted of 304 days, divided into ten months, beginning with March and going on until December. The first four months were known as Martius, Aprilis, Maius and Iunius, the rest being named according to their order (Quintilis, Sextilis were renamed later in compliment to Julius Caesar and Augustus). January and February were omitted, representing the dead season of the year when agricultural work had ceased. About 700 B.C., according to tradition, Numa Pompilius, the second of the alleged line of kings, was said to have appointed a certain Numa Marcius as Pontifex and made him responsible for the due performance of the rites at their appointed times on a lunar basis, adding Ianuarius, the month of the festival of Janus, and Februarius, the month of purification.[1]

Behind this legendary account of the pre-Caesarian situation is doubtless an oral tradition or memory of the origins of the lunar year, introduced perhaps by the Etruscan kings before the days of the Republic. Throughout the Republic the year normally had 355 days, each month containing twenty-nine or thirty days, with an additional month of twenty-seven or twenty-eight days as required after February 23rd to make up the total amount, inserted usually in alternate years. This chronology was manipulated by the *pontifices*, who often adjusted the duration to suit their own political ends in respect of impending elections, thereby throwing the calendar into confusion. To put an end to these disorders and abuses Julius Caesar undertook his reform of the calendar with the assistance of Sosigenes, a Greek astronomer of Alexandria. The lunar month was discarded in favour of a purely solar year of $365\frac{1}{4}$ days, with an extra day added to February every fourth year, as in the present reckoning.

Beginning with January an alternate sequence of thirty-one and thirty days was established, except for February which was assigned twenty-nine days, and thirty days in leap years. To

[1] Livy, i, 5-7.

bring the months into juxtaposition with the natural year, in addition to the intercalation after February 23rd two extra months, the first to consist of thirty-three days and the second of thirty-four days, were inserted between November and December, thereby enabling the Kalends, which always fell upon the first day of the month, to occur on January 1st in the year 45 B.C., and the vernal equinox on March 25th. With the intercalary month of twenty-three days, the total of the last 'year of the confusion', as the year in which the Julian reforms were introduced was called, was brought up to 445 days, and the first year of the new calendar began on January 1st in 46 B.C. From then onwards, with a small adjustment by Augustus in 8 B.C., it remained in vogue until Pope Gregory XIII in 1582 annulled ten days after the Feast of St Francis on October 5th to correct a small margin of error and make the Feast of the Annunciation on March 25th coincide with the vernal equinox. By altering the leap-year rules he prevented its recurrence. This reform was widely adopted in Western Europe but not by the Eastern Orthodox Church,[1] and in England, owing to anti-Papal bias, it was not until 1752 that eleven days were omitted after September 2nd, to the consternation of the masses who failed to understand the reason for the adjustment. With these corrections New Year's Day was restored to January 1st in the Gregorian calendar, which has remained the generally accepted reckoning of time in Western Christendom both for religious and civic purposes.

In Ancient Rome the festivals, seasonal in their origin and character, conformed in their calendrical sequence to the requirements of the agricultural year. The preservation of this conformity in the state cult of the urban civilization, however, introduced an element of unreality into the celebration of the prescribed rites which were based in the first instance upon rural conditions, very much as today a harvest festival makes a different appeal in town and country. Moreover, as in Rome the timing was in the hands of a special priesthood, who mani-

[1] In Eastern Christendom the year is now thirteen days behind that of the West.

pulated it for its own purposes, the ordinary citizen came to regard the observances very largely as a sacerdotal affair in which he had little or no part except in so far as they affected the daily routine. On the other hand, in the old agricultural *religio*, 'the religion of Numa' of the Latin farmers, they were of vital importance in the cult of the farm and of the field, where upon their due performance at the right time depended the means of subsistence and prosperity.

## THE ANCIENT AGRICULTURAL FESTIVALS

The sources of information about the old agricultural festivals are it is true inadequate. The *Fasti* of Ovid, for example, over-lays the accounts of the rural rites from January to June with purely fanciful mythology. Fragments from the forty-one books of Varro's *Antiquitatis rerum humanorum et divinarunt* (47 B.C.), which survive in quotations by St Augustine in *De Civitate Dei* (A.D. 413–426), yield a certain amount concerning rustic festivals and games, while Livy recounts traditions and legends which throw some light on earlier calendrical customs and rituals. But the pre-Julian Roman calendars, or *Fasti*, though fragmentary remain the best guides available, especially as the days and festivals written in large capital letters represent those belonging to the original Republican, as distinct from the later Republican, additions inscribed or written in smaller capitals.[1] From this record, in which a day on which the State business may be transacted (E=a *fastus*) is distinguished from an ill-omened day on which such business is unlawful (NF= *nefastus*), or only permitted in part (NP=*nefastus parte*), forty-five great festivals can be determined between March 14th and the following February 27th, the last day of the year.

### The Processions of the Salii

Thus, prior to the reforms of Julius Caesar, March was always regarded as the first month and was dedicated to Mars, whose name it bore, the oldest form of the designation being Martinsis

[1] G. Wissowa, *Religion und Kultus der Römer*, 2nd ed., Leipzig, 1912, 1, 3, 63, Appendix.

Mavors. As an agricultural god he was worshipped all over Italy from the earliest times, and was invoked to avert storms, tempests, disease, and to promote the prosperity of the crops, the flocks and the herds, and the welfare of the farmer and his household. He was also a war-god, and so became equated with the Greek Ares, and equipped with a warrior-priesthood, known as the Salii, or Leapers, who engaged in repeated dancing processions in March. The Salii occurred in many towns in Italy; in Rome they were restricted to twenty-four in number, and were divided into two groups located respectively on the Palatine and Collini hills, the former belonging to Mars, the latter to Quirinus, an ancient god associated with Mars and Jupiter in the supreme 'triad'. Everywhere, in fact, they were usually connected with the War-god, and were required to be of patrician birth, with both a father and a mother living.

In their processions they were clad in a *tunica picta*, an ancient warrior-dress, and a short military cloak (the *trabea*), a helmet (*apex*) on their heads, a breastplate and sword at the side. On their left arm they carried the *ancilia*, or 'figure of eight' shields, said to have been a gift of Jupiter to Numa, and a staff or spear. Thus arrayed, at the Agonium Martiale on March 17th, the Feast of Mars, or at the Quinquatrus on March 19th, they marched about the city, stopping at intervals to dance and clash their weapons and to sing a song the meaning of which is very difficult to determine. Each evening they rested and feasted at a different place, and hung up their arms until they resumed their processions on the next morning.

While the dancing and leaping of the Salii resemble a war-dance, it has been suggested that they may also have been intended to promote the growth of the corn sown at this time of year, March being the beginning alike of the agricultural and the campaigning season. Furthermore, their exercises were repeated in October when the grain was again sown in the autumn, and Saturn was invoked, a god who had some agricultural connexions, manifest especially in the winter revelry that bore his name (i.e. in the Saturnalia in December).[1]

[1] G.B., pt. ix, pp. 232f.

It is not improbable, therefore, that their functions, like those of the Arval Brethren, were to some extent at any rate associated with the fertility of the soil and the growth of the crops as well as with the military campaigns.

The importance attached to the rites is shown by the period of the activities of the Salii from the Calends of March to March 23rd being observed as *dies religiosi*, on which secular pursuits had to be in abeyance while they discharged their sacred duties. Only when the processions with their preliminary ceremonies, which marked the bringing of the sacred shields from their *sacraria*, had been completed, were the *ancilia* lustrated on March 19th, a ceremony corresponding to the *lustratio* of the cavalry horses at the Festival known as the Equirria on February 27th, and March 19th before the chariot-races on the Field of Mars (Campus Martius) on the north side of the old city. Then on March 23rd the trumpets were purified on the Palatine Hill at the Tubilustrium, at the beginning of the religious exercises which preceded the military campaigns in the approaching fighting season. This marked the end of the March rites and the Salii were seen no more in the streets of Rome until they resumed their functions in October. The Tubilustrium, however, was also held on May 23rd, and doubtless behind these observances lay the widespread ancient custom of driving away evil influences by lustrations and loud noises at critical junctures in the seasonal cycle. And war as well as agriculture was a seasonal occupation, beginning with the spring when farming and fighting could be resumed, and their associated rites and festivals were held to rid the fields of the forces of pollution and harmful influences, and to renew and reinvigorate them in the New Year.

## The Fordicidia

On April 15th at the Fordicidia a cow in calf (*forda*) was sacrificed to the Earth-mother (Tellus Mater) by each of the *curiae*, representing the wards of Rome, one by each of the *pontifices*, and one on the Capitol. The calf was taken from its mother by the attendants of the Vestal Virgins, and burnt, the ashes being retained by the Vestals for use at the Parilia, a shepherds' festival celebrated a few days later on April 21st in honour of Pales, the protectress of cattle.[1] This very ancient rite to secure the fertility of the crops was traditionally referred back to King Numa, who was said to have instituted it when there were bad harvests. But in all probability it was a magico-religious device to fecundate and purify the soil with a sort of magical manure before it became associated with the cult of Tellus Mater, and subsequently with that of Ceres, the Roman Demeter,[2] and was transferred from the countryside to the city, with Vestals performing their functions in it as part of the state cult.

## The Parilia

Thus Ovid, in his description of the Parilia as the sequel of the Fordicidia, though he was thinking of the later urban celebration on April 21st,[3] nevertheless actually described the original shepherds' festival, a lustral rite at the beginning of spring pasture for the purpose of purifying the cattle, the stalls and the herdsmen. Indeed, he affirmed that the Parilia was held long before the foundation of Rome, and its later use to commemorate the building of the city by Romulus,[4] when it became the *Natalis urbis Romae* in the calendars of Polemius Silvius and Philocalus.[5] Then it was kept as a public holiday with music and dancing in the streets, and the usual signs of revelry and rejoicing, like those of St George's Day, its medieval counterpart on April 23rd. But behind both these observances lay the rites connected with the turning out of the flocks and herds to the new pastures, their lustration and fumigation, the sweeping out of the stalls (as in the removal of all traces of leaven at the Hebrew Passover) culminating in the fire rites.

Thus, Ovid's narrative opens with the sprinkling of the sheep and the people with water, and towards evening when

[1] Ovid, *Fasti*, iv, 630 ff.; vi, 629 ff.

[2] Joannes Lydus, *De mensibus*, iv, 72, p. 124 (ed. Wuensch).

[3] *Op. cit.*, iv, 721–82.          [4] *Ibid.*, 807 ff.; cf. Plutarch, *Romulus*, 12, 1.

[5] *C.I.L.*, i, 262, 315; cf. Chap. vii, p. 202.

the shepherds had fed their sheep the ground was cleansed and carefully swept with brooms made of laurel twigs, the stalls were adorned with boughs and leaves, and the doors with wreaths. Sulphur was then ignited and burnt with olive wood, laurel, and rosemary, the smoke passing through the cattle sheds to the flocks and herds to purify them. Offerings of cakes and baskets of millet, and pails of milk and meat (*dapes*) were made to Pales, the pastoral and silvan goddess. Further fumigations followed, and the ashes of the bean straws and those of calves, preserved from the Fordicidia, mixed with the blood of the horse sacrificed in October, were distributed to the shepherds by the Senior Vestal Virgin. The ewes and the cows were then fumigated to make them propagate freely and provide a plentiful supply of milk. The beasts were driven through the bonfires, followed by the celebrants who jumped over them three times facing east to complete the purification, and to ensure the welfare and increase of the flocks and herds and the herdsmen and shepherds who had taken part in the rites. The festival concluded with a feast in the open air.

Although the Parilia was one of the chief festivals in the Roman calendar, marking the birthday of the city,[1] yet it remained essentially a pastoral ritual presupposing rural conditions with sheepfolds and cattle-pens, beanstalks and branches of trees, smoking fires, baskets of millet and pails of milk, as the normal equipment. Similarly, the prayers of the pastoral deity Pales were for the care alike of the flock and its masters, the shepherds, that the sheep might be free from disease and not fall a prey to wolves, and the dogs be watchful; that the grass and the vegetation might abound, the rainfall be plentiful, the udders of the cows full of milk, the rams lustful and the ewes prolific, 'that there be many a lamb in the stall', and the wool thick and soft.[2] This prayer the shepherd repeated four times looking to the east, and then washed his hands in the morning dew before drinking a bowl of milk and wine, and jumping over the fires.

[1] Cicero, *De divinatione*, ii, 47, 98; Ovid, *op. cit.*, iv, 806.
[2] Ovid, *op. cit.*, iv, 763–74.

This leaping of the shepherds and their flocks over the fire to cleanse them from every trace of pollution, taint or harmful forces is a well-known rite of purification, familiar for example in the Beltane fire ritual in Scotland and Ireland on May 1st, and later in Italy.[1] But jumping over Beltane fires was not a cathartic custom only, as the person who drew a piece of oat-cake blackened with charcoal had to leap three times through the flames 'to render the year productive of the sustenance of man and beast', and to make sure of a plentiful harvest,[2] as well as to guard against witchcraft and disease. It was, therefore, at once a cathartic and a renewal rite at which in all probability the sacral king originally was the principal celebrant. Hence the tradition that it was performed by Romulus in the first instance, and that Numa was born on the day of the festival,[3] which was subsequently observed as the annual commemoration of the foundation of the city of Rome, and so accorded a conspicuous place in the State calendar. In the present century it was revived during the Fascist régime.

## The Robigalia

On April 25th ceremonies were held, known as the Robigalia, to avert the red mildew (*robigo*) from the wheat, performed in a grove at the fifth milestone on the Via Claudia near the Milvian Bridge in honour of Robigus, the deity of mildew.[4] Ovid, in fact, claims to have been held up by the procession on his way back from Nomentum on April 25th, and to have seen a congregation all in white led by a *flamen Quirinalis* carrying *exta*, or portions of a dog and a sheep, to offer to the god in the sacred grove. Joining the procession he witnessed the ceremony and heard the prayer to Robigus not to damage

[1] MacCulloch, *The Religion of the Ancient Celts*, 1911, pp. 264 ff.; E. Hull, *Folklore of the British Isles*, 1928, pp. 248 ff.

[2] J. Pinkerton, *Great Collection of Voyages and Travels*, iii, 1814, p. 136; M. Trevelyan, *Folk-lore and Folk-stories of Wales*, 1909, pp. 22 ff.; cf. Chap. ix, p. 312.

[3] Dionysius Hal., *Ant. Rom.*, ii, 88.

[4] Ovid, *op. cit.*, iv, 905–42; Warde Fowler, *op. cit.*, pp. 88 ff.; Festus, s.v. 'Robigalia', p. 325 (ed. Lindsay).

the crops with the red mildew. He watched the priest put incense and wine into the fire on the altar, together with the flesh of the sheep and the entrails of the dog.[1] The choice of a dog as a victim was fancifully explained as averting harm to the crops from the Dog Star which was alleged to be then in the ascendant, and was thought to be hostile to the corn.[2] Actually, however, the rising of Sirius occurs on August 2nd, not on April 25th, when it disappears at sunset. In all probability the Robigalia was observed as an agricultural rite connected with the ripening of the corn before it was associated with either the sacrifice or the Dog Star.

## The Floralia

Three days later the Floralia was celebrated. This was an ancient Italian festival connected with the goddess of flowering and blossoming plants. Originally it was a movable feast controlled by the condition of the crops and flowers in any particular year at the end of April and the beginning of May.[3] It was said to have been instituted in 238 B.C. when at the instigation of the Sibylline books it was celebrated with licentious games accompanied by excessive drinking. In 173 B.C. it became an annual festival by decree of the Senate, and extended over six days (April 28th–May 3rd), after severe storms had had disastrous effects on the corn and vines.[4] In its later form courtesans are said to have appeared naked in the mimes, and to have given vent to indecent gestures, dances and utterances.[5] It is not improbable that these obscene features of the rites were relics of an earlier fertility cultus performed originally for the promotion of the fruitfulness of the earth, before it degenerated into the lewd licentiousness which gave rise to the absurd story of the origin of the Floralia recorded by Lactantius, making Flora a harlot who instituted and endowed the

[1] *Op. cit.*, iv, 901 ff.    [2] Festus, s.v. 'Catulavia', p. 39 (ed. Lindsay).

[3] Ovid, *op. cit.*, iv, 945 f.; v, 183 ff., 211–72; Varro, *de Re Rust.*, i, 1, 6; Pliny, *Nat. Hist.*, xviii, 286.

[4] *C.I.L.*, i, 144; 317; Ovid, *op. cit.*, v, 295–330.

[5] Valerius Maximus, ii, 10, 8; Lactantius, *Divin instit.*, i, 20; Seneca, *Epist. Mor.*, xcvii, 8.

games to be held annually on her birthday, and who was subsequently transformed into a goddess by the Senate.[1] In fact there is every indication that it began as a rustic feast connected perhaps with Aphrodite as the goddess of flowering plants (Antheia), held at the appropriate season at the end of April. Later when it was introduced into Rome and other Italian towns it acquired a licentious character. Finally, it gained a permanent place in the calendar, with a temple at the Circus Maxima between the Aventine and Palatine hills in Rome,[2] and a shrine on the Quirinal at which offerings of stalks of corn were made.

## THE FESTIVALS OF VESTA AND HER VIRGINS

Between May 7th and 14th three Senior Vestal Virgins gathered the first ripe ears of spelt on the odd-numbered (i.e. lucky) days. These they threshed and ground into flour by pounding them in the ancient manner. On the festival of Vesta, the Vestalia, on June 9th they made a sacred cake of meal known as *mola* which they mixed with salt prepared from brine with very great care. This *mola salsa* or salt meal, they offered presumably to their goddess Vesta in her temple, and similar cakes were prepared and treated in the same way on the Ides of September (13th), and at the Lupercalia on February 15th.[3] At the Vestalia the millstones and the asses which worked them were adorned with garlands[4] made of loaves strung together and hung round their necks in the procession.[5]

So sacred was this festival that the days immediately preceding and succeeding it were set apart as *religiosi* and *nefasti* on which all secular pursuits had to be reduced to a minimum, and marriages might not be celebrated. This suggests both its importance and antiquity. The temple of Vesta on the north of the Palatine Hill was the most ancient temple in Rome,

---

[1] Lactantius, *loc. cit.*                    [2] Tacitus, *Annals*, ii, 49.

[3] Servius, *ad Ecl.*, viii, 82; Festus, s.v. 'Mola', pp. 124f. (ed. Lindsay); Ovid, *op. cit.*, vi, 249ff.

[4] Ovid, *op. cit.*, vi, 311ff.

[5] Wissowa, 'Vesta' in Roscher's *Lexikon der griech. und röm. Mythol.*, vi, 255ff.

situated between the Via Sacra and the Via Nova, and was said to have been erected by Numa in 716 B.C.[1] on the model of the primitive round hut of the early kings, the walls made of osiers and the roof of thatch.[2] The public duties assigned to the Vestals in connexion with the fixed festivals, all of which belong to the oldest rites, again suggest that they and their cultus occupied a unique position and significance in the religion of Ancient Rome. Thus, the Pontifex Maximus was responsible for seeing that all the rites were properly performed and the festivals with which they were concerned were duly attended. These began on March 1st with the renewal of the sacred fire and of the laurels with which their shrine, the *aedes Vestae*, was decorated. On March 6th, they sacrificed to Vesta, and on the 16th and 17th they went in procession to the *argeorum sacraria*—the twenty-seven places alleged to have been consecrated by Numa scattered about Rome. A month later they took their part in the Fordicidia and the Parilia between April 15th and the 21st, and on the 28th they celebrated the foundation of the temple of Vesta on the Palatine.

On May 1st they were present at the festival of Bona Dea, a goddess described as the wife or daughter of Faunus, an ancient rustic Roman deity later identified with Pan and venerated as the giver of fertility to the flocks and their protector from attacks by wolves. The Bona Dea was similarly concerned with fertility and healing, but her oracles were revealed only to women. At her festival on May 1st the rites were conducted at night in the house of the consul or praetor for the year by one of the Vestals, all other males being rigidly excluded from the ceremonies. Originally in all probability the cult was that of the Earth-mother, like that of the Athenian Demeter Thesmophoros,[3] which later lost its rustic character when it was incorporated in the State religion and the Vestal cult organization. But according to Festus, the Bona Dea was called Damia

---

[1] Dionysius Hal., *op. cit.*, ii, 66.

[2] Varro, s.v. 'Aulus Gellius', i, 12, 9; Ovid, *op. cit.*, vi, 261-5.

[3] Ovid, *op. cit.*, v, 148 ff.; Macrobius, *op. cit.*, i, 12, 21; Pauly-Wissowa, *Realencyclopaedie*, i, 'Bona Dea', 690.

and so was identified with the Greek goddess of growth and fertility of that name, having an obvious affinity with Demeter.[1]

That a cereal vegetation cultus lay in the background of that of the Vestal Virgins and their duties is indicated, again, in their preparation of the *mola salsa* on May 7–14th, culminating on the 15th with the very primitive rite known as the Argei when twenty-seven puppets made of straw or rush were thrown by them into the Tiber at the Pons Sublicius in the presence of the Pontifex Maximus, the *pontifices* and the Flaminica Dialis, who had laid aside her bridal dress in favour of mourning, probably because the ceremony was in the nature of a purification rite at the beginning of the ingathering of the crops.[2] Various attempts have been made to explain this practice as a survival of some form of human sacrifice, either of old men thrown over the bridge, or of puppets used as simulacra of a victim.[3] On the other hand, it has been suggested that it represented the spirit of vegetation like the Jack-in-the-Green at the later May Day rites.[4] This is not very likely as they were treated as surrogates for human beings who, as Frazer maintained, may have been thrown into the river as an offering to its gods.[5] But neither of these interpretations account for the presence of the Vestals and the setting of the rite in relation to their festivals. These associations would seem to indicate a cathartic significance for the purpose of averting evil influences at a critical juncture in the seasonal cycle in which, of course, human sacrifice or 'sin-receivers' as 'scapegoats' may have played some part in the distant past when propitiation and cleaning, mourning and rejoicing were so inextricably combined in the agricultural ritual connected with the first-fruits and the harvest. Both these aspects recur in the Roman ceremonies from March to June, and again in the autumn.

---

[1] Festus, s.v. 'Damium', p. 60 (ed. Lindsay); cf. Herodotus, v, 82–8; Pausanias, ii, 30, 4.

[2] Ovid, *op. cit.*, v, 621–62; Dionysius Hal., *op. cit.*, i, 38.

[3] Ovid, *op. cit.*, iv, 91; Wissowa, in Roscher, *op. cit.*, 'Argei', pp. 211 ff.

[4] Deübner, *Archiv für Religionswissenschaft*, xxiii, 1925, pp. 299 ff.

[5] Frazer, *The Fasti of Ovid*, iv, 1929, pp. 91 ff.

They reached their climax, as we have seen, in the Vestalia which concluded with the sweeping of the *penus*, or temple storehouse of Vesta, regarded as its Holy of Holies, because in it Vesta and the Penates dwelt in their capacities as the divinities respectively of the hearth and the household, watching over the food-supplies. In it the grain was stored from which the *mola salsa* was made, and at the end of the Vestalia, before it was closed, it was cleansed with the utmost care in preparation for the first-fruits of the harvest, and the sweepings and the dung (*stercus*) were thrown down the Porta Stercovaria on the Clivus Capitolinus or into the Tiber.[1] The Vestals again made their appearance at the late harvest festivals—the Consualia and the Opiconsivia on August 21st and 24th respectively, when the grain was stored perhaps in the silos, if the custom in Greece was adopted in Italy. In that case, the Consualia and the Opiconsivia were a kind of harvest-home celebrated in honour of the gods who protected the stores of corn. But as the events were repeated on December 15th and 19th before and after the Saturnalia, it is difficult to be sure of their precise purpose, or of the function of the Vestals at them in August, and again at the vintage ceremony held on the Ides of September. Then they retired to the seclusion of the temple until they reappeared at the Lupercalia on February 15th, using up the last of the *mola salsa*.

## The Lemuria

A festival of a different nature was held on May 9th, 11th, and 13th in honour of the *lemures*, the ghosts of the dead who were devoid of kith and kin, or in some way rendered restless and dangerous to the living, as, for example, by inadequate obsequies. Unlike the *dies parentales* and the Feralia (i.e. the festival of parents and ancestors) in February, it was a private and domestic rite, at any rate in the Republic, though it may have been at one time a public festival of the dead like the 'Feast of All Souls' at the end of the year, from February

[1] Varro, *De Lingua Latina*, vi, 32; Festus, s.v. 'Stercus', pp. 310–466 (ed. Lindsay); Ovid, *op. cit.*, vi, 713.

13th to the 19th. Thus, the Lemuria seems to have been an expulsion ritual to drive away ghostly evil influences after the turn of the year in the spring when demons were always liable to be rampant, which was subsequently transformed into a private laying of the family ghosts by the father of the house-hold. Rising at midnight and after washing his hands, he walked with bare feet through the house throwing over his shoulder, or spitting out of his mouth, black beans, without looking behind him, saying, 'with these beans I redeem myself and my family'. This he repeated nine times, the ghosts, it was thought, following and picking up the beans. He then washed his hands again, and made noises with brass vessels. Repeating nine times the formula, 'ghosts of my fathers depart', he looked round and the ceremony ended.[1]

## The Parentalia

The later festival of the Parentalia, which began on February 13th and culminated on the 22nd, was also primarily a private family observance commemorating deceased parents and kins-folk to 'appease the souls of your fathers', as Ovid records.[2] It was extended, however, to include the dead in general by becoming the annual occasion on which each family visited the graves of its forebears and conducted its own rites on their behalf. The Senior Vestal Virgin performed similar functions in a communal capacity for all souls, possibly particularly to placate the ghost of Tarpeia who admitted the Sabines to the capital and was crushed to death for his treachery, and so was likely to be malevolent if not appeased.[3]

But the Parentalia was not a sinister or sad event like the Lemuria, being rather the anniversary of the feast held after a funeral, in which the mourners regaled themselves after having duly performed the obsequies. Thus, it was kept as an annual

[1] Ovid, *op. cit.*, v, 421 ff.; *C.I.L.*, i, 318; Festus, s.v. 'Faba', p. 77 (ed. Lind-say).

[2] *Op. cit.*, ii, 533.

[3] *Ibid.*, i, 261 f.; *C.I.L.*, i, 258, 309; Varro, *De Lingua Latina*, v, 41; Dionysius Hal., *op. cit.*, ii, 40.

holiday and an occasion for a family reunion in which the living and the dead joined without fear and for the benefit of both parties. At the Feralia offerings of wine, milk, honey, oil and water were made at the graves, together with gifts of flowers to adorn the tomb in a festal manner.[1] The concluding cere, mony, the Caristia, was, again, a renewal of the funeral feast, described by Ovid as a reunion of the living members of the family after they have fulfilled their duties to the dead, and characterized by mirth and good fellowship.[2] Quarrels had to be forgotten, and hostile spirits driven forth, as suggested by the story of an old hag at the Feralia who sat among the girls and performed a magical rite with a fish and black beans to shut the mouth of enemies.[3]

## The Saturnalia

The winter festival which has attracted the most attention was that known as the Saturnalia, originally held on December 17th, and later continued for seven days as a popular holiday about the time of the winter solstice in the last month of the Roman year. As its name suggests, it was observed in honour of Saturnus, traditionally regarded as the first king of Latium who introduced agriculture in the 'Golden Age'.[3] But his origin and provenance are very doubtful. Generally he has been identified with Saturnus and connected with the root of *serere*, 'to sow', or with the Etruscan family-name *satre* and so as the god worshipped by them. Usually, however, he has been described as the god of sowing and seed-corn,[4] commemorated after the completion of the autumnal sowing when the coldest season was beginning. But he was also identified with the Greek god Kronos who was said to have wandered to Italy, perhaps by way of Etruria, and to have been welcomed in Rome by Janus, where his rites were duly

[1] Varro, *De Lingua Latina*, vi, 13; Festus, s.v. 'Feralia', p. 75 (ed. Lindsay).

[2] *Fasti*, ii, 617 ff.

[3] *Ibid.*, ii, 571 ff.

[4] Varro, *De Lingua Latina*, v, 64; Macrobius, *op. cit.*, i, 7, 21–6; *C.I.L.*, i, 48; Horace, *Sat.*, ii, 7, 4 ff.; Wissowa, *Religion und Kultur der Römer*, pp. 204 ff.

performed. Having become established in the capital, the merriment and relaxations of the earlier rustic joyous harvest-home
were retained, all social distinctions and public business being
in abeyance during the festival. The law courts and the schools
were closed and the community gave itself up to feasting,
gambling with dice and the reversal of the established order of
society. Slaves were served by their masters and sat at table
with them, railing at them, wearing the *pilleus*, the badge of
freedom, and clad in their masters' clothes. Civilians and
soldiers alike joined in the festivities for no war was declared
or battle fought during the festival, just as all commercial
activities, legal business and everyday household chores ceased.

Beginning with a *sacrificium publicum* on the first day, in the
temple of Saturn in the Forum a young pig was sacrificed,
followed by the *convivium publicum*. Then the senators laid aside
their togas and assumed an undress garment, the *synthesis*,
more in keeping with the peasant origins of the Saturnalia.
Presents were exchanged, among them wax tapers (*cerei*) and
terracotta dolls (*signillaria*). These may have been a survival of
an earlier festival of light at the darkest season of the year, like the
Yule log in Northern Europe, in which, as Varro maintained,
human sacrifices were offered.[1] That in the background there
was a more sinister side of the observance is suggested by the
female cult-partner of Saturnus being Lua Mater, who was
connected with baneful (*lues*) influences, and to whom weapons
were offered.[2]

In the eastern provinces lots were cast for a mock king who
was to exercise his rule in the role of Saturn during the festival.
He performed his functions by issuing comic injunctions and
behaving in a ludicrous manner, as by carrying a flute-girl on
his back around the house.[3] It has been conjectured that this
episode represented the last relic of an annual personification
of the god by a virile young man who at the end of his brief

[1] Varro, *De Lingua Latina*, v, 64; Macrobius, *Saturn*, i, 7, 26.

[2] Livy, viii, 1–6; xlv, 33, 2.

[3] Tacitus, *op. cit.*, xiii, 15; Lucian, *Saturnalia*, 4; Cumont, *Analecta Bollandi-
ana*, 1897, pp. 5–16.

reign as a substitute for the real king was destined to have his throat cut on the altar to renew the life of nature at the winter solstice.[1] It appears, however, to have been a custom adopted by Roman soldiers stationed on the Danube, and probably represents a trait that was incorporated in the Saturnalia from Western Asian sources. It survived in the Christian era, however, as a Christian soldier, Dasius, was put to death at Ancona in A.D. 303 for refusing to play the role of Saturn at this festival.[2] But it has yet to be established that the mock king rites were an integral part of the Saturnalia, though the Lord of Misrule seems to have become a Saturnalian figure what, ever in this guise may have been his origin, provenance, and significance.[3]

## The Lupercalia

As a sequel to the Saturnalian festivities in December, the year closed with another very ancient festival on February 15th, going back to very early times when the small Roman com, munity on the Palatine Hill was composed of keepers of flocks and herds and lived on the soil and its products, before they became an urban society. Thus, the Lupercalia retained a fertility element in its ritual, in which expiation and fecundity were combined. Spring having started on February 7th (Flavonius), on the Ides (February 15th), doubtless follow, ing the example of their rustic ancestors, members of the two colleges of priests called Luperci, descendants of the oldest settlement on the Palatine, foregathered at the cave of Lupercal at the south, west of the hill where Romulus and Remus, the legendary founders of the city, were supposed to have been nurtured by the she, wolf. There they sacrificed goats and a young dog, and offered the *mola salsa* prepared by the Vestal Virgins from the first ears of the corn of the previous harvest.[4] Two youths of high rank, presumably from among the Luperci,

[1] *G.B.*, pt. ii, pp. 310f.
[2] Cumont, *op. cit.*, pp. 369ff.
[3] Seneca, *Apocolocyntosis*, 8, 2.
[4] Plutarch, *Quaest. Rom.*, 68; *Romulus*, 21; Servius, *loc. cit.*

were then smeared on the forehead with the blood of the victims, which they wiped off with wool dipped in milk. They then had to laugh. Having stripped themselves naked except for a loin-cloth made from the skins of the slain goats, and holding in their hands strips of the hides of the victims called *februa*, or Juno's cloak, they ran round the base of the Palatine settlement striking all whom they encountered, but especially the women to render them fertile and to give them easy and safe delivery of their children.[1] Livy, in fact, maintained that the chief purpose of the Lupercalia was to remedy barrenness in women,[2] though in all probability it originated as a rustic purification festival for the protection of the flocks and herds as well as for the promotion of fertility in man, beast and the crops, before it became an urban observance on the Palatine.

Thus, the encircling of the settlement by the Luperci girded with the fleece of the sacrificed goats, and carrying the *februa*, would seem to have been a beating of the bounds in order to trace a magic circle round the city to shut out the evil influences responsible for barrenness, and all other harmful things, such as wolves. But although the name Luperci suggests aversion to wolves, or protection from their ravages,[3] the meaning of the title Luperci is very difficult to determine. According to Ovid it was assigned to the priesthood of Faunus, who was primarily a deity of forests and of cattle and of herdsmen, whose festival was observed on December 5th with dancing and merry-making because he was thought to keep the wolves at bay.[4] Livy, on the other hand, made Inuus, the Greek Pan, the god served by the Luperci.[5] But as Inuus, whose name was connected with *inire*, was regarded as the fertilizer of cattle, and also the god of herdsmen, he was identified with Faunus. He

[1] Plutarch, *Romulus*, 12; Julius Caesar, 61; Ovid, *op. cit.*, ii, 267; Juvenal, *Sat.*, iv, 142.

[2] Livy, vi, p. xv; Servius on Virgil, *Ad Aeneas*, viii, 343.

[3] Arnobius, *Adversus Nationes*, v, 4, 3; Dionysius Hal., *op. cit.*, i, 32; iii, 5; i, 80, 1; Preller-Jordan, *Römische Mythologie*, i, p. 380, n. 4; Deübner, *op. cit.*, xiii, pp. 482 ff.; Mannhardt, *Mythologie Forschungen*, pp. 78 ff.

[4] Ovid, *op. cit.*, ii, 267.     [5] Livy, i, 5, 2.

too appears to have begun as a vaguely defined *numen*, or supernatural power or influence associated with the woods, as Fauni, before he was connected with the Lupercalia as the god of flocks and herds, and assumed some of the characteristic features of Mars,[1] to whom the wolf was sacred. Lupercus, as the name of a deity was almost certainly a fabrication of the ancient writers, the designation of the festival being derived from the cave of Lupercal.

So ancient was the ritual that the real name of its god or *numen* was lost in obscurity for the later Romans, who, like their successors, were reduced to conjectures. But of the importance of the event we are left in no doubt since it was on this occasion on February 15th 44 B.C. that Mark Antony in the capacity of Master of the College of Luperci offered the crown to his friend Julius Caesar, just a month before the assassination of the dictator. The scene immortalized by Shakespeare[2] was true to type and the Lupercalian tradition. Antony, scantily clad in the fashion of the Luperci, ran into the Forum, which was crowded with a mixed assembly of jubilant supporters and hostile opponents of Caesar, and presented him with a laurel diadem. In spite of his refusal of the royal emblem, Caesar was duly installed in the imperial throne, only to meet his death on the Ides of March in the Senate House at the foot of the statue of Pompey.[3]

That so conspicuous and ambitious a leader as Mark Antony became Master of the College of Luperci, and chose to make his dramatic entrance in the traditional manner at the Lupercalia, indicates the importance of the festival. In addition the Vestal Virgins were present and, according to Ovid, the Flamen Dialis officiated in spite of its association with dogs and goats, taboo to him.[4] Notwithstanding its very primitive origins and rites, belonging essentially to the pre-urban agricultural culture, it was so firmly established in the state cult

[1] Warde Fowler, *op. cit.*, pp. 113, 118.

[2] *Julius Caesar*, act 1, scene ii.

[3] Cicero, *Philip*, iii, 5, 12; xiii, 15, 31; Plutarch, *Caesar*, 61; *Antonius*, 12.

[4] Plutarch, *Quaest. Rom*, iii; Arnobius, *op. cit.*, 7, 12.

that it lived on in Rome during the Republic and the Empire. When the older cults were revived by Augustus the Lupercal was rebuilt, and the festival was re-established and given a new lease of life. So it continued to be performed until, in the Christian era, it was transformed into the Feast of the Purification of the Virgin Mary (commonly called Candlemas) by Pope Gelasius in A.D. 494.[1]

## The Terminalia

Another rustic festival was celebrated on February 23rd at the end of the old Roman year as an annual renewal of the ceremonies connected with the setting up of the boundary-stones (*termini*) marking the divisions of private and public property in the earlier 'Religion of Numa'. These rites were supposed to have been instituted by King Numa to afford a divine sanction and protection of the property of every individual. The stones were sacred to Jupiter Terminus, and offerings of the first-fruits, and subsequently of lambs and sucking pigs, were to be made to some of them (i.e. *termini sacrificales*) annually on the prescribed date and in the appointed manner,[2] as a commemoration of their erection. But before the Terminus became personified as a god and was associated with Jupiter, doubtless it had acquired sacredness by virtue of its numinous qualities, which made it taboo as the abode of indwelling supernatural power (*numen*).

In the developed state cult an ancient boundary-stone still survived in the temple of Jupiter Capitolinus on the Capitoline Hill, beneath an opening in the roof so that it could be venerated under the open sky as in the earlier agricultural cultus of the farm and the field. But nowhere on the imperial inscriptions is the Terminus described as *deus*, though Ovid invoking the boundary-stone exclaimed, 'O Terminus, whether thou art a stone or a snake buried in the field thou too hast been deified from days of old.'[3] And it was to him as the god of the boun-

---

[1] Cf. Chap. vii, p. 232.

[2] Dionysius Hal., *op. cit.*, ii, 74; Plutarch, *Quaest. Rom.*, 15; *Numa*, 16, 1; Ovid., *op. cit.*, ii, 639f., 655f., 681f.    [3] *Op. cit.*, ii, 641.

daries that the Terminalia was celebrated in the Empire with rural rites in the country districts. These included the adorn/ment of the stones with garlands, the erection of an altar on which a fire was kindled, the shaking of first/fruits into it, and the sprinkling of the blood of a lamb or of a sucking pig on the boundary/stone. A hymn to the Terminus was then sung, and the festival concluded with a feast.

Thus the ceremonies first performed at the stone's erection were repeated. In the state cult they were held at specific points, such as the sixth milestone on the Via Laurentina, doubtless formerly the boundary of the Roman State in the direction of Ostia. How the Terminus became so intimately associated with Jupiter is not very apparent, unless the temple on the Capitoline Hill was erected on the site of an ancient boundary/stone which in view of its sacredness could not be removed. However, the two gods always remained distinct and Jupiter had his own cult/status independent of the Ter/minus in his temple. It was not until just before the Christian era (*c.* 76 B.C.) that he was referred to as Jupiter Terminus when the intercalary month had been regularly inserted in the calendar after the Terminalia. This made it the last festival of the year, held on the day before the Regifugium, when it was said the flight of Tarquin, the last king of Rome, was com/memorated.[1] This was almost certainly a later interpretation of an earlier purification rite in which the Rex sacrorum may have been the principal figure.

FOREIGN CULTS AND FESTIVALS

*The Bacchanalia*

In addition to these essentially Roman and Italian festivals a host of Oriental cults made their way into the Graeco/Roman world increasingly during and after the third century B.C., following in the wake of the conquests of Alexander the Great in the previous century, and that of the Second Punic War. Among them was the worship of Bacchus (the Latin name for

[1] Plutarch, *Quaest. Rom.*, 63; Festus, s.v. 'Regifugium', p. 347 (ed. Lindsay).

Dionysus), the first trace of which in Italy occurs on an inscription from Cumae belonging to the first half of the fifth century B.C., forbidding the burial of any who were not Bacchic initiates in a cemetery reserved for its members.[1] The rites reached Rome from southern Italy, perhaps by way of Tarentum when it was captured by Fabius in 208 B.C., though Dionysus had long been known in Rome as Liber pater, a sober ancient vegetation god with a festival, the Liberalia, on March 27th, and a cult-centre on the Aventine Hill, connected with the worship of Liber, Libera and Ceres, and the Iakchos Mysteries.

In the third century the cultus underwent a fundamental change when the Bacchanalia was introduced, as Livy imagined, from Etruria.[2] This it is said was accomplished under the inspiration of a priestess, Annia Paculla, a native of Campania, who introduced men into what hitherto had been an exclusively female ritual, and altered the time of the celebration of the rites from the day to the night. It was then that licence and debauchery became rife at the nocturnal orgies held five times every month instead of three times a year. So contagious was the Bacchanalian frenzy that it spread rapidly throughout Italy, and even those of noble birth did not hesitate to embrace the esoteric movement.

There can be little doubt that behind it lay the Thraco-Phrygian Dionysiac. The excesses and anti-social effects as vividly described by Livy may have been exaggerated, but, nevertheless, apart from the orgiastic elements, the possible political and social consequences of a secret foreign cult making so strong an appeal to the populace, including as it was alleged, the slaves and criminals, raised the suspicions of the authorities. Therefore, alike on religious, moral, social and political grounds prompt action was taken to suppress it by means of drastic prohibitions rigorously enforced by the Senate in 185 B.C. No one was to be allowed to maintain a Bacchic shrine or observe the Bacchanalia, and no Roman citizen, or

[1] Cumont, *Les religions orientales dans le paganisme romain*, Paris, 1929, p. 197.
[2] Livy, xxxix, 8–19.

member of an allied state, was permitted to attend any Bacchic assembly without first appearing before the Praetor of the city and obtaining from him in the presence of not less than a hundred senators, permission to participate. This suggests that the prohibition from holding any meeting of the Bacchae was not absolute, though no Roman might become a priest or an official, no one was allowed to conduct a secret celebration of the rites, and no more than five persons might do so in public, after first having obtained permission from the Praetor.[1] These injunctions were to be proclaimed on three market days, and inscribed upon a bronze tablet where they could be most easily read.

As a result of this drastic action the Bacchic organization was broken up and its cultus suppressed, surviving only as a temporary measure in the small assemblies authorized by the Praetor. But it was not the cult of Bacchus as Liber pater that had raised the opposition to the Thracian Bacchanalia with its orgiastic esoteric rites in the grove beneath the Aventine, where in the heart of the capital frenzied women brandishing blazing torches rushed in the darkness to the Tiber to plunge them into the water and drew them out again unquenched, amid the strains of wild music, clanging timbrels and cymbals, and sinister howlings. This ecstatic delirium was completely alien and obnoxious to the state cult, and it only remained for it to be suspected of lewd and criminal practices for prompt measures to be taken to end the scandal, and to put to death all convicted of its alleged crimes, many of which in all probability were actually only symbolical Mystery rites portraying death and rebirth.

Precisely how successful the measures were is difficult to say. It was certainly some years before the Bacchanalia was extinguished in southern Italy,[2] and that the cult of Dionysus (i.e. Bacchus) survived into the Christian era is shown by the paintings in the villa Item at Pompeii, and in the scenes on the sarcophagi of this period.[3] But it never obtained official

---

[1] *C.I.L.*, i, 196, 581.  [2] Livy, xxxix, 41; xl, 19.

[3] Servius, *op. cit.*, v, 29; M. I. Rostovtzeff, *Mystic Italy*, New York, 1927, pp. 27 ff.

recognition or condonance to the extent of gaining a place in the official calendar for its observances, which always remained outside the pale in contrast to those of the Magna Mater of Phrygia.

## The Idaean Mother in Rome

It was under different circumstances that the cult of Attis and Kybele found a permanent home in the capital in the third century B.C., some twenty years before the Bacchanalian scandals were brought to light and suppressed. Rome was then becoming desperate. The Punic War had dragged on for twelve years and its end was still not in sight. Although Hannibal had only penetrated into a remote corner of Italy, there had been several ominous showers of pebble rain portending, as it was felt, some approaching calamity. These disturbing events led to the Sibylline oracles being consulted in 204 B.C., with the result, according to Livy, that it was declared that when a foreign foe had invaded Italy it could be driven out and vanquished if the Idaean Mother were brought from Pessinus.[1] It was decided, therefore, to follow this oracular counsel and an envoy was dispatched at once to the sacred Phrygian city to open negotiations with Attalus, the king of Pergamos, who had the custody of the small black meteorite in which the Goddess was embodied, for its conveyance to Rome.

After some demur the request for its removal was granted, and it was placed on a special ship which took it to Ostia where the Magna Mater has a small temple with a high priest at its head. On its arrival amid popular rejoicing strange things happened. The boat was grounded on a sandbank at the mouth of the Tiber, from which, after all other efforts to release it had failed, a Roman matron of noble birth but not unquestioned virtue, Claudia Quinta, towed it off quite easily, thereby clearing herself of the charge of adultery that had been made against her. In Ovid's account of the rest of the journey, the image sailed up the Tiber in the ship to Rome and *en route*

[1] Livy, xxix, 10-14.

it was moored to the bank for the night.[1] Livy, on the other hand, maintained that it was landed at Ostia and carried by relays of matrons to Rome.[2] In either case, on April 4th 204 B.C. it was installed in the temple of Victory on the Palatine, and there it remained until in 191 B.C. the temple of the Magna Mater was erected in her honour on the hill.[3]

As soon as the cult had been established in Rome the influence of the Phrygian Goddess was felt. The summer after her arrival produced a bumper harvest which was attributed to her presence in the city, and the following year Hannibal left Italy for Africa, having made his last stand in the mountains of Bruttium. The predictions of the Sibyls were thus fulfilled, for the enemy had left the country. It is not surprising, therefore, that the people of Rome flocked to the temple with gifts for the beneficent Goddess, and though no Roman festival was ever held between the Kalends and Nones of any month, an exception was made in this case, especially as Kybele was a foreign deity. So April 4th was set apart as a commemoration of her arrival. This took the form of a magnificent if unusual and disconcerting procession, a *lectisternium*, or sacred banquet, and *ludi* (games), to which ten years later (194 B.C.) scenic performances, known as *Ludi Megalenses*, were added.[4]

## The Megalesia

Care was taken, however, to preserve and emphasize the foreign character of the festival. It was given a Greek name, the Megalesia, and although after the erection of the temple dedicated to the Matris Magnae Idaeae on April 10th 191 B.C. it was included in the State calendar and given official recognition, it was confined at first to the precincts of the Goddess on the Palatine, and no Roman citizen was allowed to enter her service in a priestly capacity or to take part in the rites. The

[1] *Op. cit.*, iv, 326 ff.          [2] Livy, xxix, 14, 12–13.
[3] Livy, xxxvi, 13, 4; Graillot, *Le Culte de Cybèle*, Paris, 1912, pp. 25 ff.
[4] Livy, xxix, 14; xxxiv, 54.

temple was only visited by the upper classes, who gave dinner parties there on April 4th. The more extravagant aspects of the cult in public were apparently a later development.[1] Never, theless, whether or not the inevitable results were recognized from the start, it proved to be impossible to keep the rites to the Palatine indefinitely. Thus, before long the Senate was confronted with the embarrassing spectacle of the Goddess being conducted through the streets of Rome in her chariot drawn by lions with her castrated priests, or *galli*, leaping and dancing and gashing themselves amid the strains of outlandish music.

The scene has been vividly described by Lucretius:

'Borne from her sacred precinct in her car she drove a yoke of lions; her head wreathed with a battlemented crown, because embattled on glorious heights she sustains towns; and dowered with this emblem even now the image of the divine mother is carried in awesome state through great countries. On her the diverse nations in the ancient rite of worship call as the Mother of Ida, and they give her Phrygian bands to bear her company, because from those lands first they say corn began to be produced throughout the whole world. The mutilated priests they assign to her, because they wish to show that those who have offended the godhead of the Mother, and have been found ungrateful to their parents, must be thought to be unworthy to bring offspring alive into coasts of light. Taut timbrels thunder in their hands and hollow cymbals all around, and horns menace with harsh, sounding bray, and the hollow pipe goads their minds in the Phrygian mode, and they carry weapons before them, the symbols of their dangerous frenzy, that they may be able to fill with fear through the goddess's power the thankless minds and unfilial hearts of the multitude. And so as soon as she rides on through great cities, and silently blesses mortals with unspoken salutation, with bronze and silver they strew all the path of her journey, enriching her with bounteous

[1] Livy, xxxvi, 36; Cicero, *De haruspicum responsis*, 12, 24.

alms, and snow rose-blossoms over her, overshadowing the Mother and the troops of her escort. Then comes an armed band, whom the Greeks call the Curetes, whenever they sport among the Phrygian troops and leap in rhythmic movement, gladdened at the sight of blood and shaking as they nod their awesome crests upon their heads, recall the Curetes of Diete.'[1]

Making due allowance for Lucretius having borrowed much of the embellishment of his narrative from the songs of 'learned poets of the Greeks in the days of old', as he himself affirms, in fact he described substantially what took place in Rome in the second century B.C. on April 4th at the annual celebration of the Megalesia, as is supported by the shorter account of the proceedings given by Ovid.[2] He too records the procession, the blowing of the Phrygian flutes, the beating of the drums, the clashing on the cymbals by the 'eunuch priests of Kybele' who cut their limbs in their frenzy as she rides in her lion-drawn car from the Palatine to the Circus where the *ludi* were held and the plays produced in the presence of the Praetor urbanis, representing the State and doubtless keeping a strict watch on the proceedings.[3]

Although every effort had been made to keep the ecstatic procession and its accompaniments within bounds and under Phrygian control, its abandon became all too easily contagious, and like the Bacchanalia, made a strong appeal to the Roman populace. This put the civil authorities in a quandary, specially as in response to their urgent request the Goddess had come to their aid, and demonstrated her power in delivering Rome from the Carthaginians, and giving fruitful seasons. Now the choice lay between showing her the respect and veneration that she merited by the services she had

---

[1] Lucretius, *De rerum nat.*, ii, 600–30 (ed. C. Bailey), O.U.P., 1947, pp. 267 ff.

[2] *Op. cit.*, iv, 181–6, cf. 221–44.

[3] Cf. Livy, xxxiv, 54, 3; Valerius Maximus, ii, 4, 3; Dionysius Hal., *op. cit.*, i, 19, 4.

rendered, and the maintenance of dignified, decent and orderly behaviour on the part of the citizens. It was clear that the rites could neither be ignored nor suppressed, and so having provided the Goddess with a temple and a retinue of her own priests and priestesses, mainly brought over from Anatolia for the purpose, the Megalesia was tolerated as a public festival under the restraining eye of the Praetor. These regulations and limitations, restricting the performance of the rites to her own people, had the effect of isolating the cult and its observances as a foreign intrusion which provided an unusual if not very edifying spectacle for the Romans. Thus, though some of the Archigalli bore Roman names as their numbers greatly increased, the ritual was normally performed by Phrygians, and in course of time, when the novelty had worn off, the Megalesia was little more than a holiday celebrated in honour of the Magna Mater. By the end of the Republic, indeed, it had so far declined in public esteem that when a high priest from Pessinus appeared in the Forum arrayed in his vestments and ornaments to demand a public expiation for an alleged profanation of the statue of the Goddess, he was mobbed by the populace.[1]

Nevertheless, the cult was revived with the establishment of the Empire, and given a new status by Augustus in 22 B.C. In its original observance in Rome it had been primarily a recognition of the deliverance from the invader by the aid and intervention of the Idaean Goddess, in a series of ceremonies extended to six days, beginning on April 4th with the procession and ending with the games and plays and circuses at the season when rejoicing and feasting were the normal course of events. Under the Empire the ceremonial was increased and a greater emphasis was given to the fertility significance of Kybele and the fruitfulness of the earth. Her temple on the Palatine, after having been burned down in A.D. 3, was rebuilt, and the Attis myth with which her cult-legend had always been associated was dramatically enacted in a series of festivals in March. The first mention of these

[1] Diodorus Siculus, xxxvi, b; Plutarch, *Marius*, 17.

ceremonies is by Lucan (A.D. 39–65),[1] but so integral was the story of the death and resurrection of Attis, the Phrygian counterpart of the Syrian Adonis, in the cult of Kybele that it would be surprising if the worship of her lover or son was not brought with her on her arrival in Rome in 204 B.C. Thus, her *galli* doubtless emasculated themselves in imitation of Attis who, according to the version of his demise current in Pessinus, unmanned himself under a pine-tree and as a result bled to death. Elsewhere he was said to have been killed by a boar like Adonis.

## The Hilaria

In any case it was this event and its sequel that were celebrated at the Spring Festival called Hilaria when the cult was incorporated in the State religion of Rome in the reign of Claudius (A.D. 41–54).[2] The proceedings opened on March 15th with a procession of reed-bearers (*cannophori*) in commemoration of the finding by Kybele of the youthful mutilated Attis in the reeds of the Phrygian river Sangarius. A six-year-old bull carried in procession was sacrificed by the *archigallus*, and after a fast from meat for a week a pine-tree was felled in the wood of Kybele outside Rome on March 22nd. It was wrapped in linen to represent the dead Attis, and hung with wool and garlanded with violets because violets were said to have sprung from the blood of Attis. To its stem his effigy was tied, and then it was taken in procession by the tree-bearers (*dendrophori*) to the temple on the Palatine.[3]

When these ancient agrarian rites of Phrygian origin had been duly performed, on the next day, when trumpets were blown, a strict fast was observed in preparation for the solemn celebration of the Day of Blood (*Dies Sanguis*) on the 24th.

[1] Lucan, i, 599; cf. Suetonius, *Otho*, 8.

[2] That the Emperor was the later Claudius Eothicus who came to the throne in A.D. 258 has been argued with more ingenuity than conviction by Domaszewski in *The Journal of Roman Studies*, i, 1911, pp. 56f.

[3] Arnobius, *op. cit.*, v, 7, 16, 39, 167f.; Julian, *Orat*, v, 168; Firmicus Maternus, *De errore prof. rel.*, vi, 27; Graillot, *op. cit.*, pp. 117ff.; Cumont, *Les religions orientales*, pp. 89ff.; Hepding, *Attis*, pp. 86, 92f., 96.

The death of Attis was then mourned with loud and bitter lamentation, which included the blowing of pipes and the uttering of piercing cries, culminating in the *archigallus* cutting his arm in order to draw blood as an offering symbolizing the self-mutilation of the neophytes in the earlier Phrygian rite.[1] Worked into a state of frenzy by the clashing of cymbals, the beating of drums, the blowing of horns, and the screeching of flutes, the rest of the *galli* gashed themselves with knives, like the priests of Baal on Carmel, in a wild dance to unite their blood in a common offering to the Mater Dolorosa sorrowing for her dead lover, and to restore him to life at the vernal equinox.[2]

In the evening the lamentation was renewed and continued during the night of fasting and vigil (*pannychis*) probably in conjunction with the laying of an image of Attis in a tomb.[3] At a given moment, presumably at the dawn of March 25th, the empty sepulchre was opened and the *archigallus* proclaimed the longed-for gracious message: 'Be of good cheer, neophytes, seeing that the god is saved; for we also, after our toils, shall find salvation.' Sorrow then gave place to joy, and weeping to rejoicing, because the initiates were now united with the Goddess in the relationship of a new Attis, and shared in his triumph over death both in this world and beyond the grave. Therefore, on this joyful vernal equinox the resurrection of Attis was celebrated as a carnival with feasting, merriment, masquerades and Saturnalian licence. The Hilaria as a festival of joy on March 25th, has given its name to the Spring Festival, as Easter, the climax of Holy Week and Good Friday, occupies much the same position in the Christian liturgical year.[4]

After a much-needed day of rest (*requietia*) on March 26th, these jubilations were brought to a close with the *Lavatio* on

[1] Tertullian, *Apol.*, 25; Apuleius, *Meta*, viii, 28.

[2] Lucian, *Deorum Dialogi*, xii, i; Hepding, *op. cit.*, pp. 158f.

[3] Diodorus Siculus, iii, 59; Arnobius, *op. cit.*, v, 16; Firmicus Maternus, *op. cit.*, 3, 22.

[4] Macrobius, *op. cit.*, i, 21, 10; Cumont, *Les religions orientales*, pp. 89ff.

March 27th. This began with the image of the Goddess being conveyed in the morning on a wagon drawn by oxen to the river Almo, outside the Porta Capena, preceded by barefooted nobles, to the accompaniment of pipes and tambourines. On reaching the banks of the river near the walls of Rome the *archigallus*, vested in purple, washed the silver image and the wagon and the other sacred objects in accordance with an ancient rite. The wagon and oxen, still adorned with spring flowers, returned to the Palatine with the mysterious image in its silver setting to replace it in its shrine, where it remained in isolation until the crude Phrygian drama was re-enacted at the Spring Festival the following March.[1]

## The Taurobolium

Closely associated with these Attic rites was the grim baptism of blood, or Taurobolium, which after the second century A.D. was held in Rome on March 28th in conjunction with his Mysteries. It first appeared in the West from Asia Minor in the cult of Venus at Puteoli in about A.D. 134.[2] Its origin is obscure, but it was a crude importation from Phrygia requiring the initiate into the Attic Mysteries, as an adjunct to the spring rites, to stand in a pit beneath a grating over which a garlanded bull was stabbed to death with a consecrated spear. Saturated with its blood he emerged cleansed from every stain of impurity and reborn for twenty years, or, according to a later inscription, in *aeternum renatus*.[3]

Foreign as it was to the Roman religious tradition, nevertheless, like the rest of the Attis-Kybele cultus, having become established in Rome at her sanctuary on the Vatican Hill, it spread to Ostia, Narbonensis, Aquitania, Spain and North Africa.[4] During the Julian pagan revival in the second half of

[1] Arnobius, *op. cit.*, vii, 32, 49; Lucretius, *op. cit.*, ii, 608-12; Ovid, *op. cit.*, iv, 337-46.

[2] Dessau, *Inscriptiones Laternae Selectae*, 4271, cf. 4099; Cumont, *Les religions orientales*, pp. 100ff.

[3] Dessau, *op. cit.*, 4152, 4271; *C.I.L.*, vi, 510.

[4] Dessau, *op. cit.*, 4145, 4147, 4153; *C.I.L.*, xiii, 1751; Wissowa, *op. cit.*, 323, n. 4, 6-10.

the fourth century A.D. it became very popular, and was adopted by Mithraism, possibly to some extent as a counter-balance to the Christian sacrament of baptism. This may explain the combination of a barbaric rite with lofty spiritual ideas, as in the Jewish Day of Atonement observance, and the reason why persons of the highest rank in the Empire and its priesthood underwent the grim experience. Originally, how-ever, there can be little doubt that it arose as a seasonal sacri-ficial slaying of a bull in which the blood was drunk and applied sacramentally to secure a renewal of the process of regeneration in nature and in mankind. So regarded it would readily become associated with the cult of the Magna Mater, and her Spring Festival would be the appropriate occasion for its celebration.

## The Isis Ritual

Like the other foreign cults, the worship of Isis came into the Roman world in the first instance as a private and secret ritual. In the third century B.C. it reached Sicily, and having estab-lished itself in a syncretistic form at Syracuse and Palermo, it passed on to Pompeii and Pozzuoli, and to part of the Campania, in the next century. In combination with the Apis bull the Hellenized Isis found a home in the temple of Serapis by 105 B.C. In the next century altars to Isis were destroyed in the capital in Rome by consuls on five consecutive occasions, between 59 and 48 B.C.,[1] when an attempt was made by the Senate to suppress the cult which had become far too popular, and, as was alleged, was having a harmful influence on the Republic, and consequently on the Empire when Antony and Cleopatra were connected with it.[2] These efforts at repression having failed, Gaius reversed the decree of Augustus on his accession in A.D. 37, and it may have been in his reign that the Isiac was first celebrated in a temple in the Campus Martius in Rome.[3] It was not, however, until A.D. 215 that Aurelius

---

[1] *C.I.L.*, x, 1781; Tertullian, *Apol.*, 6; *ad nat.*, i, 10.

[2] Cicero, *De divinatione*, i, 58, 132; Die Cassius, xlvii, 15, 4.

[3] Mommsen, *C.I.L.*, i, 2, pp. 333 f.; Apuleius, *op. cit.*, xi, 26.

Caracalla gave Isis a place in the Roman pantheon with a magnificent temple on the Capitoline Hill.[1]

Although, as we have seen, Isis was not the Mother-goddess in Egypt, in her Hellenized syncretistic guise she was equated with the Magna Mater, and personified the female principle in its various aspects as 'the goddess of ten thousand names', the source of all life and beneficence.[2] Notwithstanding the suspicion in which it was held by the Roman Senate, her cultus escaped the orgiastic elements in its Anatolian counterparts. Indeed, it made considerable demands on the chastity of its female votaries, to the despair of their husbands who viewed with apprehension the approach of the annual *puri dies* when abstinence from sexual intercourse was required, their spouses sleeping apart on their chaste couches in preparation for the Isiac.[3]

Sexual abstinence, however, was not the only requirement for participation in 'the pure rites of the Goddess'. Thus, in the graphic if fanciful account of initiation into the priesthood of the cult, Apuleius explains how his hero, Lucius, who was really himself, had first to abstain from 'profane' and 'evil' foods, wine and the flesh of animals, and to undergo the prescribed lustrations, before taking part in the Spring Festival of Isis.[4] But while originally these were no doubt the customary taboos which had to be observed before initiation ceremonies and seasonal festivals, they had acquired a spiritual and moral significance in the Roman Empire, involving personal purity and piety rather than mere ritual prohibitions and cathartic purifications.[5] Thus, when Lucius had passed through the three stages of his initiation, received from the Goddess the secret revelations which he was not permitted to disclose, and been admitted to her service, he is represented as having obtained a new and higher quality of spiritual life carrying with it the hope of everlasting bliss.

This priestly vocation was the highest degree in the worship of Isis and made heavy demands on those who embraced it.

[1] Minucius Felix, *Octavus*, 22, 2.     [2] Plutarch, *de Iside et Osiride*, 53.
[3] Propertius, iv, 5; Tibullus, i, 3, 23–6; Ovid, *Amores*, iii, 9, 33.
[4] *Op. cit.*, xi, 21.     [5] Plutarch, *de Iside et Osiride*, 8; Juvenal, *op. cit.*, vi, 522 ff.

At a lower level there was the usual round of festivals, the chief of which occurred on the last day of October and the first three days of November, to celebrate the search of Isis and Nephthys for the dismembered body of Osiris amid lamentation and grief (the Heuresis), culminating on November 3rd with feasting and rejoicing when his restoration by Anubis was proclaimed. Although Saturnalian licence was not a recognized feature of the Hilaria, nevertheless, scandals were apparently not unknown among the 'procuresses' for Isis, and they may have been a contributory factor in the suppression of the cult in 48 B.C. and by Augustus.

On March 5th a festival known as Isidis Navigium, or Ploiaphesia, marked the opening of the season of navigation. A ship laden with spices was sent out to sea at Cenchreai near Corinth as an offering to Isis. This was preceded by a procession through the streets of the town with women in white carrying flowers and wearing them in their hair, men masquerading as soldiers, hunters and gladiators, and behind them women bearing mirrors facing the image of the Goddess to enable her to see those taking part in the procession. Others held ivory combs for her toilet, and one strewed the streets with balsam and unguents. Following them were men and women with tapers and musicians with flutes and pipes, a chorus of youths clad in white, and veiled women with anointed hair and jingling sistra of Egyptian appearance and extraction. Then came the chief ministers of the Great Gods bearing their insignia, the first carrying a lamp, the second models of altars, the third a palm tree with golden leaves and a *caduceus*, a fourth a libation jar with a breast design and containing milk, and the fifth a winnowing fan. After the priests of other Egyptian divinities like Anubis and Hathor, with their symbols, came a chest containing esoteric sacred objects and a curious divine effigy, followed by a priest with sistrum and roses. The ship having been duly dispatched, the priests and mystics returned to the temple of Isis with the sacred emblems, and this brought the proceedings to a close.[1]

[1] Apuleius, *op. cit.*, xi, 7–17.

Widespread and exceedingly popular as was the cult in the
Graeco-Roman world it was essentially Egyptian in origin and
in its professional priesthood, and the use of Nile water for
libations. Nevertheless, it had become so highly Hellenized in its
externals, and Isis herself was such a syncretistic figure, having
assumed the form and absorbed the qualities and functions of
so many goddesses with Greek and Asiatic names, that she was
able to secure and retain the allegiance of all and sundry,
especially of women who found in her worship and Mysteries
the satisfaction of their emotional and spiritual needs.[1] But the
dissemination of the cult was chiefly where Egyptian influences
were felt (e.g. in North Africa), and like Mithraism, in military
centres. Thus, except at Alexandria and Philae her temples
were small, and the worship in them often was localized and
continued to be not beyond suspicion in Roman official circles.

## The Mithraic Cultus

The appeal of Mithraism differed from that of the Isis cult,
being almost exclusively male and confined very largely to the
military. It was, however, no less of foreign extraction, having
been introduced into the Roman Empire just before the
Christian era, from Western Asia, derived from Iranian
sources with Babylonian astrological and occult accretions. By
this time Mithras, from being an Indo-Iranian god of light, had
acquired the nature and status of a Mystery divinity with ethical
attributes and a sacramental cultus. As the invincible god of
celestial light, the *sol invictus*, who never grew old, died or lost
his vigour, he was at once the creator of the world and the
inaugurator of the new order destined to last for ever—the first
and final cause of all things, the upholder of justice and truth.
Therefore he was an inspiring figure calculated to stir the
devotion of his initiates, especially of the soldiers who flocked
into the sect to find strength to fight victoriously not only on the
field of battle but also against their own passions and tempta-
tions. Moreover, when the earthly struggle was over they were
assured of a blessed immortality.

[1] Dessau, *op. cit.*, 4362; *C.I.L.*, v, 4007.

Mithraism was always essentially a private cult; but though it was confined to male initiates, it was essentially syncretistic, as is shown by the inscriptions and monuments recently discovered at Dura-Europos on the Euphrates, and it erected its *mithraea* in close association with other shrines, as at Augusta Treverorum and Poetovio. But, nevertheless, in spite of the imperial favour it enjoyed, especially under the Antonines and during the Julian interlude in the middle of the fourth century A.D., it never acquired a definitely civil status or a place in the *sacra publica* in the Roman Empire,[1] and its cultus did not contain an Annual Festival at which a death and resurrection drama was enacted, as in so many of the other Oriental Mysteries, because Mithras did not die to be reborn in the spring or the autumn.

The central act of worship of Mithraism appears to have been the sacrifice of a mysterious bull, the prototype of which was the slaying of the bull by Mithras himself, from which all creatures were supposed to have sprung. This sacrificial offering before he ascended to heaven is depicted in the *tauroctonus* represented in relief in every Mithraic sanctuary, notably in that at Neuenheim near Heidelburg, showing the young god in Persian costume with a peaked cap kneeling on the bull and plunging his dagger into his neck. A dog springs up on its hind legs towards the wound, a serpent licks up the blood, a raven sits near by, serpents occupy the foreground, and two youths in Persian attire stand on either side with torches in their hands. From the tail of the dying bull emerge germinating ears of corn, and blood gives life to the vine, the fruit of which was used in the cultus for wine at the sacramental banquet with the Sun-god. In one scene Mithras stands beside the slain bull holding a drinking-horn in his left hand, receiving a bunch of grapes from Ahura Mazda, the Iranian supreme deity.

Though by this sacrificial act Mithras was a life-giver, since he did not himself pass through death to life there is a marked difference between the Mithraic and the Attis initiations. As Miss Weston says, 'the Attic initiate dies, is possibly buried, and

[1] Nock, *Journal of Roman Studies*, xxviii, 1937, p. 108.

revives with his god: the Mithraic initiate rises direct to the celestial sphere, where he is met and welcomed by his god.'[1] Having ascended by the seven degrees during the process of initiation, he is destined at length to attain full communion in the beatific vision in the supreme heaven, where he partakes of the celestial banquet of which the sacramental communion of bread, water and wine, consecrated by priests called 'fathers' and administered to the votary on his admission to the higher degrees, depicted on a relief in Bosnia, was a counterpart.[2]

These esoteric rites were celebrated in small *mithraea* constructed wholly or partially underground, as, for example, at Ostia and Capua, rather than in commodious temples erected for public worship and seasonal observances. These subterranean vaults were described as *spelaea*,[3] and were often established in caves or grottoes, as in the case of the one on the north side of the Capitol at Rome, beneath the church of Santa Maria in Aracoeli. Usually, however, they were approached by a stairway below ground, as in the well-known chapel of Mithras under the lower church of San Clemente in the Via di San Giovanni in Laterano between the Colosseum and the Lateran. The damp dark chamber as it is seen today, below this very fine basilica served by Irish Dominicans hardly suggests the scene as it must have appeared when the initiates entered the Mithraic sanctuary. Then it was brilliantly decorated and illuminated with the *tauroctonus*, which still remains in the apse of the small oblong chamber, with the stone benches on either side on which initiates sat to behold the rites and in all probability partake of the sacred beverage. Then it would doubtless have been adorned with the statues of the lion-headed Kronos and his mystic symbols, smaller effigies of Mithras being born from the rock, and other sculptures. Torch-bearers stood at the entrance to the aisles of the sanctum.

[1] *From Ritual to Romance*, C.U.P., 1922, pp. 157ff.

[2] Cumont, *Les Mystères de Mithra*, Brussels, 1913, p. 159; E. Wust, in Pauly-Wissowa, *Realencyclopaedie*. xv, ii, 1932, cols. 2131-5; Dieterich, *Eine Mithrasliturgie*, Leipzig, 1903.

[3] *C.I.L.*, iii, 1096.

It is unfortunate that from the texts and monuments so little is known of the Mithraic liturgies.[1] In the Hermetic literature a few references occur related to the beginning and end of the world with Mithras as the first and final cause, and the inaugurator of the new order destined to last for ever. But of the cult-legend culminating in the slaying of the bull all that remains is enshrined in the iconography depicting various scenes representing the birth of Mithras, his investiture by the Sun-god, the *tauroctonus*, the mystic banquet and figures of the gods and goddesses associated with the cult.

In addition to the initiation rites, the 'fathers' and the 'clergy' seem to have been responsible for tending the sacred fire on the altars, to have said offices daily to the Sun at dawn, noon and dusk, and on appointed days offered special sacrifices to higher and lower gods in vestments resembling those of the Persian Magi, and to have exposed the *tauroctonus* (normally concealed by a veil) for the veneration of the votaries. At a particular place in the *mithraea* the planet to which the day was sacred was invoked, the first day of the week, dedicated to the Sun, being the most holy. The middle day of the month may have been devoted to Mithras, while December 25th (the *Dies Natalis*, or *solis Invicti*) was commemorated as his birthday, coinciding as it did with the winter solstice. The initiations, however, were held in the spring, in March or in April, beginning with baptismal lustrations and a solemn sealing on the forehead with a red-hot iron as an indelible mark of the sacramental oath of perfect loyalty to Mithras and his fraternity, which he then made. That these striking similarities with Christianity led the Early Fathers of the Church to regard them as a devilish parody of their own sacramental ordinances is hardly surprising.[2] To this parallel round of fast and festival in Christendom we must now turn.

[1] Cumont, *Textes et monuments figurés relatifs aux mystères de Mithra*, Brussels, 1896–99.

[2] Tertullian, *de Praescr. Haer.*, 40; Justin Martyr, *Apol.*, i, 86.

## CHAPTER VII

# The Christian Liturgical Year

WHEN in the fourth century A.D. the Emperor Constantine threw the weight of his office and its prestige on the side of the Christian Church as the spiritual dynamic and unifying centre of the Empire only about one-tenth of the population was even nominally Christian. And this small minority was confined mainly to the eastern section. After his campaign which ended with his victory over Maxentius at the Milvian Bridge in 313, in spite of his own Christian predilections Constantine reigned over what continued to be a pagan world, and the only practicable policy was a recognition of the parity of all religions. As had been already agreed with his ally Licinius at Milan earlier in the year, all men were to have the right to follow freely whatever religion they wished to practice, 'so that thereby whatever of Divinity there be in the heavenly seat may be favourable and propitious to us and to all who are placed under our authority'.[1]

This secured for Christianity the privileges of a *religio licita* (a 'licensed cult'), and opened the way for it to become the State religion in due course when with the accession of Theodosius in 378 paganism was formally and finally abolished. In 381 an edict was issued denouncing participation in forbidden pagan rites, and in 438 this decree was followed by the prohibition of *auspicia* and offerings of any kind to lares, penates, or any genius or pagan deity, with fines of twenty pounds in gold, or confiscation of property on conviction of worshipping an 'image constructed by human hands', or 'performing any acts of pagan sacrifice' in public temples or shrines.[2] Along with this prohibition of pagan cults and their priesthoods and

---

[1] Lactantius, *De mort. pers.*, 48; Eusebius, *Eccles. Hist.*, x, 5; N. H. Baynes, *Proceedings of the British Academy*, 1929.

[2] *Codex Theodosianus*, xvi, 7; 10, 8; 10, 12, 14.

rituals went the abolition of the Roman calendar and in its place the institution of a Christian calendar based on the ecclesiastical festivals and commemorations of martyrs and saints.[1]

## THE EARLY ECCLESIASTICAL CALENDARS

During the preceding centuries the germs of a Christian calendar had emerged, derived ultimately from the Roman calendar which it gradually superseded. As has been explained,[2] the Julian chronology remained unchanged but annual commemorations of those who gave their lives for the Faith in the persecutions under Diocletian and his reforming predecessors took place; lists of martyrs had been drawn up and preserved in the diptychs of local churches for celebration among the memorials of martyrs as their anniversaries recurred.[3] Similar lists of festivals have been found among chronological documents belonging to A.D. 354, but going back probably to the previous century, as this is stated to have been a republication of an edition of 336.

Commemorations of the dead, in fact, in the opening centuries of the era were made on tombstones as *memoria* or *epitaphs*, and on the diptychs, or two-leaved wooden tablets coated with wax or parchment, on one of which waxed sides was inscribed the names of the baptized, living bishops, benefactors, or outstanding members of a particular church, and on the other side those of the faithful departed, martyrs and other deceased. These were read by the deacon from the ambo at the Eucharist followed by a *commendatio*, or general oration, by the celebrant.[4] The care and veneration bestowed upon the dead, especially on those who were held in great esteem is shown by the representation of the deceased as an *orante* with outstretched arms and hands turned to the sky in the act of

---

[1] *Cod. Theod.*, bk. ii, *De Feriis.*
[2] Chap. vi, pp. 159 ff.
[3] Cyprian, *Ep.*, xxxiv, 37; Tertullian, *De Corona*, xiii.
[4] St Augustine, *De Cura pro Mortuis gerenda*, iv; *Confessiones*, ix, 15.

intercession. In the case of the martyrs this solemn commenda-tion was repeated at the grave or place of martyrdom on the eve of the anniversary of his death, with a *commendatio* in the church on the following day.[1]

## Martyrologies

These *panegyries* were collected together in due course as *martyrologies*, or Acts of the Martyrs, and were soon extended to contain the birthdays of all the saints preserved as permanent records of the whole Church, whereas the calendars, or *menologion*, as they were called in the East, were texts of the feasts kept in particular districts with their dates in an orderly arrangement of months and days. The earliest of these lists of festivals occurs in a compilation of chronological documents dated A.D. 354, as the republication of an edition of 336 by a Roman Christian calligrapher, Furius Dionysius Philocalus. Beginning with a civil calendar of the pagan festivals, the Christian week of seven days is distinguished by the letters A–G, prefixed to the sequence of the days, from that of eight days (the *nundinae*) represented by the letters A–H. Of two lists of anniversaries in the order of the months, the one, *Depositio Episcoporum*, sets out the burial-days of the Popes from Lucius (255–257) to Silvester (314–357); the other, *Depositio Martirum*, those of twenty-nine martyrs. In the second list December 25th is described as 'Natus Christus in Betleem Judaeae', implying probably some liturgical observance marking the beginning of the Christian year.[2]

This and similar local lists formed a conspectus of the shrines which from the second century A.D. occurred in the subterranean galleries that were excavated beneath the farms and estates of Christians outside the walls of Rome. Thus, in the Via Ardeatina, Flavia Domitilla, a niece of the Emperor Domitian, allowed portions of her property to be used for Christian burial and the interment of the bones of the martyrs, as did Priscilla, wife of the Consul Acilius Glabrio, and one

[1] Cyprian, *op. cit.*, xxxiv.
[2] H. Lietzmann, *Die Drei Ältesten Martyrologien*, Bonn, 1903, pp. 3 ff.

Commodilla on the Via Ostiensis. To these catacombs the faithful resorted for the celebration of the Eucharist at the funeral and on anniversaries of the martyrdoms until at the end of the penal times the relics of the martyrs were transferred to the city churches.

## The Philocalian Calendar

Since the dates of the first Roman bishops in the Philocalian calendar to be commemorated in this way are in the third century—Callistus on October 14th, 222, and Hippolytus and Pontanus on August 13th, 235—it seems that the practice began about that time. June 29th is dedicated to 'Peter in the cata-combs and to Paul in the consulate of Tuscus and Bassus on the Ostian Way', commemorating the translation of their bones in 258. But it is also stated that in 354 St Peter was commemorated at the catacomb of St Sebastian on the Appian Way, and St Paul on the Ostian Way. It is possible that this anomaly may have arisen owing to the graves of the two Apostles having been located on these two highways, while during the Valerian persecution the bodies were taken to the catacomb of St Sebastian for security. There the cultus began in the middle of the third century, and at the cessation of the persecutions the relics were restored to their respective resting-places, and churches erected in which their martyrdom was celebrated jointly on June 29th.[1] The other Philocalian fixed feasts were the Chair of St Peter on February 22nd, and those of the North African martyrs St Cyprian on September 14th and St Perpetua and St Felicitas on March 7th.

The oldest exclusively Christian calendar is a Gothic frag-ment of a list of martyrs, apparently prepared in Thrace at the end of the fourth century, containing the last eight days of October and the whole of the month of November. Two days are assigned to New Testament saints, two from the Goths, and three from the rest of the Church.[2] In 448 the calendar of Polemius Silvius supplied a complete list of all the days of the

---

[1] Cf. Lietzmann, *op. cit.*
[2] *P.L.*, xviii, 878.

year, mention being made of those on which the Roman Senate sits, when the pagan festivals are held (the Lupercalia, Terminalia, Parilia etc.), and the games in the Circus. Historical events with their dates (e.g. the capture of Rome by the Gauls on the Ides of February), and the days on which legal business can be transacted, are recorded, together with the Christian commemorations, which include Christmas and Epiphany, Passiontide, Easter, and several saints, also Virgil and Cicero. Here the two civilizations have been combined in a production resembling an almanac.[1] In the *Historiae Francorum* of Gregory, Bishop of Tours (*c.* 540–594) Christmas, Epiphany, Easter and the Ascension are marked as the chief festivals with vigils, and the list of fasts and station days from Quinquagesima to the Nativity of St John the Baptist on June 24th, instituted in the diocese of Tours by Bishop Perpetuus (461–490). At the end of the fifth century or the beginning of the sixth century in North Africa the 'Calendar of Carthage' was promulgated containing the names of local bishops and martyrs, beginning with Cyprian (*d.* 258) and ending with Eugenius (*d.* 505), spread over seventy-nine days. Eighteen are those of foreigners, nine of whom are Roman saints. In addition to the aforementioned festivals, St Stephen, the first martyr, St John and St James and the Holy Innocents followed immediately Christmas Day, as now in the West, St Luke on October 13th, St Andrew on November 29th, and the Maccabees on August 1st.

The beginning of the liturgical year with the season of Advent on the Sunday nearest to November 30th may have been an attempt to wean converts from the pagan New Year observances, though originally the Christian year began either on Christmas Day or the Feast of the Annunciation on March 25th. Advent is first mentioned in Spain and in Gaul, but it did not reach Rome apparently until the time of Leo the Great in the fifth century, and subsequently became a preparation for Christmas as the counterpart of the Lenten fast before Easter, though it was kept with less strictness.

[1] *P.L.*, xiii, 676; Mommsen, *C.I.L.*, i, 335.

## Calendrical Confusion

A compilation from Oriental and Arian sources preserved in Syriac from the fifth century, and arranged according to the Roman months (assigned Syriac titles), had a much wider range, containing the commemorations of martyrs of Nicomedia, Antioch and Alexandria, and St Perpetua and St Felicitas in Africa, arranged in order of their ecclesiastical status. As some of the martyrs during the reign of Julian are included it cannot be earlier than 362, and probably it was written in Nicomedia in Greek, and passed from there to Antioch and Edessa where it was translated into Syriac, with Persian augmentations to the lists. The Epiphany and Easter are the only festivals mentioned besides those of the martyrs and saints. The Apostolic commemorations are confined to those of St Peter and St Paul, St John and St James and St Stephen. In the West, in spite of the prestige of the Roman calendar, the diversities in the calendars and their chronologies were augmented by the intercourse of the churches in Rome with those of North Africa, Gaul and Spain, the widespread veneration of local saints and martyrs, and the discrepancy in the dating of the commencement of the year, varying from January 1st in the Julian calendar, March 25th in Florence, France and the British Isles, to September 1st in the Byzantine Empire and December 25th in Scandinavia and the Low Countries, Prussia and Central Europe. Moreover, no less than five methods were in use for indicating the day of the month, beginning with the Roman Kalends, Ides and Nones, and ending with the designation of the day by the feast held on it.

## The Easter Controversy

Easter being the principal event in the Liturgical year the variation in the date of its observance in different parts of Christendom was a major cause of the confusion, and the calendrical controversy that rent the Church in twain in the second century and onwards. The dispute arose in the first instance about keeping the festival on a Sunday regardless of the date, or, as in Asia, following Jewish custom, holding it on the fourteenth day (i.e. the full moon of the first lunar month after the spring equinox whatever day of the week it might be).[1] These Quartodecimans included Polycarp of Smyrna, Melito of Sardis, and Blastus of Rome, who traced their tradition back to the Fourth Evangelist and St Philip, and they refused to be persuaded by Pope Anicetus (*c.* 158) to conform to the practice of Rome and the West. So the controversy dragged on until Victor ascended the Papal chair about 190 and resorted to less conciliatory methods than his predecessor. Deeming it intolerable that the churches of Asia Minor should differ from the practice of Rome, the mother of all the churches, in such an important matter as observing Easter on the first day of the week, thereby throwing the movable feasts dependent upon it out of line with the rest of Christendom, Victor threatened to excommunicate the Asians unless they abandoned their custom. It is not clear whether or not he did actually ex-communicate them in 198,[2] but in any case he was reproached by Irenaeus for his precipitate action, and eventually, through his intervention, peace was restored until the question was reopened at the Council of Nicaea in 325.

Then it was urged by Constantine that the festival should be held by all always on a Sunday independent of a par-ticular phase of the moon and of Jewish precedents,[3] but the Quartodecimans survived among the Syrians. Furthermore, owing to the difficulties in computation it was by no means easy to arrive at a correct determination of the date of Easter on the Sunday following the fourteenth day of the Paschal moon after the vernal equinox. This task was assigned to the Alexan-drians by the Council of Nicaea, they being the most skilled in astronomical calculations. Ultimately it was determined on the basis of a system of cycles of nineteen years containing 6940 days, devised by an Athenian astronomer Meton in 433 B.C. which dropped a day every fourth cycle to correct the

[1] Eusebius, *op. cit.*, v, 23–5; Hippolytus, *Refut.*, viii, 18; Epiphanius, *Contra Haer.*, l.

[2] Eusebius, *op. cit.*, v, 23; Socrates, *Hist. Eccles.*, v, 22.

[3] Eusebius, *Vit. Constant.*, iii, 18; Socrates, *op. cit.*, i, 9.

margin of error. For a while Rome retained its own date, but in the sixth century it adopted the Alexandrian computation through the instrumentality of a Scythian monk Dionysius, who slightly modified the Alexandrian computation in 525. In this form it was universally accepted both in Western and Eastern Christendom, though the isolated Celtic Church in Britain was very slow to fall into line, having observed an eighty-four-year cycle of its own for keeping Easter on a Sunday between the 14th and the 20th of Nisan. It was not until Wilfrid (634–709), Bishop of York, persuaded the Council of Whitby in 664 that the Roman system was accepted,[1] and even then it was only very slowly adopted in the north and in Ireland, while in Gaul a divergent use continued until the time of Charlemagne towards the end of the eighth century.

Trivial as this protracted controversy may seem, it shows what a very crucial place in the calendar and its observances the Easter Festival held, and the fundamental importance that was attached to it. Some of the confusion was caused by the term *Pascha*, which in the second century was applied to Good Friday and the Passion, and was later used to denote Easter Day. Moreover, in the Gospel narratives there is a discrepancy between the Synoptic and the Johannine chronology. In the first three accounts of the Last Supper it was on 'the first day of unleavened bread when they sacrificed the Passover' (i.e. on the 15th of Nisan) that the Apostles were assembled in the Upper Room at Jerusalem (St Mark xiv, 21; St Luke xxii, 13; St Matthew xxvi, 18). The Fourth Gospel, on the other hand, maintained that the gathering took place 'before the Passover', and alleged that the bodies were taken down from the crosses on the 'Preparation' to prevent their remaining at the scene of execution over the feast 'for the day of the Sabbath was a high day' (St John xiii, 1; xix, 31 f, cf. 14; xviii, 28).

That it was on the first day of the week that the Resurrection occurred is not in dispute in the Biblical narratives, and it was in commemoration of this signal event that in Christian tradition Sunday became the festal holy day of worship, while

[1] Bede, *Hist. Eccles.*, ii, 2, 4, 19.

Friday was observed as the weekly fast in memory of the Crucifixion. The Jewish Christians continued to keep the Sabbath on Saturdays in the prescribed manner in addition to the weekly Sunday assembling together for 'the Breaking of the Bread' (i.e. the Eucharist), exhortation, conference and social intercourse.[1] As St Paul recognized, Sabbath observance was not incumbent on the Gentile converts,[2] and when the Church ceased to be a Jewish sect, it soon abandoned it altogether. Attention then became concentrated more and more upon the complex calendrical system in the Roman world, although the Jewish antecedents remained a permanent heritage inasmuch as the 'cult-legend' was centred upon the incarnate life of Christ in Palestine and its Messianic setting. Therefore, it was his Birth, Death, Resurrection, and Ascension, and the other outstanding episodes recorded in the New Testament narratives, that constituted the principal commemorations in the Christian liturgical year.

FESTIVALS

*The Christian Passover*

The starting-point and principal feast in this sequence being the annual commemoration of the Resurrection as the central event in the drama of Redemption, it occupied a unique position as the 'queen of festivals'. Even Christmas was said to be celebrated only as a preparation for Easter, the *festum festorum*,[3] and all the movable feasts were determined by it. Moreover, its Paschal associations made it the connecting link with the Jewish calendar, whether it was Good Friday and the Crucifixion, or Easter Day and the Resurrection that the *Pascha* commemorated. Sometimes the term was extended to cover Holy Week, and even the whole of Lent as the preparation for Passiontide and its sequel on the 'third day', very much as the Jewish Passover as the Spring Festival included the Exodus, the sacrifice of the firstling of the flock, the slaying of the first-born

---

[1] Acts xx, 7–11; St John xx, 19, 26; 2 Cor. xvi, 2; Rev. i, 10.
[2] Col. ii, 6.
[3] Leo, *Sermo*, xlvii, *in Exodum*.

of children, and the agricultural Feast of Unleavened Bread. Clement of Alexandria equated it as the first day of the fifty days of rejoicing for the victory over sin and death with the Jewish prototype, connecting the rising of Christ from the dead on 'the sixteenth of Nisan' with 'the first day of the week of harvest on which the priest offered the first sheaf according to the Law'.[1]

Exactly how this observance became the principal event in the Christian calendar is not clear. St Paul referred to Christ as the Paschal Lamb and exhorted the Christians in Corinth to keep the feast with 'the unleavened bread of sincerity and truth', attaching to it a specifically Christian symbolism.[2] That Easter had become an established institution in the second century is indicated by the acute controversy, discussed above, about the date of its observance, and this is confirmed by the prominence given to the festival in the ancient liturgical documents of the next century. From these sources it appears that it was a nocturnal ritual on the night of Holy Saturday, the Eve and Vigil of Easter, consisting of a series of lections concerning the Exodus and the Passover in Israel and the Death and Resurrection of Christ, interspersed with chants after the blessing and lighting of lamps, and followed by a sermon by the bishop. Then came the Baptism and Confirmation of the catechumens before the celebration of the Easter Mass at which they made their First Communion with the rest of the faithful, after having undergone a preparatory fast and daily exorcism for a fortnight.[3]

As Gregory Dix has emphasized, this Christianized re-enactment of the Jewish Passover was essentially 'the feast of the Christian redemption effected by the Passion and Resurrection of Christ in combination, viewed as a single act'.[4] It was apparently not until towards the end of the fourth century in

---

[1] *Chronicon Paschale* (ed. Dinforth) i, 14.
[2] Cor. v, 7 ff.
[3] Hippolytus, *Apostolic Tradition*, xx, 7–9; xxi, 1–5.
[4] Dix, *The Treatise on the Tradition of St. Hippolytus of Rome*, i, 1937, pp. 73 f.; *The Shape of the Liturgy*, 1945, pp. 338 ff., 348 ff.

Jerusalem that Good Friday and Easter Day were kept as separate commemorations in the great drama of Holy Week and Easter from Palm Sunday to Low Sunday.[1] In the third century the entire Mystery was represented as an undivided whole, with the solemn baptism of the new converts as the central feature, interpreted as the act whereby they were buried with Christ and reborn as new creatures.[2]

As recorded by Tertullian, the African contemporary of Hippolytus, the rite at this season of the *Pascha* began with an invocation of the Holy Spirit, or *epiklesis*, upon the water. The neophytes after their period of fasting, exorcism and confession, made an act of renunciation before being immersed in the water three times, and making a profession of faith in the form of answers to the interrogations of the celebrant. The anointing with oil (chrism) followed as an act of consecration, and the laying on of hands of the bishop to bestow the Holy Spirit in Confirmation. After their communion the newly baptized were clothed in white garments and fed with milk and honey, and for a week they had to abstain from their usual daily bath.[3]

This *Pascha* formed the basis of the subsequent Holy Satur‑day and baptismal developments, however much the details may have varied in different localities. Tertullian after becom‑ing a Montanist continued to refer to the initiatory anointings, signings, imposition of hands, and communion,[4] and in Syria, and among the Nestorians, the same rite was in use to the end of the sixth century, consisting of unction, baptism, and com‑munion.[5] In Africa it continued to be a nocturnal festival, preceded by a fast stricter than those at other seasons and occasions, but this was not an innovation of the rigorist Montanist sect,[6] being in agreement with the practice of Rome

[1] F. E. Brightman, *Journal of Theological Studies*, xxv, 1924, p. 257.

[2] Rom. vi, 3 f.; Col. ii, 12; Shepherd of Hermas, *Simil.*, ix; xvi, 4.

[3] Tertullian, *De Baptismo*, vi–viii; xix; *De Corona*, iii; Hippolytus, *Apost. Trad.*, xxi.

[4] *De res Carn.*, viii.

[5] *Older Didascalia*, iii, 12; Connelly, *Liturgical Homilies of Narsai*, 1909, pp. 43 ff.

[6] Tertullian, *De Jejunio*, ii.

described by Hippolytus and in the third-century manuals of worship.[1] As St Augustine affirmed at a much later period, 'once in the year, namely at Easter, all Christians observe the seventh day of the week by fasting in memory of the mourning with which the disciples, as men bereaved, lamented the death of the Lord'.[2]

## The Drama of Holy Week

Although it might be postponed until the Eve of Pentecost, Holy Saturday was the prescribed time for the great Christian initiation ceremony performed, like that in the *telesterion* at Eleusis, in the darkness of the night. As the ritual developed, in Jerusalem by 385 the drama of Holy Week seems to have been given greater prominence than in Rome. Thus, the course of events leading up to the Passion and the Resurrection was portrayed, beginning with a solemn procession from the Mount of Olives on Palm Sunday afternoon bearing branches of palm and entering the city in triumph. After the nightly visits to the Mount of Olives, on Maundy Thursday the Eucharist was celebrated in the chapel of the Cross with a general communion, and, again, in the evenings at the church of Eleona on the Mountain. Gethsemane was visited after midnight, and in the morning of Good Friday a return was made to the city for the reading of the Passion narratives and the veneration of the relics of the True Cross. On Calvary a watch was kept from noon until 3 p.m., with lections and prayers amid great devotion. In the evening a final visit was made to the Holy Sepulchre for the reading of the gospel of the entombment. Then on Holy Saturday the Easter Vigil began with its lections, baptisms, and the First Mass of Easter.[3]

Thus, at Jerusalem the Holy Week ceremonies were established before the end of the fourth century, and gradually they were adopted substantially in this form throughout Catholic Christendom. Thus, in the Roman Sacramentary known as

[1] *Didascalia Apostolorum*, 180.    [2] *Ad Casulanus*, xxxv, 31.

[3] Dix, *The Shape of the Liturgy*, p. 348; Duchesne, *Christian Worship*, 5th ed., 1923, pp. 491 ff., 553 ff.

'Gelasian', as it was attributed to Pope Gelasius I (492–496) though actually it was written probably in the seventh or early years of the eighth century, the Vigil office consisted of twelve lections, or 'prophecies', recording the Creation, the Fall of man, the Deluge, the sacrifice of Isaac, the crossing of the Red Sea, as an ancient type of baptism, Ezekiel's vision of the valley of dry bones, together with the story of Jonah, both typifying the Resurrection, Isaiah's prediction of baptism in the parable of the vineyard, and other similar prophetic themes in the Old Testament. When these had been read a procession headed by the Pope or a bishop made its way to the baptistery, where the font and the water in it were blessed with the holy oils, breathings, and imposition of tapers. After the congregation had been asperged the catechumens were interrogated by the archdeacon and then baptized with triple immersion, and signed by priests with the oil of chrism before putting on new white robes and being conducted to the bishop to be con-firmed. Easter Day having by now dawned, the procession returned to the church for the First Mass of the feast.[1]

In Rome, however, the Holy Week ceremonies were re-latively simple by comparison with those of Jerusalem, and it was from Byzantine, Spanish and French sources that the later developments in the Papal rite were introduced, including the blessing, distribution and procession of Palms, the singing of the Passion, the consecration of the chrism and the altar of repose on Maundy Thursday; the veneration of the Cross, the Reproaches and the Mass of the Presanctified on Good Friday; the blessing of the New Fire and the Twelve Prophecies on Holy Saturday. These accretions appeared first in the parish churches in Rome and elsewhere, and gradually, between the seventh and fourteenth centuries, they were incorporated in the Papal rite.

That this dramatic representation of the central mystery of the Christian Faith should have found a ready response among the masses in an age of vivid symbolism and deeply laid Mystery ideas is not surprising. Thus, the Emperor Constantine,

[1] H. A. Wilson, *The Gelasian Sacramentary*, O.U.P., 1894, pp. 82 ff.

according to Eusebius, caused Jerusalem to be illuminated during the night of the Vigil of Easter, and St Cyril refers to it as 'that night whose darkness is like day'.[1] In the West St Patrick records that in the sixth century large bonfires were lighted in Ireland on the Eve of Easter.[2] Three lamps are said to have been hidden away on Maundy Thursday in Rome during the consecration of the chrism, and kept alight until Holy Saturday. From them the candles and lamps were lighted by a priest for illumination at the baptismal ceremonies. The only account of these proceedings, however, is in the thirteenth Epistle from Zacharias to Boniface. The blessing of the Paschal Candle of large dimensions, preceded since the eleventh century by the making and blessing of the New Fire, was an ancient custom, sanctioned, according to the second edition of the *Liber Pontificales*, in the *suburbicarian* diocese of Rome. In the Gelasian Sacramentary it was blessed and lighted from one of the lamps by the archdeacon at the end of the litany, sung in procession at the beginning of the Vigil ceremonies.

In the more complicated Gallican liturgy, which displays many Eastern characteristics, the later deveoplments of the ceremonial became more apparent, until by the Middle Ages the Holy Week symbolism was complete. On Maundy Thursʹ day the drama of the Passion began with a solemn commemoration of the institution of the Eucharist in a festal High Mass and general communion followed by the stripping and washing of the altars and a procession of the Host to the place (often at first the sacristy) where it was to be reserved in an urn until it was consumed at the Mass of the Presanctified on Good Friday morning. With the development of the cultus of the Blessed Sacrament the altar of repose was transferred to the church, and at it a watch was kept by the faithful throughout the interval. In the Gelasian Sacramentary three Masses were provided—(1) for the reconciliation of penitents; (2) for the consecration of the oils; (3) for the memorial of the institution

---

[1] *Procat.*, 15.

[2] Zacharias, *Ep. 13 ad Bonifacium*, P.L., lxxxix, 95.

of the Eucharist and the betrayal by Judas. When the number was reduced to a single Mass, all priests as well as the laity received communion at it, a custom that was retained, though since 1951, when the Holy Week services underwent considerable revision, the solemn Mass of the Lord's Supper is now celebrated in the evening, and all clerics attached to a church are expected to assist and communicate.

From the eighth century there was a tendency to bring the services forward, partly no doubt to meet the requirements of the fast before communion. Thus, after the ninth century the Maundy Thursday Mass was sung in the morning instead of the evening, and was followed by the *Mandatum* ('commandment', the opening word of the first antiphon), from which the English word 'maundy' is derived, and referring to the washing of the feet of the disciples by Christ on this day,[1] perpetuated by the custom of the bishop, abbot or prior washing the feet of thirteen people. In England this practice, originally performed by the reigning sovereign, has been replaced by a gift of money, especially minted for the purpose, to as many poor elderly men and women as there are years of the king or queen's life. This is done on Maundy Thursday, until recently at Westminster Abbey, either by the monarch in person wearing an apron, or by a minister of state appointed by him. The moving forward of the rites from the evening to the morning on this day had an anomalous effect on the Easter Vigil ceremonies. In the eighth century they had been transferred to the afternoon, and later to the morning of Holy Saturday. As a result much of the symbolism lost its significance, as when the celebrant spoke of 'this night in which Christ burst the bonds of death', and the New Fire was kindled, and the Paschal Candle as the 'light of Christ' shone forth not in the darkness before the dawn but in broad daylight.

To remedy these anachronisms in a ritual full of archaisms, on February 9th, 1951, the Sacred Congregation of Rites in Rome issued the *Acta Apostolicae* granting permission by the Holy See for the Holy Saturday ceremonies to be held in the

[1] St John xiii, 34.

late evening of that day so that the First Mass of Easter would begin at or about midnight, with corresponding alterations in the times of the rest of the services from Maundy Thursday onwards. After an experimental period of four years during which careful instruction was given in the reasons for and the significance of the revisions, on Palm Sunday, 1956, it became an obligation for all who belong to the Roman rite to conform to the restored order of Holy Week. Therefore, except in churches in which the Chrism Mass is celebrated on Maundy Thursday, where the morning offices of Matins and Lauds, known as Tenebrae, may be sung by anticipation on the previous evening as heretofore, they are to be recited in the early hours of the actual day, following the rubrics of the Breviary. In practice this means that so far as the laity are concerned, Tenebrae with the extinguishing of a candle at the end of each psalm until one only is left alight, and this finally is concealed behind the altar at the end of the *Benedictus*, symbolizing the death of Christ and the darkness of dereliction, is now no longer a feature of the Triduum Sacrum (i.e. the services of the last three days of Holy Week). The Chrism Mass, at which Holy Communion is not given, is usually celebrated only in cathedrals, and, therefore, in parish churches 'the Mass of the Lord's Supper' is now sung between four o'clock in the afternoon and nine o'clock in the evening, with the general communion of the whole congregation, including any priests present.[1] On Good Friday the liturgy is celebrated in the afternoon, preferably about three o'clock, the traditional hour of the death of Christ, or at any convenient time from midday to 9 p.m. But it has ceased to be the Mass of the Presanctified, becoming rather a simple 'Communion service', preceded by the Veneration of the Cross.

The Easter Vigil function now begins after sunset so that the

---

[1] Where the washing of the feet is performed, it may now take place within the Mass. The ciborium containing the Hosts to be reserved for Good Friday is carried in solemn procession to the place of repose as heretofore before the stripping of the altars. The bells continue to be rung at the *Gloria in Excelsis*, and then are silenced until the Easter Vigil Mass.

Mass starts about midnight to enable Easter communion to be made in the early hours of the Festival of the resurrection. In this way the original time of the Holy Saturday ceremonies and their symbolism have been restored, and some of the later additions have been eliminated. The blessing of the New Fire and of the Paschal Candle as the image of the risen Christ have been retained in a somewhat simplified form at the entrance to the church. Then the procession in the darkened nave and chancel makes its way to the sanctuary with the chanting of *Lumen Christi* as the candles held by the celebrant, the clerks and acolytes, and finally those of the congregation, are lighted, together with the lamps, producing a sudden blaze of light symbolizing in a striking manner the glory of the Easter Festival. The *Exultet* in praise of the Paschal Candle and all that it signifies, is then sung by the deacon. This is followed by the reading of the Prophecies, reduced from twelve to four, the first part of the Litany of the Saints, and the blessing of the water, now usually in the choir, and the procession to the font, where the renewal of baptismal vows is made. At the conclusion of this act of renewal so characteristic of transitional rites at seasonal festivals, the second part of the Litany is sung, but without the former prostrations, while the altar is being prepared and the candles lighted for the solemn Easter Vigil Mass. This reaches its conclusion in a general communion. A fast has been maintained since ten o'clock (p.m.), notwithstanding the ancient rule that the Eucharistic fast begins at midnight.

At the annual re-enactment of the drama of Redemption at the Easter Festival which constitutes the climax of the liturgical year, this very ancient ceremonial and its symbolism has preserved and reproduced to a striking extent the characteristic features of the New Year Festival. In the long process of representation and re-evaluation in terms of the Death and Resurrection of Christ, the crudities of the earlier observances have disappeared but the fundamental structure has been retained. Thus, it was at the full moon nearest to the spring equinox, between March 21st and April 25th, that the oldest and greatest festival in the Christian year was celebrated, approximating in time to the New Year Festival in Mesopotamia in the month of Nisan, and its counterpart in Israel and else-where in the Near East. After the preparation in Lent and Passiontide, varying in length from two or three days before Easter to forty days, the special ceremonies of Holy Week culminated in the initiation of the catechumens as a process of rebirth through a death and resurrection ritual. In its more developed form, the blessing of the New Fire at the beginning of the rites, practised in Ireland at any rate from the seventh century, and perhaps from the time of St Patrick,[1] apparently represents a survival of the widespread custom of holding fire-festivals at this season of the year at which new fire was kindled, and renewal rites were performed in connexion with it.[2] In this context the consecration of the Paschal Candle is true to type with its solar associations and life-giving symbolism. The blessing of the fire in all probability reached Rome, by way of the Carolingian Empire with its pagan background, and ultimately from the Holy Sepulchre at Jerusalem where Latin monks may have been stationed by Charlemagne (*c.* 799–801).[3] So although the Paschal Candle appears to go back to the second half of the fourth century, it was not blessed in Rome until the ninth century, having been introduced from southern Italy, a region steeped in pre-Christian customs and beliefs, like the countries of the Gallican rite and North Africa, where it was also prominent in the preceding centuries. At first it may have acquired a survival value largely for utilitarian reasons as it serves to provide illumination for the performance of the nocturnal Vigil rites, before the ancient symbolism was reinterpreted to express the victory over sin and death and the powers of darkness.

In the *Exultet* in praise of the Paschal Candle, likened to a sacred pillar, or menhir, a commemoration was made of the

---

[1] Cf. L. Gougaud, *Christianity in Celtic Lands*, 1932, p. 322; Stokes, *Tri-partite Life of St. Patrick*, 1887, p. 278.

[2] *G.B.*, pt. x, pp. 106 ff.

[3] Wordsworth, *Ministry of Grace*, 1903, pp. 384 f.

story of creation brought into relation with redemption effected by the Death and Resurrection of Christ the King. This mystical rebirth of the world was compared with the passage of the Israelites through the Red Sea when they were delivered from bondage in Egypt. Every incident in the ritual, in fact, was based on some episode in the traditional history of the Hebrews, regarded as a prototype or prefiguration of the Easter Festival and the establishment of the New Dispensation for 'the re-creation of the new people whom the font of Baptism brings forth'. The cult-legend having been recited in these terms in the reading of the Prophecies, it was given ritual expression in the blessing of the font and the bestowal upon the water of its regenerative powers by the inbreathing of the Holy Spirit operating through the solemn infusion of the breath of life, the commixture of the oil of chrism and the oil of unction, and the introduction of the Paschal Candle as the sacred pillar kindled by the shining fire.

Like the sacral king at the Annual Festival, the candidates were admonished concerning the responsibilities of the new life and status in which they had been installed, and they or their sponsors had made their profession of faith. They were then consecrated, vested in their chrysom, and anointed in the presence of the congregation, as the king was presented to his people and proclaimed as their duly crowned and enthroned sovereign. Having been exorcized to purge the evil of the former 'earthly' condition and its 'original sin', they were given a new name as a citizen of the eternal world, a member of the Mystical Body of Christ, the Church, and an inheritor of the Kingdom of Heaven. To complete the *rite de passage* and their union with the divine order, they made their first communion at the Mass celebrated in honour of the Resurrection that immediately followed.

## The Feast of the Ascension

Forty days later the withdrawal of Christ into the heavenly realms was celebrated at the Feast of the Ascension, though in the ancient liturgical calendar prior to the fourth century no mention is made of it. There is some ambiguity in the gospels about its occurrence as the account in St Luke xxiv, 50–53 seems to suggest that it was on the evening of Easter Day that he was 'carried up into heaven' after he had blessed his disciples at Bethany. But in the Acts of the Apostles, which is also attributed to St Luke, it is made clear that it was not until forty days later, at the end of the Resurrection appearances, that he gathered them together on the Mount of Olives and a cloud received him out of their sight (Acts i, 1–11). On the other hand, the Epistle of Barnabas at the beginning of the second century rested the observance of Sunday on its having been the day on which Christ rose from the dead and ascended into Heaven.[1] In the *Apology* of Aristides, another second-century document, it is said that 'after three days Jesus arose and ascended into heaven',[2] and in the apocryphal Gospel of Peter the Ascension on Easter Day is described in a fanciful manner.[3]

The earliest reference to the Feast in the *Peregrinatio Etheriae* in about 380, states, on the other hand, that 'the fortieth day after Easter' was kept as Ascension Day at Jerusalem in conjunction with Pentecost. In Cappadocia and Antioch it was known as ἐπισωζομένη, denoting that by ascending into his glory Christ completed the work of redemption.[4] That the Festival was established by the fifth century is shown by St Chrysostom's reference to it as an ancient and universal festival, and in the West St Augustine declared that it was of Apostolic origin and celebrated throughout the world.[5] Socrates says that it was kept as an established custom in a suburb of Constantinople in the year 390,[6] and Etheria, who was on a pilgrimage to Palestine about this time, records that she went to the Basilica of Bethlehem built over the grotto where Christ was believed to have been born, and where he frequently conversed with his disciples, to take part in the combined celebration of Pentecost and the Ascension. In the afternoon the people

[1] Epistle of Barnabas, xv, 8.   [2] *Apol.*, ii.   [3] Gospel of Peter, 35–42.
[4] Gregory of Nyssa, *P.G.*, xlvi, 690; Chrysostom, *P.G.*, i, 441–52; ii, 188.
[5] *P.L.*, xxxviii, 1202 ff.   [6] *Op. cit.*, vii, 26.

assembled at the Mount of Olives for the reading of the Ascension narratives, and the Old Testament prophecies concerning them, in the Eleona, the traditional site of the Ascension now marked by the church erected there in its honour.[1]

In the West, when the festival acquired its own status independent of either Easter Day or Pentecost, it marked the close of Eastertide. This was marked by the extinguishing of the Paschal Candle after the Gospel at the Mass, and in the liturgical scriptures of the day the emphasis has been on the completion of the work of redemption and the victorious return of Christ the King to his celestial throne at the right hand of the majesty on high, exalted as a prince and a saviour. There, having accomplished his work of salvation, he reigns in his glorified humanity. After the commemoration of the faithful departed in the canon of the Mass, beans, grapes and the first-fruits were blessed, the deacon and subdeacon wearing mitres. The ceremonies concluded with a triumphal procession outside the churches symbolizing ascent to the heavenly realms.

In Transylvania it has been the custom after Mass on Ascension Day to make a sheaf of threshed corn into a figure depicting death, and to dress it in the festal attire of a peasant girl. It is then placed at a window where it may be seen by all on their way to Vespers. After the singing of the office a procession forms, led by two girls carrying the effigy and followed by the rest of the girls singing the hymn *Gott mein Vater, deine Liebe, Reicht so weit der Himmel ist*. Having paraded through the streets of the village, they enter a house and strip the figure of its ornaments. The truss of straw is then thrown out of the window to the boys waiting outside who run with it outside the village and throw it into the brook. Meanwhile one of the girls puts on the clothes and ornaments of the image and is led in procession through the streets singing the same hymn. They then retire to the house of the leader where a sumptuous feast has been prepared for

[1] Duchesne, *op. cit.*, pp. 491, 515.

them. Children it is believed may then eat fruit without ill effects.[1]

Similarly, in Munich until the end of the eighteenth century a man disguised as a demon was chased through the streets on the Eve of the Ascension by pursuers dressed as witches and wizards with crutches, brooms and pitchforks. When he was caught he was ducked in puddles and rolled on dung hills, till on reaching the royal palace he put off his disguise and was given a good meal as a reward. The costume he had worn was stuffed with straw and taken to the Frauenkirche where it was hung up in a window in the tower all night, painted black with horns. Before Vespers on Ascension Day it was thrown down to the crowd outside the church, and a tremendous struggle ensued to obtain possession of it. Finally, it was carried out of the town by the Isar Gate and burned on a hill to drive away evil from the city.[2]

## Rogationtide Processions

It was, however, in the three days before the Feast of the Ascension that litanies had been ordered to be said out of doors in solemn processions at a time of earthquake by Mamer-tus, Bishop of Vienne, in 470. These litanies called Rogations, were extended to the whole of Gaul by the first Council of Orleans in 511, and in about 800 reached Rome where they were reorganized by Leo III.[3] The 'Major Rogation' held on April 25th was an earlier Christianized version of the former Robigalia at the fifth milestone on the Via Claudia to preserve the crops from the red mildew,[4] enjoined by Gregory the Great in 598 as a counterblast to the Roman rites. Later the Feast of St Mark was commemorated on that day in the liturgical year, with which it had no connexion historically. The litany which

[1] J. H. Schuller, *Das Todaustragen und der Muorlef, ein Beitrage zur Kunde sächsischer Sitte in Siebenbürgen*, Hermannstadt, 1861, pp. 4 ff.

[2] Curtius, 'Christi Himmelfahrt', *Archiv. für Religion-wissenschaft*, xiv, 1911, p. 307.

[3] Gregory of Tours, *Hist. Franc.*, ii, 34; Sidonius Apollinaris, *Ep.*, v, 14; vii, 1; *Liber Pontificalis*, ii, p. 35, n. 17 and p. 40, n. 58.

[4] Cf. Chap. vi, p. 168.

replaced the pagan procession started from the church of San Lorenzo in Lucina, the nearest to the Flaminian Gate, and after making a station at San Valentino-fuori-le-mura, and at the Milvian Bridge, turned left towards the Vatican instead of proceeding along the Claudian Way to the ancient site. After pausing at a cross, and in the Atrium di San Pietro, it reached its final destination at the basilica where the last station was held.

Behind this procession, therefore, there was a long vegetation tradition, going back to the Robigalia and its associated spring rites to promote the growth of the newly sown crops and to avert harmful influences attacking them. Similarly, the Rogations before the Feast of the Ascension had the same purpose and significance, corresponding to the ancient Ambarvalia, or *lustratio*, on the three days in May to prevent blight, and to invoke the blessing of Ceres on the fruits of the earth.[1] It is probable that the beating of the bounds at Whitsuntide with its Lupercalian background is another survival of these rites. This affords a reason for the medieval practice of erecting an altar at the boundary stones where Mass was said for the fruits of the earth, and for the custom of reading the liturgical gospel at 'Gospel Oaks'. Since fasting and asceticisms are an important feature in ritual observances of this nature, that the Rogationtide processions have assumed a penitential character with 'fastings, prayers, psalms and tears', as Sidonius Apollinaris says, is in keeping with their purpose. To give new life to the crops it was appropriate to approach the festivities which have been of common occurrence at Ascensiontide and Whitsuntide with the Rogation austerities and penitential processions.

## Whitsun

While in the liturgical year Ascension Day marked the end of the Easter Festival, the fifty days from Easter to Pentecost were kept as a time of rejoicing in celebration of the Mystery of the Resurrection. Indeed, it was so closely bound up with Easter

[1] Chap. vi, p. 165.

that it seems to have been primarily regarded as the termination of Eastertide. Nevertheless, the descent of the Holy Ghost upon the Apostles as recorded in the second chapter of the Acts of the Apostles in the New Testament hardly could fail to give it a Christian significance independent of the Jewish festival of the first-fruits of wheat harvest.[1] Moreover, after the institution of Ascension Day in the fourth century, this specifically Christian aspect of the feast was brought into greater prominence. Thus, in the second half of the century it was regarded as a festival of long standing, and at the Council of Elvira (*c.* 300) the obligation of its observance, as distinct from Ascension Day, was stressed in its forty-third canon.

Once it became firmly established it attained almost equal status with Easter Day as the second festival in the calendar with an octave assigned to it in the Gelasian and Gregorian Sacramentaries. In the West on the Vigil the ceremonies of Holy Saturday were repeated with the omission of the blessing of the New Fire and the Paschal Candle, and the reduction of the Prophecies from twelve to six.[2] It has been suggested that the title 'Whitsun' was derived from the practice of the catechumens wearing white vestures at their baptism on this day, but this is merely a conjecture and the white chrysom was not peculiar to this baptismal season. The liturgical colour, in fact, is red indicative of the tongues of fire that were said to have descended upon the Apostles on this day. In commemoration of this event in Italy rose leaves have been scattered from the ceiling of the churches at the festival to symbolize the descent of the Holy Ghost in fiery form. As a result in Sicily and elsewhere the day has been known as *Pascha rosatum*, or *Pascha rossa*. The blowing of trumpets during the Mass in France was said to commemorate the sound of the mighty rushing wind accompanying the charismatic descent, but in all probability it was really a survival of the widespread custom of blowing sacred trumpets to make trees bear fruit in abundance,

[1] Tertullian, *De Idol.*, xiv; *De Baptismo*, xix; *De Corona*, iii; Origen, *Adv. Celsum*, viii, 22.

[2] In the revised liturgy the Whitsun ceremonies have been omitted altogether.

and to avert the powers of evil, as for example, at the Jewish Feast of Purim, enacting the Esther story as its cult-legend.[1]

As will be considered later,[2] the fifty days from Easter to Whitsun, coinciding with the ancient Spring Festival in the agricultural calendars, were marked by a number of folk obser-vances, some of which acquired an ecclesiastical character by becoming absorbed in the liturgical year and its feasts. But it was primarily the cult-legend (using the term in its technical sense) of the risen and ascended incarnate Saviour of mankind and trium-phant Redeemer-King, that was celebrated in a succession of rites and festivals, structurally akin to those which marked the victory of the ancient sacral king over his enemies at the Annual Festival. Thus, the great forty days of Eastertide were brought to a conclu-sion with penitential processions and contests, rejoicings and the signs of victory, in line with the ritual pattern of the seasonal obser-vances, re-evaluated in terms of the Christian concept of the spirit-ual victory of Christ over sin and death leading to the birth of the Church as his Mystical Body at Whitsun for the express purpose of inaugurating a new era, henceforth designated *Anno Domini*.

## Corpus Christi

From Pentecost, or, as in the Anglican Communion, from its octave known as Trinity Sunday, the rest of the Sundays of the year until Advent are numbered. The connecting link between the round of fasts and festivals in the first half of the calendrical sequence, and the subsequent Pentecost or Trinity succession of events in Western Christendom, is the Feast of Corpus Christi. This is a relatively late introduction, arising in Belgium in the middle of the thirteenth century. About 1280 when she became the prioress of her Order, a nun, Blessed Juliana, believed that she had had a vision encouraging her to use her influence with the ecclesiastical authorities for the institution of the feast. In 1246 the Bishop of Liège ordered the day to be kept in honour of the Blessed Sacrament in his diocese, and his successor petitioned Pope Urban IV to make it a universal celebration. This request met with success and in 1264 a bull

[1] Chap. iv, p. 121.　　　[2] Chap. ix, pp. 305 ff.

was published setting apart the first Thursday after Trinity Sunday for this purpose. Before its execution, however, Urban died, and it was not until 1311 that it was authorized by Clement V at the Council of Vienne. Seven years later a procession of the Host was enjoined by John XXII, the next Pope.

Since on Maundy Thursday the Passion is the principal preoccupation a high festival in honour of the central act of Christian worship could hardly be held then. Therefore, it seemed desirable and appropriate that the first available Thursday after the prolonged Easter celebrations should be assigned to this commemoration, especially at a time when the controversy about the doctrine of the Real Presence of Christ in the Eucharist provoked by Berengar of Tours (999–1088) and his followers eventually had led the Vatican Council in 1215 to promulgate the dogma of Transubstantiation as *de fide*. The office for the new feast and its octave were drawn up by St Thomas Aquinas at the request of Urban, and the festival became a day of obligation. As soon as the procession was instituted it became the most conspicuous event in the observance. The carrying on the Thursday after Trinity Sunday of the ciborium containing the Host through the highways of medieval Europe, thronged with adoring crowds venerating the Blessed Sacrament, and accompanied by princes, magistrates and members of Guilds and of Religious Orders, was a spectacle which caught the popular imagination, specially when in the fifteenth century it was followed by a Mystery play. To this even so scoffing an observer as Naogeorgus bore witness in his description of the scene, adding a reference incidentally to the reading of the Gospel at the stations during the procession 'keeping the corn from the wind and rain and from the blast'.[1] If this was a traditional belief it must have been an importation from the Rogations, and possibly from the secular Spring Festival at that season of the year.

Be this as it may, the Corpus Christi celebrations formed a fitting conclusion to the series of commemorations which

---

[1] Naogeorgus (Kirchmeyer), *The Popish Kingdome, or reigne of Antichrist*, 1570, (ed. R. C. Hope, 1880), pp. 53 ff.

reached their climax in the Holy Week and Easter ceremonies, and the inauguration of their sequel in the second half of the liturgical year. Furthermore, they were true to type in the age-long pattern of seasonal ritual. The relation of the festival to Maundy Thursday brought it into association with the Death and Resurrection of Christ as the suffering but triumphant Saviour-King, incarnated once and for all in order ever after to rule over the souls of men, invested in a scarlet robe, a crown of thorns, and a reed for a sceptre, and dying to live on a cross which was destined to become symbolized as the tree of life.[1] Therefore, the sacrifice offered on Good Friday, ratified on Easter Day, and perpetuated in the Eucharistic offering, was triumphantly proclaimed in the Corpus Christi rites when the consecrated Host was borne in solemn procession as a mystical representation of the age-long victory which the king must win on ascending the throne, be he, as in the pagan ritual, the reigning sacral sovereign, or, as in Christianity, the incarnate Son of God.

## The Nativity of St John the Baptist

The next calendrical event in the liturgical year which was essentially of a seasonal character is the Nativity of St John the Baptist which in the West since the fifth century has been kept on June 24th, thereby coinciding with the summer solstice. The date suggested by the account of the birth of the herald of Christianity in the Lucian narrative (St Luke i. 36) was placed just six months before the Christmas Festival. This was fixed in the Roman calendar on June 24th[2] instead of on the 25th, but in the East and in Gaul it was held in January soon after the celebration of the Baptism of Christ at the Epiphany.[3] The earliest reference to it occurs in St Augustine's Sermons[4] early in the fifth century (*c.* 430), when in contrasting the birth of Christ with that of the Baptist he discussed the appropriateness of keeping the feast at midsummer when the days were about

---

[1] Hocart, *Kingship*, O.U.P, 1927, p. 16.; James, *Christian Myth and Ritual*, 1933, pp. 242f.

[2] *Kal. Jul*, viii.    [3] Duchesne, *op. cit.*, p. 270.    [4] 287, *P.L.*, xxxviii, 301.

to shorten, whereas after Christmas, as in the Eastern practice, they were slowly lengthening.

This was one of the oldest festivals in honour of a saint in both the Greek and Latin liturgies, and the choice of the date and the commemoration of the birth rather than the death of St John the Baptist were in all probability influenced by the summer solstice on which it was fixed. As on Christmas Day three Masses were ordered to be said on June 24th, the first at midnight, the second at daybreak and the third in the morning at the third hour, against a background of general rejoicing and the lighting of midsummer fires on mountains and hills where/ ever these were available. This date is the turning/point in the sun's course on the horizon, when after climbing higher and higher in the sky it begins, at first almost imperceptibly, to retrace its path until on Christmas Day it reaches its lowest place, before repeating the cyclic operation in the New Year. As the lighting respectively of bonfires and Yule logs on these two occasions is a very ancient and widespread custom in solar ritual and long antedates the Christian observances at the summer and winter solstice, only a very thin veneer of Christianity has been given to them on these two occasions. Thus, the midsummer ceremonies include, in addition to the fires on eminences, processions with torches round the fields, rolling burning wheels down hills, and sometimes making foul smoke from burning bones and rubbish, presumably to drive away evil influences at a very critical juncture in the annual cycle, as well as to stimulate the life and energy of the sun at the beginning of its downward course. These ancient calendrical practices readily lent themselves to reinterpretation in terms of the herald of the new era, himself destined to decrease as the one whose advent he foretold and prepared increased.

## Michaelmas

Similarly, at the approach of autumn when the sun's declining rays were becoming more apparent, with the reciprocal effects in nature, leading men's thoughts to death and doom, the Feast of St Michael, the oldest of the Angel festivals, was held on September 29th. Around this angelic champion of Jews and Christians alike, who was regarded as the protector against the devil, especially at the hour of death when he escorted the souls of the faithful to the perpetual light of the divine presence, a cultus developed at an early period in Phrygia and Western Asia, and passed to the West before the fifth century. Thus, in the Leonine Sacramentary St Michael is mentioned in four of the five Masses celebrated on September 30th at the dedication of a church to him in the Via Salaria, six miles from Rome. At first the festival was confined to the churches under his patronage, but as his fame and veneration increased and became firmly established throughout the whole of Christendom, Michaelmas was a fitting introduction to the autumnal struggle with the forces of darkness and death.

*All Saints and All Souls*

It was, however, in the month of November that this aspect of the seasonal decline eventually found expression in the liturgical year, when November 1st was set apart in the ninth century for the commemoration of the saints, largely to Christianize the pagan All Hallows' Eve Festival in Northern and Central Europe. It was then that Beltane fire rites were held, as also in May when, as early as the fourth century in Eastern Christendom the first Sunday after Pentecost was appointed for the commemoration of the martyrs. In the sixth century a similar festival of the saints was introduced in Rome when the Pantheon was dedicated to Santa Maria del Martiri by Boniface IV on May 13th 609 or 610. Henceforward this day became the annual commemoration of All Saints, until it was transferred to November 1st by Gregory IV in 835 to supplant the autumnal pagan rites.

The commemoration of all the faithful departed on the following day (i.e. the solemnity of All Souls on November 2nd) was established about the same time in the Benedictine Religious Houses under the influence of the Abbot of Cluny, Odilo, in 988, and the observance was rapidly adopted throughout the Western Church. At first the dead, as we have seen, were entered in the lists of names of the living and departed Christians, known as the diptychs, and commemorated in the liturgy. This practice was continued and developed in both the Eastern and Western early liturgies, while the anniversaries of martyrs and saints eventually passed into an annual special commemoration of all the faithful departed which by the thirteenth century, as is shown by Durandus, had become adopted everywhere in the West. Around it some of the popular customs connected with the Festival of the Dead have survived, such as the lighting of lamps on graves, the burning of candles in the houses, tolling of the bells till midnight, and in Brittany a procession to the charnel-house after Vespers of the Dead on the Eve of All Souls, chanting a dirge in Breton. On returning to their houses they keep a large log alight all night on the hearth, around which the family talk of their departed relatives, and 'singers of death' parade in the streets reminding the people in the houses to pray for the souls in purgatory. Food is provided for the holy souls in the kitchen as they are supposed to return and warm themselves by the fire.[1] Like the processions with lighted candles, the offering of soul-cakes to the dead on the Eve of All Souls Day has been widely practised in Northern and Central Europe.[2]

### The Feast of the Nativity and the Epiphany

Most of the popular customs connected with this season, however, have accumulated round the winter solstice which in the Christian liturgical year found its centre in the Feast of the Nativity. From time immemorial the turn of the year in mid-winter had been the occasion of *rites de passage* as a precaution against the supernatural forces thought to be then rampant, and to ensure the renewal of the waning power of the sun, as has been considered in relation to the Saturnalia in the Roman World.[3] In Scandinavia, Iceland and Germany, as has yet to be

---

[1] Cf. A. le Braz, *La Légende de la Mort en Basse-Bretagne*, Paris, 1893, pp. 280 ff.

[2] Reinsberg-Düringsfeld, *Calendrier Belge*, ii, Brussels, 1861-2, pp. 236 ff.; *Fest-Kalender aus Böhmen*, pp. 493 ff.; E. H. Meyer, *Badisches Volksleben im neunzehnten Jahrhundert*, Strassburg, 1900, p. 601.        [3] Chap. vi, pp. 175 f.

discussed in its proper setting in a later chapter,[1] Yuletide extended from the middle of November to the beginning of January. Therefore, the Church was confronted with a very firmly established and highly developed calendrical ritual, though it was not until towards the end of the fourth century that it was associated with the birth of Christ.

The date of the Nativity was a matter of speculation in the opening centuries of the Christian era as no clear indication is given in the Gospels when it occurred. Even the year is uncertain, leave alone the month and the day, and no reference exists to the observance of a festival to commemorate the event prior to the fourth century when in the Philocalian calendar, drawn up in Rome in 336, December 25th was set apart for this purpose. In the Eastern Empire, on the other hand, on January 6th the Feast of the Epiphany was held, in the first instance apparently to celebrate the Baptism of Christ. To this commemoration the Nativity was added, especially in Syria, by the middle of the fourth century. It is by no means certain, however, whether the institution of a feast confined exclusively to the Nativity arose first of all in the West or in the East. According to Usener it was kept everywhere on January 6th until in 353 Pope Liberius in the West, without discarding the Epiphany, transferred Christmas Day to December 25th, perhaps to counteract the Saturnalia and the Mithraic *Natalis Solis Invicti* in honour of the birth of the Sun, then still prevalent in Rome. From the West, on this view, it spread to the East.[2] Conversely, Duchesne maintains that originally Christmas was a festival peculiar to the Latin Church, and from the beginning the Eastern churches universally observed the Epiphany, or 'Manifestations', on January 6th as a commemoration of the Baptism of Christ, as among the Gnostic Basilidians at Alexandria, including in the observance in the fourth century the Nativity and the visit of the Magi. He agrees, nevertheless, that December 25th in the East was derived from Rome.[3]

[1] Chap. ix, pp. 292ff.
[2] Usener, 'Das Weihnachtsfest', *Religionsgeschichtliche Untersuchungen*, Bonn, 1889, 2nd. ed. by Lietzmann, 1923.        [3] Duchesne, *op. cit.*, pp. 259ff.

More recently Dom Bernard Botte has contended that in Jerusalem at the end of the fourth century, the Epiphany commemorated the Incarnation and that there is no indication that the baptism was then associated with it. Between 424 and 458 Christmas was established, and after being discarded, it reappeared in the middle of the sixth century between 565 and 578. From Rome it had passed to Antioch as early as 386, and in the following year the Epiphany was kept as the feast of the baptism, without having previously had a place in the Syrian calendar. In Asia Minor both festivals were observed by the end of the fourth century as in Antioch, but Armenia, where the Epiphany was called 'the Coming of the Son of God into the Temple', never adopted it, and did not include the baptism till the eighth century. In the West, Christmas having been established independently of the Epiphany, this commemoration (i.e. the Epiphany) was introduced in the fifth century and confined in the Roman liturgical year to the visit of the Magi. As it gradually became a universal observance, the Baptism (and sometimes the Transfiguration) was mentioned, together with the Miracle at Cana of Galilee. But the limitation of the story to the Magi was of Western origin, assigned by Botte to Spain, or possibly Gaul, whence it passed to Rome and the rest of the West.[1]

That a historical tradition lies behind either of the two dates, he thinks, is highly improbable, and he is inclined to the view that December 25th was selected for the Nativity as the Christian counterpart of the pagan festival because it was then at the winter solstice that it was most appropriate to set the birth of the sun of righteousness as the true Light of the World against the pagan *Natalis Invicti*. The supposed relation of Christmas to the Saturnalia as suggested by Epiphanius, Bishop of Constantia in Cyprus in 362, was the result of a confusion of the *Natalis Invicti* with the Saturnalia regardless of the fact that the Saturnalia ended on December 23rd, however much the two events may have reacted on each other. Furthermore, he placed the birth of Christ thirteen days after

[1] Botte, *Les Origines de la Noël et de l'Epiphanie*, Louvain, 1932.

the solstice, and so made it coincide with the Koreion at Alexandria, the celebration of the birth of Aeon from Kore. According to Botte, Christmas and Epiphany were both based on solstice festivals, the discrepancies arising from the defective, ness of the dates in the Alexandrian calendar. Originally, he contends, the winter solstice in the Egyptian calendar of Amenhotep I of Thebes was on January 6th, but by the beginning of the Christian era it was observed on December 25th while January 6th also retained its earlier celebration.[1]

However these calendrical conundrums are explained, the Feast of the Nativity was in fact observed at the season of the winter solstice and, therefore, it was brought into very intimate association with the mythological victory of light over darkness and of the rebirth of the sun as the author and giver of life. Indeed, the Syrians and Armenians who continued to keep Christmas on January 6th, the winter solstice of the Julian calendar and incidentally the birthday of Osiris in Alexandria, accused the Latins of sun-worship in observing the feast on December 25th. Nor apparently was the accusation wholly without justification since Leo the Great condemned customs practised on this occasion in Rome in the fifth century as indistinguishable from sun-worship, and launched a vigorous campaign against these pagan accretions.

Nevertheless, they lingered on, especially in Northern and Central Europe where Boniface had to deal drastically with them as late as the eighth century, and three hundred years later in spite of constant denunciations in canons, homilies, capitu, laries and penitentials, Burchardus, Bishop of Worms from 1000 to 1025, refers to their having still persisted in his day. Even as far away from the ancient centre of the Empire as the British Isles in the so-called Penitential of Egbert (*c.* 766) there is reference to the Kalends showing that the celebration was not unknown in these islands. Thus, around the Christmas Festival, a great variety of ancient seasonal customs and beliefs from a number of different sources clustered, originally observed from the beginning of November to the end of January, particularly

[1] Norden, *Die Geburt des Kindes*, Leipzig, 1924.

those connected with the winter solstice rites on December 25th and the Kalends of January, the Roman New Year's Day, characterized by rejoicings, the decoration of houses with greenery and lights, carousals, well-laden tables and fire rites. With them were combined Dionysian elements from the festival of Dionysus on January 5th, and perhaps from Osirian sources associated with the birthday of Osiris in Alexandria, which found expression in relation to the Miracle at Cana of Galilee and the Baptism of Christ as features of the Epiphany.[1]

## Candlemas

Finally, forty days after the Feast of the Nativity, the Presentation of the Christ Child in the Temple was commemorated with a procession on February 14th, the Quadragesima de Epiphania, in the church of the Anastasia in Jerusalem from about 350. When Christmas Day was observed on December 25th it was brought forward to February 2nd by the Emperor Justinian in 542, and ordered to be kept on this day in Constantinople as a thanksgiving for the ending of a plague. According to Baronius (1538–1607) it was first introduced into Rome by Pope Gelasius (492–496) to counteract the pagan Lupercalia,[2] but, as we have seen, this occurred on February 15th as a *lustratio* and does not seem to bear any resemblance to the Christian festival which has become known as Candlemas. Encircling the bounds and beating the bystanders savour of Rogationtide rather than the blessing, distribution and carrying of candles on February 2nd in memory of the entrance of Christ as the 'True Light' into the Temple and the prophecy of the aged Simeon in the *Nunc Dimittis* (Luke ii, 22, 39).

The feast is first described by Etheria in the *Peregrinatio* under the name Quadragesima de Epiphania before the Christmas Festival had been adopted at Jerusalem, and was celebrated in relation to the Presentation without reference to the Purification of the Blessed Virgin Mary. The designation *Purificatio* appears first in the Gelasian Sacramentary in the seventh century, suggesting that this aspect of the feast had a Gallican

[1] Cf. Chap. ix, pp. 293 ff.    [2] *Martyrologium Romanum*, 1586, p. 87.

origin. That it came in the first instance from the East is indicated by the title *Hypapante* (i.e. the meeting of the Christ Child with Simeon and Anna), which was retained in the West until the ninth century. The procession was introduced by Pope Sergius at the end of the seventh century, but no mention of this adjunct occurs in the Gregorian tradition in the next century. It would seem, in fact, that the procession to the Liberian basilica in the time of Sergius was the ordinary 'station' rather than a liturgical ceremony as it later became. It is possible that as Sergius, though a Sicilian, was of Syrian extraction, he may have introduced the carrying of candles, but this was not a characteristic feature in common use in the West until the eleventh century.

Since the Feast of Lights had long been observed on February 1st with a highly developed fire ceremonial in which perambulations with lighted torches, connected with the return of the Goddess from the underworld and the rebirth of nature in the spring, played a prominent part, it is by no means improbable that this ancient festival lay in the background of the Candlemas liturgical rites, especially in Jerusalem and the East.[1] Indeed, its customs survived in the Christian era long after their original significance had been abandoned and probably forgotten. In Scotland, for example, the sacred fire of St Bride, or Bridget, was carefully guarded and on the Eve of Candlemas a bed made of corn and hay was surrounded with candles as a fertility rite,[2] the fire symbolizing the victorious emergence of the sun from the darkness of winter.

As candles were emblems of the divine vitalizing power of the sun, and were carried in procession at the beginning of February as a protection against plague, famine, pestilence and earthquake, in the pre-Christian Feast of Lights, it would not be inappropriate for them to be blessed, distributed and similarly treated at the end of the Christmas Festival to

[1] Baumstark, *Liturgia Romana e Liturgia dell' Esarcato*, Rome, 1904, Chap. viii, 2, pp. 166f.
[2] Brand, *Popular Antiquities*, i, p. 50; J. Ramsay, *Scotland and Scotsmen in the Eighteenth Century*, ii, Edinburgh, 1888, p. 447.

commemorate the presentation of the 'Son of righteousness' in the Temple of his heavenly Father. Furthermore, as the sacred light became a symbol of the Christ Child who was declared to be 'the light to lighten the gentiles and the glory of his people Israel', so Mary as the Theotokos came into greater prominence as the 'light-bearer', and she too had her place and part in Candlemas since it celebrated also her 'purification'. The procession depicted the entry into the world of the 'True Light'; the blessing and distribution of the candles, to be carried in the penitential manner anticlockwise, indicated his illumination of the whole world; and the Mass, the Purification of the Blessed Virgin Mary which followed, brought the Incarnation, 'translating mankind from the power of darkness into the clear light of his beloved Son', into relation with the 'light-bearer'. The penitential character of the procession was in accord with the purificatory preparation in the ancient ceremonies, while the candle ritual was derived from the torch and light symbolism brought into conjunction with that of the Presentation in the Temple. Taken collectively this was a fitting conclusion to the Feast of the Nativity.

## The Annunciation

In addition to the Candlemas procession, Sergius instituted a stational procession on March 25th from the church of St Adrian to the basilica of Santa Maria Maggiore on the occasion of the Feast of the Annunciation. Exactly when the appearance of the Archangel Gabriel to Mary to announce her virginal conception was accorded a festival is not known. Once, however, the date of the Nativity had been fixed on December 25th the prior event could be observed most appropriately on March 25th. But this raised a problem in the East as the Council of Laodicea in the fourth century forbade the keeping of holy days in Lent, except on Saturdays and Sundays.[1] This situation was relieved by an exception being made in favour of its observance as a concession at the Council of Trullo in 692. In the West when it was first kept in Spain it

[1] J. D. Mansi, *Sacrorum Conciliorum Collectio*, ii, Florence, 1759, p. 572.

was held on different dates in different places, until the Council of Toledo in 656 fixed December 18th as the date to avoid its occurring in Lent or Eastertide. But in the Mozarabic rite the same Mass was appointed for both December 18th and March 25th.[1] This procedure was later adopted in Rome, but no mention of the Feast was made in the list of festivals ordered by the Council of Metz in 813.

As it was not known apparently at the Synod which assembled at Laodicea in 327, and the first mention of it in the West is in the Gelasian Sacramentary in the seventh-century manuscript, and in a manuscript of the Gregorian Sacramentary in the next century, in Rome it may have arisen in the seventh century.[2] In the East it would seem to have been a product of the fifth century about the time of the Council of Ephesus in 431, and soon after this it was observed in Spain. At first, like Candlemas, it was a Dominical Festival since it commemorated the virginal conception of Christ, and it was not until the Marian cultus developed after the Council of Ephesus that it was held primarily in honour of the Mother of God. In the West originally it was observed only in countries of the Gallican rite and then it was held in the middle of January.[3] Therefore, as a special commemoration the Annunciation has never been rigidly fixed to March 25th, in spite of its date in relation to Christmas Day. In the Ambrosian rite in Milan it was assigned to the first Sunday in Advent, while the Armenians kept it on the Eve of the Epiphany until they transferred it to April 7th.

## The Assumption of the Blessed Virgin Mary

Of the remaining Marian festivals, the Assumption or Dormition (i.e. the Falling Asleep) of the Blessed Virgin Mary, is said by Nicephorus Callistus (*c.* 1256–1335) to have been instituted by the Emperor Maurice (580–602),[4] though it may have been observed in Syria and Palestine in the previous century, and at Antioch in the fourth century. In Egypt and

---

[1] *P.L.*, lxxxv, 170, 734.   [2] Duchesne, *op. cit.*, p. 262.
[3] *P.L.*, lxxi, 713.   [4] *Hist. Eccles.*, xvii, 28.

Arabia, and in the Gallican liturgy, it was celebrated on January 18th in association with the Epiphany in the sixth century, but although it became the principal Marian Festival—'*Natalis sanctae Mariae*'—as it was called in the lectionary of Würzburg—its universal observance was only very gradually established outside Byzantium.

In all probability the festival arose as a commemoration of the dedication of a church on August 15th rather than, as has been suggested, by decree of the Council of Ephesus, or introduced into Rome by St Damascus. But behind it lay a long tradition of apocryphal and Gnostic speculation concerning the mysterious death of the Virgin and the miraculous assumption of her body either on the way to burial or after three days. Thus, in a Collyridian legend of her death her body was said to have been wafted on a cloud to Jerusalem and in the presence of the Apostles her soul was taken from it to Paradise by the Archangel Gabriel. When her mortal remains were laid in a tomb in the valley of Jehoshaphat Christ appeared and reunited them with her soul which had been brought back from Paradise for the purpose by St Michael.[1] This apocryphal story recorded in the *De Obitu S. Dominae* and in *De Transitu Virginis Mariae Liber* was refuted by Epiphanius who maintained that while her death and burial were surrounded with the honour due to her sanctity, and her body was 'blessed and glorified, no one knows her end'.[2]

It was not until after the Council of Ephesus in 431, when in reaction to the Nestorian heresy which appeared to belittle the divinity of Christ by asserting that Mary gave birth to a man who was subsequently united with the Son of God, she was declared to be the Theotokos, the Mother of God, that in due course her corporeal assumption became a widespread pious belief. With the development of her cultus the fabulous traditions in the apocryphal books and in heretical treatises were uncritically accepted, until in the sixth century Gregory of Tours incorporated the Collyridian legend in the Gallican Mass for August 15th. Soon the feast was designated the

[1] *Bibliotheca Patrum Maxima*, ii, p. 212.  [2] *Panarion*, 78, 11, 24.

'Assumption', a title that first appeared in the canons of Bishop Sonnatius of Rheims about 630.

Like the other three festivals of the Virgin, the Purification, the Annunciation, and the Nativity, the Assumption was in all probability of Eastern origin, imported into the West from Byzantium.[1] In the Gallican Sacramentary the feast is des-cribed as the '*Assumptio*' but no reference is made to the legend. This may suggest that a Mass commemorating the death of the Virgin was said on August 15th, since the feast seems to have been observed in Rome at Santa Maria Maggiore in the sixth century. By the time of Sergius it was a major festival, and in the ninth century it was provided with a vigil and an octave, except in the Ambrosian rite at Milan. It was not, however, until as recently as 1950 that the doctrine of the corporeal assumption was declared *ex cathedra* by Papal decree to be a *de fide* article of faith, though the belief had been increasingly widely held in the West as well as in the East since it was first formulated by Gregory of Tours in the sixth century.

The choice of August 15th for the principal Marian Festival gave it a seasonal significance inasmuch as its celebration coincided with the ingathering of harvest in southern Europe. Indeed, the feast became known as Our Lady in Harvest, held in honour of the triumphant Assumption of the Queen of Heaven to be reunited with her divine Son as the 'Bride of Christ'—a status inherited from that of the 'Bride Church'.[2] In this capacity she exercised her intercessory functions in the celestial realms on behalf of struggling humanity on earth. She shared in her Son's victory over sin, concupiscence and death, so that her aid was readily sought for all the needs of mankind, material and spiritual alike. In an age accustomed to the supernatural control of natural forces, the Mother of the Redeemer as Theotokos occupied a key position in this process. Her chief festival, therefore, occuring at the time of harvest, became a significant seasonal event in the liturgical calendar

[1] Duchesne, *op. cit.*, pp. 271f.
[2] James, *The Cult of the Mother Goddess*, 1959, pp. 202ff.

corresponding in time and content to its pagan predecessors, and deriving some of its symbolism from the earlier harvest rituals. Thus, in Italy it ousted festivals like that of Diana on August 13th, at the height of summer when the fields were golden with corn, the trees laden with fruit, and the vines with bunches of ripening grapes. Then was the moment to rejoice for the beneficence of the bountiful Mother, greeted not inappropriately as Our Lady in Harvest, and to seek her protection against the destructive forces lest the kindly fruits of the earth should fail to come to maturity and be safely gathered.[1] Farther north where the harvest was delayed until the autumn, or after the summer rains, harvest rites were dedicated to her; at the feast of her Nativity on September 8th.

[1] E. Lucius, *Die Anfänge des Heiligenkultes in der Christlichen Kirche*, Tübingen, 1904, pp. 488f., 521.

# CHAPTER VIII

# The Drama of the Medieval Church

## THE DRAMATIZATION OF THE LITURGY

In the Middle Ages the seasonal festivals frequently included a sacred drama arising out of the liturgical year, portraying the events proper to the occasion. The antiphonal singing of the sentences, usually from the scriptures, before and after the psalms in the divine office and at the *Introit* in the liturgy, and their responses, took the form of dialogues. Similarly, the gestures of the sacred ministers in the Mass, itself a ritual representation of redemption in its various aspects, were in the nature of a drama, interpreted in relation to the Feast of the Nativity, Good Friday, Easter and Whitsun, culminating in the Corpus Christi processions and Mystery plays. It was within this framework, as the Christian counterpart of the earlier death and resurrection ritual, that the medieval drama emerged, though as Professor Young has pointed out, dramatic externalities of this kind must not be mistaken for genuine drama itself in which the essential element is not forms of speech and movement, but impersonation.[1] Moreover, some of the plays were composed from Biblical and other sources expressly for the purpose by individual authors.[2]

## THE NATIVITY PLAYS

Nevertheless, from the ninth century the practice arose of supplementing the sentences of the psalms used as the *Introit* in the Mass appointed for certain festivals like Christmas and Easter by additional words and melodies, sung by the choir in the form of a question calling for a response from the congregation. This antiphonal singing, like the Greek Mystery acts of Dionysus, helped to develop the drama. For instance, on

[1] *The Drama of the Medieval Church*, ii, O.U.P., 1935, p. 80.
[2] O. Cargill, *Drama and Liturgy*, New York, 1930.

Christmas Day an amplification or embellishment known as a trope, ascribed to Tutilo of St Gall, was as follows: 'Today must we sing of a Child, whom in unspeakable wise His Father begat before all times, and whom within time, a glorious mother brought forth.' Then came the *interrogato*, 'Who is this Child whom ye proclaim worthy of so great laudations? Tell us that we also may praise Him.' The response follows, 'This is He whose coming to earth the prophetic and chosen initiate into the mysteries of God foresaw and pointed out long before and foretold.'

This dialogue was elaborated into a symbolic drama with two deacons behind the altar singing, 'Whom seek ye, say ye shepherds?', and two cantors in the choir in the guise of shepherds replying. In due course was added a long series of Old Testament characters and incidents in the form of *Prophetae* leading up to the Nativity, portrayed by the placing of the *bambino* in the crib (commonly known as the *praesepe*) behind the altar, and the visit of the Magi to Bethlehem. Singing boys concealed in the triforium played the role of the heavenly host breaking forth into an exultant *Gloria in Excelsis* at the appropriate moment as the shepherds in the persons of five cantors advanced towards the *praesepe* where two mid-wives awaited them. Two priests with two *obstetrices* met them singing *quem quaeritis*, and the play closed with the adoration of the shepherds.[1]

### The Stella Plays

In the *Ordinarium* of Amiens (1291) the *bambino* was placed in the crib, and with the growth of the Stella drama, in addition to the visit of the shepherds the journey of the Three Kings was symbolized by the movement of the Star across the choir. The simplest Stella version of the Epiphany plays is from Limoges, and consists of a ceremonial entry of the Magi to the choir with their gifts of myrrh representing suffering and death, gold and incense typifying life and resurrection. Following the star to

[1] E. K. Chambers, *The Medieval Stage*, ii, O.U.P., 1903, pp. 8ff.; C. Davidson, *English Mystery Plays*, Yale, 1892, pp. 50ff.

the high altar they presented their offerings, each contained in a gilt cup. The birth of Christ was then announced by a boy, and the royal visitors retired to the sacristy.[1] In the Rouen *Officium Stellae* belonging to the fourteenth century, the three were directed to approach from the east, north and south of the church meeting at the altar where they embraced and sang *Eamus ergo, et inquiramus eum, offerantes ei munera; aurum thus et mirrbant.* A procession formed, apparently before the Mass, immediately after the *Te Deum* at the end of Matins,[2] and went to the nave while the star was lighted over the altar near an image of the Virgin. The Magi moved towards it singing *Ecce Magi ab Oriente venerunt Jerosolymam,* and at the altar of the Cross arranged as a crib, were met by two of the assistants in dalmatics, with whom they engaged in a dialogue. While the congregation offered their gifts the Magi fell asleep and were warned by an angel to return home another way. This was enacted by the procession going to the choir by a side aisle, and the Mass then began.[3]

An imposing procession was a feature of the Stella play at Milan in 1336, and as the drama developed it assumed more elaborate proportions.[4] To the procession of the Three Kings with their gifts guided by the star, and the reading of the liturgi-cal gospel, in due course were added other scenes connected with the Nativity, such as the Massacre of the Innocents and the meeting with Herod.[5] This led to the fusion of the three Christ-mas plays—the *Pastores,* or Shepherds' play, the Rachel play depicting the killing of the Innocents, and the Stella play—into one great Nativity drama. Thus, in the Strasbourg play the Magi met the shepherds on their way home from Bethlehem after leaving Herod, who incidentally assumed increasing import-ance as an impersonation of the principle of evil represented

---

[1] Martene, *De Antiquis Eccles, Retibus,* iii, Venice, 1788, p. 44.

[2] *P.L.,* cxlvii, 43.

[3] Davidson, *op. cit.,* pp. 50 ff.

[4] Chambers, *Book of Days,* i, 1863, p. 62.

[5] E. K. Chambers, *Medieval Stage,* ii, pp. 47 ff.; L. Petit de Julleville, *Les Mystères,* i, *Histoire du Théâtre de France en Moyen Age,* Paris, 1880, pp. 52 ff.

as a raging tyrant. In the Freising texts the three episodes are combined, the scene opening with the angelic salutation from one of the *Pastores*, followed by the meeting of the Magi with Herod, the Dream of St Joseph, the Flight into Egypt and the grief of Rachel weeping for her children after the Massacre of the Innocents. But the Stella play is absent in this manu‑ script although the first text devotes much of its space to the Magi and their relations with Herod.[1]

## *The Prophetae*

Finally, the *Prophetae*, based on the *Sermo contra Judaeos Paganos et Arianos de Symbolo*, attributed in the Middle Ages to St Augustine but actually the work of a sixth‑century author, presented dramatically a series of Messianic prophets which included Moses, David, Isaiah, Jeremiah and Daniel, together with Simeon, Zacharias, St John the Baptist, and three pagans, Virgil, Nebuchadnezzar and the Erythraean Sibyl, each giving his testimony foretelling the coming of Christ. The utterances appear to have been delivered by a single person who recited the expositions. In addition to this sermon there were other versions of the *lectio* used at Matins on Christmas Day, narrated by several speakers, as is shown in the homily printed in 1594 from the cathedral of Salerno, recited at the end of the first Mass at dawn on Christmas morning. After reading the introductory passage addressed to the Jews, the lector summoned the thirteen witnesses in turn to give their testimony.[2]

In another version from the monastery of St Martialis at Limoges, set to music but with no stage directions, in place of Zacharias Israel was substituted, and Elizabeth, the wife of Zacharias, was added. Otherwise the speakers and the Pro‑ phecies were practically the same, but as they were arranged in

[1] E. du Méril, *Origines latines du Théâtre moderne*, Paris, 1896, pp. 156, 162, 175.

[2] M. Sepet, 'Les prophètes du Christ', *Bibliothèque de l'École de Chartres*, xxviii, 1867, pp. 1 ff., 211 ff.; Young, *op. cit.*, ii, pp. 133 ff.; Chambers, *Medieval Stage*, ii, pp. 52 ff.

the correct chronological order it would appear to have been a revision of the former documents. This is also apparent in the thirteenth-century *Prophetae* from the cathedral of Laon containing a list of characters and descriptions of their appearance, and mode of dress, Moses carrying the tables of stone, Isaiah bearded, Daniel depicted as a youth, Elizabeth in a state of pregnancy and John the Baptist wearing a hair shirt. Virgil was to have a crown of ivy and the Sibyls to be in a state of frenzy. At the end the reception of the Holy Child by Simeon at the Presentation in the Temple was portrayed, and Balaam and his ass dramatically entered in an animated scene, the ass being impersonated by a boy. The Balaam episode was further developed in the Rouen version in the *Festum Asinorum*, and the story of the casting of Shadrach, Meshach and Abednego into the fiery furnace, recorded in Daniel iii, 24–35, was dramatized with an actual furnace.[1]

## Benediktbeuern Christmas Play

As scenic effects and properties were increased the liturgical tropes and ceremonial offices developed into Mystery and Miracle plays in which the emphasis was on the story portrayed rather than on the liturgical action, designed for the purpose of instructing the masses ignorant of Latin in the mysteries of the Christian faith at the appropriate seasons of their commemoration. Thus, as the drama on the Nativity and childhood of Christ was gradually shaped out of the Christmas liturgy and offices, the story of the Nativity in its various aspects was dramatically represented from its foreshadowing in the Old Dispensation to its fulfilment in the sequence of events centred at Bethlehem. This is shown in the somewhat confused and incomplete but comprehensive Christmas play produced by the *scholares vagantes*, as the wandering scholars were called, from the abbey of Benediktbeuern in Bavaria in the thirteenth century. Here the *Prophetae*,

[1] Chevalier, *Ordinaires de l'Église cathédral de Laon*, 1897; Young, *op. cit.*, ii, pp. 145 ff., 154.

the Annunciation, the *Pastores*, the Stellas, the Massacre of the Innocents, the Herod episodes, the Flight into Egypt, and the death of Herod, were combined. The prophets, with St Augustine in the centre, foretold the coming of Christ in the prologue presenting the general theme of the *Ordo Prophetarum*. Isaiah, Daniel, the Sibyl, Aaron and Balaam stood at the right, and on the left the chief of the synagogue and a group of Jews, in active opposition. After each of the prophets had sung their prophecies and the Sibyl made her gesticulations gazing at the star above her, the Archisynagogus ridiculed their utterances, stamping his feet. The Boy Bishop called upon St Augustine to refute the Jews, and an animated debate ensued concerning the probability of the Virgin Birth, the choir of prophets replying *Res miranda* and that of the Jews *Res neganda*. The Annunciation followed as a dialogue between the Virgin and the angel, this scene being an essential feature of the Christmas cycle between the *Prophetae* and the *Pastores*. It was sometimes performed, however, independently as a liturgical drama on either March 25th or on the Wednesday after December 13th in the Advent Ember week, with considerable elaboration at Tournai and Hildesheim in the thirteenth century, in the cathedral at Cividale in Italy, in Germany in the fourteenth, and in Belgium and Holland in the fifteenth century.[1]

After the representation of the visit of Mary to her cousin Elizabeth, the accouchement of Mary and the appearance of the star were enacted, the choir hailing the birth of Christ. The Three Kings appeared from different directions, each repeating four stanzas concerning the meaning of the star, and proceeding on their way were confronted with the messengers of Herod, who, after consultation with the leader of the synagogue received them and allowed them to depart towards Bethlehem. The shepherds now appeared for the first time, and the angelic choir having sung the *Gloria in Excelsis*, they proceeded to the *praesepe* to adore. On the way home they met the Magi, told them of what they had heard and seen, and sent

[1] Young, *op. cit.*, ii, pp. 245 ff.

them too to Bethlehem to make their offerings to the Christ Child. Their return by another route to avoid Jerusalem, and the command of Herod to slaughter the infants were enacted vividly, followed by the death of Herod and his being carried to hell by demons. Then came the dispatch of Joseph to Egypt with the Young Child and his mother, the falling down of the idols on their arrival, and the conversion of the Egyptian priests, the play ending with a hymn of vengeance against Herod and the Jews.[1]

In this combination most of the dramatic forms connected with the Christmas season were included—the *Prophetae* were reduced in number to five, and St Augustine and the Archi-synagogus were introduced to represent the Church and the Jews. The Boy Bishop was a new character borrowed from the Holy Innocents' Day revels as St Augustine had been derived from the apocryphal *Sermo contra Judaeos* of the *Prophetae* attributed to him, and the similar pseudo-Augustinian discourse, *De Altercatione Ecclesiae et Synagogae Dialogus*.[2] The Annunciation scene with which the play proper began, came from the Marian group, and the Nativity, the arrival of the star and the Magi, the Herod episodes, the Shepherds, and the return of the Kings, were derived from the Christmas cycle with the addition of the devil apparently from the Passion plays, and foreshadowing the Moralities. The laments of the mothers over their slain infants belonged to the Rachel *Ordo* set in metrical form, as did the Flight into Egypt, but the grim presentation of the death of Herod was a new element having a counterpart in the *Martyrology* of Bede.[3] Therefore, it was a composite production perhaps belonging to the wandering scholars (*vagantes*) with some attempt at sophistication, as in the discussion among the Magi about the new star, combined in the antics of the leader of the synagogue with humour, which was conspicuously absent in the assurance of the refutation by the Boy Bishop, who elsewhere was a comic figure. Some of the

[1] du Méril, *op. cit.*, p. 187; Young, *op. cit.*, ii, pp. 172 ff.
[2] *P.L.*, xlii, 1131–40.
[3] *P.L.*, xciv, 1144.

scenes (e.g. the death of Herod) presupposed realistic production and more properties than were likely to have been available. Therefore, in all probability they had to be considerably modified in presentation, and it is not very probable that the Benediktbeuern was played in church, though doubtless it was performed in some building such as a monastery school.

## THE EASTER AND PASSION PLAYS
### The Burial of the Host and of the Cross

It was around the elaborate liturgical observances of Holy Week, Good Friday and Easter that the drama of the medieval Church became most highly developed. The Mass itself being the anamnesis of the Death and Resurrection of Christ as Redeemer perpetuating for all time all that this signified in Catholic theology, there could be no more suitable occasion for interpolations in the liturgical text in the form of tropes to occur. Thus, the Easter play, or *Resurrexi*, emerged from the *Quem quaeritis in sepulchro Christicolae*, with its response, *Jesus Nazarenum crucifixum, O coelicolae. Non est hic, surrexit sicut praedixerat; Ite, nuntiate quia surrexit de sepulchro. Resurrexi.* This was combined with the *Depositio*, or burial of the Host in a *sepulchrum* after the Mass of the Presanctified on Good Friday morning or Vespers in the afternoon. There it remained until it was taken up before Matins on Easter Day as a symbolic representation of the Resurrection. Although it was an extra-liturgical ceremony, it provided a dramatic element which was in line with the *Quem quaeritis* trope in the Easter Mass and its subsequent developments, and made a popular appeal. Thus, a watch was kept at the *sepulchrum* until Matins on Easter morning when the Host, sometimes accompanied by the Cross that had been venerated on Good Friday and buried with the 'Most Holy' (i.e. the reserved Host), was carried back to the altar amid great rejoicing, as at the Hilaria in Ancient Rome. Three priests in copes and carrying censers, representing the Three Marys at the empty tomb, were asked by an Angel,

'Whom seek ye?'. After making the proper reply they were told to proclaim far and wide that the Lord had risen. Thereupon they sang the antiphon *Surrexit enim, sicut dixit dominus, Alleluia.*[1]

The *Depositio* and *Elevatio* would seem to have arisen out of the custom of carrying the Host after the Mass on Maundy Thursday to the place of 'repose' other than the altar on which It had been consecrated and depositing It in an 'urn'. This was not far removed in idea from the *Depositio* notwithstanding the denial of the Sacred Congregation of Rites of the identification of the *reposoir* (i.e. the place of repose) with the sepulchre of Christ.[2] But whatever may have been the origin of the burial of the Host and of the Cross, it arose within the context of the Maundy Thursday and Good Friday ceremonial and its symbolism, and when it became an established, though not universal practice in the Middle Ages it was closely associated with the *Quem quaeritis* trope, which was sung not later than the tenth century at the Mass of Easter. The stage was now set for the Easter drama. To the simple symbolical enactment of the Death and Resurrection of Christ in the *Depositio*, the *Elevatio*, and the trope was added the representation of the visit of the Three Marys, the Angel and the Apostles St Peter and St John to the tomb; and the meeting of the Risen Lord with St Mary Magdalen in the garden. Illustrating these aspects of the Easter story more than four hundred tropes and offices are known in the extant texts,[3] and to them other scenes in due course were added, such as the *Peregrinus*, or journey of the two Apostles to Emmaus on the afternoon of Easter Day and their meeting with the Risen Christ, which was appended to Vespers of Easter Monday in France, Germany and England in the twelfth century.

[1] du Méril, *op. cit.*, pp. 96 ff.; Young, *op. cit.*, i, pp. 112 ff.; Chambers, *Medieval Stage*, ii, pp. 16 ff.; N. C. Brooks, *The Sepulchre of Christ in Art and Liturgy*, Urbana, 1921, pp. 33 ff., 49 ff.          [2] *Decreta*, iv, 419 ff.

[3] Young, *op. cit.*, i, pp. 239 ff., 576; for bibliography cf. C. Lange, *Die lateinischen Osterfeiern*, Munich, 1887; Chambers, *Medieval Stage*, ii, pp. 9 f., 306 ff.

*The Resurrection Drama*

Starting from the *Quem quaeritis* trope addressed by the Three Marys to the choir, the visit to the tomb, portrayed by the altar, was enacted by such acts as the Marys vested in copes raising the frontal, or peering behind it, with the Angel wearing an alb sitting near by in silence until he said, *Venite et videte*, and after a pause, *non est hic*. They then returned and proclaimed the Resurrection, after which the *Te Deum* was sung, concluding with the refrain, *Alleluia, resurrexit Dominus*. This procedure with many variations was gradually enlarged in the eleventh century by the dramatization of the Sequence after the Epistle, the *Victimae paschali* being sung in dialogue, each of the women singing one of the sentences and then, in response to the inter- rogation of the cantor, the reply. The procession sometimes was extended to include visits to the side altars *en route* to the high altar, occasionally repeating the *Surrexit, non est hic*, in spite of their not having been made aware of the Resurrection before their arrival at the tomb. When the *Visitatio* was combined with the *Depositio*, as at Laon, a priest emerged from the sepulchre with a Host in a chalice which was carried in procession to the crucifix while *Resurrexit Dominus* and *Cum rex gloriae* were sung, together with *Christus resurgens* and *Discant nunc Judaei* at the crucifix. Then the priest placed the chalice on the high altar. A similar ceremony recurred near by at Soissons where after the announcement of the Resurrection the Host was taken from the sepulchre to the high altar before Matins on Easter Day.

In the next stage in the development St Peter and St Paul made their appearance to confirm the report of the Marys after this had been duly announced, hastening to the tomb after the dismissal of the women by the Angel. The grave-clothes now began to be displayed, and congregational singing in the vernacular to take the place of Latin after the *Te Deum*. In the version from the church of St John the Evangelist, Dublin, the Marys carried pyxes for boxes of ointment to anoint the body, and when they met the Apostles on leaving the sepulchre the Magdalen sang the first part of the Sequence. They then went to the tomb and with their testimony the play closed.[1] The grave-clothes were omitted, whereas in a version from the monastery of St Lambrecht they were given considerable prominence, being wrapped over the arms and head of the Cross, and displayed by the Marys when they elevated the Cross.

The final stage was reached, probably in the twelfth century, when Christ himself was introduced conversing with Mary Magdalen in the garden. At first this scene, known as a *Hortulanus*, based on the narrative in St John xx, 11–18, recorded in the antiphons, took the place of the appearances to the Apostles. In the Rouen version after the Marys had withdrawn the Magdalen approached the high altar and a canon impersonating the Risen Lord entered from the left side. The dialogue then began in which the other Marys took part in unison. It would seem that the Christus must have been expected to leave when this discourse was finished as he was directed to reappear to all three of the women at the right end of the altar with the words, *Avete, nolite timere* taken from the Matthaean narrative. When he had left the stage the Marys turned towards the chorus singing *Resurrexit Dominus*.[2]

In most of the *Visitatio* texts which contain this scene there is a good deal of confusion in the presentation of the incidents as a result of the intermixture of verses in the antiphons and offices, taken from the several accounts of the post-Resurrection appearances in the Gospel narratives, involving discrepancies in their dramatization. Moreover, each of the plays has a history of its own with special liturgical features in the text, such as the laments of the women, the introduction of a second angel, the order of the appearances of the Christus to St Mary Magdalen alone and to the Three Marys together. The fusion with the *Elevatio* and the *Quem quaeritis*, and the addition of other scenes (e.g. the *Peregrinus*, and the Supper at Emmaus, which give rise to a separate play of the incredulity of St Thomas), inevitably produced complications. Nevertheless, taken collectively the Easter drama enacted the principal events

[1] Chambers, *Medieval Stage*, ii, pp. 315 ff.; Young, *op. cit.*, ii, p. 347.
[2] *Ibid.*, pp. 370 ff., 660 f.

connected with the Resurrection, from the sealing of the tomb, the setting of the watch, the visit of the Marys with their embalming spices and ointments, to the Resurrection (i.e. the *Quem quaeritis*) and its announcement to Pilate, the appearances to St Mary Magdalen alone and to the Three Marys together, their return to the Apostles, the journey to Emmaus, and the St Thomas incident.

## The Play of the Ascension

Finally, the forty days of Eastertide were brought to a close with the dramatization of the Ascension on the Thursday after the fifth Sunday after Easter, which eventually became known as Ascension Day. The Mass provided the *Introit* trope, *Quem creditis super astra ascendisse, O Christicolae?* but there is no indication of its having developed into a play like that in the liturgy for Easter Day. It was rather in conjunction with the processions considered in the last chapter that symbolic actions were employed to give effect to the festival, as when a cross was lifted up by two priests at the words *Ascendo ad Patrem* during the course of the procession before the Mass, or clerics climbed on to a raised platform at this point, or, again, mounting the pulpit at the singing of the response *Non vos relinquam*. In the sixteenth century a figure of Christ was introduced and raised up three times at the end of None and placed on a platform in front of the choir, where it was censed and asperged during the singing of *Ascendo ad Patrem* and *Viri Galilaei*. Then it was drawn up through an opening in the roof and water and fragments of wafers were thrown down.[1]

An earlier (fourteenth-century) text from Moosburg in Bavaria, printed by Young,[2] conforms more closely to the liturgical pattern. The ceremony, it is stated, occurs after Vespers on Ascension Day in a specially constructed enclosure called *tentorium* in the middle of the nave, representing the Mount Horeb or Sinai, not the Mount of Olives as in the Biblical narrative (Acts i, 12). Within is an image of Christ to which

[1] *Agenda Bambergensia*, Ingolstadt, 1587, pp. 627 ff.
[2] *Op. cit.*, i, pp. 483 ff.

ropes are attached and a ring of flowers enclosing the representa‑ tion of a dove, and another in the likeness of an angel. Twelve of the choir play the role of the Apostles, each with his name on his crown and carrying his symbol. The Virgin is clothed as a widow and two angels have wings and chaplets of flowers. Proceeding from the sacristy to the *tentorium* they sing the response *Post passionem*, to which reply is made in the words of the antiphon, *Pater*, *manifestavi* and *Ascendo*, by the person care‑ fully concealed who impersonates Christ. The image is then drawn up towards the roof and the dove and the angel are lowered over it while the Apostolic choir sing a liturgical text. A dialogue between Christ and Philip ensues, the antiphon *Ascendo* is repeated, and the effigy is raised higher. Mary sings the hymn *Jesu, nostra redemptio*, and the Christus and the Apostles sing additional antiphons. After the *Ascendo* has been sung for the third time the image is drawn through the roof, the two angels sing *Viri Galilaei* and the Apostles withdraw.

Although the scenic effects, which include this realistic treatment of the effigy in the act of ascension, brings the representation definitely within the category of a play, yet it retained a liturgical setting with its antiphons and versicles, and passages arranged and rendered in the customary manner based on the Mass, the trope bearing a very close resemblance to that of the Easter *Quem quaeritis*. And there does not appear to be any particular reason for supposing that it did not follow a similar line of development into a liturgical drama, and finally into a Mystery play when some of the incidents in the non‑ liturgical ceremonies connected with the feast were introduced.

## Pentecost

The culmination of the Resurrection theme was reached with the enactment of the Descent of the Holy Ghost upon the Apostles at Pentecost, fifty days after the beginning of the Easter Festival. This event lent itself to dramatic symbolization in a variety of forms, and it was these which characterized the Whitsun drama rather than the liturgical setting. Nevertheless, the ceremonial was associated with the liturgy and the divine

office, as at the other important seasonal festivals, being performed either in conjunction with the Mass or after one of the
offices. Thus, the widespread use of the dove lowered into the
church from the hole in the roof during the singing of the
*Veni Creator* (the office hymn at Terce at Whitsuntide), or in
the course of the Mass, sometimes accompanied with flowers,
water, burning tow, wafers and leaves, and with the swinging
of a huge censer up and down the nave.[1] On the roof an antiphon was sung by two choir boys, but no attempt appears to
have been made to dramatize the assembly of the disciples in
the Cenaculum, or Upper Room, at Jerusalem, or the actual
descent upon them of the tongues of fire.

## The Passion Play

Similarly, although Holy Week afforded exactly the background for the development of a Passion drama, no attempt
was made to introduce a dramatic representation of the Passion
narratives in the Maundy Thursday and Good Friday liturgies.
The Mass being the divinely ordained perpetuation of the
sacrificial immolation of the Saviour of mankind, doubtless
no further demonstration of this supreme offering was felt to
be required, or indeed, desirable, at this solemn season. The
procession of palms and the singing of the Passion on Palm
Sunday; the *Mandatum*, the ceremonies connected with the
altar of repose and the stripping of the altars, and Tenebrae on
Maundy Thursday; and the singing of the Passion, the Veneration of the Cross, the Reproaches and the Mass of the Presanctified on Good Friday, supplied sufficient dramatic enactment
of the events in the official services of the Church without any
further embellishment or dramatization. This in all probability explains the absence of Passion plays earlier than the
thirteenth century, though the extra-liturgical *Depositio* and
*Elevatio* paved the way for the Easter sepulchre rites, as did the
Reproaches for the *Planctus*, or laments of the Mater dolorosa,
and those who suffered with her on Calvary at the foot of the
Cross, and on their approach to the tomb on Easter morning.

[1] Chambers, *Medieval Stage*, ii, p. 66.

Nevertheless, the number of representations of the Crucifixion in the medieval Church were surprisingly few, and late in making their appearance. Holy Week reaching its climax on Easter Day already was so very fully equipped with visible and audible representations of the solemn season commemorated and its sequence of events, that little or no opportunity remained for the introduction of a Passion play as an independent entity. It sufficed to elaborate the *Planctus* on Good Friday giving greater emphasis to the expressions of intense emotion on the part of the Virgin, such as occurred in the Laments of Mary in the apocryphal Gospel of Nicodemus.[1] The Laments almost certainly were the local beginning of the Passion play which established itself beside the drama of the Resurrection.[2] In addition to these lamentations typical of a mourning ceremonial, the Descent from the Cross, the healing of Longinus the centurion, the entombment and the setting of the Watch, were introduced, together with the figure of Pilate, St Mary Magdalen and her companions.

It was apparently from concentration upon the burial of Christ in the tomb of Joseph of Arimathea that the Passion play emerged as a prelude to the Easter Resurrection plays. This is shown in the case of the Benediktbeuern Resurrection play in the *Carmina Burana* Manuscript. This opens with the entry of Pilate with his wife and escort, Herod and his attendants, the high priests, the merchant and his wife and Mary Magdalen. After a few short scenes in the life of Christ representing the calling of St Peter and St Andrew, the colloquy with Zachaeus and the healing of Bartimaeus, extracts from the Palm Sunday processionals are sung. The meal in the house of Simon the Pharisee is next portrayed, together with the career of Mary Magdalen, first as a courtesan and then as a penitent anointing the feet of Jesus and receiving absolution from him before she departs in a state of grief for her past sins. Further short scenes represent the raising of Lazarus, Judas' visit to the high priests, the Last Supper, the trials and the Crucifixion, in which the

[1] Tischendorf, *Evangelia Apocrypha*, 1879, pp. livff.
[2] Julleville, *op. cit.*, ii, p. 40.

Laments of Mary are the principal feature, ending with the piercing of the side of the dying Christ by Longinus amid the mockery of the Jews.

Throughout the stress is laid on the Magdalen's dual capacity as 'the woman who was a sinner' and the sister of Lazarus. This leads up to the anointings in the Easter plays. Next to her Mary, the Mother of Jesus, is the dominant figure whose grief at the Cross is given great prominence and full vent in the form of a *Planctus Mariae*. But the composition is not well conceived and the scriptural order often is abandoned, while the abrupt ending is indicative of its not being a complete and independent play in itself. In a briefer version of this play in laboured prose without any embellishments the sequence of events from the Last Supper to the Entombment is portrayed, the text largely taken from the Vulgate of the Gospels with the Matthaean narrative as the basic source. Here again, the Marian *planctus* at the death of Christ is the most arresting feature of the play, possibly with utterances from the other Marys and St John. Two scenes are given simultaneous representation, Judas withdrawing to confer with the high priests, and the Last Supper continuing in silence, instead of the traitor having previously arranged for the betrayal as in the Gospel narrative (St Matthew xxvi, 14–16). Whether the play was in fact performed in association with the liturgy is not clear, but immediately following the text an Easter play begins, probably at Matins.

As the Passion play developed it attached to itself the Easter play as a sequel, and the Creation drama formed a prelude, to complete the story of Redemption. Thus, the Vienna Passion play, which is one of the oldest known dating from the beginning of the fourteenth century, starts with the Creation and the rebellion and expulsion of Lucifer, and his fallen angels, followed by the Fall of man. Prominence is given to the Devil and the temptation of Eve, but although it ends with the Last Supper in the extant version, originally it may have continued to the end of the Easter triumph like the Frankfort, Feising and Augsburg plays, which open with the creation of man and close with the descent of the Holy Ghost.[1] It is to this cycle that the great Bavarian and Tyrolese Passion plays belong, the most familiar survival of which is the well-known enactment of the Passion and Death of Christ at Oberammergau in Upper Bavaria, performed for the first time in 1633 in gratitude for the cessation of a plague, when it was vowed to repeat the performances every tenth year until 1674, and from 1680 onwards in the decimal years. In this class of drama the Creation story is made the basis of the mystery of Redemption, the Crucified and Risen Christ being represented as the Second Adam.

## The Harrowing of Hell

Closely connected with the introduction of Adam and Satan into the Passion play, sometimes in a humorous vein suggesting secular influences, the Harrowing of Hell often became a popular feature, based on the *Descensus Christi ad infernos* and his conquest of Satan to liberate Adam and the Old Testament saints from Limbo. This story from the apocryphal Gospel of Nicodemus, assigned to the second or third century, gives an account of the interval between the death of Christ on Good Friday afternoon and his resurrection on Easter morning, spent in Limbo in bursting the gates of Hell which adjoined the abode of souls awaiting the beatific vision. This accomplished, the patriarchs and the rest of the faithful awaiting his arrival were released and Satan was bound.[2] This event is related in the English poems by Caedmon and Cynewulf, but an earlier medieval version occurs in a dialogue in East Midland dialect dating from the end of the thirteenth century. But, as Chambers has shown, there are reasons for thinking that this narrative was intended for recitation rather than for dramatic representation.[3] In two of the three manuscripts the opening words of the

---

[1] R. Froning, *Das Drama des Mittelalters*, Stuttgart, 1891, pp. 340 ff.

[2] W. H. Hulme, *Harrowing of Hell and the Gospel of Nicodemus*, 1907, pp. 3 ff.; 23 ff.; Harnack, *Geschichte der altchristlichen Literatur*, i, Leipzig, 1893, pp. 21 ff.; Tischendorf, *op. cit.*, pp. 397 f.

[3] *Medieval Stage*, ii, p. 74.

prologues, 'Alle herkneth to me nou, A strif wille I tellen our, of Jesu and of Satan', indicate that it was recited probably by one person, doubtless an *astrif* or *débat* on a subject familiar in the Miracle play.[1] Hence the confusion of the poem with the Mystery play ever since the scene was incorporated into the Easter cycle in the thirteenth century and onwards.[2]

The scene is laid in Limbo whither Christ descends to succour the souls who had died in faith but been held captive since the beginning of the world, as related in the Gospel of Nicodemus. After the prologue, a dispute between Dominus and Satan ensues before the gates of Hell which ends with the janitor fleeing and the felling of the gates by the Christus. He enters and is welcomed by Adam and Eve, Abraham, David, John the Baptist and Moses, whom he proceeds to release after they have done homage to him as the Lord of Life. Then follows a prayer:

> *God, for his moder loue*
> *Let ous neuer thider come!*
> *Louerd, for this michele grace*
> *Graunte ous en heuene one place;*
> *Let ous neuer be forloren*
> *For no sinne, Crist icoren;*
> *Ah bring ous out of helle pine,*
> *Louerd, ous and alle thine;*
> *And gif ous grace to liue and ende*
> *In this seruice and to heuene wende. Amen.*

This episode occurs in the thirty-seventh of the York plays, in the nineteenth of the Chester series, and in 1487 it was played before Henry VII at Winchester by the choir boys of Hyde Abbey and St Swithin's Priory. It afforded an opportunity for some topical allusions and such scenic effects as red fire and demoniac display. The theme is in line with the pre-Christian

---

[1] *Medieval Stage*, i, p. 81.

[2] Pollard, *English Miracle Plays, Moralities, and Interludes*, O.U.P., 1923, pp. 3–21, for the text.

ritual combat, reinterpreted in terms of the victory of the Cross vanquishing Hell and Christ becoming Lord of the dead as well as of the living. The Creation catastrophe had been over-come and Adam and Eve were released as the first-fruits of Calvary. A final prayer is made for the participation in these inestimable benefits by redeemed humanity, represented by the assembled audience. Having wrestled with the powers of evil in the underworld, and 'preached to the souls in prison, which sometime were disobedient, when once the long-suffering of God waited in the days of Noah' (1 St Peter iii, 19f.), authori-ties and powers had been made subject to the triumphant Risen Lord. Therefore, the Harrowing of Hell narrative and its dramatic representation belonged to the *Elevatio* rather than to the *Depositio* in the sepulchre ceremonial, as a prelude to the Resurrection and all that the bursting of the tomb involved and implied in the gospel of Redemption enacted in the Easter drama.

## THE CORPUS CHRISTI CYCLE

The same theme runs through the Corpus Christi plays on the Thursday after Trinity Sunday at the festival in honour of the institution of the Eucharist, transferred from Maundy Thurs-day. At this important point at the beginning of the second half of the liturgical year, coinciding with the first-fruits of the early harvest in the cradleland of the sacred drama, the whole Christian scheme of salvation and regeneration was enacted, from the Creation and the Fall, through the Annunciation, the Nativity and the Passion, to the Resurrection, the Ascension and the Descent of the Holy Ghost, and concluding with the victorious return of Christ as the judge of the living and the dead at Doomsday when the Antichrist would be finally destroyed. The Corpus Christi plays, therefore, covered the entire content of the Christian faith as it was then understood and enacted in the sequence of feasts and fasts throughout the liturgical year.

After the establishment of this festival in the thirteenth

century, early in the next century the plays hitherto held at Whitsun were transferred to it, and, as we have seen, were brought into association with the procession of the Host. These composite productions combining in an all-inclusive cycle a number of earlier plays, required a very considerable cast, literary skill, powers of production and the co-operation of performers and organizers, very different from the earlier liturgical tropes or the later folk plays. The Feast of Corpus Christi, in fact, was adopted by many of the guilds as their Annual Festival, and as the weather was generally favourable from the middle of May to the later part of June, it was an excellent time of year for an outdoor event on a grand scale, as it soon tended to become. Thus, each craft might become responsible for its own scene held in conjunction with the procession. Sometimes to save time the play was given in stages at the stations, but so lengthy did some of them become that they could not be performed in their entirety each year. The Coventry play, for instance, was divided into two parts, the first twenty-eight scenes covering the period from the Creation to the Betrayal by Judas being given one year, and the rest the next year. Similarly, the number of stations at which the plays were held varied. At York there were from twelve to sixteen; at Beverley six; at Coventry probably only three or four. At Chester they occupied three days at Whitsuntide instead of at Corpus Christi, though the event was called the 'Corpus Christi', suggesting that originally it was held on the day of the Feast and later was transferred to the previous week, perhaps to avoid clashing with the procession.[1] At Newcastle this difficulty led to the pageant going round with the procession in the morning, the actual play being deferred until the afternoon of the Feast.

That Corpus Christi became the focus of the great medieval dramas in their most developed form is not surprising in view of the place occupied by the liturgy and the sacrifice of the Mass in the evolution of the Mystery play, apart from the favourable time of year. Long before the dogma of transubstantiation was

[1] Chambers, *Medieval Stage*, ii, p. 138.

formulated and promulgated, the daily offering of the Holy Sacrifice constituted a dramatic representation of the fundamental beliefs in Christian faith and practice, commemorated at the prescribed fasts and festivals in the liturgical year but brought together daily at the altar. As the office of Holy Week declares, 'the Church commemorates every day the bloody sacrifice of Jesus Christ on the Cross, by a true and real unbloody sacrifice in which she offers to God the same body and blood that were given for the sins of the world'. This being the predominant conviction of the medieval Church, and, indeed, of Catholic Christendom at all times, the desire to set forth as vividly as possible all that the belief involved found expression and satisfaction in the Feast of Corpus Christi and its observances. Here under the most advantageous climatic conditions was an opportunity to enact the life of Christ as the incarnate Redeemer-King, beginning with the story of Creation and the Fall of man as the root cause for the Nativity, the Death and Resurrection, and the subsequent Ascension to 'the right hand of the Majesty on high' where 'the eternal High Priest after the order of Melchizedek' exercised his royal and priestly office.[1] Since the Mass was the daily re-enactment on earth of the eternal sacrifice before the throne of God in Heaven, the Feast of Corpus Christi, being the annual commemoration of the central act of Christian worship, was the proper occasion for the most elaborate dramatization of the Eucharistic sacrifice.

Thus, the Corpus Christi cycle constitutes an ambitious literary scheme bringing into a composite whole the theological interpretation of the universe, as it was then understood and accepted, from the dawn of creation to the final consummation, in a series of scenes which developed from the very simple liturgical embellishments and dramatic additions in the earlier Mystery plays. Once the practice of enlarging the scope and contents of the original enactments was established, the process rapidly developed. To the Creation story was added the revolt and expulsion of Lucifer from heaven, the Flood, the sacrifice of Abraham and the revelations of the Hebrew patriarchs and

[1] Cf. James, *The Nature and Function of Priesthood*, 1955, pp. 166ff.

prophets. Similarly, at the other end, the Harrowing of Hell was staged together with the Easter episodes, the Assumption of the Virgin and Doomsday.

## THE MARIAN PLAYS

Occasionally the Corpus Christi plays were transferred to another festival, as for example, to St Anne's Day on July 24th at Lincoln in the fifteenth century. At Coventry the Assumption was portrayed separately on August 15th, generally because particular guilds were responsible for the scene appropriate to this or some other Marian feast, especially in a city where the Virgin was greatly venerated. This applied mainly to those plays which were performed in her honour as distinct from those in which she occurred in the liturgical commemoration of the Nativity, the Presentation in the Temple, the Annunciation, the Purification, the Passion and the Resurrection. These were all primarily Dominical festivals in which, although the Mother of God featured prominently, Christ was the central figure. Even the Annunciation originally belonged to this class of feast because it was an integral part of the Nativity sequence marking the beginning of the incarnate life of Christ in which Mary was the human instrument.

## *The Annunciation*

Nevertheless, as it was around Mary in her capacity as the Theotokos that the Marian cultus arose, plays held in her honour, whether as part of the Gospel story of the Birth, Death and Resurrection of Christ, or as her personal history and significance as recorded in the apocryphal literature (e.g. the Gospel of the Nativity of Mary and the Gospel of Nicodemus), can hardly be rigidly distinguished in the context of medieval drama where they were so interwoven. The primary purpose of these plays was to give honour and veneration to Mary in her several roles, on the day appointed for the celebration of the particular event in her unique career and status. The calendrical significance of the Annunciation on March 25th has already been considered,[1] and the play connected with it belonged to the Christmas *Prophetae* and the Nativity cycle, not primarily intended for her special commemoration, and held at different times in the year—either in Advent in Spain, or in Lent in Rome. The dramatic presentation, as we have seen, was associated with the reading of the liturgical Gospel at the Mass or in Matins. In the sixteenth century at Tournai this was performed in the December Ember Week, embellished with scenes portraying the appearance of the Archangel Gabriel at the singing of the *Gloria in Excelsis*, and with the dialogue sung at the Gospel by the two impersonators of Gabriel and Mary, who bowed to each other three times. At the words *Spiritus sanctus superveniet in te* the image of a dove descended before the Virgin and there remained until it was drawn up after the *Agnus Dei*.

This was clearly a later development of an earlier simpler dramatization of the Gospel of the day, with the impersonations extended throughout the Mass, and the introduction of the dove to give visible effect to the descent of the Holy Ghost upon her. At Padua in the fourteenth century a more elaborate ceremonial was adopted which included Mary, Elizabeth, Joseph, Joiachim and Gabriel in their respective roles. The part of the angel was played by a boy, and he and Mary sang their verses in the Gospel, and a dove descended as in the Tournai version, but it was concealed by her under her cloak to symbolize her virginal conception by the Holy Ghost. Next followed the visitation to Elizabeth indicated by Mary going to the place where Elizabeth and Joiachim stood, and there she sang the *Magnificat*. The Cividale text from Italy also includes the Annunciation and Visitation, and ends with the singing of the *Magnificat*, but without any further embellishments or directions concerning scenic effects. The text of the Vulgate is preserved in the speeches in this rendering.

### The Purification

The Purification of the Blessed Virgin Mary forty days after the Nativity, as has been considered, was a Dominical festival of

---

[1] Chap. vii, pp. 234f.

Eastern origin—the Byzantine *Hypapante*, or meeting of the infant Christ with Simeon and Anna at his Presentation in the Temple (St Luke ii, 22, 38)—which brought to an end the Christmas celebrations in a blaze of glory, as it coincided with the ancient Feast of Lights. When it reached the West in the fifth century and the Candlemas rites became a feature of the event in and after the seventh century, the symbolism of Christ as the Light of the World and Mary as the 'light-bearer', took on a variety of modes of expression in the liturgy and its procession. Thus, during the singing of the antiphon a priest in the guise of Simeon entered the church carrying on a cushion either a book containing the Gospel of the festival, or an image of the Holy Child, or of Mary with him in her arms. By the end of the fourteenth century processions of guilds to churches dedicated to Our Lady were led by members impersonating Simeon, Joseph, and two angels in front of a statue of the Mother and Child, while in the church the effigy of the infant Jesus was presented to Simeon at the high altar by someone in the role of Mary. This dramatic action was elaborated at Padua by Mary carrying the Child in her arms, Joseph bearing a basket on his shoulders, Anna holding a parchment in her hand, accompanied by four prophets and three angels, proceeding to the altar of SS. Fabian and Sebastian, behind which the Presentation was enacted. The antiphon, *Ave, gratia plena, Dei genitrix virgo*, having been sung, she made her offering of two doves. These were inspected and approved by Simeon as being without blemish, two more antiphons were sung by the angels, and the play ended with the *Nunc Dimittis* precentored by Simeon as the characters returned to the sacristy.

In other versions he received a message from the Holy Ghost warning him of the approach of the Saviour to the Temple. But apart from particular incidents of this nature, the action of the play was concentrated on the Presentation and its principal characters.[1] Its close association with the Christmas Festival often led to it being merged with the Nativity plays, and as a

[1] K. Young, 'Dramatic Ceremonies of the Feast of the Purification', *Speculum*, v, 1930, pp. 97 ff.

result it was detached from its own feast on February 2nd, and performed in conjunction with the Christmas cycle as a simple adjunct requiring little in the way of properties, stage effects, or utterance beyond the singing of the antiphons. Humorous incidents were sometimes introduced in the dove episode, as in the Chester plays (XI), or in theological disquisitions. In both the Chester cycle and the Coventry Weavers' pageant the play portraying Christ disputing with the Doctors in the Temple at the age of twelve was united with that of the Puri-fication, and the one follows the other in the Towneley cycle. That the two events were separated by twelve years would not be of any concern for the producers in the fourteenth and fifteenth centuries.

## The Presentation of the Blessed Virgin Mary

Of the plays that were devised and produced exclusively in honour of Mary, as distinct from those in which she was the outstanding figure as the Theotokos, her own Presentation in the Temple celebrated on November 21st, and her Assumption on August 15th, attracted dramatic ceremonies in the later Middle Ages. The first of these, the Presentation, arose from the story of her unaided ascent of the steps leading to the Temple when she was taken there by Joiachim and Anna when she was three years of age, recorded in The Book of James, an apo-cryphal Infancy Gospel. Having made a vow of virginity there she remained as one of the virgins, and was the recipient of daily visits from angels, and herself had heavenly visions. When she reached her fourteenth birthday the high priest, seeking divine guidance, was led to assemble the young men of the House of David, and promised to give Mary to the one whose rod should blossom, and upon whom the Holy Ghost should descend in the form of a dove. It was to Joseph that these signs were vouchsafed.[1]

The tradition was commemorated in a feast in Eastern Christendom which was first observed in the eighth century

[1] Tischendorf, *op. cit.*, pp. 14ff., 115ff.; M. Zalan, *Ephemerides Liturgicae*, xli, Rome, 1927, pp. 188f.

and became definitely established by the beginning of the twelfth century.[1] Subsequently it was introduced into the West by Philippe de Mézières (c. 1326–1405), a devout French nobleman and diplomat, who became acquainted with it in the Near East, and brought back a transcript of the liturgical office to Italy and France. In Venice he secured the observance of the festival and at it a dramatic performance of the events in the tradition. With the interest and approval of the Pope (Gregory XI, 1370–1378) it was celebrated at Avignon on November 21st, 1372, and by 1385 it had become an elaborate representation in which twenty-two characters appeared. The Virgin herself was impersonated by a little girl of about three years of age, accompanied by fourteen other small girls, with Joiachim and Anna, and a group of angels, including Gabriel, Raphael and Michael. These all moved towards the altar in procession, with Mary ascending the fifteen steps to be presented by her parents to a priest in the guise of the high priest. The Mass then proceeded, Mary occupying the stall next to the cardinals.[2]

From the *Ordo* it appears that the rendering involved two stages or platforms, one erected in the nave of the church and approached by wooden steps on the east and west sides, with a railing extending round the top. On the rectangular platform seats were provided for Mary in the middle and for Joiachim and Anna on either side of her. Facing Joiachim was a stool for the actor impersonating the Jewish synagogue (the Synagoga), and opposite to Anna one for the Ecclesia. Gabriel stood at the north-west corner with the musicians at the other two corners. Against the north wall of the choir, between the choir stalls and the high altar, the smaller platform was erected. This also was provided with a seat for Mary and a kneeler for use during the Mass.

[1] Holweck, *Calendarium Liturgicum Festorum Dei et Dei Matres Mariae*, Philadelphia, 1925, p. 386.

[2] Young, 'Philippe de Mézières, Dramatic office for the Presentation of the Virgin', in *Publications of the Modern Languages Association of America*, xxvi, 1911, pp. 181 ff.

Those taking part in the procession assembled and vested in the chapter-house, and then passed through the cloister to the west door of the church, into the nave, headed by the bishop, the deacon and the subdeacon, followed by the angels, the Synagoga, the Ecclesia, the musicians, and the two maidens, with Gabriel and Raphael on the right and left of Mary. Behind came Joiachim and Anna, Michael and Lucifer, and the lay members. The bishop went to his throne beyond the platform beside the high altar, Mary mounted the steps to the rectangular stage carrying her dove and a candle, and the rest went to their appointed stations. The nine angels ascended the steps on the west to sing the *Laudes Mariae*, and made their exit by those on the east side, as Anna, Joiachim and Ecclesia took their places and uttered their verses of praise. Synagoga then gave vent to a lament and was pushed down the west steps by Gabriel and Raphael. Dropping her banner and the tables of the Mosaic Law, she fled in tears from the church amid laughter. Lucifer was brought howling on to the platform by Raphael, humbled before Mary, and was then thrown down the west steps to the ground by Michael, Gabriel and Raphael. During the singing of a hymn Mary was conducted to the bishop by Joiachim and Anna to symbolize her Presentation in the Temple, and when she had been received in his arms she was taken by Gabriel and Raphael to her seat on the smaller platform at the north wall of the choir for the Mass. Before the *Introit* she released her dove, and at the end of the liturgy she was carried from the church.[1]

This very detailed account of the proceedings recorded by Philippe de Mézières gives a clear picture of the play as it was performed at Avignon in 1372. While it was still in very close association with the liturgy, nevertheless, it had acquired the form and setting of a genuine sacred drama. Therefore, it constitutes an important link between the liturgical and the vernacular plays which eventually emerged as independent productions while still preserving their sacred themes in relation to the liturgical year and its seasonal observances.

[1] Young, *Drama of the Medieval Church*, ii, pp. 227 ff.

## The Assumption

That the principal Marian Festival—the Assumption on August 15th—was not accompanied by a dramatic celebration is surprising in view of the development of the cult-legend of the feast and its procession, and its connexion with the harvest, since it was first established in Rome by the eighth century, and widely distributed in both Eastern and Western Christendom in the Middle Ages. This is the more remarkable as in the fourteenth-century Miracle plays of Our Lady were so abundant. In the so-called Hegge plays, the *Ludus Coventriae*, the death, assumption and coronation of the Virgin as narrated in the apocryphal Gospel of Nicodemus are portrayed, describing Mary calling to her death-bed the Apostles from all parts of the world. Thus it is related that St Thomas was carried to her from India on a cloud, but notwithstanding this miraculous transference he still refused to believe when he saw her ascend to Heaven before his eyes until she sent down her girdle to him to touch. Then at last he was convinced. Similar popular plays in honour of her Dormition and Coronation recur in the York cycle, and probably they were also in the Towneley and Chester cycles, though they are now lost. This doubtless applies to many others.

In the *Ordo* from Halle of the sixteenth century a liturgical drama has been preserved which was held after None on the feast, consisting of a procession in the church at the ending of which an image of the Virgin on a platform before the high altar was drawn up through an opening in the roof, as in the Ascension plays. There is no indication, however, of any impersonation, and the clerics officiate in their choir vestures, the antiphons being sung in the normal manner. The liturgy does not appear to have been dramatized, perhaps because the revelry associated with the harvest, against which the *Ordo* gave warning, had penetrated the feast of the Assumption. Thus riotous behaviour occurred, for example, in its celebration in the chapel of Notre Dame-du-Jardin in Rouen cathedral. There the Brotherhood of the Assumption arranged a garden with grotesque figures of the Twelve Apostles and the Devil, and

held in it a procession and a dramatic performance of a scur-
rilous nature. In what they consisted is not disclosed but the
proceedings are referred to with disapproval in several acts of
the Chapter between 1460 and 1521.[1]

## THE MEDIEVAL STAGE AND ITS EFFECTS

As long as the liturgical drama took place in church as a
supplement of the liturgy or the offices, this acted as a restraining
influence both as regards the content and temper of what was
said and done, and on the dramatic setting. The nave, the choir
and the sanctuary were then utilized for the dramatic action and
staging, and even when between the thirteenth and fourteenth
centuries the drama began to leave the church and to become
laicized, it by no means lost its original character. In the
market-place and the street the course of the ecclesiastical
procession continued to be followed, halting at stations *en route*,
as within the sacred precincts. At each station the group taking
part gathered together, or was collected on wagons, and
performed its scenes. Each craft had its own movable stage
erected on either four or eight wheels, and divided into an
upper and lower compartment. The performance was given on
the upper platform which represented the earth, corresponding
to the choir in the church, where most of the action took place.
Above were the celestial realms (i.e. the sanctuary in the
church), sometimes separated from the platform by a canopy,
arches and battlements. Below, the lower room used for dressing
and waiting for cues, and furnished with ladders leading to the
stage through trap doors, represented Hell, like the nave in the
church setting.

From the platform in the chancel, in fact, the stage developed
when the plays left the church and began an independent
career in the open air, or in the porch, or in the graveyard, as in
the case of the Adam play of Death with elaborate stage
directions which required more space than the church afforded.
Before this transition there was a tendency for the performances

[1] P. le Verdier, *Mystère de l'Incarnation et Nativité de Notre Sauveur er Rédemp-
teur Jésus-Christ représenté a Rouen en 1474*, ii, Rouen, 1885, pp. xl–xliii.

to spread from the choir to the nave, and once the church was abandoned altogether, the length and elaboration of the setting rapidly increased.[1] When the entire action was on a level stage, Hell was located at one end and Heaven at the other, to enable the incidents to be seen by the audience. These 'mansions' were then canopied with sun and moon, and similar celestial emblems, and rude attempts at scenery were made with a series of painted cloths. Thus, in the Creation scenes the sky was repre-sented by a cloth with stars and the names of the planets on it, and the separation of light from darkness was portrayed by a cloth divided into two halves, one painted white, the other black. A hut was used for a stable at Bethlehem in the Nativity scenes, and for the palace of Herod. An embattled tower constituted Hell's mouth, which sometimes assumed the form of a dragon with staring eyes, a huge nose, and movable jaws out of which fire and smoke belched forth.

The three-storied plan of the stage representing the earth, the heavenly sphere and the underworld, resembled the setting of the coronation drama in Ancient Egypt recorded in the Ramesseum Papyrus, performed at 'stations' during the royal procession on the banks of the Nile, at which the ascent of Osiris was symbolized by the setting up of a ladder to the sky.[2] Thus, in the medieval plays the three stages were connected by ladders, the ascent from the stage to the raised platform at the back representing the transference of the dramatic action from earth to Heaven, as in the story of Jacob at Bethel.[3] As in the Egyptian drama the king re-enacted the coronation ceremony and the funerary ritual of his predecessor, so in the Miracle and Mystery plays the birth, death, resurrection and ascension of Christ, and the coronation of the Mother of God, were repre-sented to assist the faithful in the deepening of their mystical union with him, and to enable them to share in his victory as mem-bers of regenerated humanity. Moreover, the dramatization of the resurrection story was brought into relation with that of the

---

[1] Chambers, *Medieval Stage*, ii, pp. 79 ff.

[2] Sethe, *Dramatische Texte zu altaegyptischen Mysterienspielen*, Leipzig, 1928, pp. 96 ff.    [3] Gen. xxviii, 12.

creation, and of final rewards and punishments at Doomsday in the great Corpus Christi cycle and its procession. Thus, the sacred drama of the medieval Church with its origins in the liturgy never ceased to be fundamentally and essentially a reproduction of all that was enshrined and enacted in the Mass, extended over the whole course of sacred history, making explicit what was already implicit in liturgical worship.

## THE SECULARIZATION OF THE MIRACLE PLAYS

The transference from the church to the market-place and guild-halls, the introduction of lay actors from the Guilds and of amateur players, the use of the vernacular, and the development of burlesques and comic episodes, undoubtedly had a secularizing effect. This sometimes led to wanton observances, as at Rouen, and eventually to ecclesiastical opposition and prohibition, as in the case of Grosseteste, Bishop of Lincoln (1235–1253), who forbade his clergy to participate in any plays or May Day games. But in fact it was only the folk plays, burlesques, the Feast of Fools, and the Feast of the Ass, that were suppressed at all effectively until the Reformation,[1] and then only within certain limits, and surviving in the folk drama. Thus, in spite of Grosseteste's stringent regulations, even in Lincoln cathedral the Miracle plays continued to be performed, as elsewhere.

One of their purposes always had been to afford a counter-attraction to the pagan seasonal revels, little changed from pre-Christian times. Therefore, unedifying frolics were tolerated to some extent as a relaxation from restraint under ecclesiastical control. To eliminate such a very popular pastime, so deeply rooted in both the religious and cultural tradition of medieval society would have been a very difficult if not impossible procedure, especially as many of the plays were still performed in churches and retained some of their earlier liturgical features. Therefore, it was only certain plays that were condemned, whether they were held within or without a church,

[1] H. C. Gardiner, *Mysteries' End. An Investigation of the Last Days of the Medieval Religious Stage*, New Haven, 1946, pp. 1–19.

because they had incorporated licentious and comic elements from the secular drama which were positively indecent and wanton, and definitely irreverent and indecorous.

The Abbess of Hohenberg in the twelfth century, while commending the Epiphany play of 'The Old Fathers of the Church' depicting the star leading the Magi to Bethlehem, the Massacre of the Innocents, the accouchement of the Virgin and other incidents connected with the Nativity, deplored the practice current in her day of priests dressed as soldiers feasting and engaging in buffoonery in the church, coupled with lewd jesting and the presence of shameless women; a disorderly assembly, as she affirmed, that seldom ended without quarrelling.[1] Similarly, the introduction of the Devil was an occasion for a good deal of coarse by-play in very long plays, which became tedious and failed to hold the attention of the audience. Any interludes that livened the proceedings were welcomed, and as these were held at seasonal festivals and on festal days, often as adjuncts of fairs, the people were in a mood for merry-making and relaxation. For many centuries before the advent of the Miracle play the drama and the circus often had been inseparably combined, as we have seen, when not infrequently vice was so rife that Christians had been forbidden to take any part in them. The tradition lingered on after the Church had herself instituted her own liturgical dramatic representations as an integral part of public worship and the offices. It is not surprising, therefore, that when the Miracle and Mystery plays were secularized, buffoonery and the cruder forms of banality were gradually reintroduced and became increasingly associated with the portrayal of the most sacred events. To the popular medieval mind the incongruity of the amalgamation was not apparent in spite of recurrent attempts to initiate reforms and issue prohibitions.

Towards the end of the fourteenth century the Morality play in the form of a dramatized allegory, such as the Dance of Death, began to make its appearance. Unlike the Mystery

[1] K. Pearson, *The Chances of Death and Other Studies in Evolution*, ii, C.U.P., 1897, pp. 285f., cf. Chambers, *Medieval Stage*, i, p. 318.

plays, based ultimately on the liturgical scriptures in the Mass and the Divine Office, and the Miracle plays depicting the lives and legends of the saints—e.g. those of St Nicholas, St Thomas and the French *Miracles de Notre Dame*, associated particularly with their annual commemorations but including many new themes, the Moralities dealt with abstractions. Virtues and vices were personified in their *dramatis personae* in scenes set in familiar surroundings and under contemporary conditions. In the Anglo-Dutch *Everyman*, belonging to the beginning of the sixteenth century but based on an earlier allegory in the legend of Barlaam and Josaphat, the four 'last things' (i.e. death, judgment, heaven and hell) were dramatized with a remarkable realism that has never failed to grip an audience, and even under present-day conditions it is still 'good theatre'. It is, however, hardly typical of the Morality class of drama which deals exclusively with the way of salvation allegorized as a journey in quest of holy dying, with great earnestness and no lighter reliefs. But the Morality plays do not belong to the seasonal sequence, and therefore, lie outside the scope of our present inquiry.

## CHAPTER IX

# Folk Drama, Dances and Festivals

### FOLK DRAMA

If there is little to suggest the direct merging of the Miracle and Mystery plays with the secular folk drama, both arose out of seasonal rites with a deeply laid death and resurrection theme, and satisfied the same primitive instincts. In the peasant cultures of medieval Europe the need to secure the means of subsistence by the performance of vegetation ceremonies may not have been as urgent as it had been at the time when the *ludi* of the folk first came into being. Nevertheless, the ancient customs survived in the popular round of fast and festival, not infrequently to the embarrassment of the ecclesiastical authorities who, as has been considered, did not regard the growing secularization of the Mystery plays with approval, even though the less offensive accretions were tolerated. In Northern and Central Europe the medieval religious drama came to an end in the sixteenth century, under pressure from Puritan and other anti-Papal reactions against the presentation of sacred events on the stage, and, indeed, against any forms of acting. There were exceptions to this general trend, and in France and other Catholic countries the plays went on little changed long after the Reformation suppressions.[1]

Although in England professional actors were branded as 'rogues and vagabonds', and despite Puritan opposition to acting and dancing, some of the Mysteries continued to be held during the reign of Elizabeth I (1558–1603), if they escaped the suspicion of being 'pro-Papal' in their content (e.g. some of the Coventry cycle, and the Towneley plays with emendations), together with country dances. Indeed, the Queen herself excelled in the courtly *covanto* and in the vigorous *volta* from Provence. During the Renaissance, especially in the south of Europe, the

[1] Cf. A. Brown, *Folk-Lore*, lxiii, 1952, pp. 65 ff.

mime, dance, song and acrobatics had been interwoven into the popular drama performed by wandering players with the aid of masks, gestures, and impersonations often in mockery of the tragedies of the poets. Thus, at the public festivals Mummers wearing masks or animal disguises, and clad in fantastic garments, serenaded outside houses, or played their roles in the folk plays of St George, portraying the antithesis of winter and summer, spring and autumn, in a folk version of the ancient seasonal ritual.

## The Mummers' Play

The central feature in the Mummers' play is the fight between Saint (or King) George and his adversary who is killed or wounded and then restored by the Doctor. The play opens with a prologue introducing the performers, often spoken of as 'merry boys', and as each enters he announces his name and describes his role. St George, for example, proclaims,

> *In come I, Saint George, the man of courage bold;*
> *With my broad axe and sword I won a crown of gold.*
> *I fought the fiery dragon, and drove him to the slaughter,*
> *And by these means I won the King of Egypt's daughter.*
> *Show me the man that bids me stand;*
> *I'll cut him down with my courageous hand.*

Then enters Bold Slasher in the guise of Turkish Knight, to fight St George. An altercation between them follows, both boasting of their prowess, and they draw their swords for the fight, challenging each other, 'one shall die and the other shall live'. The struggle ensues and Slasher falls to the ground, whereupon the Presenter, as the father of the defeated Slasher, calls for a doctor to restore him and heal his deep and deadly wound, offering 'a thousand pounds if a doctor can be found'. When he appears, having come, as he asserts, 'from Italy, Sicily, Germany, France and Spain', and 'been three times round the world and back again', he describes all the diseases he can cure:

> *The itch, the stitch, the palsy and the gout,*
> *Pains within and pains without.*

Producing a bottle containing 'elecampans', he pours 'a drop on his head, a drop on his heart', saying, 'rise up, bold fellow, and take thy part'. Then the rest of the cast enter—Big Head with his little wit who dances a jig; Beelzebub carrying a club on his shoulder and holding a dripping-pan in his hand; Johnny Jack with his wife and large family; and little Devil Dout demanding money on pain of sweeping everybody to the grave.[1]

While the various versions have their own variations and features, and nowhere does a perfect play exist, in their general structure, incidents and dialogue they conform to this pattern. Additional characters may be introduced, such as a Fool or Clown, the Doctor's man, often called Jack Finney, the Man-woman, the Lawyer, Valiant Soldier and Rumour or Room.[2] In the Ampleforth play the chief characters are the King, Queen and Clown, the King being the Clown's son who is killed in a Sword dance in which he takes the part of the foreman. The person killed, however, may be a spectator, but it would seem that originally it was the King himself who became the victim, since the Clown addresses the dead man as his son. In other plays the role of the old year is played by Father Christmas, or the King of Egypt, and that of the hero by Saint or King George who challenges his antagonist, Turkey Knight or Rumour, to fight in deadly combat. Sometimes the role of King George is reversed, as at Longborough, Gloucestershire, near Stow-in-the-Wold, where the Turkey Champion strikes down Prince George in a battle with swords, and the Headman proclaims:

> *Horrible, terrible, what has thou done?*
> *Thou hast killed my only dearly beloved Son,*
> *Is there a doctor to be found*
> *To cure him of his deep and deadly wound.*[3]

[1] R. J. E. Tiddy, *The Mummers' Play*, O.U.P., 1923, pp. 144 ff.: Chambers, *The English Folk Play*, O.U.P., 1933, pp. 6 ff.

[2] Rumour or Room is a medieval term for the floorspace for dancing and action, and the formula 'Room, room, brave gallants, give me room to rhyme' in Elizabethan English later became 'Room, room, and gallons of room' in the Overton play, and 'A room, a room, a garland room' at Sudbury; and finally a character called Room or Rumour.          [3] Tiddy, *op. cit.*, p. 181.

This aspect of the Mummers' play, called by Chambers the Lament, in which the 'only son', or 'eldest son', is slain by the antagonist, would seem to contain a more serious element inherited from the pre-Christian and Mystery traditions. As Tiddy says, 'if we are justified in making any deductions from the folk plays that survive, we may take it as certain that the pagan ritual included a heroic figure who slew his antagonist and this antagonist afterwards was revived'.[1] Moreover, there appears to be a connexion between the St George players and the Sword dancers with their mock death and revival as its central point, the performers being clad in animal disguises.[2] No doubt this similarity in the secular and the sacred themes was one of the primary causes of the prohibitions of the *ludi* at the seasonal festivals from the thirteenth century onwards, as the two could hardly fail to react on each other. Thus, traces of the vaunts of St George and his opponents, and of the cure by the Doctor, may be detected in the language of Octavian and Herod, of Pilate and Caiaphas, and later of the Mercador episode in the Easter play.

Nevertheless, although there was this assimilation, the folk drama certainly was not a product of its liturgical counterpart. Behind it lay a very long and independent tradition which goes back to Graeco-Oriental pagan sources associated, as we have seen, with Dionysus, at whose festival and in whose temple the plays were performed.[3] Here again, the death and resurrection motif was prominent, the essence of Greek tragedy being the πάθως-θρῆνος (violent death and lamentation) of the hero finding expression in a funerary ritual, and that of comedy (the κῶμος-γάμος) in the resurrection-nuptial revel symbolism of victory over death and decay. Because its purpose was to give life and renewal, the *epiphania* of the god, or in the plays of Euripides, as in most tragedies, the deification of the hero, was a fitting conclusion to the drama. The Old King was driven forth that the Young King might reign in his stead.

[1] Tiddy, *op. cit.*, p. 74.    [2] Chambers, *op. cit.*, p. 211.
[3] Chap. v, p. 140.

In a modern folk play discovered by Professor Dawkins in the Viza region of Thrace, this ancient Dionysian myth and ritual have survived. In the last week of Carnival all the houses in the village are visited by two men in goats' skins and masks, one carrying a cross-bow and the other a wooden phallus, with which to knock at the doors. Two boys dressed as brides, a man in female attire and an old woman called Babo carrying a baby of unknown paternity in a *liknon*, or winnowing basket, together with a 'gipsy' and his wife, also as a Man-woman, policemen with swords and a man with bagpipes, make up the rest of the characters. The 'gipsies' visit all the houses and per-form obscene acts outside each of them, while the man with the phallus knocks on the doors. The 'policemen' brandish their swords in the dance that follows. In the afternoon the play begins. The gipsy, now called the 'smith', and his wife forge a mock ploughshare, and a plough is hitched and drawn round the village square, a man walking behind scattering seeds.

After these preliminaries the old woman called Babo (i.e. unmarried mother) with the *liknon* containing the swaddled seven-months-old illegitimate infant declares that it is getting too big for its basket. It has now developed an enormous appetite and demands a wife. One of the brides is pursued by the masked goatman who carries the cross-bow, and brought to the child who has now grown to maturity. After their marriage the second goatman appears and engages in a fight with the bridegroom and kills him. The bride thereupon loudly bewails her slain husband, and without the intervention of a Doctor he is restored to life. As an epilogue the two brides are yoked to a plough which they drag round the village widdershins while the spectators cry, 'May wheat be ten piastres the bushel! Amen, O God, that the poor may eat! Yea, O God, that the poor folk be filled!'[1]

A similar play has been recorded from Thessaly by Mr Wace which differs in some respects from the Thracian version. Thus, instead of the goatman who assumes the role of the adversary being an exact double of the hero in name and

[1] *J.H.S.*, xxvi, 1906, pp. 191 ff.

appearance, in the Thessalian version the two characters are quite distinct. Furthermore, the resuscitation of the dead man is performed by a Doctor (γιατρός), and the play ends in an obscene pantomime between the bride and the bridegroom.[1] But despite these differences in detail in the respective local presentations, the essential features are the same. The central action is the ritual combat between the two contestants in which the hero is killed and brought to life again, and then engages in a marriage as the culmination of the play.

As the introduction of the plough shows, it was an early spring ritual dramatizing the story of Dionysus which, as we have seen, was of Thracian origin.[2] The bastard wonder-child of seven months was born of the Earth-mother (Babo) and laid in a *liknon*, just as Dionysus was called Liknites, 'He of the winnowing fan.' His illegitimacy may be a relic of his miraculous birth, just as the virgin birth tradition, according to the Johannine narrative, probably caused Christ to be similarly libelled (St John viii, 41). The incredibly rapid growth to maturity, followed by his marriage, death and restoration, leading up to the consummation of the union to bring about a renewal of life and fertility 'that the poor may eat', are all in line with the Dionysiac and its underlying vegetation cultus. The phallic procession in the village, the obscene pantomime, the circumstances surrounding the mysterious child and his mother, the ritual combat, the reanimation ceremony, and the marriage, connect the festival and its carnival with the Dionysiac on the one side and the Mummers' plays and Sword dance on the other, thereby indicating the line of development of the folk drama from the ancient Mystery cults. In the process they lost their earlier serious purpose and significance. From being the *dromenon*, the sacred action done, they became the *drama* performed at best for edification, instruction and worship, as in the Miracle, Mystery and Moral-ity plays, or merely for recreation, amusement or 'luck', as a pastime or seasonal revel.

[1] Wace, *B.S.A.*, xvi, 1909–10, p. 233.
[2] Cf. Chap. v, p. 145.

The introduction of burlesque into sacred solemnities, for example in the St Nicholas plays on December 6th, which in Germany were originally very largely Christianized forms of folk dramas, with grotesque figures resembling the Fool of the Morris dances, represents an intermediate phase in the trans/formation. This became more apparent in the election of a Boy Bishop on this day, or on Holy Innocents Day (Childer/mas) on December 28th, chosen from among his fellows at a choir school or grammar school. Arrayed in episcopal vest/ments, he sang Vespers and occasionally even celebrated a mock Mass, and attended by subordinates in priestly vestures, went from house to house. His position was recognized to the extent that Edward I allowed the holder of the office to sing Vespers in his presence on December 7th, 1299 at Heaton near Newark. The custom in England was suppressed by Henry VIII, revived by Mary Tudor, and finally abolished by Elizabeth I, though it lingered on for some time in the villages.[1]

## The Feast of Fools

Closely connected with these extravagances was the Feast of Fools, the Lord of Misrule and the Feast of Asses, when in certain French towns a donkey played a prominent part in the dramatization of the Flight into Egypt. Thus, at Beauvais on January 14th the central figure was a girl seated on an ass with a baby in her arms, impersonating the Virgin. The congre/gation proceeded from the cathedral to the church of St Etienne, and on its arrival was directed to bray like an ass three times at the *Introit*, and again at the *Kyrie*, the *Gloria in Excelsis* and at the *Ite missa est*, the celebrant doing likewise. These and similar fantastic customs survived in many places until the sixteenth century, despite the efforts of the hierarchy to suppress them.

As late as 1664 the Feast of Fools was celebrated on Holy Innocents Day at the monastery of the Cordeliers, where it was witnessed and described in scathing terms in a letter to Pierre

[1] Chambers, *The Medieval Stage*, i, pp. 336ff.

Gassendi.[1] This mock-religious festival held on or about January 1st from the twelfth century onwards, especially in France, was an occasion of excessive buffoonery and extra-vagance incorporating New Year and Saturnalian customs, some of which were borrowed from the folk plays. Attempts were made to correct the abuses, as, for instance, at Notre Dame in Paris when in 1199 the canons were ordered not to leave their stalls on the Eve of the Feast of the Circumcision to prevent the officiants at the Feast of Fools taking their places, and prohibiting *chansons* and masks, and curtailing the cere-monies connected with the handing over of the *baculus*, or precentor's staff, to the leader of the feast during the singing of the *Magnificat*. Similar action was taken at Sens in connexion with the Festum Assinorum. In 1207 Innocent III directed the discontinuance of masks and *ludi* in churches in Poland, and in the fifteenth century the Faculty of Theology in the University of Paris issued an encyclical to all the French bishops to put down the Feast of Fools. This suggests how little effect the previous endeavours to eliminate the observance had had.

The persistence of these strange and unedifying burlesques is an example of the survival and revival of the buffooneries, crude jesting and absurdities which were so prominent in the seasonal festivals and installation rites, throughout the ages. It is not surprising, therefore, that at the beginning of the New Year a *festum stultorum* was held, and found a place among the medieval ecclesiastical counterparts of the secular revelries at the turn of the year of the Lord of Misrule. At Beverley, Vienne, Noyon and Besançon such a burlesque figure was actually called, and treated as, Mock King. In this context the Christmas Mummers' play is true to type. The leader of the mighty forces of evil there becomes a farcical figure, a 'jolly old man' carrying a dripping-pan or club. The reanimation of the slain or wounded hero is performed by a burlesque Doctor described as a 'quack', and the masked personifications of the gods are now merely clowns with bladders, blackened faces

[1] J. B. L. du Tilliot, *Mémoires pour servir à l'histoire de la Fête des Foux*, Paris, 1741–51; L. Schneegans, in Müller's *Zeitschrift für Deutsche Kulturgeschichte*, 1858.

and calves' tails. The all-important ritual marriage is performed in conjunction with the functionless Man-woman or Boy-girl character. The Hobby-horse when it occurs may belong to the same category, unless it is a relic of an animal sacrifice as an integral element in the seasonal ritual.

## The Sword Dance

The combat and its sequel, together with the Sword dance, gives the clue, however, to the primary purpose and significance of the folk drama in its original form. From times beyond memory the sacred dance has been an outstanding feature in seasonal ceremonial and observances, the expression of *joie de vivre* in rhythmical activity and physical exuberance on occasions of public rejoicing, often accompanied by singing, clapping and other noises. Indeed, song and dance are so interwoven, as is shown in our own day by their amalgamation at Cecil Sharp House in London, that the one cannot be separated from the other in a common ritual or pastime of perpetual recurrence. Thus, from the cradle to the grave, and from season to season, in the primitive and peasant cultures the entire group, domestic and social, have been united as a harmonious whole in a common activity, welded together by collective emotions as a corporate unified entity. Therefore, the dance has found its rightful place in all the principal celebrations in the cycle of human life and of the seasons—initiation, puberty, marriage, death; planting and sowing, harvesting and vintage, and at the turn of the year. Also on such important occasions as going to war, or to the chase or at the gathering of the clans for peaceful intercourse to promote solidarity and mutual goodwill.

In the more primitive dances the mimic element is very prominent, in which the behaviour of animals, fertility processes, natural phenomena (e.g. rain, clouds, etc.), and warlike activity, are represented in a realistic manner in order to gain control over the supernatural forces governing the objects and events portrayed. In addition to this more serious function of vital importance to all concerned, communal dances afford an opportunity for social intercourse, bringing people together for 'fun and games' as adjuncts to ritual observances. As this lighter side increased with the secularization of the ancient folk drama, and in the Middle Ages gradually became divorced from ecclesiastical influences and controls, the plays and dances acquired a serio-comic character.[1] With the break-up of the medieval synthesis at the end of the fourteenth century, and the rise of the Tudor drama, the folk element, largely in this form, came into its own again. The more joyous aspects of the Nativity plays were transferred to the popular festivals, and as the Passion tended to overshadow the Easter cycle in the ecclesiastical tradition,. so a more sombre element, inherited from tragedy, was latent in the folk drama. In the carol *The Holly and the Ivy*, for example, which appears to have originated in the sixteenth century, the struggle between the male and female principles in nature was transformed into a Christian meditation on the significance of the crown of thorns, symbolized in the holly's red berries, prickles, and bitter bark. In the refrain, however, are allusions to the sun and the deer, on the one hand, and, on the other hand, to the choirs and organs, appropriate in a dance-song in which elements have been incorporated from the Nativity and Passion mimes with a folk refrain. This represents the burlesque of sacred solemnities in reverse.

In the folk drama the serious and the comic, the joyous and the tragic, dance and song, are combined, and have been concentrated upon one or other of the seasonal festivals, notably Christmas and Easter. This has resulted in a combination of rites, observances and celebrations, so that in Christmas plays we have Yule-tide and Christian rites, customs, traditions and dances, along with dramatic reminiscences of the legend of St George, and figures more closely associated with the Easter Pace-Egg plays and the Plough Monday play at the beginning of January. But common to them all is the Sword dance, very frequently recurring as an interlude in each of them, often to the accompaniment of a song by the principal character as a

[1] Cf. A. Brown, *loc. cit.*; E. O. James, *Folk-Lore*, lviii, 1947, pp. 364 ff.

sort of personification of the ancient chorus, characterizing each of the actors at their entrance. This is most apparent in Durham and the north-eastern counties in England, though not un-known as far south as Devon. Indeed, it is a feature of seasonal observances everywhere, especially at midwinter, usually performed by five, six or eight men carrying a sword, called a 'rapper', in one hand, and holding the point of that of his neighbour in the other hand.

The swords vary in length, and may be made either of steel with a wooden handle at one end, or sometimes merely wooden laths, as at Flamborough in Yorkshire. Occasionally sticks or pilgrim staves are used, particularly on the Continent. The origin of the short sword, or rapper, as of the dance itself, is by no means clear. The name 'rapper' suggests a rapier, but this hardly can have been its original character if, as is very probable, the dance and its implements are of great antiquity, when the object held may have had a phallic significance and symbolism. Be this as it may, the setting of the dance is that of a fertility seasonal ritual with its Fool or Clown, Doctor, Man-woman, Hobby-horse and Bessie or Dirty Bet, as stock characters, and refer-ences to the killing of a bullock. Its performance requires skill, especially in the short sword variety where the acting is con-gested with tap-dance interludes. In them all the Fool or Clown or Medicine-man is the principal figure accompanied by his assistants with blackened faces as a disguise, but very far removed from the court jester of later Tudor drama. Sometimes the King acts as the leader and the Queen as the man dressed in women's attire, though the Man-woman usually is the Bessie.

The King, Clown, the Bessie or the leader generally opens the dance with a call for 'room', and an introduction, or 'calling-on', of the characters. These may include well-known persons (e.g. Nelson, Wellington, or Napoleon), or local types (e.g. Dick the cobbler, Tim the tailor, Ale the vintner, Coal Hewer, or Tom the tinker). After some rustic foolery and the reference to killing a bullock, a quarrel ensues which ends in a fight in which the Clown, or his equivalent, dies and is restored in the customary Mumming manner. The dance then proceeds to its climax, the men standing in a circle with their swords interlocked in a chain, the hilt under the point of his neighbour's making star-shaped figures ranging from a pentagon to an octagon, according to the number of dancers. This is called Rose, Lock, Shield, Nut (Knot) or Glass. The symbol is displayed by the leader, or placed round the neck of the dancer who is symbolically decapitated.

In the several fragments and versions of the play of which the dance was once an integral part, the characters and their roles differ very considerably, but a mimic death of a victim and his subsequent resurrection by a magical cure are common to them all as the central feature. In the earliest and least corrupted English example preserved in a manuscript dated October 20th, 1779 from Revesby in Lincolnshire, there are six Sword dancers represented as the sons of the Fool, who introduces them and himself plays the chief role. After commending the play to the generosity of the audience he calls his sons who say that they intend to cut off his head. Though he is reluctant to die, he expresses his willingness to submit for the good of them all. Kneeling down with the swords round his neck he falls on the ground, and the dancers walk once round him and perform a figure of a Sword dance making a ring round him, to make the Knot or Lock or Glass, in the form of a star made by linking the swords together. The dance is repeated and ends again in making the Glass and threatening to decapitate him. Playing for time he makes his will leaving his horse to one of the sons, his cow to another, his sow to the third, his dog to the fourth, and his ram to the fifth. When all his efforts fail to appease or flout them, he is killed by their swords but immediately rises from the floor explaining that he was not slain after all. The dance, the incidents and the figure are then repeated with the same results, the Fool again coming to life, returning as it were from a journey. Finally, there is a love scene in which he and his eldest son vie with each other for a woman, Ciceley, whom the Fool wins.[1]

[1] Chambers, *English Folk Play*, pp. 105–21.

Here the theme has points of contact with the Dionysiac in Thrace with its goat men dancing and singing in a circular orchestra, and the Titans killing Dionysus while he was looking at his own reflection in a mirror, very much as the Lock is called the Glass in which the Old Fool sees his face before he dies at the hands of his five sons; also the Titans disguised themselves by whitening their faces as the dancers blackened them with soot. In both the motif is the death and resurrection dramatically represented. In the Revesby play it is the Fool who is killed by his own sons, whereas in the compli⸍cated Ampleforth play and its Sword dance, as collected by Cecil Sharp,[1] the King fights the Clown after the Queen has rejected him in favour of the Clown, and asks the dancers to kill him. Actually at the conclusion of the dance it is a hand⸍some young foreigner who is slain, when all kneel round him and sing a 'psalm' over his corpse. A Doctor is then called to cure him but in spite of many pretensions and much patter he fails, and it remains for the Clown to restore him to life with his sword.

This compilation, originally published in 1913 as it was recorded by an elderly Darlington railway man who himself had played the part of the Clown in it, has incorporated several motifs and subsidiary songs and dialogue, together with highly complicated figures in the dance. It is, in fact, one of the most elaborate English productions of this kind in existence, containing a number of elements borrowed from various sources but descended ultimately from a common original ritual performed at the winter solstice, like the Mummers' play and the Plough Monday plays, with which it has many points of contact. As Cecil Sharp recognized, the chief interest lies in the dramatic dialogue, of which the dance is the central feature, rather than in the actual dance. It is unfortunate that now at Ampleforth College only the dance is performed instead of the entire play. The original team of six dancers and two musicians (a fiddler and a drummer) have long since been disbanded.

[1] *The Sword Dancers of Northern England*, iii, 2nd. ed., 1951, pp. 50ff.

*The Morris Dance*

With regard to the closely related but independent Morris dance we are rather more fortunately placed as this tradition has been kept alive by teams of 'Morris men', particularly in England in Oxfordshire, Gloucestershire, Warwickshire and Northamptonshire. Although the term is applied sometimes to Mummers, or those who perform Sword dances, as used by Cecil Sharp it is confined to the folk dance that he first discovered in the Cotswold country at Whitsuntide, of which perhaps the best-known example is that held on Whit-Monday at Bampton in Oxfordshire. In this pleasant little town on the edge of the Cotswolds between Witney and Lechlade year by year according to time-honoured custom the six men take possession, wearing white garments, jingling bells, fluttering ribbons, carrying white handkerchiefs, accompanied by the Fool with his bladder, and the cake- and sword-bearer, his sword decorated with ribbons and flowers and with a tin at its end containing a cake. Crowds from the surrounding district still foregather to watch the seasonal dance, and perchance to obtain at a price, for 'luck' or even for a future husband, a piece of the cake on the tip of the sword.

The actual Morris dance is much simpler than the Sword dance, having no elaboration of a figure, though the steps are varied and the rhythm is complex requiring a good deal of skill both in the dance and in the rhythmic manipulation of the handkerchiefs. While these movements conform to the Morris type of folk dance each village or town has its own tradition. Thus, in the Oxfordshire district, at Ducklington, a few miles from Bampton, the ritual opens with a rhythmic dance by 'green garters' round the village garlanded Maypole 'for luck' before the Morris men set out on their rounds; and the raising of the Maypole early in the morning is a ceremonial event of considerable importance. This accomplished, the dancers are duly summoned by blasts blown on horns made of the bark of withy trees. At Kirtlington, on the north side of Oxford, in Whit Week at the annual Lamb Ale the Morris men preceded by a shepherd in a white smock leading a lamb adorned with ribbons went out each morning and danced 'green garters' round the shepherd and the lamb. At the end of the festival the lamb was killed and made into pies which were eaten by the dancers. This appears to have been a survival of a sacramental meal as the pie containing the head with the wool intact was thought to have particular potency as a life-giving agent. At Bampton, and on Headington Hill where Cecil Sharp first saw a group of Morris dancers on Boxing Day 1899, and was so impressed that he was led to devote the rest of his life to the collection, study and revival of the art, the performances have survived little changed in their ancient rustic setting, except that at Headington cricket caps are worn by the dancers. The Fool, from whose grandfather Sharp learned the Morris technique and its tunes, wears a straw in his hair, and the *dramatis personae* follows the normal Cotswold pattern, including the Man-woman and the Fool, but otherwise with very little dramatic action.

On the opposite bank of the Thames in Berkshire, at Abingdon, the six men in white wear top hats and bells on their legs, and carry an ox-head with horns on the top of a pole. Formerly a Mock Mayor was elected by those who lived in Ock Street, and having seated him on a chair ornamented with evergreens, they carried him up and down the street in triumph, accompanied by the Fool, the dancers and the musicians, the ox-head, together with the former mayor carrying a wooden chalice called 'the glass', having the bull's heart in silver as the emblem. Now that Abingdon has become overshadowed by Harwell and developed into a flourishing quasi-industrialized town, the Ock Street Morris dance has survived only in a very diminished form, as in so many other places that have suffered a similar fate.

In former times the Morris dance had a wide distribution in England, by no means confined to the Midlands and the Cotswold region, but extending from Herefordshire and Cheshire to the Thames valley, Wiltshire, Somerset, and the Forest of Dean.[1] In the rest of Europe it was known in France,

---

[1] The very ancient Horn dance at Abbots Bromley in Staffordshire is in the Morris tradition but as it has shifted its date to the beginning of September it is difficult to place it in the seasonal sequence.

Spain, Italy, Flanders, Switzerland and Germany. Although the derivation of the name is very obscure, it may have some connexion with the French form *Mauresque*, brought to England perhaps by soldiers who had seen the dance in France during the Three Hundred Years War; or with the Spanish *Moresco*, a name that may have arisen because the dancers blackened their faces and so were thought to look like Moors.[1] It was not, however, of Moorish origin as its wide distribution extended far beyond the regions under Moorish influence. The blackening of the face was a ritual disguise in the first instance to conceal the identity of the dancers, a tradition that has lingered on as Cecil Sharp was told by one of the Morris men 'so that no one shan't know you sir',[2] or again, as a Hampshire Mummer explained when he covered his face with paper streamers, 'they musn't know who I be'.[3]

The Morris dance may have been introduced into England from France or Spain, where country *Moresco*, often in the form of Sword dances, have been held at fixed seasons ever since the Moors were driven out of the Peninsula in the twelfth century.[4] But although John of Gaunt's troops, or their successors, may have brought the name, the dance is very much older, and, as Chambers maintained, it may have been a derivative of the Sword dance as the two dances so often occur together at the same folk festival with some of the same characters in both of them, while swords or their substitutes occasionally feature in the Morris dance.[5] The bells, on the other hand, are not used in Sword dances while the sacrificial victim is not a Morris characteristic, though traces of sacrifice may have remained in the Kidlington and Kirtlington Lamb Ales, and in the Abingdon ox horns.

In any case, the source of both dances must be sought in the rhythmic rites connected with the food supply and the sequence

[1] Chambers, *The Medieval Stage*, i, p. 199.
[2] M. Karpeles, *Folk-Lore*, xliii, 1932, p. 134.
[3] Alford, *Pyrenean Festivals*, 1937, p. 224.
[4] *Ibid.*, pp. 217 ff.; F. Douce, *Illustrations of Shakespeare*, ii, 1809, pp. 433 ff.
[5] Chambers, *The Medieval Stage*, i, p. 200.

of the seasons, around which in due course communication with the potent supernatural forces controlling the natural order and its processes found a variety of modes of expression. These had been so firmly established in the remote ages of antiquity that by the time they come on the horizon of folk drama and dances they had lost their earlier significance and functions, and survived as adjuncts of the rustic seasonal festivals mainly for amusement, social intercourse and good cheer. Nevertheless, they were still often associated with the religious feasts in the liturgical year, particularly Christmas, Easter, Whitsuntide, and May Day (a month that eventually became dedicated to the Madonna), and so retained a link with their original purposes against the background of the Miracle and Mystery plays. They were, however, essentially secular events, notwithstanding the predominance of the symbolic death and resurrection drama, so conspicuous in the mid-winter Mumming contests at the turn of the year, and in the spring dances with their simulated killing and restoration of the hero.

## Robin Hood

The introduction of such characters as Robin Hood and his band, Maid Marian and Friar Tuck in Tudor times in England, represents a further development in the Morris dance and its themes associated with the Green Man, or Jack-in-the-Green, as the annual victim in the vegetation drama, the prototype of the Fool garlanded in greenery.[1] This figure has a long history in agricultural festivals, recurring in some of the forms and symbolisms that have been considered. The cult is widespread as the Al-Khider, or 'green thing', in the Indus valley in India; in Palestine and Syria, in relation to the Elijah story; in Mesopotamia and Western Asia in the Tammuz theme and its cultus; and later as St George of Cappadocia, the hero of the Dragon, Perseus, and Andromeda story, until at length he became the Saint or King George of the Mum-

[1] E. E. H. Welsford, *The Fool: His Social and Literary History*, 1935; Lady Raglan, *Folk-Lore*, l, 1939, p. 45 ff.

mers' play, and the personification of the Maypole on the village green. In this context Robin Hood, accompanied in the revels by Maid Marian and Friar Tuck and the rest of the merry men in Sherwood Forest, found a place with the Fool and the Hobby-horse in the Morris tradition in and after the fourteenth century. The earliest reference to Robin Hood the ballad hero, is in Langland's *Piers Plowman* about 1377, and in the next century his fame spread throughout the Midlands and northern counties when he became the patron of the cult of the long bow.[1]

Up to a point no doubt he was the creation of the ballad muse, but his equation with the Green Man and the May Day revels and Maid Marian brought him into the fertility drama and its seasonal death and resurrection ritual. As its central figure he had to die by the chance flight of an arrow and like Adonis to bleed to death, and then be restored to life, while Maid Marian assumed the role of the Man-woman. In the capacity of the Robin-of-the-Wood, he was essentially a vegetation sacral hero rather than the leader of the robber band in the forest, or the highly skilled archer of the ballad and romance, or even the shepherd of the French *pastourelles*. His name and Maid Marian's may have been introduced by the minstrels into English, and having been so adopted by the May Day games they were identified with the Nottinghamshire outlaws, the Robin-of-the-Wood being confused with the robber of the rich on behalf of the poor.[2] But while closely connected, the Morris and the Robin Hood teams were not always identical, even though the respective actors and dancers may have been interchangeable, and both represent versions of the same original seasonal ritual.

## The Masque

As in the sixteenth century the *Moresco* tended to become a court dance as well as a folk dance, so from the fourteenth century onwards the Masque developed in France and England

[1] W. H. Clawson, *The Gest of Robin Hood*, 1909.
[2] Chambers, *The Medieval Stage*, i, p. 176.

out of Mummings and dance revels, when kings and their courtiers whiled away the long dark winter evenings with theatrical performances based on the folk drama. Arrayed in richly ornamented and fantastic costumes, the actors portrayed mythological and comic characters, and at the conclusion the spectators were invited to join in a dance. It was this intimacy between the performers and the spectators, as Chambers has pointed out, that differentiates the masque from the drama. Henry VIII himself at the beginning of his reign invaded the queen's chamber at Westminster in the guise of Robin Hood, with his men in 'green coats and hose of Kentish Kendal', and a Maid Marian. Such masquerades continued in court circles throughout his reign, disguising being an integral element in the masked Tudor revels.[1] Having taken their rise in Mumming, they had a seasonal background connected essentially with the winter festal events, but as court performances they tended to become dancing interludes for entertainment as occasion required irrespective of the cycle of the calendar, based on the Italian neo-classical mould of Renaissance pageantry and dancing. Therefore, the Masque hardly falls within the domain of the present inquiry except as a sophisticated offshoot of the folk drama.

## The Country Dance

At the other end of the social scale the country dance of the peasantry was a product of the May Day celebrations, and rapidly became a purely social recreation on occasions of revelry. Divorced from the Maypole with its sacred associations, or the tree of life and the boundary processions, it lost its original significance in becoming a secular form of amusement. Some of its earlier fertility aspects survived in licentious practices which led to prohibitions at Oxford and elsewhere in the thirteenth century. But although the so-called country dance arose within the seasonal ritual and became particularly associated with the peasantry in the village communities, it was in fact popular with all sections of society. As the court Masque

[1] Chambers, *The Elizabethan Stage*, i, O.U.P., 1923, pp. 149 ff.

was a recognized form of indoor Tudor entertainment, so the country dance was an outdoor recreation which in the time of Elizabeth I in England was adopted by courtiers as well as by the common people in preference to the French and Italian more sophisticated dances. So great was its popularity that in 1650 John Playford, a music publisher, produced and sold in considerable numbers at his shop in the Inner Temple in London his handbook on the dances, entitled *The English Dancing Master*. In it were more than a hundred dances with their tunes, consisting of series of figures chosen to fit a particular tune and various formations, some of the Longways type, others in Rounds, and Squares for eight dancers. These, however, gave place in the eighteenth century to the Longways 'for as many as will', and as the earlier Rounds from the Maypole dropped out, the parallel lines of dancers became the traditional type, engaged in as a pastime and devoid of any seasonal or sacred significance.

## FOLK FESTIVALS AND CALENDAR CUSTOMS

Rustic seasonal festivals were by no means confined to the folk drama and its dances. Like the feasts of the liturgical year in the ecclesiastical calendar, they gave ritual expression to the fundamental themes in the annual sequence of winter and summer, of seedtime and harvest, upon which the rhythm of life depended. This has been most apparent in the peasant communities, where many of the ancient seasonal customs have been preserved to a greater or less extent throughout the ages, especially at the solstices. Thus, at midwinter the coincidence of the Christian Feast of the Nativity in its several aspects and manifestations with the solar and agricultural folk customs centred in the turn of the year, has brought together in a complex and composite pattern the various observances connected with both these significant events.

### Folk Festivals

Thus, with the influx of the Northern barbarians Germanic folk customs were incorporated in the Christmas Festival, though since the Teutonic and Celtic calendars were not regulated in relation to the winter solstice their New Year rites belonged to November rather than to December and January. It was when fodder and pasturage became scarce at the approach of winter and the cattle were slaughtered in consider, able numbers that a great banquet was held on the fresh meat, accompanied with fire rites and the usual expressions of autumn, nal rejoicings, coupled with the placation of the dead and the ancestral spirits. The date no doubt was determined originally by the first appearance of snow on the pastures. Eventually it was fixed in the Germano, Celtic calendar in the middle of Novem, ber (11th or 12th),[1] under such designations as *Jiuleis*, *Giuli*, and in Scandinavia *Yule*, a name which still perplexes philologists.

## The Yule Feast

In the absence of a solstitial feast in the Germano, Celtic calen, dar, it is not very likely that Yule originally had this meaning and application. Nevertheless, after the transference of the winter festival from November to the Christmas season of the Roman World when the Northern tribes had penetrated into Gaul, Britain and Central Europe, where the turning, point of the year occurred later, the Teutonic Yule Festival was celebrated in the darkest period (i.e. from mid December to mid January). Yuletide then became equated with Christmas and the midwinter solstice, and its festival included the earlier feasting of the November rites, together with the cult of the dead, and its other observances. These were combined with the solstitial solar and transitional rites connected with the turn of the year, the rebirth of the sun and the renewal of the processes of fertility. Under Christian influence the folk festival was brought into relation with the Nativity commemorations proper to the Christmas season. Therefore, Yuletide became a highly complex observance combining Nordic pagan elements with those derived from the Christian calendrical tradition with its Graeco, Roman background. In this form were celebrated

[1] A. Tille, *Yule and Christmas*, 1899, pp. 18, 24, 78, 107.

the dark ancestral spirits, the lengthening of the days with the return of the sun at a critical juncture in its career, and hopeful anticipation of new life emerging from the darkness and death at the decline of the year, brought into relation with the Christmas message of a new dispensation in the spiritual sphere. The food and fellowship in which the ghostly members of the family joined, the Yule log and Yule cakes, the greenery and the fir-trees, the wassailing and carols, the gifts and greet-ings, all bore witness to the several aspects and commemora-tions of the festive season which, as the Nativity became the dominant feature, were given a deeper interpretation in terms of the Incarnation of 'the true Light of the World'.

## Yule Candles

That fires and light should play such a conspicuous part in the Yuletide and Christmas observances is to be expected since the festival has been fixed at the darkest and coldest time in the year when the two essential requirements are warmth and illumination. In Sweden the festivities began with 'Little Yule' on December 13th, St Lucia's Day, when a Lucia Queen or Bride was elected in the village. Dressed in white and carrying on her head lighted candles, she set forth in the dark with a man on horseback and a cortège of maids of honour, and with 'star-boys' representing demons and trolls conquered by the reviving sun, to visit the houses, farms and stables, as the harbinger of the return of life and light. The youngest girl of a family might assume the role of St Lucia in her own home, adorned with a candle-crown and going the round of the house with coffee and singing songs. These perambulations were followed by breakfast in a brightly illuminated room, and the animals were given extra fodder. In a somewhat modified form these customs still prevail in Scandinavia and the adjacent Northern countries (e.g. Finland).

On Christmas Eve a large candle resembling in dimensions the Paschal Candle in the Holy Saturday ceremonies, was lighted and allowed to burn either throughout Christmas Day, or like its Easter counterpart, during the whole of the festival until Twelfth Night or New Year's Day, when it was extinguished by the head or eldest member of the household. An ancient stone candle-socket with the figure of the *Agnus Dei* that contained the Yule candle which was burnt in the Hall of St John's College, Oxford, during the twelve nights of the festival, is still preserved in the buttery. The candles on Christmas trees placed in the windows of houses are the last relic of the Yule candle once so widespread, and of the Christian legend concerning the Holy Child being guided in the darkness to the lighted house to bless all who dwelt therein. In 1926 the practice was revived at the Regency Campden Hill Square in London, where in every window a lighted candle stood on Christmas Eve.

*Yule Log*

The Yule log has been even more persistent. As the domestic midwinter counterpart of the communal midsummer bonfires a log, sometimes decorated with greenery and ribbons, was placed on the hearth on Christmas Eve and kindled with the remains of its predecessor which had been carefully preserved throughout the year for this purpose. It had to be kept alight until Twelfth Night to promote the fruitfulness of the new crops, and so tended that a portion remained for preservation, while the ashes might be scattered on the fields to make them productive, or kept in the house as a protection against lightning and fire. Its purpose, however, was primarily to give light and warmth to the spirits of the dead.

In Yugoslavia the logs were sawn from oaks which were felled on Christmas Eve before sunrise, and were decorated with red silk, leaves and flowers before they were carried ceremonially to the houses in the twilight with lighted tapers. As they were taken over the threshold corn and sometimes wine were thrown over the first log and it was greeted in personal terms. It was then placed on the fire by the oldest male member of the family. The floor was strewn with straw by the mother, a Yule candle was lighted in the middle of a sheaf of wheat, the father praying for the blessing of God upon the household, its fields, cattle, sheep, bees and the crops, before they all sat down to a meal. The night was spent in keeping the log burning brightly, and early the next morning a pig was roasted on the fire while the family anxiously awaited the arrival of a boy, called the *polaznik*, who threw a handful of wheat on them with the words 'Christ is born.' They replied 'He is born indeed', and the mother threw wheat over this mysterious visitor. He then struck the log and wished 'good luck, prosperity, progress and happiness' to the household and its beasts. By sitting on the floor he was thought to fix his wishes into the ground, and to ensure a good supply of thick cream he was wrapped in a thick blanket.[1]

In France the Yule log (*tréfoire*) was a prominent feature in Provence, the Dordogne and in Dauphine. Thus, Frédéric Mistral, the Provençal poet, speaking of his boyhood recalled the cutting of the Yule log from a fruit-tree and the bringing of it to his home, in single file beginning with the eldest and ending with the youngest. Three times a tour of the kitchen was made and the log was then laid on the hearth, his father pouring a glass of wine over it with the words 'Joy, joy, May God shower joy upon us, my dear children. Christmas brings us all good things. God give us grace to see the New Year, and if we do not increase in numbers may we at all events not decrease.' In chorus they replied, 'Joy, joy, joy!', and lifted the log on the fire dogs. Then as the first flame leapt up the father crossed himself saying, 'Burn the log, O fire,' and they all sat down to the table.[2] In Périgord in the Dordogne plum-tree, cherry and oak were regarded as the best wood for logs, as they burnt well and slowly which was a good omen, and they made excellent charcoal and ash, required for healing swollen glands. The part of the trunk which was not burnt was used to make the wedge for the plough, as it was believed that it caused the seeds and poultry to thrive.[3]

In Italy in the Val di Chiana a great log was gathered and when it was ignited the children were blindfolded and set to

[1] Chelo Mijatovich, *Servia and the Servians*, 1908, pp. 98 ff.
[2] *Memoirs of Mistral*, E.T. by C. E. Maud, 1907, pp. 29 f.
[3] Mannhardt, *Baumkultus*, 1875, pp. 226 f.

beat it with tongs. In a book printed in Milan probably in the fifteenth century, an account occurs of the father calling together his family on Christmas Eve for the placing of the log on the fire with juniper under it and money on the top which was afterwards given to the servants. Wine was poured on the fire three times, and the ashes were preserved as a protection against hail, or more recently for the benefit of the silk worms.[1] In Germany and in England the ritual conformed to this general pattern, the log being lighted generally from a fragment of its predecessor, and kept burning on Christmas Day. The ashes were used to protect the house, the crops and the fruit-trees from insects and to increase fertility.[2]

*Bonfires*

Besides these private or domestic Yule celebrations a mid-winter fire-festival occasionally was kept as a public observance in Northern and Central Europe. Thus, in Thuringia a huge bonfire was kindled on the Antonius Mountain on Christmas Eve by young people, in defiance of all efforts by Church and State to suppress the custom. Around it other smaller fires were lighted and torches were swung, the night being spent in revelry until at length the company dispersed and went to Mass.[3] In Scotland where Christmas customs have been transferred to the New Year, on the Eve of the event known as Hogmanay enormous crowds gather outside the Tron Kirk in Edinburgh at midnight. As the clock strikes the hour all engage in handshaking, toasting, health-drinking and good wishes. Hats are thrown into the air, and to the strains of wild music by the bagpipes, dancing and revelry begin. First-footers go off to bring luck to the houses they enter if they are dark-haired strangers, and all the pent up energy of the delayed

[1] Gubernatis, *Storia Comparati degli Usi Natalizen*, Milan, 1878, pp. 112f.

[2] A. Witzschel, *Sagen, Sitten und Gebräuche aus Thüringen*, Vienna, 1878, p. 172; A. Kuhn, *Sagen, Gebräuche, und Märchen aus Westfalen*, ii, Leipzig, 1859, pp. 319ff.; Brand, *Popular Antiquities*, i, pp. 245ff.; Herrick, *Hesperides*, 'Ceremonies for Christmasse'.

[3] Witzschel, *op. cit*, pp. 171ff.

Christmas Festival spends its force on the night of New Year's Eve in phenomenal feasting and drinking. At Biggar in Lanarkshire the Old Year is burnt out with bonfires, while at Burghead on the Moray Firth on Hogmanay, or on January 11th, the old New Year's Eve, a tar-barrel called the Clavie is set on fire by blazing peat, and hoisted on a pole known as the Spoke. No metal may be used in its preparation and only local men may be employed in its production. The Clavie is carried by young men, round the village and its fishing boats, to the top of the Doorie Hill, down the sides of which eventually it is rolled. As it passes the houses the doors are opened to allow brands to be thrown in to bring luck, and from them the house fires are lighted. Should one of the bearers of the Clavie stumble during the procession it portends his death in the course of the year, and ill-luck to the town. The crowd scramble for the embers, and keep them as charms against witchcraft and other evil influences.[1] The persistence of this ancient festival and the taboo on the use of metal suggests the great antiquity of the observance in a town containing a mound surrounded with unique ramparts made of earth, stone and logs in the manner of pre-Roman Gaul.

*Plough Monday*

On Monday after the Epiphany when work in the farms was resumed after the Christmas recess ending with Twelfth Night, the ploughs to be used in the preparation of the fields for the spring crops were blessed and decorated and carried round the village by young men called Plough Bullocks, or Plough Stots, accompanied by the Fool and Bessy of the Mummers' plays and the Sword dances, which were performed on this day by the farm-labourers, especially in Lincolnshire and the East Midlands in England. In these plays the ancient ritual combat was dramatically enacted in the violent dances and imagery centred in the death and revival theme, symbolizing the renewal of vegetation at the approach of spring in the

[1] Chambers, *Book of Days*, ii, 1886, pp. 789ff.; *Folk-Lore*, vii, 1889, pp. 11ff.

seasonal sequence. On this occasion, as the plough was the central feature, the dance was held round it. In recent years this ancient custom has been restored in many English villages by a plough being taken to the parish church on the Sunday after the Epiphany, and there blessed by the incumbent at Evensong in the presence of the local farmers and ploughmen, as a token of divine beneficence on the agricultural work of the forth-coming season.

### The Haxey Hood

At Haxey in northern Lincolnshire not far from Doncaster the struggle between winter and spring is still displayed on January 6th in a tussle that goes back at least to the thirteenth century, and in all probability is a relic of the ancient spring contest. The ceremony in its present form begins with a pro-cession headed by the Fool with his face smeared with soot and red ochre, clad in trousers of sackcloth with red patches on them, a red shirt and a flowered top hat with goose's wings adorning it. In his hand he carries a whip, and a sock filled with bran on the end of a thong to take the place of his bladder. With him are the twelve players called Boggans, their leader being known as the King Boggan, also clad in red coats with top hats and red armlets. The leader or King carries a wand of thirteen willow rods bound together, and a roll of rope encased in leather and sacking called the Hood. When the contestants reach the church their approach is heralded by the ringing of the bells, and the Fool, who mounts the stone at the base of the Cross near the wall of the churchyard, calls upon the assembly to engage in the ancient struggle. He alleges that two bullocks and a half have been killed, the other half having been left running about the field, and announces the rules of the game:

> Hoose agen hoose, toone agen toone,
> If tho meets a man, knock 'im doone
> But dont 'ut im!

Jumping down from the stone he leads the crowd to the half-acre field where after a short struggle for sham hoods, the real

Hood is thrown into the air and the genuine scramble begins in an endeavour by all the participants to seize it and carry it off to their own village. It is the business of the Boggans to prevent the Hood leaving Haxey, and if one of them is able to get it, or even to touch it, it is considered 'dead' and has to be thrown up again. For several hours the fray continues, the swaying mass of struggling humanity moving first this way and then that, regardless of walls, hedges and onlookers in their path, until at length it is forced into the village of the strongest section.[1]

It seems very likely that originally the Hood was the half or head of a bull sacrificed to fertilize the newly ploughed fields, and, therefore, eagerly sought by those who could secure it to vitalize their crops. Now by way of explanation of the custom an aetiological story is told of a Lady Mowbray of the local Manor who lost her hood on a windy day and gave the land on which the Sway takes place in trust for the twelve men who restored it to her. But this is the usual fictitious interpretation of an ancient rite the real origin of which has long been forgotten. The reference to the bullocks in the Fool's speech, the Plough Monday associations, and formerly, a final 'smoking' of the Fool, either after his oration or on the following day, over a fire of damp straw as a ritual fumigation—a practice now abandoned—are all indicative of a transitional rite at the end of the midwinter festival. It has every appearance of being the folk survival of the last stage of a ritual combat between local groups, and there can be little doubt that originally the Hood was the sacrificial victim, it too having been formerly roasted at the fire in the inn as the Fool was smoked by being dangled over a damp fire.

*Shrovetide Contests*

Moreover, contests of this nature have been an integral element in seasonal ritual for the purpose of promoting fertility and conquering the malign forces of evil, especially at the approach

[1] E. H. Rudkin, *Folk-Lore*, xliii, 1932, pp. 294 ff; cf. vii, 1896, pp. 189, 330; viii, pp. 72, 173.

of spring. This is apparent in the many ball games that have survived throughout the ages which originally had a ritual significance akin to the Haxey Hood. Not infrequently these have occurred in the opening of the year, and have persisted in association with the carnival, revelries and merry-making after the Epiphany and before the austerities of Lent begin on Ash Wednesday. The rites, however, belong to the Spring Festival rather than to that of the winter solstice, Shrovetide looking forward to Easter, not backwards to Christmas. And the popular customs connected with Shrovetide were not confined to the day before Ash Wednesday when the faithful might be expected to be occupied with more serious exercises in view of the requirements of shriving before Lent on this day. Thus, Barnaby Googe (1540–1594) says that Shrovetide feasting and hilarity lasted for four days from the Saturday before Quinquagesima to Shrove Tuesday, and in Britain contests became a feature of the final phase of these Mardi Gras celebrations which in the sunnier Latin south were characterized by greater gaiety though certainly not by more determination and local hostility.

In England it became the custom for parishes to divide themselves into two opposed groups at this season of the year, which usually coincided with Shrove Tuesday, to engage in 'rough and tumbles', such as those at Ashbourne, Alnwick, Chester-le-Street, Dorking and Yetholm in Roxburghshire, to mention but a few of the forty-two towns or districts in which they have been recorded, and in which they have survived to within recent memory. So seriously was the event taken in 1928 at Ashbourne that the Duke of Windsor, who was then Prince of Wales, started the match by throwing up the ball, and in Wales in the parish of Lampeter the combatants assembled in church before the contest, which incidentally took place there on Christmas Day rather than on Shrove Tuesday. So highly esteemed was victory in Scotland that a Bro of the Highlands or a Blaenau of the Lowlands would as soon lose a cow from his cow-house as the football from his portion of the parish.[1]

[1] A. B. Gomme, *Dictionary of British Folklore*, i, pt. i, pp. 136f.

The earliest record of Shrove Tuesday Football is at Chester in 1533 when an unsuccessful attempt was made to suppress it as a public nuisance.[1] It was not, however, until the eighteenth century that accounts occur of local struggles between two opposed groups as seasonal events centred at Shrovetide, often in association with cock-fighting, hen-thrashing, and similar brutal sports, as, for example, at Derby in 1790. There it is said to have been carried to 'the barbarous height of an election contest', the hero being 'chaired through the streets like a successful member, although his utmost elevation of character was no more than that of a butcher's apprentice'.[2] From subsequent accounts the order of events seems to have con-sisted in a contest between the parishioners of All Saints, with their goal at Nun's Mill, and those of St Peter's whose goal was at Gallows Balt on the Normanton road. The players were young men from eighteen to thirty or upwards, but people from the rest of the town joined in the fray. The game commenced in the market-place where the two sides were marshalled about noon. A large ball was thrown up in the midst of them and the violent struggle began, each side endeavouring to secure the ball and carry it to their respective goals—the St Peter's men to the Morledge brook into the Derwent; the All Saints party to urge it westwards to their domain. 'Broken shins, broken heads, torn coats and lost hats', we are told, were 'among the minor accidents of this fearful contest.' A French-man who witnessed the scene remarked that 'if Englishmen called this playing, it would be impossible to say what they would call fighting'. Encouraged by the respective supporters of the two contestant groups among the surrounding mob, and reinvigorated with oranges and 'other refreshment' (the nature of which is not specified), the fray and the numbers increased till they exceeded a thousand in the streets crowded with on-lookers, with 'two or three hundred of the men up to their chins

[1] F. P. Magoen, *Shrove Tuesday Football*, Harvard University Press, 1931, p. 13.
[2] W. Hutton, *A History of Derby, from the Remote Ages of Antiquity to the year MDCCXCI*, 1791, pp. 218f.

in the Derwent continually ducking each other'. The town, in short, presented the appearance of 'a place suddenly taken by storm'.[1]

According to the local tradition this violent event celebrated the driving out and slaying of a cohort of Roman soldiers marching through the town of Derventio in 217 by the unarmed Britons. But, however it may have arisen, it was so deeply laid in the traditional life of the town that to suppress the observance in 1846 'it required two troops of Dragoons, a large levy of special constables and the reading of the Riot Act to secure the desired result'.[2] It claims to have been much more ancient and firmly established than its counterpart at Ashbourne to the north-west of Derby, though in a song sung by a comedian at the Ashbourne theatre on February 21st, 1821 the Shrove Tuesday contest between Upwards and Downwards was likened to the battle of Waterloo as an established feature of the 'neat little town'.[3] The dividing line of the two sides was a bridge in the centre of Ashbourne, those living north of it constituting one group and those to the south of it the other, with goals three miles apart marked by the mills at either end, each one and a half miles from the bridge. To score the ball had to touch the mill and the player had to swim across the millpond and touch the building himself. At two o'clock the ball made of cork covered with leather and painted red, white and blue, was thrown up in the air and some two hundred combatants began their efforts to rush it through the streets of the town to the stream. When at length this was accomplished the players continued their struggles in the water, ducking each other and paying off old scores, until one or other of the mills was reached.[4]

In County Durham a traditional Shrovetide match between

---

[1] S. Glover, *The History, Gazetteer, and Directory of the County of Derby*, i, Derby, 1829, pp. 310f.

[2] A. W. Davidson, *Derby; its Rise and Progress*, 1906, pp. 210ff.; cf. William Andrews, *Bygone Derbyshire*, 1892, p. 220.

[3] Llewellyn Jewitt, *Ballads and Songs of Derbyshire*, 1867, pp. 284ff.

[4] E. Dudley, *The Field*, lxxi, 3 March, 1888, p. 304.

tradesmen and countrymen was played at Sedgefield throughout the nineteenth century in the presence of several thousand spectators, though occupying less than an hour. At Chester-le-Street in this district it was a more violent affair, and in 1887 a lamp-post was broken by the Up-streeters in their struggle with the Down-streeters.[1] At Dorking in Surrey in the same year, a decade before it was stopped as a public nuisance, two thousand people were said to have joined in the game during the last hour when the struggle was at its fiercest. The game commenced at two o'clock, the object of each side being to have the ball in its own quarter of the town when the clock struck six. The shops in the High Street were barricaded to prevent damage to the windows and their contents, though according to the accounts accidents were few and in spite of rough play good temper usually prevailed.[2] At Stonyhurst College in Lancashire in the last century football matches in which sixty or seventy boys took part, representing 'English' and 'French', were played on the Thursday before Quinquagesima Sunday, and on the following Monday and Tuesday. Flags were flown and cannons fired while the games were in progress, and on Shrove Tuesday extra pancakes were given to those who distinguished themselves in them.[3]

At Ludlow in Shropshire a tug-of-war on a grand scale took place on Shrove Tuesday between the inhabitants of the Broad Street Ward and the Corve Street Ward, with a rope three inches thick and thirty-six yards long, having a red knob at one end and a blue knob at the other. At four o'clock the shops shut and put up their shutters as a precaution against broken windows, and the Mayor with his retinue went to the Market Hall to suspend the rope out of one of the windows. Below, a vast concourse of townsfolk, numbering thousands, assembled to take part in the contest, and as soon as the rope was lowered it was seized by the competitors in the hope of

[1] W. Andrews, *Bygone Durham*, 1898, p. 210.

[2] *Notes and Queries*, 3rd Series, i, 1862, p. 224; 6th Series, 1880, p. 154; J. S. Bright, *A History of Dorking and the Neighbouring Parishes*, Dorking, 1884, p. 48.

[3] *Notes and Queries*, 10th Series, i, 1904, p. 435.

pulling it to the boundary of their respective wards. When this had been achieved, the winners, often with clothes torn to ribbons in the process, and some of their allies badly injured, returned the rope to the Market Hall, after having dipped it in the river Teme if they were the Red Knob side. It was then given out again and returned by the victors in the same manner until the same side had been twice successful. Then the rope was bought back from them by public subscription and the money was spent on drinking and feasting.[1] The conduct and accidents to which it gave rise caused it to be discontinued in 1851. A similar custom has been recorded from Presteign in Radnorshire between the Upper and the Lower portions of the town, which survived long after the suppression of the Ludlow tug-of-war.[2]

Seasonal games and contests of this nature were almost universal in England and elsewhere in Europe at the approach or beginning of spring, until they were prohibited on the ground that they were dangerous to life and limb and property, as indeed they were. With the rapid growth of the population in the nineteenth century this was an increasingly serious consideration. In a few favoured small towns, such as Ashbourne and Chester-le-Street, they were able to survive to the present century, like St Giles' Fair in Oxford, or the Mummers' at Bampton. But seasonal customs involving horseplay and ferocity have been condoned and tolerated only within certain limits. When they have run to excess they have become unendurable, and have been greatly modified or entirely suppressed either by public opinion or by legal procedure. This applies in particular to those that have lost any serious and useful function and significance.

*Eastertide Diversions*

Around the Easter Festival a number of less strenuous and destructive ball games have collected, such as stool-ball, played especially by girls and women. The meaning and purpose of

[1] Brand, *op. cit.*, i, p. 92.
[2] C. S. Burne and G. F. Jackson, *Shropshire Folk-Lore*, 1883, pp. 321f.

these pastimes may be gleaned from an Easter verse in *Poor Robin's Almanack* for 1740:

> *Now milkmaids pails are deckt with flowers,*
> *And men begin to drink in bowers.*
> *The mackerels come up in shoals*
> *To fill the mouths of hungry souls;*
> *Sweet sillabubs, and life-lov'd tansy*
> *For William is prepared by Nancy;*
> *Much time is wasted now away,*
> *At pigeon-holes and nine-pin play,*
> *Whilst hob-nail Dick and simp'ring Frances,*
> *Tip it away in country dances;*
> *At stool-ball and at barley-break,*
> *Wherewith they harmless pastime make.*

Similarly, contests with eggs, symbols of new life and resurrection, have been common on Easter Day. The game consists in a hard-boiled egg being held by one player and struck at by the other, like the chestnuts in the autumn game 'conkers'. The egg that first breaks is won by the striker, and this process is repeated till all the eggs have been disposed of.[1] Brightly coloured eggs decorated in yellow, red or gilt, and other tints artistically blended in an elaborate pattern or with furze or broom flowers, are rolled down hills by children in Switzerland and in the north of England until they are broken, and then eaten. On Easter Eve boys and men in Lancashire used to tour the towns and villages as 'Pace-eggers' begging for eggs and performing the St George Mummers' play, or the Pace-Egg (i.e. Pasch play) version of it, transferred from the Christmas Festival, with the same characters and words except for local peculiarities, to obtain money for those taking part. The custom declined at the end of the last century but survived until recently in the Lake District and at Blackburn. Disguises were a feature of the play, and a female called Old Miser Brown Bags, played by a boy, was sometimes introduced.

[1] *Journal of American Folk-Lore*, xii, 1899, p. 107; xvi, 1903, p. 138.

The earlier magico-religious significance of these games survived in a very modified form by the egg becoming a symbol of the Resurrection, and so being consecrated in church and distributed as sacred emblems. At Chester the bishop and dean are said to have engaged in an egg-throwing match with the choir boys in the cathedral, and, according to Hone, a ball was produced on Easter Day when the antiphon was being sung, and the dean began a dance taking the ball in his hand. At intervals it was passed to each of the choristers, and at the end of the proceedings all the participants, who included the lord of the manor and the archbishop, withdrew for refreshment.[1] It is possible there may have been some connexion between this custom and the tradition that the sun danced round and round for joy at dawn on Easter morning, which lay behind the widespread and ancient practice of going to hills at sunrise to see the sun whirling around, as it was firmly believed and constantly affirmed to do.

Again, making a special brew of strong ale for the churchwardens to drink in church and sell to the parishioners at Easter for the benefit of church expenses, or other charitable purposes, may have been the relic of an earlier sacred meal, like the Church Ales at Whitsun, Midsummer and Christmas. It was also customary in some villages for the poor to be given feasts in church on Easter Day, and in 1637 a complaint was made to Archbishop Laud by the parishioners of Clunganford in Shropshire because their Easter Feast was not held.[2] Cakes were also distributed from the parish church to the young people until the practice was generally abolished in the sixteenth century, though it survived where special bequests had been left for doles of cakes, bread and cheese to the poor annually at Easter.[3]

Among secular customs, 'heaving' on Easter Monday was practised until the later part of the last century, especially in the northern counties in England, and occasionally it still survives

[1] W. Hone, *The Every Day Book*, i, 1839, p. 429.
[2] S. O. Addy, *Church and Manor*, 1913, pp. 332f.
[3] *Notes and Queries*, 2nd Series, ii, 1856, pp. 404f.

in some of the industrial towns. As described by Brand, quoting from a record dated 1290 and communicated to the Society of Antiquaries in 1805, Edward I was lifted by ladies of the court on Easter Monday, and paid them fourteen pounds according to custom, the person lifted always being required to pay a small tribute to those performing the 'heaving'. In Manchester, Bolton and Warrington parties of women surrounded any man they met and lifted him three times above their heads. The next day the process was reversed, the men lifting the women in the same manner. In one case cited by Brand in 1798, on Easter Tuesday a man at the Talbot, Shrewsbury, was invited by the female servants of the house to sit in a chair decorated with coloured ribbons, and they then hoisted him well above their heads and each of them kissed him. There it was the custom for women to lift the men on Tuesday instead of on Easter Monday when the men performed their functions. Sometimes in Shropshire the person lifted was asperged by means of a bunch of flowers dipped in water.[1] Brand thinks that the custom was intended to represent the Resurrection, but it seems to be more likely that it was originally a spring rite to promote the growth of the crops, as in the leaping of the Salii in Rome during March.[2]

## Hocktide

On the following Monday after Low Sunday, called Hocktide, women armed with ropes caught and bound any man they encountered and demanded a forfeit, while the next day the men retaliated. From the church accounts it would seem that this was a lucrative form of amusement, the amount of money collected and passed over to the wardens being quite considerable, particularly from the women. As well as the extraction of dues and forfeits, Hocktide was an occasion for boisterous sports, whipping passers-by, sprinkling and binding with ropes, and the performance of the Coventry Hock play. As

[1] Brand, *op. cit.*, i, pp. 181ff.; *Notes and Queries*, 6th Series, i, 1852, p. 194; Burne and Jackson, *Northern Folklore*, p. 84.

[2] Cf. Chap. vi, p. 164.

this had a Sword dance and fight but no Doctor and his cure, it seems to be in line with the Shrovetide football and to derive from the age-long struggle for the fertilizing victim in the Spring Festival rites, rather than with the St George tradition.[1] In July 1575 it was revived for the entertainment of Queen Elizabeth when she visited the Earl of Leicester at Kenilworth, and represented the portraying of the massacre of the Danes by Ethelred on St Brice's Day 1002, when they had been led captive by the English women. This was one tradition of its origin; another connected it with the sudden death of Hardicanute at the end of the Danish usurpation. But these are only aetiological attempts to give a historical origin to what in fact was a seasonal rite.

At Hungerford in Berkshire, Hocktide is still observed on the Tuesday after Low Sunday in the traditional manner. Early in the morning the landlords and householders are summoned to assemble for the festival by the Town Crier wearing a scarlet and grey uniform, and a tall hat ornamented with gold lace. At eight o'clock (a.m.) he blows his horn from the balcony of the Town Hall, the horn being a replica of that presented to Hungerford by John of Gaunt and still in its possession. At nine o'clock a jury is sworn in at the Town Hall for the purpose of electing a High Constable, Bailiff, Portreen, Tithing or Tuttimen, and other functionaries. The High Constable then gives the Tuttimen the tutti poles adorned with blue ribbons and flowers (i.e. 'tutties' in the form of posies), and equipped with an adequate supply of oranges they tour the town, collecting money from the men and kisses from the women, climbing ladders and mounting balconies to reach windows to receive their dues. In return they distribute their oranges for 'luck' and 'plenty'. When this is over, at the invitation of the retiring High Constable the jury repair to the Three Swans Hotel for luncheon. Afterwards the guests and newcomers undergo an initiation rite performed by two 'farriers' who seize them and pretend to drive nails into their shoes until they have paid for drinks all round by way of

[1] Chambers, *The Medieval Stage*, i, p. 187.

ransom. They then become 'townsmen'. On the following Friday the officials are sworn in and in the evening are given a banquet by the new High Constable, at which the toast to the memory of John of Gaunt is drunk in silence. On the next Sunday in their official capacities they attend the morning service in the parish church.[1]

Like Michaelmas, Hocktide was formerly the occasion for the payment of rents and other dues, but the contests between men and women on their respective days (the men Hocking on the Monday and the women retaliating on the Tuesday, or vice versa), which included the taking of hostages and the payment of ransoms, suggest that in the background of these folk observances lay seasonal rites in which sacrificial victims were offered to secure the rebirth of nature at the Spring Festival, later redeemed by the payment of money as in Ancient Israel (Ex. xiii, 13, 15). There may be an inkling of what took place in the past in the form of the survival which in 1450 was described as 'disgraceful sports and amusements practised on the days commonly called Hock-days', when the Bishop of Worcester issued an order to the Almoner of the Cathedral for their suppression.[2]

## May Day Celebrations

Rather different in their character but more persistent, and performed for much the same purpose, are the May Day celebrations at the beginning of summer, centring in the May King or Green Man, his Queen and his symbol, the Maypole, decorated with greenery. As the sacred pine tree representing the self-emasculated Attis was taken in procession by the *dendrophori* from Kybele's wood to her temple on the Palatine Hill in Rome at the Spring Festival on March 22nd,[3] so in many parts of peasant Europe youths have repaired to the woods after midnight at the dawn of the month of May for a similar purpose. Having engaged in unrestrained love-making and games they

[1] *Folk-Lore*, ix, 1898, pp. 282ff.
[2] J. Noake, *Worcester in Olden Times*, 1849, p. 136.
[3] Cf. Chap. vi, p. 189.

cut down a tree, lopped off the branches leaving a few at the top. They then wrapped it round with purple bands, after decorating it with violets like the figure of Attis. At sunrise, blowing horns and flutes, they have taken it back to the village with young trees or branches to fasten over the doors and windows of their houses. The Maypole has been erected on the village green, or in some other central place often near the church, as it still is throughout the length and breadth of rural England and elsewhere. Sometimes a doll has been fixed to the tree in the middle of a garland, like the image of Attis, or carried in a basket or cradle from house to house by young girls, or dangled in the centre of two hoops at right angles to each other, and decorated with flowers as the May Lady.[1]

The Maypole sometimes stood more than sixty feet high, and, like Kybele in her car drawn by lions or oxen, it has been conveyed in a wagon drawn by from twenty to forty oxen, each adorned with garlands on its horns, followed by men, women and children. On its arrival at its destination it has been erected near the church amid rejoicing, very much as the pine-tree was exposed for veneration and set up near the temple of the Magna Mater on the Palatine. Around it dances have always been held, sometimes confined to lovers but generally engaged in by all the young people in the village. In England long streamers are now attached to the top of the pole, each held by a child, and as they dance round it the ribbons are entwined, until they are unplaited when the dancers reverse. These may be a survival of the bands of wool on the Attis tree. The May Queen herself is often taken to the village green in a decorated cart drawn by youths or maids of honour, headed by the Maypole. On her arrival she is crowned and enthroned before the dances begin, and sometimes they are performed before her throne rather than round the Maypole. During her year of office she is supposed to preside at all the gatherings

[1] T. F. Thistleton-Dyer, *British Popular Customs*, 1876, pp. 251 ff.; R. Chambers, *Book of Days*, i, 1886, p. 577, col. i; W. Hone, *Every Man Book*, xi, 1820, pp. 615 ff.; Brand, *op. cit.*, i, pp. 212 ff.; E. Hull, *Folklore of the British Isles*, 1928, pp. 253 f.

and revels of young people.[1] Similarly the May King has been represented by a man, usually a chimney-sweep, clad in a wooden framework covered with leaves in the guise of the Jack-in-the-Green. He too has been taken to the scene of the revels either on horseback with the pyramid over him, or on a sledge, surrounded by a cavalcade of young men.[2]

The representation of the May Queen and the May King as bride and bridegroom is reminiscent of the sacred marriage in the Magna Mater Festival; and as Kybele was responsible for the flowering of the fields, so the May Queen sat in an arbour wreathed with flowers, or in the porch of the church similarly adorned, like her Romano-Phrygian counterpart seated in her mountain abode and receiving floral offerings from her votaries.[3] Her spouse the Green Man has been treated in the same manner because he has played the Attis role in the folk tradition. In short, they have both survived true to type in their essential features and the general setting of the May celebrations, in spite of the observances having now lost their earlier significance, becoming an occasion for merry-making and the collection of *pourboires*. The principal parts are now generally played by children, and in Warwickshire the Queen is a small girl wheeled in a 'mail-cart', or perambulator, by an older girl. The Maypole is carried by four boys, and a young girl takes the money box as the children go from house to house singing their traditional songs and collecting money for their tea in the afternoon.[4] But although they are now picturesque pastimes and childish diversions, often acquiring local colour and customs, the fact that they have persisted so little changed and true to type in their respective roles, shows how very deeply laid was the myth and ritual of the Spring Festival in its diffusion from the Ancient Near East, where upon it was believed to depend the rebirth of nature in the spring.

[1] Thistleton-Dyer, *op. cit.*, pp. 270ff.; Wright and Lones, *British Calendar Customs*, ii, 1938, pp. 224ff.

[2] Mannhardt, *op. cit.*, p. 322; W. D. Rouse, *Folk-Lore*, iv, 1893, pp. 50ff.

[3] Chap. vi, pp. 185f.; cf. C. B. Lewis, *A Miscellany of Studies to L. E. Kastner*, 1932, pp. 330ff.

[4] *G.B.*, pt. ii, p. 88.

*The Beltane Fire Festival*

In Scotland and Ireland the ancient Celtic practice of lighting
bonfires at the beginning of May as part of a sacrificial rite
lingered on until the eighteenth century in the observance
known as Beltane or Bealtainn. The name is derived from the
Gaelic *tein-eigin*, 'need-fire', and *Beil*, possibly connected with
the Celtic god Belenos whose worship was widespread in
Gaul and perhaps in Britain, rather than with the Semitic Baal
or Bel. Whether or not this deity was a solar god, both Beltane
and Belenos mean 'bright fire', and the practice of lighting
sacred fires, often on hills, at the beginning of the second
division of the Celtic year was for the purpose of stimulating
the sun as the life-giving agent at the commencement of
summer. On November 1st a similar observance, the Samhain,
was held to usher in winter with all its perils and privations, to
drive away evil influences when the sun was waning, as at
Beltane, or May Day, the corresponding rites were a precaution
against witchcraft and other sinister forces rampant at the
beginning of summer.

Thus, on Walpurgis Night, the Eve of May Day, branches
of rowan or buckthorn were fastened to the houses and cattle-
stalls to keep away the witches, and the gorse was set on fire
at the break of day to burn them out.[1] Fires were extinguished
and rekindled with appropriate ceremonies as on Easter Eve in
the liturgical calendar, the antiquity of which custom is
indicated by the use of earlier methods of fire-making by
friction, tinder and flint and steel being employed for the
purpose. When the Beltane bonfire had been lighted from the
'need-fire' (*tein-eigin*) branches were lit at it and carried into the
house to ignite the new fires in the grates. In the Highlands of
Scotland this was the only occasion when the peat-fires were
put out and relighted (by the friction method) like the annual
renewal of the sacred fire in the temple of Vesta on March 1st
by the Vestal Virgins.[2]

[1] J. Rhys, *Proceedings of the British Academy*, iv, pp. 55 ff.; Reinberg-Dürings-
feld, *Fest-Kalender aus Böhmen*, Prague, 1861, p. 210.

[2] Chap. vi, p. 171.

That the Beltane fires were regarded as cathartic and regenera-tive is suggested by the custom of driving cattle through them to protect them from disease, and of girls and women jumping across them either to secure husbands or to have safe deliverance in childbirth. The burning of the skull or bones of a horse in it may have been a survival of the sacrifice of the horse at the ancient Celtic festival, while the scattering of the embers on the fields to produce good crops was clearly a fertility rite, as was also the dance held on Walpurgis Night in which, following the example of the Salii, the warrior priests of Mars in Rome,[1] those who took part leaped as high as they could to make the crops grow to their fullest capacity. In the Beltane rites it was customary to dance round the fire sunwise, and in the same manner to run round the fields with burning brands to stimu-late the fecundity of the soil and of the crops sown in it, as well as to drive away the witches.

Large round cakes of oatmeal as a solar symbol have been rolled down a hill or through the fields in some districts. Sometimes a tree was carried through the fields or by the dwellings and afterwards burned. At the end of the proceedings the Beltane cake was divided among the company. The person who received the piece that was marked with charcoal was called *cailleach-beal-teine*—i.e. the Beltane carline, a term of reproach—and an attempt was made to put him into the fire. From this fate he was rescued, though he might have to leap over the fire three times, or in some places to be laid on the ground to undergo a mock quartering as a sacrificial victim. Afterwards he was pelted with egg-shells, and for the rest of the year he retained the odium of his office. For a time he was spoken of as dead.[2] Originally there appear to have been two fires and between them the Beltane victims were immolated to make the year productive and to drive away the witches.[3]

[1] Chap. vi, p. 164.

[2] J. Ramsay, *Scotland and Scotsmen in the Eighteenth Century*, ii, Edinburgh, 1888, pp. 439ff.; J. G. Dalzell, *The Darker Superstitions of Scotland*, 1834, pp. 176ff.

[3] M. Martin, *The Western Isles of Scotland*, 1873, p. 105.

To counteract these evil influences associated with the Spring Festival sprigs of rowan were carried round the fire, fastened to the tails of cattle, or attached to houses.[1]

## Midsummer Fires and Customs

The principal season for fire-rites, however, was the summer solstice when on Midsummer Eve (June 23rd)—equated with the Feast of the Nativity of St John the Baptist in the liturgical calendar on June 24th[2]—the Beltane celebrations reached their climax, and were brought into relation with the solar observances, Midsummer Day being the turning-point in the career of the sun. It was then that its energy had to be renewed as it was about to begin its downward course across the horizon. Therefore, bonfires were lighted, torches were carried in procession, and burning wheels were rolled down hills and through the fields, just as in the Celtic dual seasonal calendar these rites belonged to the May celebrations. Even the May King and Queen occasionally have appeared as the Summer Lord and Lady, unless these are independent and more ancient characters like the Jack-in-the-Green, as it is not at all improbable. In Sweden and Bohemia a Maypole or Midsummer-tree was erected and burned on the bonfire around which dances were held, the people jumping over it.[3]

The custom of dancing round and leaping over fires, and passing cattle through them, was, in fact, equally a prominent feature in May and Midsummer ceremonial,[4] and had the same purpose and significance; namely, to purify and protect from witches and other evil influences, and to ensure the well-being of the sun in its course in the heavens. To these ends the festival fires have been lighted everywhere on the Eve of Midsummer, as in Celtic lands on that of May Day, as is clear from the medieval records in which frequent reference is

[1] C. Rogers, *Social Life in Scotland*, i, Edinburgh, 1884, p. 13.

[2] Cf. Chap. vii, pp. 225 f.

[3] L. Lloyd, *Peasant Life in Sweden*, 1870, pp. 257 ff.

[4] Brand, *op. cit.*, i, pp. 298 ff.; Naogeorgus (Kirchmeyer), *The Popish Kingdome, or reigne of Antichrist*, 1570 (ed. R. C. Hope, 1880), p. 54.

made to the practice.[1] That the summer solstice should be the principal occasion, when the period of solar decline with its withering effects on vegetation is about to begin, is understandable. Moreover, since this was regarded as a critical season when witches and noxious dragons were thought to be abroad and particularly active, poisoning wells and rivers among other machinations, proper precautions had to be taken to keep them at bay. Thus, foul smoke sometimes was produced for this purpose by burning refuse, the name 'bonfire' possibly having arisen because in the first instance fires were made largely of bones. Brooms similarly were placed outside houses, and fern seed (spores)[2] worn, as protective devices. Midsummer was also a time when hempseed was sown by young women in search of a lover, the means of causing him to appear being to go to the porch of the church at midnight on the Eve of the festival and there scatter the seed saying,

> *Hempseed I sow, hempseed I mow,*
> *He that will my true love be*
> *Come rake this hempseed after me.*

The future husband would then be seen following her, mowing or eating the seed. Sometimes she had to walk round the churchyard twelve times without stopping, repeating the words and performing the same action. Another device has been for a girl blindfolded to pick a rose at midnight on Midsummer Eve, or at noon on Midsummer Day, keep it in a sheet of paper until Christmas Day when it should be as fresh as when she gathered it. Then if she places it against her bosom the man she is to marry will come and take it from her. The same may be done with St John's wort, the withering of which during Midsummer night is a very bad omen both for matrimonial and other prospects, as it is a preventive against demons and witches. On Midsummer Eve parishioners may be seen, it has been thought, going in and out of the parish church in ghostly

[1] Grimm, *Deutsche Mythologie*, Berlin, 1875–8, pp. 502, 510, 516.

[2] 'Fern seed' is believed also to have the property of making the wearer invisible, and to assist diviners of matrimonial and other affairs.

form at midnight. By sitting in the porch and watching the apparitions it is possible to determine who will die or marry during the year, as those who come out again will live, while those who do not will die.

## Samhain and Hallowe'en Observances

Although Midsummer fires may still be seen burning brightly on hills and mountains in many parts of Europe, in England, except perhaps in isolated cases in Cornwall, they have burned themselves out almost completely. In the British Isles fire festivals have survived for longest in or near the Celtic districts though in fact in the Celtic world attention was concentrated upon the spring and autumn festivals rather than on those at the solstices. Thus, it was at the beginning of its year on November 1st, when, as we have seen, the cattle were brought back from the pastures to the stalls, that the Samhain (i.e. 'summer ends') rites were held to counteract the blight of winter with its fears and dangers for man and beast alike. This was the Celtic turning-point in the seasonal sequence celebrated with fire festivals which had a pastoral rather than a solar or vegetations ignificance. It was then that the herdsmen repeated their spring Beltane rites to usher in winter, and the Church in its liturgical year associated the ancient pastoral observances with its own Feast of All Saints and solemnity of All Souls.

Thus, in the Isle of Man November 1st (Old Style) was regarded as New Year's Day, 'Hogunnas', when the Mummers used to sing songs in Manx, and all land tenures and service agreements ended and were renewed. In Ireland, Lancashire, Yorkshire, Devonshire and other places, fires were lighted to commemorate the New Year, drive away witches and other malign forces, and many forms of divination were practised appropriate to the beginning of the year. In Ireland at Tara, the General Assembly or open-air parliament (*Feis*), was held at Samhain 'because the crops and fruit were ripe,' and then was the time to renew the laws every three years, and to write up the annals and genealogies, after sacrifice had been offered to all the gods.[1] Like Beltane and Midsummer, omens, auguries, games and ceremonies were observed, some of which were brought into relation with the cult of the dead, so very deeply laid in November ritual.[2]

These customs were associated with love and marriage, health and wealth, blight, decline and death. In Scotland those connected with the Cailleach or 'hags' were combined with those belonging to the month of the dead when the activities of witches and demons were most dreaded, and the dangers of cutting the last sheaf were apparent. It was essentially however, a New Year Festival with a pastoral setting and some agricultural elements transferred from the harvest and threshing season. The extinguishing and relighting of fires, the feasting and merriment, the licence, divination and omens, and the last sheaf rites, are all indicative of a festival of beginnings and renewal at a time of decline. But eventually many of them were transferred from Samhain to the Yule Feast at Christmas, as we have seen. The feasting on animals slaughtered in November when the fodder was becoming restricted, originally in all probability had a sacrificial significance involving perhaps a human victim as a kind of 'scapegoat', and remotely connected with the slaying of the the anthropic animals and possibly of the Corn-spirit. Thus, in Gaul to assimilate themselves to the sacred species animal disguises were worn by those taking part in the processions at Samhain, made from the heads and skins of animals slaughtered at the Kalends.[3] Throughout the Celtic area masquerading has been a prominent feature at the festival and still lingers on in the Scottish Highlands.[4]

While Samhain was primarily a pastoral observance, the crops as well as the flocks and herds had to be protected from the dangerous and demonic influences rife at the turn of the

[1] E. Hull, *op. cit.*, pp. 228 ff.

[2] Wright and Lones, *op. cit.*, iii, pp. 107 ff.; Banks, *British Calendar Customs* (Scotland), iii, 1941, pp. 108 ff.

[3] Chambers, *Medieval Stage*, i, Appendix; *P.L.*, xxxix, 2001.

[4] Banks, *op. cit.*, pp. 107 ff.; Rhys, *Celtic Folklore*, i, O.U.P., 1901, pp. 225 ff.; *Celtic Heathendom*, 1888, pp. 460, 514 ff.

year and the ingathering of harvest. As the May King and Queen presided over the Beltane celebrations, so the Corn-mother or Corn-maiden connected with the last sheaf seems to have had a place, however obscure and shadowy, as the 'Queen' or 'Yule wife' in the Samhain rites.[1] The slaying of sacrificial victims on a grand scale doubtless was not only to seek pro-tection from malevolent forces. In all probability it was also directed to promotion of fecundity and fertility in which vegetation had its normal place in the calendrical ritual when the powers of growth were at their weakest at the beginning of winter. It was then that the chthonic divinities, the Matres, or Earth-goddesses, and the spirits of the corn, together with the spirits of the dead, were feasted and placated and their aid was sought to bring life and light out of the prevailing death and darkness, anticipated at Samhain and later transferred to the Yule Festival at the winter solstice.

When this was accomplished, the several traditions were merged in a composite festival in which the perennial struggle between the Old and the New Year for the possession of the fruitful earth was enacted as the days shortened and the nights lengthened, and the fates were still in the balance. In the folk feasts the ancient ritual performed with such deadly earnestness in the Fertile Crescent before it passed into peasant Europe by way of the Eastern Mediterranean, the Danube and the Atlantic littoral, survived in masquerades, dances, and customs, partly serious and partly frivolous, but retaining the essential features and structure of the earlier observances. In the process of diffusion it lost much of its stern reality and more sinister elements, becoming the occasion for popular relaxation, dancing, games, feasting, carnival and revelry in a serio-comic vein. The introduction of the Miracle and Morality plays in the thirteenth century as a component part of the liturgical year in its offices and central act of worship, gave a more serious and religious significance to medieval sacred drama. But with the break-up of Christendom in the sixteenth century, the secu-larized folk plays rapidly degenerated into burlesques and

[1] Hazlitt, *Dictionary of Faiths and Folklore*, 1905, pp. 97f.

Mumming, and the seasonal feasts into periodic opportunities to engage in boisterous behaviour and revels which had out-lived their original purpose and function.

Isolated from the prevailing pattern of society, its beliefs, institutions and practices, they tended to become diversions and pastimes, picturesque but otiose relics of bygone ages. In recent years, however, serious attempts have been made to recover this lost heritage which, as the present inquiry has demonstrated had been a potent stabilizing factor and consolidating dynamic in the social structure long before seasonal feasts and festivals became folk observances. Thus, the revival of folk drama and dances, besides affording an opportunity for healthy and pleasant recreation has made some contribution to the restoration of the rhythm of communal country life, so sadly lacking in our over-industrialized age. Furthermore, the importance of collecting the rapidly disappearing data in this field for scientific study is now widely recognized and encouraged, not least because of the light that thereby may be thrown upon the function of these time-honoured observances in maintaining the solidarity and sense of continuity in the communal life of a community.

# ABBREVIATIONS

| | |
|---|---|
| *A.B.* | *Anat-Baal texts.* |
| *A.J.A.* | *American Journal of Archaeology.* |
| *A.N.E.T.* | *Ancient Near Eastern Texts relating to the Old Testament,* ed. J. B. Pritchard, 2nd ed., Princeton, 1955. |
| *B.A.S.O.R.* | *Bulletin of the American Schools of Oriental Research.* |
| *B.S.A.* | *Annual of the British School of Athens.* |
| *C.G.S.* | *Cults of the Greek States,* L. R. Farnell, O.U.P., 1896–1909. |
| *C.I.G.* | *Corpus Inscriptionum Graecorum.* |
| *C.I.L.* | *Corpus Inscriptionum Latinarum.* |
| *E.R.E.* | *Encyclopaedia of Religion and Ethics,* ed. Hastings, 1908–1926. |
| *G.B.* | *The Golden Bough,* J. G. Frazer, 3rd ed., 1911–1917. |
| *J.A.O.S.* | *Journal of the American Oriental Society,* New Haven. |
| *J.E.A.* | *Journal of Egyptian Archaeology,* London. |
| *J.H.S.* | *Journal of Hellenic Studies,* London. |
| *J.N.E.S.* | *Journal of Near Eastern Studies,* Chicago. |
| *J.R.A.S.* | *Journal of the Royal Asiatic Society,* London. |
| *K.U.B.* | *Keilschrifturkunden aus Boghazköi,* Berlin, 1921–1938. |
| *P.G.* | *Patrologia Graeca,* Migne. |
| *P.L.* | *Patrologia Latina,* Migne. |
| *P.T.* | *Pyramid texts.* |
| *S.B.E.* | *Sacred Books of the East,* O.U.P., 1879–1910. |

# BIBLIOGRAPHY

The books listed in this selected bibliography are suggested for further study of the subject in its various aspects. References to the source material and to the more technical publications are given in the documentation in the text. Except where otherwise stated the books are all published in London. English translations are indicated by the letters E.T., and those by the Oxford and Cambridge University Presses by O.U.P. and C.U.P. respectively.

## CHAPTER I

*Four Hundred Centuries of Cave Art* by Abbé H. Breuil (E.T. by M. E. Boyle, Montignac, Dordogne, 1952) is the most exhaustive account of Cave Art in France and Spain, fully illustrated under the guidance of F. Windels. Among other useful works are *Lascaux* by A. Laming, E.T. by E. F. Armstrong in Penguin Books, 1959; *The Lascaux Cave Paintings* by F. Windels, 1949; *Lascaux, A Commentary* by A. H. Brodrick, 1949; *The Art of the Cave Dweller* by G. Baldwin Brown, 1928.

A general survey of hunting seasonal ritual under Palaeolithic conditions will be found in *Prehistory* by M. C. Burkitt (C.U.P., 2nd ed., 1925); *Early Man* by A. H. Brodrick, 1948; *Prehistoric Religion* by E. O. James, 1957; *The Art and Religion of Fossil Man* by G. H. Luquet (E.T. by J. T. Russell, O.U.P., 1930); *Les Religions de la Préhistoire* by Th. Mainage (Paris, 1921); and *Fossil Man in Spain* by H. Obermaier (E.T., Yale University Press, 1925).

Among the accounts of modern primitive people living virtually in a Palaeolithic state of culture attention may be called to: *The Native Tribes of Central Australia* (new ed., 1938); *The Northern Tribes of Central Australia*, 1904; and *The Arunta*, 2 vols., 1927, by Spencer and Gillen; *The Native Tribes of South-east Australia* by A. W. Howitt, 1904; *The Australian Aborigines* by A. P. Elkin (Sydney, 1938); *The Eskimo* by K. Birket-Smith, 1936; *The Eskimo* by E. H. Weyer (New Haven, 1932); *Aboriginal Siberia* by M. A. Czaplicka (O.U.P., 1914); *Elementary Forms of the Religious Life* by E. Durkheim (E.T., 1915); and in a rather higher state of culture, *Nuer Religion* by E. E. Evans-Pritchard (O.U.P., 1956).

The rise of civilization in the Ancient Near East is surveyed by V. G. Childe in *New Light on the Most Ancient East*, brought up to date in the

4th edition in 1952, and in a more popular form and wider range from the Stone Age to the Roman Empire in his *What Happened in History* (Pelican Books, 1946). In *The Birth of Civilization in the Ancient Near East* H. Frankfort gives a concise account of the process and its social innovations in Egypt and Mesopotamia. The worship of the Great Mother is discussed by Miss G. R. Levy in *The Gate of Horn*, 1948; by G. Contenau in *La Déesse Nue Babylonienne* (Paris, 1914), and by E. O. James in *The Cult of the Mother Goddess*, 1959. For the male aspects see *Ideas of Divine Rule in the Ancient East* by C. J. Gadd; *The Sky-Religion in Egypt* by G. A. Wainwright (C.U.P., 1938); the monumental work *Zeus* by A. B. Cook in three volumes (C.U.P., 1914-38), and more concisely *The Greeks and their Gods* by W. K. C. Guthrie, 1950.

## CHAPTER II

The literature on the Egyptian calendar and the seasons is enormous; a very full selection of this is appended to the article 'Calendar (Egyptian)' in the *E.R.E.*, iii, pp. 104ff. For a short account see J. H. Breasted, *History of the Ancient Egyptians*, 1908; R. A. Parker, *The Calendars of Egypt* (Chicago, 1950); P. Montet, *Everyday Life in Egypt* (E.T., 1958). The local festivals are described in outline by J. H. Breasted in *Ancient Records of Egypt* (Chicago, 1906-7); by S. A. Mercer in *The Religion of Ancient Egypt*, 1949; and by E. Erman in *Life in Ancient Egypt* (E.T., 1894). The Osirian festivals have been examined in great detail by E. A. W. Budge in *Osiris and the Egyptian Resurrection*, 1911; and useful discussions of them occur in *Du caractère religieux de la royauté pharaonique* (Paris, 1902) by A. Moret and in his *Le rituel de culte divin journalier en égypte* (Paris, 1902) and in *Mystères égyptiens* (Paris, 1912), and *The Nile and Egyptian Civilization* (E.T., 1927). In *Medinet Habu III, Festival Scenes of Ramesses III* by J. A. Wilson (Chicago, 1940) the festivals of Soker and Min are studied exhaustively. For the various festivals of Min see also *Les fêtes du dieu Min* (Cairo, 1931) by H. Gauthier. The position of the king is considered by Frankfort in *Kingship and the Gods* (Chicago, 1948), and the periodic feasts are described by E. Drioton in *Les Fêtes égyptienne* (Cairo, 1944), those of the Nile, Anubis, Apis, etc. by Budge in *The Liturgy of Funerary Offerings*, 1909, and the New Year Festival of Opet by A. M. Blackman in *Luxor and its Temples*, 1923. The texts of the Sed Festival have been translated by Moret in *Du caractère religieux de la royauté pharaonique*, where the Accession rites are also described. The Hatshepsut reliefs are depicted in *The Temple of Deir el-Bahari* by E. Naville, 1895–1908, and the Mystery play of the Accession is recorded by K. Sethe in *Dramatische Texte zu altaegyptischen Mysterienspielen* (Leipzig, 1928). For their repetition in the daily temple liturgy and its ceremonies see Moret, *Le rituel du culte divin journalier en Égypte* and the fully documented article by A. M. Blackman in *E.R.E.*, xii, pp. 776 ff.

CHAPTER III

The influence of the environment and climatic conditions on the seasonal cultus in Mesopotamia is discussed by Th. Jacobsen in *The Intellectual Adventure of Ancient Man* (Chicago, 1946), reprinted in Pelican Books under the title *Before Philosophy*, 1949, and further developed with special reference to the New Year Festival by A. J. Wansinck in 'The Semitic New Year and the Origin of Eschatology' in *Acta Orientalis*, i, pp. 169 ff. The formation and methods of intercalation of the calendar are dealt with by S. Langdon in *Babylonian Menologies and the Semitic Calendar* (Schweich Lectures, 1933, O.U.P., 1958); by Sidney Smith in *Myth, Ritual and Kingship* (edited by S. H. Hooke, O.U.P., 1958); by Fr Hommel in *E.R.E.*, iii, pp. 73 ff. For the position of the king in the calendrical ritual: *Caractère religieux de la royauté assyro-babylonienne* by R. Labat (Paris, 1939); *Sumerische und Akkadische Königinschriften* by F. Thureau-Dangin (Leipzig, 1907); *Kingship and the Gods* by Frankfort (Chicago, 1949); *Studies in Divine Kingship in the Ancient Near East* by I. Engnell (Uppsala, 1943); and the article by C. J. Gadd in *Myth and Ritual* (O.U.P., 1933). The Tammuz myth, ritual, and liturgies are discussed by S. Langdon in *Tammuz and Ishtar* (O.U.P., 1914); *The Babylonian Liturgies* (Paris, 1913), and by M. Witzel 'Tammuz-liturgien und Verwandtes', *Analecta Orientalia* (Rome, 1935).

For the New Year Festival in Babylon see *The Babylonian Akitu Festival* by S. A. Pallis (Copenhagen, 1926); *Rituels Accadiens* by F. Thureau-Dangin (Paris, 1921); *Babylonian Epic of Creation* by S. Langdon, 1923; *Babylonian and Assyrian Religion* by S. H. Hooke, 1953, and *The Origins of Early Semitic Ritual* (Schweich Lectures, 1933); Frankfort, *Kingship and the Gods*; *A.N.E.T.*, edited by J. B. Pritchard (2nd ed., 1955) for the texts.

CHAPTER IV

For the geographical and archaeological background of the Palestinian festivals, *Archaeology and the Religion of Israel* by W. F. Albright (3rd ed.,

Baltimore, 1953) together with his *Archaeology of Palestine* in Pelican Books, 1954. *The Cuneiform Texts of Ras-Shamra-Ugarit* by C. F. A. Schaeffer, 1939; *Les Textes de Ras Shamra-Ugarit* by R. de Langhe (Paris, 1944–5); *Ugaritic Literature* by C. H. Gordon (Rome, 1949); *Thespis* by T. H. Gaster (New York, 1950); *Canaanite Myths and Legends* by G. R. Driver (Edinburgh, 1956); and the texts in *A.N.E.T.*, for the literary source material of the Ugaritic cult-drama and its rituals, in the middle of the second millennium B.C.

For the background of the Hebrew festivals and their cultus see *From Joseph to Joshua* by H. H. R. Rowley (Schweich Lectures, 1950); *Hebrew Origins* by J. T. Meek (2nd ed., New York, 1950); *From the Stone Age to Christianity* by W. F. Albright (new ed., Doubleday Anchor Books, New York, 1957); *Israel, its Life and Culture* by J. Pedersen, vols. i–iv, 1947; *Biblical Calendars* by J. Van Goudoever (Leiden, 1959) which covers the whole range of Israelite and Christian calendars and their festivals in a Biblical setting. For the Passover see *The Jewish New Year Festival* by N. H. Snaith, 1947; *Sacrifice in the Old Testament* by G. B. Gray (O.U.P., 1925); *The Religion of the Semites* by W. Robertson Smith (new ed., 1927); *The Golden Bough*, pt. iv by J. G. Frazer; and *Myth and Ritual* (O.U.P., 1933) article by Oesterley, where, as also in Snaith's *Jewish New Year Festival* The Feast of Tabernacles is also discussed, as by A. R. Johnson in *Sacral Kingship in Ancient Israel* (Cardiff, 1955); in *Die Thronfahrt Jahves am Fest der Jahreswende* by Hans Schmidt (Tübingen, 1927); P. Volz, *Das Neujahr Jahves* (Tübingen, 1927); S. Mowinckel, *Psalmenstudien II* (Kristiania, 1922); and J. H. T. Thackeray, *The Septuagint and the Jewish Worship*, 1921. For the Day of Atonement ceremonial see G. Buchanan Gray, *Sacrifice in the Old Testament*, (O.U.P., 1925), and W. O. E. Oesterley, *Sacrifices in Ancient Israel*, 1937. The later Jewish feasts are discussed by O. S. Rankin in *The Origins of the Festival of Hanukkah* (Edinburgh, 1930); J. van Goudoever in *Biblical Calendars* (Leiden, 1959), and in the case of Purim by M. Jastrow in *E.R.E.*, x, pp. 505 ff.; by L. B. Paton in *A Critical and Exegetical Commentary on the Book of Esther* (International Critical Commentary, 1908), and by I. Abrahams in *Jewish Life in the Middle Ages*, 1896.

CHAPTER V

The principal references to Hittite seasonal festivals occur in a useful article on 'Hittite Religion' by H. G. Güterbock in *Forgotten Religions* edited by V. Ferm (New York, 1949); in *The Hittites* by O. R. Gurney

(Penguin Books, 1954), and in his article on 'Hittite Kingship' in *Myth, Ritual and Kingship* (O.U.P., 1958). The two fragmentary versions of the cult-legend of the *Purulli* Festival are translated by A. Goetze in *A.N.E.T.*, pp. 125ff., and in his *Kleinasien* (*Kulturgeschichte des alten Orients, Handbuch der Altertumswissenschaft*, Munich, 1930) where they are discussed. In *Thespis*, 1950, Dr Gaster represents the myth as the libretto of an ancient Hittite ritual play. The Telipinu myth as the Hittite counterpart of that of Tammuz and its cultus is recorded by Goetze in *A.N.E.T.*, pp. 126ff. and also by Gaster in *Thespis*. For the Kumarbi theogony with its Hesiodic affinities see Güterbock in *Kumarbi Efsanesi* (Ankara, 1945); Otten in *Mythen vom Gotte Kumarbi* (Berlin, 1950), and Goetze in *A.N.E.T.*, pp. 121ff.

The Greek calendar in its various aspects is described and discussed by M. P. Nilsson in *Primitive Time Reckoning* (Lund, 1920); and in *Grundriss der antiken Zeitrechnung* (Leipzig, 1928); by G. Thomson in *J.H.S.*, lxiii, 1943, pp. 53ff.; by A. Mommsen in *Chronologie* (Leipzig, 1883). The literature on Hellenic agricultural festivals is very considerable. The standard work on the Cretan background is Nilsson's *The Minoan-Mycenaean Religion and its Survival in Greek Religion* (2nd ed., Lund, 1950); and for Greece the five volumes of *The Cults of the Greek States* by L. R. Farnell (O.U.P., 1896–1909) should be consulted, and the appropriate sections (see Index) of *The Golden Bough* (Frazer). See also, *Prolegomena to the Study of Greek Religion* by J. E. Harrison (3rd ed., C.U.P., 1922), and her *Themis* (C.U.P., 1927), and *Ancient Art and Ritual* (Home University Library, 1913); *Psyche* by E. Rhode, 1925; *Primitive Culture in Greece* by H. J. Rose, 1925; *Pausanias's Description of Greece* by J. G. Frazer (2nd ed. in 6 vols., 1913); and *Griechische Feste von religiöser Bedeutung* by M. P. Nilsson (Leipzig, 1906). The Athenian festivals are given special attention in *Feste der Stadt Athen* by A. Mommsen; *Attische Feste* by L. Deübner (Berlin, 1932); and *Studia de Dionysus atticis* by Nilsson, 1900, and in *Geschichte der griechischen Religion* (Munich, 1941). For the origins and significance of Greek drama see *The Dramatic Festivals of Athens* (O.U.P., 1953), and *Dithyramb, Tragedy and Comedy* (O.U.P., 1927) by A. Pickard-Cambridge. *The Origins of Attic Comedy* by F. M. Cornford, 1914; and W. Ridgeway, *Origin of Tragedy*, 1910. The Eleusinian festivals are described by Farnell in *C.G.S.*, iii; Nilsson, *Geschichte der griech. Rel.*; F. Noack, *Eleusis* (Berlin, 1927); and the cult-legend has been translated by T. W. Allen, E. E. Sykes and T. W. Halliday in *The Homeric Hymn* (3rd ed., O.U.P., 1936). A fully illustrated account of the Panathenaia is given by B. Ashmole in *A Short Guide to the Sculptures of the Parthenon* (new ed., 1950); and by E. N. Gardiner in his *Greek Athletic Sports and Festivals*, 1910, and more fully in *J.H.S.*, xxxii, pp. 179ff.; see also his *Olympia* (O.U.P., 1925).

## CHAPTER VI

Fragments of the Ancient Roman calendars have been collected by Th. Mommsen in his Commentary on *Fasti divini* in *Corpus Inscriptionum Latinarum*, vol. i, and the formation of the Julian calendar is explained by W. Warde Fowler in *The Roman Festivals* (2nd ed., 1908); by F. Altheim in *A History of Roman Religion*, 1938; and by G. Wissowa in *Religion und Kultus der Römer* (2nd ed., Leipzig, 1912). The festivals are described and discussed in detail by Warde Fowler, *op. cit.*; by Frazer in his translation of and Commentary on *The Fasti of Ovid* in 5 vols., 1929; and in the appropriate articles in *Lexikon der griechischen und römischen Mythologie* by W. H. Roscher, and Pauly-Wissowa, *Realencyclopaedie der classischen Altertumswissenschaft*. See also *Phases in the Religion of Ancient Rome* by C. Bailey (O.U.P., 1932); *The Religion of Numa and other Essays on the Religion of Ancient Rome* by J. B. Carter, 1906; *Primitive Culture in Italy* by H. J. Rose, 1926, and his *Ancient Roman Religion*, 1949; *A History of the Vestal Virgins of Rome* by Sir Thomas Cato Worsfold, 1932.

The Oriental and Mystery cults are described by F. Cumont in *Les religions orientales dans le paganisme romain* (4th ed., Paris, 1929, which is better documented than the E.T. in 1911); also by Wissowa in *Religion und Kultus der Römer*; C. Bailey, Chap. vi, Warde Fowler, *Religious Experience of the Roman People*, 1911; A. D. Nock, *Conversion* (O.U.P., 1933); and in *Cambridge Ancient History*, xii, 1939; H. Graillot, *Le Culte de Cybèle* (Paris, 1912); H. Jeanmaire, *Dionysos, Histoire du Culte de Bacchus* (Paris, 1915); H. Hepding, *Attis, seine Mythen und sein Kult* (Giessen, 1903); R. Reitzenstein, *Die hellenistichen Mysterien-religionen* (Leipzig, 1927); Cumont, *Textes et monuments figurés relatifs aux mystères de Mithra* (2 vols., Brussels, 1896–99); *Les Mystères de Mithra* (2 vols., Brussels, 1913), E.T., 1903; A. Dieterich, *Eine Mithrasliturgie* (3rd ed., Leipzig, 1923).

## CHAPTER VII

For the early Christian calendars and Martyrologies: De Rossi-Duchesne,'Martyrologicum Hieronymianum', *Acta Sanctorum* Nov.vol. 2, 1894; H. Lietzmann, *Die Drei Ältesten Martyrologien* (Bonn, 1903); J. Dowden *The Church Year and Kalendar*, 1910; F. Cabrol, *Les origines liturgiques* (Paris, 1906); Article 'Calendar' in *E.R.E.* (bibliography); and article 'Calendar' in *The New Schaff-Herzog Encyclopaedia*, vol. ii, and in *Catholic Encyclopaedia*, vol. iii.

For the Easter controversies: L. Duchesne. 'La question de la Pâque au concile de Nicée', in *Revue des Questions Historiques*, xxviii, Paris, 1880; F. E. Brightman, 'The Quartodeciman Question' in *Journal of Theological Studies*, xxv, 1924. For the Easter Festival and its ceremonies consult: G. Dix, *The Treatise on St. Hippolytus of Rome*, 1937, and *The Shape of the Liturgy*, 1945; L. Duchesne, *Origines du culte chrétien* (Paris, 1909) (E.T. *Christian Worship*, 5th ed., 1923); and *Le Liber Pontificalis* (Paris, 1886); H. A. Wilson, *The Gelasian Sacramentary* (O.U.P., 1894); *The Gregorian Sacramentary* (O.U.P., 1915); J. B. O'Connell, *The Ceremonies of Holy Week*, 1957; and Appendices IV, V of *Liturgy of the Roman Church*, A. A. King, 1957; J. Wordsworth, *The Ministry of Grace*, 1903. Rogation Days and the Ascension: D. de Bruyne, in *Revue Benedictine*, xxiv, 1922; G. Kretschmar, in *Zeitschrift für Kirchengeschichte*, xlvi, 1956, pp. 209 ff.; Corpus Christi: P. Browne, in *Jahrbuch für Liturgiewissenschaft*, viii (Münster, 1928); *Textus antiqui de Festo Corporis Christi* (Münster, 1934); All Saints: L. Eisenhofer, *Handbuch der Katholischen Liturgik*, i, 1932, pp. 606f. Christmas: H. Usener, 'Das Weihnachtsfest' (Bonn, 1889; 2nd ed. by Leitzmann, 1921); L. Duchesne, *Christian Worship* (5th ed., 1923); F. Cabrol and H. Leclercq in *Dictionnaire d'Archéologie Chrétienne et la liturgie*, xii, 1935, pt. i, cols. 910–34; B. Botte, *Les Origines de la Noël et de l'Epiphanie* (Louvain, 1932); Candlemas: Duchesne, *Christian Worship*; *Liber Pontificalis*; D. de Bruyne, *Revue Bénédictine*, xxiv, 1922; E. de Moreau, 'L'Orient et Rome dans la fête du 2 février' in *Nouvelle Revue Théologique*, lxii, 1935, pp. 5 ff. See also bibliographies in articles 'Feasts and Festivals' in *E.R.E.*; *The Catholic Encyclopaedia*; *The Evolution of the Christian Year* by A. A. McArthur, 1953; and *Christian Myth and Ritual* by E. O. James.

CHAPTER VIII

The most outstanding works on sacred drama in the Middle Ages are *The Mediaeval Stage* by Sir Edmund Chambers (2 vols., O.U.P., 1903), and *The Drama of the Medieval Church* by Karl Young (2 vols, O.U.P., 1935). To these may be added, *Mysteries' End: An Investigation of the Last Days of the Medieval Religious Stage* by H. C. Gardiner (New Haven, 1946); *Les Mystères* (vol. i, *Histoire du Théâtre de France en Moyen Age*) by L. Petit de Julleville (Paris, 1880); *Origines latines du Théâtre moderne*, by E. du Méril (Paris, 1896); and the exhaustive bibliography of the literature in *The Bibliography of Medieval Drama* by C. J. Stratman (Berkeley and Los Angeles, 1954), and that appended to the chapter on 'The Early Religious Drama' by W. Creizenbach in *The Cambridge History of English Literature*, v, C.U.P., 1910, pp. 36 ff., 387 ff., and to the section on Medieval Drama in *The Cambridge Bibliography of English Literature*, i, C.U.P., 1940, pp. 271 ff.

For the Liturgical Drama see also *The Liturgical Element in the Earliest Forms of the Medieval Drama with special reference to the English and German Plays* (University of Minnesota Studies in Language and Literature, iv, 1916); *Drama and Liturgy* by O. Cargill (Colombia University Studies in English and Comparative Literature, New York, 1930); *Origines catholique du théâtre moderne* by M. Sepet (Paris, 1901); and his *Le Drame Chrétien au Moyen Âge*, 1878; for regional studies of English medieval drama see *The English Religious Drama of the Middle Ages* by H. Craig (O.U.P., 1955); *English Mystery Plays* by C. Davidson (Yale, 1892); *Early English Stage, 1330–1660* by G. Wickham, 1959; *English Miracle Plays, Moralities and Interludes* by A. W. Pollard (O.U.P., 1923); *English Nativity Plays* by S. B. Hemingway (New York, 1909); *The Role of the Virgin Mary in the Coventry, York, Chester and Towneley Cycles* by C. Luke (Washington, 1933); medieval French drama is discussed by Mrs Grace Frank in *The Medieval French Drama* (O.U.P., 1954); and *Le Théâtre en France du Moyen Âge* by G. Cohen, 1928. For the Moralities and Interludes see *Cambridge Bibliography of English Literature*, i, pp. 513–17; *The Cambridge History of English Literature*, v, pp. 391–4, and Stratman's *The Bibliography of Medieval Drama*, pp. 166 ff.

CHAPTER IX

Vol. i of Chambers' *The Medieval Stage* (O.U.P., 1903) remains the basic work on Folk Drama, supplemented by the new material in his *English Folk Play* (O.U.P., 1933) and in *The Mummers' Play* by R. J. E. Tiddy (O.U.P., 1923). The subject has been discussed in a general article on 'The English Folk Drama' in *Folk-Lore*, iv, 1893 by T. F. Ordish, and more recently by S. Piggott in 'Berkshire Mummers' Plays' in *Folk-Lore*, xli, 1930; by D. A. N. Tod, 'The Christmas Mummers' Plays' from Gloucestershire in *Folk-Lore*, xlvi, 1935, and by Mrs E. H. Rudkin, 'Lincolnshire Plough Play' in *Folk-Lore*, l, 1939 and 'Plough-Jack's Play from Willoughton', 'The Pace-eggers' Play in England' in *Folk-Lore*, xlix, 1938, and 'The Soul-caking Play' by M. W. Myres in *Folk-Lore*, xliii, 1932. The Feast of Fools is dealt with in considerable detail by E. K. Chambers in *The Medieval Stage*, i, Chaps. xiii–xviii. See also *Mysteries' End* by H. C. Gardiner; J. B. L. du Tilliot, *Mémoires pour servir à l'histoire de la Fête des Foux* (Paris, 1741–51); and E. E. H. Welsford, *The Fool: His Social and Literary History*, 1935.

Folk dances are discussed by Curt Sachs in *The World History of the Dance*, 1938; by W. O. E. Oesterley, *The Sacred Dance*, 1923; and Cecil J. Sharp in *The Dance*, 1924, gives a historical survey of dancing in Europe. In *Sword Dances of Northern England* he describes the Sword dances with their tunes in particular districts, and Douglas Kennedy discusses the English dances from the standpoint of the Director of the English Folk Dance and Song Society in his *England's Dances*, 1949. Miss Karpeles has a useful article on 'English Folk Dances' in *Folk-Lore*, xliii, 1932, which is elaborated in her book with L. Blake on *Dances of England and Wales* in the Handbook of European National Dances Series, 1950. See also *The Traditional Dance* by V. Alford and R. Gallop, 1935; and her *Introduction to English Folklore*, 1952; *The Lancashire Morris* by M. Karpeles, 1930; *The Country Dance Book* by C. Sharp in six parts from 1909 to 1922, and *The Morris Book* in five parts from 1909 to 1913; *The Court Masque* by E. E. H. Welsford (O.U.P., 1927). The Robin Hood story is considered by F. J. Child, *English and Scottish Ballads*, 1899; W. H. Clawson, *The Gest of Robin Hood* (Toronto, 1909), and J. H. Gable, *Bibliography of Robin Hood* (Nebraska, 1939).

The Seasonal Festivals and Calendar Customs in the British Isles are catalogued in the volumes on *British Calendar Customs* published by the Folk-Lore Society by A. W. Wright and T. E. Lones (England) and by M. M. Banks (Scotland) between 1936 and 1946. Miss V. Alford has described the calendar customs, dances, and drama in the Pyrenees in her *Pyrenean Festivals*, 1937; while *The Golden Bough* is a mine of information about the relevant material in Europe (see Index). For the Yule Feast and Christmas customs see C. A. Miles, *Christmas in ritual and tradition, Christian and Pagan*, 1912; C. Hole, *Christmas and its Customs*, 1957; T. G. Crippen, *Christmas and Christmas Lore*, 1923; for Plough Monday observances in addition to Chambers see Brand, *Popular Antiquities*; T. F. Thistleton-Dyer, *British Popular Customs*, and Mrs E. H. Rudkin in *Folk-Lore*, xliii, 1932. The literature dealing with Shrove-tide Contests is recorded in *Shrove Tuesday Football* by F. P. Magoen (Harvard University Press, 1931); and for Easter games and diversions see the references given for Pace-egging and Hocktide. May Day celebrations are fully discussed by Chambers, Frazer, Thistleton-Dyer,

Brand, and Hone (*Every Day Book*), and in *British Calendar Customs*, and by Mannhardt and by L. Whistler, *The English Festivals*, 1947; P. H. Ditchfield, *Old English Customs*, 1896, and in the Beltane literature listed in the text. Midsummer, Samhain, and Hallowe'en customs are also described in the same sources, together with *Celtic Folk-Lore* by J. Rhys; J. A. MacCulloch, *The Religion of the Ancient Celts*, 1911; C. L. Paton, *Manx Calendar Customs*, 1942; J. Ramsay, *Scotland and Scotsmen in the Eighteenth Century*, 1888; A. Macbain, *Celtic Mythology and Religion*, 1917, and E. Hull, *Folklore of the British Isles*, 1928.

# INDEX

ABRAHAM, 103
Adad, 98
Adonis, 96, 97, 101, 123
Agriculture, beginnings of, 30f.
Akitu Festival, the, 79ff., 82ff.
Albright, W. F., 35, 103, 106, 323f.
Alcheringa, the, 28ff.
Aleyan-Baal, 94ff., 105
Alford, V. A., 287
All Hallows, Festival of (cf. All Saints and Hallowe'en)
All Saints, Feast of, 227f.
All Souls, commemoration of, 227f.
Altheim, F., 189
Ampleforth play, the, 274
Amon-Re, 42, 48, 63f., 67
Anat, 95f., 99f.
Annunciation, Feast of the, 234f.; play, 260f.
Anthesteria, the, 139f.
Anu, 95, 129
Aphrodite, 170
Apollo, 121, 134, 147
Apsu, the, 80f., 130
Apuleius, 193f.
Arpachiyah, Tell, 34; figurines, 35f.
Arunta tribe, the, 24ff.
Ascension, Feast of the, 217ff.; play of the, 250f.
Ashbourne contest, 302
Asherah, 96, 99
Ashmole, B., 154
Ashur, 81
'Asith, Feast of, 113ff., 118
Assumption of the B.V.M., Feast of, 235f., 266f.
Astrology, 91

Athena, 153
Atonement, ritual of, 83f., 118ff.
Attis, 96, 128, 189f., 191, 196, 310f.
Augustine, St, 210, 245

BAAL (cf. Aleyan-Baal)
Bacchanalia, the, 181f.
Bampton Morris men, the, 285
Baptismal rites, 209ff.
Bégouën, Count, 16f.
Beltane Festival, the, 168, 227, 312ff.
Benediktbeuern Christmas play, 243f.
Blackman, A. M., 47, 50, 54, 59, 66f.
Bonfires, 296f. (cf. Yule, Midsummer, Hallowe'en)
Boy Bishop, the, 278
Botte, B., 230f.
Brand, J., 233, 296, 304, 310, 319
Breasted, J. H., 45, 60, 62
Breuil, Abbé H., 17, 20f.
Brightman, F. E., 209
Brooks, N. C., 247
Budge, E. A., 57, 322
Busiris, 55

CALENDAR, the,
Babylonian, 74ff., 89f.; Ecclesiastical, 200f., 204, 231; Egyptian, 45ff.; Gregorian, 162; Julian, the, 47, 161ff., 200; Lunar, 107, 116; Peasants', the, 45; Philocalian, 202f., 229; Roman, 159f., 200; Solar, the, 45f.; Syrian, 97; Zodiacal, 91
Candlemas, Feast of, 180, 232ff.; play of, 262f.
Cargill, O., 239

331